The Civil Wars of General

JOSEPH E. JOHNSTON,

Confederate States Army

Volume I: Virginia and Mississippi, 1861–1863

RICHARD M. MCMURRY

SB

Savas Beatie

California

Library of Congress Cataloging-in-Publication Data

Names: McMurry, Richard M., author.
Title: The Civil Wars of General Joseph E. Johnston, Confederate States Army
 / by Richard M. McMurry.
Description: El Dorado Hills, CA: Savas Beatie, [2022-] | Includes
 bibliographical references and index. | Contents: V. 1. Virginia and
 Mississippi, 1861-1863 — v. 2. Georgia, the Carolinas, and the Years
 Since the War 1865 to the Present. | Summary: "Joseph Eggleston Johnston
 was one of the original five full generals of the Confederacy. This
 title unlocks Johnston the general and represents a lifetime of study
 and thinking about the officer, his military career, and his
 simultaneous battles with the government in Richmond in general, and
 with President Jefferson Davis in particular. Sometimes he even fought the Yankees.
 McMurry also sheds fresh light on old controversies and examines Johnston's relationships
 and their impact on the course of the war"— Provided by publisher.
Identifiers: LCCN 2022024771 | ISBN 9781611215922 (hardcover) |
 ISBN 9781954547117 (ebook)
Subjects: LCSH: Johnston, Joseph E. (Joseph Eggleston), 1807-1891. |
 Generals--Confederate States of America--Biography. | Confederate States
 of America. Army–Biography. | United States–History–Civil War,
 1861-1865–Campaigns.
Classification: LCC E467.1.J74 M87 2022 | DDC 973.7/3092
 [B]–dc23/eng/20220531
LC record available at https://lccn.loc.gov/2022024771

First Edition, First Printing

SB

Savas Beatie
989 Governor Drive, Suite 102
El Dorado Hills, CA 95762
916-941-6896 / sales@savasbeatie.com
www.savasbeatie.com

Savas Beatie titles are available at special discounts for bulk purchases in the United States.
Contact us for more details.

Proudly published, printed, and warehoused in the United States of America.

For the Fab Five, my wonderful grandchildren
Sarah, Sam, Kai, Nate, and Liam

Every day you guys show your dads how much they mean to me.

Love,
Grandpa M

GENERAL JOSEPH E. JOHNSTON (center),
flanked by President Jefferson Davis (left) and General Robert E. Lee (right).

Contents

Contents (continued)

List of Maps

Photographs

Foreword

A Fresh Assessment

by Stephen Davis

The ancient Romans had a phrase, *sui generis*, meaning "of its own kind." Today, we would probably say "one of a kind." Both of these compliments apply to Richard M. McMurry's *The Civil Wars of General Joseph E. Johnston, Confederate States Army*.

Joseph Eggleston Johnston (1807-1891) was a complicated character and controversial figure in Confederate history. Dr. McMurry offers an analysis of his extremely important role in the War for Southern Independence. Part military history, part biography, part psychological profile, this study offers boundless benefits to those who wish to know how Joe Johnston ticked, and why he acted in ways that so often hurt—and certainly did not help—the Confederacy's hopes for military victory and political sovereignty.

McMurry argues that Joseph E. Johnston was "the central military figure in the history of the Southern Confederacy," and by doing so immediately stakes out why this book is so achingly overdue. Johnston commanded both major Confederate field armies (those in Virginia and in the Western Theater) and through the course of the war commanded more Confederate troops than Lee did in Virginia. He also surrendered more troops in the Carolinas than Lee did at Appomattox Courthouse. Countless biographies have been written about Marse Robert; Old Joe has all of three.

When McMurry describes Johnston as "the most controversial of the Confederacy's wartime military figures," he places his subject in the uncomfortable company of, say, Braxton Bragg, but his point is a cogent one. And when Richard declares that his subject's "long, bitter feud with President Davis [was] arguably *the* key reason for the Rebels' failure to attain independence," you know this is going to be a hard book to put down.

McMurry makes it clear that his is not a traditional biography of Joe Johnston; Hughes' *Johnston* (1894), Govan's and Livingood's *A Different Valor* (1956), and

Symonds's *Joseph. E. Johnston* (1992) have already done that. Rather, this is a study of Johnston's generalship in the context of his relations with Jefferson Davis and Robert E. Lee.

Fascinating.

McMurry makes a strong argument that "Johnston placed his reputation above more important matters." For instance, early in the war he wanted to evacuate Harpers Ferry, but waited for an order so as to escape criticism for a retreat. McMurry rightly calls out Johnston for his "incessant whining" over the issue. Our author explains the spat over rank between Davis and Johnston in September 1861 with surgical precision. (Who else but Johnston would have written, "I outrank General Lee"?) McMurry is not afraid of bold judgments. When he writes that Johnston's argument with Davis about seniority "was to have a profound effect on the history of the Confederate States of America and therefore on the history of the United States," he is making just the kind of imaginative declaration one expects in a book like this.

Another example is the author's judgment of "the general's extreme, often unwise, sometimes intemperate, usually petty and childish, and always foolish hypersensitivity with regard to his status and reputation in the Confederate military establishment." Johnston's recalcitrance, October 1861-May 1862, in the face of the administration's orders to reorganize his regiments into single-state brigades is so demonstrative of the general's political obtuseness—and so telling as another coffin-nail in the Davis-Johnston relationship–that McMurry devotes a full chapter to the imbroglio. (In contrast, Robert E. Lee did not like the reorganization idea either, but he went along with it anyway; after all, Davis was president and commander-in-chief.) "The prickly general" also failed to cooperate when Richmond asked that he write often as to his tactical situation.

The author's perspective shrewdly includes Jefferson Davis. His assessment of the Confederate president is sharp, but well supported by the primary evidence and Davis's biographers. Davis, concludes McMurry, was intelligent and committed to the cause, but not averse to picking squabbles that "made him a divisive force in Confederate political and military affairs." The President's role as War Department micro-manager is also well known. Not so is our author's claim that in the spring of 1862 Johnston angrily offered to resign, but that Davis refused to accept it. McMurry argues convincingly that one of Davis's chief failures as war president was that he only gave suggestions, not orders to his army commanders, and that too many times he seemed incapable of making a strong decision.

Then there is General Lee. McMurry posits that Lee embodied Steven Covey's precepts of character and practiced Covey's habits of effectiveness, while Johnston exhibited "old patterns of self-defeating behavior." The author's analysis of Lee's and Johnston's complicated relationship in the decades before the war is nothing less than fascinating. Then, when Lee succeeded Johnston in command of the Confederate army in Virginia, Johnston began to exhibit a quiet, smoldering jealousy toward his fellow Virginian, West Point classmate, and prewar friend.

After Johnston recovered from his Seven Pines wound in November 1862, the President sent him to Tullahoma, Tennessee (Bragg's base) to command the "Department of the West," a super department that placed Johnston in nominal charge of Bragg's army in Tennessee, John C. Pemberton's in Mississippi, and E. Kirby Smith's force in east Tennessee. McMurry aptly relates Johnston's frustration with this awkward command structure, one in which he served until the spring of 1863.

Louis T. Wigfall emerges as a secondary character in McMurry's analysis of the complex relationship of Johnston and Davis, such as when the Texas senator advised the general in the fall of 1862 to keep "careful records to protect himself later against possible accusations by the Davis administration." Johnston's wife Lydia also figures into the mix when, in November of 1862 she told her husband that Davis "hates you & he has power & he will ruin you." When Johnston wrote his friend Wigfall that "nobody ever assumed a command under more unfortunate circumstances," McMurry agrees: "Johnston found himself tossed into the rapidly escalating command chaos and confusion" of a theater command split between Bragg and Pemberton, and an administration that could not declare to Johnston that Tennessee was more important than Mississippi (or vice versa). Worse, Pemberton communicated directly with Richmond—a practice that Davis did not try to stop. The new department commander rightly worried about his new situation, but he did not help himself, either. As McMurry demonstrates, "it is also a damning comment about his almost completely passive approach to high-level command that he did almost nothing to advise the government about his fears"—much less do anything to try to quell them (like relieving Pemberton).

The author finds related importance in the fact that during his trip in December 1862 through Tennessee to Mississippi, the President did not meet with Georgia governor Joseph E. Brown. Given Brown's loud-mouthed objections to conscription and criticisms of the Davis administration over habeas corpus and other issues, McMurry is on-the-spot in seeing this episode as another example of Jefferson Davis's "failure to think like a national war leader."

By the start of 1863, "Johnston's nagging suspicion that the Davis government was hostile to him had grown," as our author declares. Worse, so too had his sense of self-doubt in the face of daunting challenge. "I cannot direct both parts of my command [Bragg, Pemberton] at once," he wrote on January 6, 1863. At the same time, McMurry recognizes that "Johnston's refusal . . . to communicate meaningfully with the government lay at the heart of his many self-inflicted difficulties."

Not all of Johnston's difficulties were self-inflicted, and McMurry is alert to these as well. He pays attention, for example, to the Confederate railway system, which was already deteriorating by early 1863 and thus influencing Johnston's thinking about how to transfer reinforcements from Bragg's army to the Vicksburg garrison. And while McMurry is frequently critical of Johnston, at times he defends the general's decisions, such as that to abandon Jackson, Mississippi, on May 14, 1863. Johnston has been accused of timidity by Davis and others, but McMurry exonerates him: "with only 6,000 men, Johnston could do nothing at the time to reinforce or relieve Vicksburg."

When Major General U. S. Grant headed toward the Mississippi River fortress, Johnston implored Pemberton to unite with the forces he was then gathering near Jackson. Had Pemberton done so, the Confederates could have turned on Grant before he received heavy reinforcements in June. Instead, Pemberton tried to take Grant on himself and was routed. The result, concludes Richard, was that the combat of Champion Hill on May 16 was "arguably the most important battle of the war." Eventually Johnston gave up even trying to coordinate strategy with the Vicksburg commander (three times Pemberton refused to obey Johnston's orders). McMurry sympathizes with Johnston in making this decision, calling attention to "an almost complete failure on the part of the government to comprehend the enormity of the difficulties facing Johnston in Mississippi." By early June Johnston had built his Army of Relief up to around 30,000 troops. By then, Grant was besieging Vicksburg. Even if Johnston attacked Grant from the east, McMurry believes the general stood little chance of driving the Federal army away so Pemberton could escape. This is the kind of judgment you don't often see in Civil War books.

Related to the crisis out West was General Lee's decision after the battle of Chancellorsville to march his Army of Northern Virginia north into Pennsylvania instead of sending, say, George Pickett's infantry division to Mississippi. We know how all that worked out . . .

Then there was the argument between Johnston and Davis over the general's departmental authority. Johnston believed that when he was ordered from Tennessee to Mississippi, he ceased to command troops in the former state; Davis contended it did no such thing. Our author has little patience for either participant in this little tiff, and at one point criticizes Johnston's "long and silly letter" as well as Davis's "foolish screed."

With a trained military historian's keen eye and sure hand, McMurry outlines all the factors that doomed the Southern forces at Vicksburg: Grant's numbers (70,000); geography—especially how the Yazoo and Big Black rivers pinched Johnston's avenues of approach; Federal river gunboats; no timely communication between Pemberton and Johnston once the former had become besieged; and, the garrison's physical weakness ("exposure, malnourishment, and sickness"). All of these did not keep Confederates trapped inside the Vicksburg fortifications from hoping that Old Joe would come and save them.

Johnston learned of Pemberton's surrender on July 5. He had seen it coming: "I consider saving Vicksburg hopeless," he had written on June 15. In the end, McMurry fairly and accurately apportions blame for the fall of the river fortress on both Jeff Davis and Joe Johnston. Relations between the two men had sunk into mistrust, suspicion, and rancor. That the Confederacy's Chief Executive would in just six months' time once more turn to General Johnston in a command crisis says much about Davis's lingering respect for the general's military ability and experience. Or maybe the President had simply run out of officer options. It is a story we will look forward to Richard telling us in Volume II of his *magnum opus*.

Until then, we may conclude that in this work, his assessment of Confederate General Joseph E. Johnston is one of the most scathing that exists in the voluminous Civil War literature.

Preface

Jeff, Bob, and Joe

" . . . it seems it is only a fight between Joe Johnston and Jeff Davis."
— Mary Chesnut, December 27, 1864

During the 1960-1961 academic year I was a first classman (senior) at the Virginia Military Institute. By then I knew that I wanted to pursue graduate work specializing in the field of Civil War history. At the suggestion of several of the VMI professors I had applied for admission to the history graduate program at Emory University in Atlanta. By some incomprehensible miracle (or more likely an egregious administrative blunder) the school accepted me into the program. I had even begun to correspond with Bell I. Wiley, Emory's Civil War historian, about possible thesis/dissertation topics.

Since I had grown up in the Atlanta area and had a longstanding interest in the Civil War in that region, the great 1864 struggle for that key Confederate city quickly emerged as the obvious subject for my specialized graduate work. Owing to this fortuitous convergence of circumstances, I was able to take some very preliminary steps toward that end during my final year at the Institute.[1]

Both John Barrett's class, "The Civil War and Reconstruction," and Tyson Wilson's course in "American Military History" involved much outside-the-classroom work of one kind or another. By taking the Atlanta Campaign as the subject of as much of that work as possible, I had the opportunity to begin what I—perhaps erroneously—like to think of as a serious study of what became my

---

1 At that time the best—indeed, the only—book on the 1864 campaign in North Georgia (not counting *Gone With the Wind*, of course) was Jacob D. Cox's 1882 *Atlanta*, a volume in Scribner's "Campaigns of the Civil War" Series. Cox's then-outdated work was at best a short, very general narrative, and it devoted undue attention to the part of the Union force with which he had served in 1864. Note: full bibliographical data for works cited in these notes will be found where those data belong—in the Bibliography that will appear in Volume II. The short titles used in the notes are in a key word/words in context format. The ones that are not obvious are listed in a short title index incorporated alphabetically into the Bibliography.

major area of Civil War interest. In one way or another I have been studying that military operation and the people who waged it ever since.

GENERAL JOSEPH EGGLESTON Johnston clearly became the central figure on the Confederate side of the 1864 campaign in North Georgia—in terms both of what happened (the facts of the campaign) and of how both the general public and serious students of the war have understood those events (the memory and history of the campaign). Owing to this fact much of my work with the campaign has revolved around a study of Johnston, his personality, and his conduct of the 1864 defense of North Georgia and the crucial city of Atlanta.

Such an undertaking inevitably expanded to include investigations of other periods of Johnston's life, his other Civil War military operations, his relations with other prominent Confederates—notably President Jefferson Davis and Generals Robert E. Lee, John C. Pemberton, and John Bell Hood—and his standing in the general history of the war.

OVER THE DECADES I have come to two conclusions about Johnston and his place in the war and its history. First, he stands, I have come firmly to believe, as the central military figure in the history of the Southern Confederacy, not just of the 1864 operations in North Georgia. To be sure, Robert E. Lee is clearly the most prominent Southern military figure in both the popular mind and in Confederate military historiography (Confederate military history as it has been written).[2] Lee's role in the *ultimate military outcome* of the war, however, was not as important or as consequential as was that of Johnston.[3]

2 A. L. Long (*Lee*, 161), who had served on General Lee's staff, called the general "the central figure of the war."

3 Lee's importance as far as the war's history goes, it seems to me, lies in his 1862-1864 military successes in Virginia. Those victories prolonged the war by two or three years. As the war lengthened, its overall nature changed—as the nature of wars so often does—and those changes led to more and more far-reaching results. The most obvious example can be seen in the growth of "radical" sentiment among Northern Republicans with regard to slavery, then to emancipation, and finally to citizenship and equality for black Americans. Would those developments have come about when they did, had the war ended in, say, June or July 1862—as it may well have done had President Jefferson Davis not named Lee to command the army defending Richmond? Historian Allan Nevins commented: "Had fighting ended in the spring of 1862 it [slavery] might have survived for years" (*Ordeal of the Union*, VI, viii). Was Lee's role, in fact, that of the Great Emancipator? (See my *Fourth Battle of Winchester*, 80.) Lee also occupies the key military spot in the white South's postwar mythmaking that far surpasses that of any

Lee still served as a staff officer in Richmond in July 1861 when Johnston commanded the victorious Confederate army in the war's first major battle. Johnston commanded another Confederate army in the field for more than two weeks after Lee surrendered in 1865.

Johnston commanded major Rebel armies in Virginia, Tennessee, Mississippi, Georgia, South Carolina, and North Carolina. In addition, smaller units in Alabama, Florida, and East Louisiana came under his authority at one time or another. He, in fact, was the only officer to command both principal Confederate field armies. More individual Confederate soldiers served in forces under Johnston's direct control than under the authority of any other Southern general.[4]

Johnston commanded the Rebel troops in the war's two most *militarily* crucial campaigns—Vicksburg in 1863 and Atlanta the following year. His long bitter feud with President Jefferson Davis runs like an angry scar through the history of the Southern Confederacy. It was certainly a key reason—arguably *the* key reason—for the Rebels' failure to attain independence. In May 1864, the well-known Confederate author Mary Chesnut wrote of "the Joe Johnston disaffection eating into the very vitals of our distracted country." Seven months later under date of December 27 she commented, "We thought this was a struggle for independence—Southern states against odds—in the U. S. A. Now it seems it is only a fight between Joe Johnston and Jeff Davis."[5]

Second, I have come to believe that for most of the past 160 years or so, Johnston's role in the war, especially his part in the great operations of 1863 and even more so in those of the following year, has often been misunderstood. That misunderstanding, in turn, has led to what I believe to be a badly flawed view of the war in general and of its military history in particular. Indeed, that misunderstanding carried over into the post-1865 history and memory of the war as the

---

other former Confederate. Neither of these facts, however, means that Lee's role was as great as was that of Johnston in determining the war's *military* outcome.

4 Gen. P. G. T. Beauregard commanded the Army of Tennessee (then known as the Army of the Mississippi, sometimes without the "the") for a few weeks in the spring of 1862 and is the only other possible claimant to having commanded both major Confederate armies. Beauregard, however, commanded only one of the predecessor units of the Army of Northern Virginia. He never commanded the entire army. Technically, of course, all Rebel soldiers served under Lee's command once he became general-in-chief of Confederate land forces in February 1865. That appointment, however, came much too late to affect the course of the war, and Lee in person commanded only one major Rebel field army.

5 Chesnut, *Chesnut's Civil War*, 609, 698.

conflict came to be understood in the mind of white America in general, and especially in the mind of the white South. The influence of that misunderstanding lingers yet in the national cultural, social, intellectual, and political life.

If these conclusions are valid, it follows that to *understand* the military history of the Confederacy, and hence of the war itself, both as it was fought and as it has been remembered and written, we must reach a better understanding of Joseph E. Johnston's wartime role and of his place in overall Confederate military history—even in the larger fields of Confederate and Civil War history. Indeed, one could construct a reasonable argument that the story of Johnston's Confederate career *is* the story of Confederate military history.

This book is a report on my clumsy efforts to explore and understand these topics.

I BEGAN WORK on this project many years ago with the happy and naïve assumption that it could take the form of a simple, if long biographical essay, chronologically tracing Johnston's Confederate career with extended pauses every so often to analyze what he had done in this or that situation as it arose in the course of the war. At one time I had completed about two-thirds of such a book. That manuscript, however, became less satisfactory as it grew longer.

Eventually I concluded that to have even a chance of understanding the part Joseph E. Johnston played in the Civil War—not to mention the even larger part he played (and in some cases still plays) in our understanding (misunderstanding?) of the war—I would have to start all over. The account of Johnston's role had to be put into the larger context of Confederate military policy, of the overall political history of the Confederacy itself, and particularly into that of Johnston's decades-long relationship with Jefferson Davis and Robert E. Lee. As persevering readers will see, Davis came to occupy a great many of these pages. Lee, too, eventually received much more coverage than I had originally intended for him. In fact, at one time, the working title of this project was "Jeff, Bob, and Joe."[6]

6 Historian Joseph T. Glatthaar observed, "One cannot analyze the Davis-Johnston relationship . . . without delving into the Confederate president's dealings with Lee" (*Partners in Command*, viii). To this, I would add one must also delve into the Lee-Johnston, Johnston-Pemberton, and Johnston-Hood relationships. Hood does not emerge as an important factor in this matter until Volume II of this work.

This study—the product of that realization (revelation?)—is not a collective biography of the three men, although it has much biographical material and even presents some new, if minor, biographical facts about Johnston. It comprises instead a series of discrete essays covering in chronological order Johnston's different Confederate command assignments with frequent, but I hope relevant, flashbacks to analyze the situations in which the general found himself, and how he, and frequently Davis and Lee, reacted to them. At times, Davis and/or Lee take center stage and Johnston disappears—as in the account of the summer and fall of 1862 when he goes off to recover from his wounds, and in the case of the crucial spring 1863 "Gettysburg decision" in which he played no part. A final section offers my speculations as to why Johnston behaved as he did, and some thoughts on his place in the war and its history.[7]

INEVITABLY SUCH AN approach has produced some overlaps in which the same matter is discussed in two or more of the essays. In each such case I believe the practice justified and I have tried to keep the overlapping sections as short as possible. In every such instance the purpose of the overlap is to view the topic under discussion from a different perspective or in the context of a different, larger, subject. This approach will also spare readers the need to flip around in the pages to refresh their memory, and each part of the work can stand on its own—so far as it deserves to—as a separate study of one of Johnston's four periods of Confederate command.

I also felt it necessary to insert into the text at several points some long quotations. These permit readers to experience the writings and something of the emotions of Johnston, Davis, and others in their own words. In so doing, they offer insights directly into the minds of the principals and present the precise language of the laws and other documents about which they differed, as well as the language of their efforts to justify their decisions and actions. I apologize if these long quotations unduly interrupt the flow of the narrative. Be assured, gentle reader, that I have used them only where I believe them necessary to a full understanding of the matter under discussion.

---

7 To hold down the length of this book, I have omitted treatment of several minor, if interesting events in Johnston's life that did not affect his relationship with other Confederates. Examples include his possible role in designing the South's battleflag and in the early use of observation balloons as well as the story of his wartime meeting with an elderly slave who had been his nurse when he was an infant.

READERS will also notice a major difference in the subject matter emphasized in Book One and that covered in the remainder of the work. Book One deals with Johnston's 1861-1862 tenure as commander of the main Rebel force in Virginia. It focuses on the origins and early development of the Davis-Johnston quarrels and is virtually devoid of any treatment of events on the battlefield. The 1861 and 1862 military operations in Virginia did not become the subjects of major disputes between the President and the general, and they do not tell us very much about Johnston the general or Johnston the man. Book Two (and Books Three and Four in the second volume of this study), on the other hand, present considerably more detail about Johnston's 1863-1865 military operations, his role as an army commander, and the military events about which he and Davis quarreled, or which affected him in some significant way.

Books Two and Three, especially, reflect this change of emphasis. Book Two deals with Johnston's 1862-1863 period of command in the West. Most of what historians have written about that period is devoted to events in the field during the long struggle for Vicksburg. Since this work concentrates on Johnston, I have had to cover his activities during those weeks in much more detail than have those writing about the field operations with which he had almost nothing to do. For the reasons mentioned in the opening paragraphs of the second chapter of Book Three in Volume II and elsewhere in the second installment, I have covered Johnston's activities in the first six-and-one half-months of 1864 in much greater detail than I had originally planned.

THE overall interpretation presented in these pages, I need to say at the outset, has as its general framework my very strong conviction that the Confederates lost the war on the Western battlefields; the Federal government did not win it.

Ever since the war ended in the spring of 1865, whole battalions of historians have eked out a living producing books and articles in which each argues that this, or that, or something else brought about the national military triumph. In truth, almost all the reasons put forth to explain Confederate defeat had little, if anything, to do with bringing about the Rebels' *military* downfall.

Many of the suggested reasons for the failure of secession were in whole or in part, directly or indirectly, the *products*, not the causes, of defeat on the battlefield. Examples include inflation of the currency, civilian suffering on the home front, and the unsuccessful efforts to gain support and diplomatic recognition from European governments.

Virtually all the other reasons put forth to explain Confederate failure involve factors that *might* well have (probably would have?) brought about *eventual* Federal victory had the Confederates not managed to propel themselves so far along the road to ruin before those factors became crucial. The naval blockade of the Rebel coast and the oft-cited Northern population and industrial superiority (the famous "overwhelming numbers and resources," as General Lee put it in the well-known "Farewell Order" to his army of April 10, 1865), are examples of Union advantages that played at most a very slight role in the key events of 1861-1863 that launched the Secessionists on and carried them far along the path to defeat. Perhaps this concept would be better put if phrased "the Confederates managed to lose the war before the Yankees could manage to win it, and they lost it in battles fought between the Appalachian Mountains and the Mississippi River."[8]

Late in 2011, many years after launching this project and many more before completing it, I was pleased to come across the following observation in Julia Stern's *Mary Chesnut's Civil War Epic*: "Chesnut documents throughout her narrative the ways this feud [between Davis and Johnston] registered among wives and other officers; and this small chapter of the war is a story that could comprise an entire book in itself."[9]

This work, I hope, is that book.

---

8 See my *Fourth Battle of Winchester*, especially 57-79; and (with others) "The Union Didn't Win the War, the Confederacy Lost It."

9 Stern, *Mary Chesnut's Civil War Epic*, 310 n7.

Acknowledgments

AS MENTIONED IN the Preface, this book has taken shape over some six and a half decades. Throughout those years I have benefitted greatly from the help of (literally) many thousands of people.

This vast multitude includes teachers of long ago classes (not all of them, by any means, history classes); archivists and librarians all over the country; attendees at various gatherings sponsored by many different organizations from California to New Hampshire and Minnesota to Florida; collectors of Civil War letters and other documents who have shared copies of items in their collections or family papers; members of Civil War Round Tables as well as several state and local historical and heritage societies; National Park Service rangers and historians; students; participants in Elderhostel (now ROAD Scholars) programs; as well as amateur and professional historians (many of the amateurs, by the way, do excellent work).

Comments, questions, insights, and criticisms from these folks have added much to my knowledge and understanding of the war and of the people who waged it, as well as of the lives of those who simply sought to survive it. A goodly number of these helpful people have become personal friends as well as fellow Civil Warriors. Many of them, alas, have crossed over the river (to paraphrase Stonewall Jackson) and are no longer with us.

To list all these people is impossible. To list the ones whose names I remember would yield a long roster that would still omit many names. At several places in the footnotes, I have thanked individuals who provided documents, information on particular subjects, or specific help with certain matters. To all, a hearty "thank you." You have done your best to make this a respectable work. The many faults that doubtless remain are my responsibility and mine alone. It is a pleasure and privilege to know (or to have known) all of you. Additional acknowledgments will appear in the second volume.

To those who slog through these volumes, take heart. The Army of the Potomac survived the Mud March. The Army of Tennessee fought well after Franklin and Nashville.

Richard M. McMurry
Spring 2022

Prelude

A Meeting on the Hudson

"... the triangular relationship among Davis, Johnston, and Lee."
— Stephen Newton, 1998

THE young Mississippian first saw the two Virginians sometime in the summer of 1825. The two were then among the eighty-seven newcomers beginning their four-year cadetships at the United States Military Academy at West Point, New York. The Mississippian was already there, a seasoned and veteran cadet—a "third classman," in Academy jargon—with one year's experience at the school under his belt.

Perhaps that initial meeting occurred when the Virginians first came ashore at the boat landing and climbed the steep path leading from the majestic Hudson River to the austere buildings of the Academy. It might have come a bit later, maybe after the new boys had passed their admissions tests and were struggling to fit themselves into the unfamiliar uniforms the school required them to wear.

If the three did not meet earlier, they doubtless did at the summer encampment called "Camp Adams" that year to honor newly inaugurated President John Quincy Adams. All members of the Academy's Corps of Cadets except those entering their third year at the school (the rising "second classmen," who got to go home for an all-too brief summer furlough) spent most of July and August "in the field." There they learned and practiced various aspects of soldier life. During those weeks the old cadets put the new fourth classmen through what amounted to basic military training.

WE SHALL NEVER know the circumstances in which the young Mississippian and the two Virginians first saw one another, for their initial meeting went unremarked and unrecorded. When that summer 1825 encounter took place, they were three intelligent high-spirited college boys at the beginning of a new school year and a new life. They were at an early stage of their adulthood and at the very commencement of their professional careers. Forty summers later they were three old gray men standing amid the ruined hopes of their people.

Over the course of the four decades after they met the strands of their personal lives and of their professional careers came to resemble nothing so much as the long fronds of an underwater plant moving in the invisible currents. Sometimes the fronds sway in unison; at other times they appear to move independently. Occasionally they bump against one another; then, again at times, they seem to be on more or less parallel planes. Always, however, they have common roots and a common destiny.

So it was to be with the young Mississippian and the two Virginians. Their common roots were found in their backgrounds and at the Military Academy on the Hudson. The three found their common destiny forty years later amid the rubble of the Confederate States of America.

To a large extent both their destiny and the fate of their people had been determined by what the three of them did and did not do during the American Civil War—by "the triangular relationship among Davis, Johnston, and Lee."[1]

---

[1] Newton, *Johnston*, 69. As noted in the Preface, this work is not a conventional biography. For that reason, as well as to shorten the book and to minimize pedantry, I have not cited sources for well-known facts, biographical or otherwise. The planet is already cursed with, among many other things, too many footnotes. Unless otherwise noted, the biographical material is from the standard works: Cooper, *Davis*; W. Davis (no kin to his subject), *Davis*; Govan and Livingood, *Different Valor*; Symonds, *Johnston*; Freeman, *Lee*; Guelzo, *Lee*; Korda, *Lee*; Pryor, *Lee*; and Thomas, *Lee*.

The Civil Wars of General Joseph E. Johnston

Book One

Virginia, 1861-1862

Chapter One

JEFFERSON DAVIS AND JOSEPH E. JOHNSTON:
The General's Rank

PART I

"The army's iron-clad respect for seniority."
— Wayne Wei-Siang Hsieh, 2009

IN the spring 1861 crisis brought on by secession, Southern-born officers of the United States Army faced the question of whether their primary loyalty lay with the national government or with their individual State (as everyone would have written the word at that time). The dilemma constituted a terrible ordeal for many of them—the better the officer, the more terrible the ordeal. A few decades later one veteran of both the antebellum army and the Civil War recalled, "it was a trying time for all Southern officers . . . many, even from South Carolina, resigned with bitter tears."[1]

One by one those officers who came down on the State side of the question submitted their resignations to the War Department; balanced their accounts; closed their books and completed other administrative and housekeeping tasks; turned their duties over to their replacements; took leave of their comrades; and, finally, departed for their homes to offer their services in defense first of their State and then of the newly established Confederacy. Since initially only the seven States of the Deep South had declared themselves out of the Union, officers from the

---

1 Stanley, *Memoirs*, 61. Chapter XXV of volume I of Freeman's *Lee*, "The Decision He Was Born to Make," 431-447, is the classic account of an officer's struggle with this dilemma, but keep in mind Freeman's semi-worshipful attitude toward Lee.

border slave States were spared, but only temporarily, the agony of making that decision.[2]

The outbreak of war in mid-April forced the eight slave States remaining in the Union to reconsider their earlier decisions against secession. Four of them—Arkansas, North Carolina, Tennessee, and Virginia—opted to join their Deep South sisters in the Confederate States of America.

Virginia's secession on April 17 led two of the most distinguished officers of the national army to conclude, after much agonized thinking, that they could not fight against their State and that duty compelled them to leave the army in which they had served so well for more than thirty years and to take up arms in defense of the Old Dominion. Colonel Robert E. Lee submitted his resignation from the United States Army on April 20; Brigadier General Joseph E. Johnston handed in his two days later.[3]

After brief service in the Virginia State Army (the Old Dominion had not yet joined the Confederacy), both Lee and Johnston received from President Jefferson Davis appointments as brigadier generals in the Confederate Regular Army. (At the time brigadier general was the highest grade authorized by Confederate law.) The Rebel Chief Executive assigned Johnston to command Secessionist troops gathering at Harpers Ferry, Virginia (now in West Virginia). Lee wound up as a military adviser to the President with his office in Richmond.

By early fall Johnston found himself commanding Secessionist forces spread along Virginia's northern frontier. Lee at that time had charge of the defenses of far-off western Virginia and would soon take command on the South Atlantic coast. By then both men held the grade of full general (equivalent to a modern "four-star general") which the Rebel Congress on May 16 had created as the highest in the Confederate Army.[4]

THE general Joseph E. Johnston, who directed the defenses of northern Virginia in 1861 and early 1862, embodied a massive bundle of high-strung

---

2 James Longstreet, *Manassas to Appomattox*, 29-30, gives some hint of this course of events in an officer's life.

3 One writer remembered that Joseph E. Johnston was so overcome with emotion when he submitted his resignation that he had to be helped from the room. See Pryor, *Lee*, 284-285.

4 'Grade" and "rank" are often (and incorrectly) used interchangeably. Strictly speaking, an officer holds a certain grade (captain, colonel, and so on) within which he (and, in modern times, or she) is ranked by seniority. Except in quotations, this strict meaning will be used in this study. Officers in higher grades, of course, "outrank" those in lower grades.

JOSEPH E. JOHNSTON
in the United States Army.
Carlisle Barracks

contradictions. He was to prove the most controversial of the Confederacy's wartime military figures. By April 1861 when he left the "old army" to "go South," he had shown himself to be a knowledgeable and unusually competent officer in no fewer than five different branches of the army—artillery, topographical engineers, infantry, cavalry, and quartermaster. A brave as well as an accomplished officer, he had twice been wounded in combat—by Indians in Florida in 1838 and by Mexicans nine years later.[5]

In the Civil War Johnston was to prove himself a general who could win—or at least receive—and frequently retain the loyalty, and even the devotion of, tens of thousands who served under his command. At the same time, he could demoralize thousands of other troops as well as many civilians even as he alienated, frustrated, and disgusted some other people—especially if they held authority over him.[6]

On occasion Johnston displayed a grasp of the Confederacy's general military situation and an understanding of the war's general military strategy far surpassing that of most other Rebels. He could, at the same time, show himself to be vain, self-centered, extremely petty, passive, parochial, and—most important of all—unbelievably dense and obtuse with regard to the importance of personal relations with his superiors and colleagues. He seems to have been almost indifferent regarding such crucial matters as his government's political, diplomatic, economic, logistical, and psychological (public opinion) needs. This last trait was to play the most significant role in shaping Johnston's part in the Confederacy and his place in American military history.

Almost all of this, however, lay in the unknown future in early September 1861, when General Joseph E. Johnston sat down at his desk in his Manassas, Virginia, headquarters, began to sort through the contents of a packet of mail recently

---

5 One of Johnston's admirers, writing just after the general's death in 1891, proclaimed that in 1861 he had been "the best soldier in the Army of the United States, accomplished in all the knowledge of the art of war and capable of directing great affairs and great armies. He was master of the art of logistics, the art of managing great armies. Robert E. Lee, by contrast, had not had the scientific training that Johnston had." Johnson, *Memoir of Johnston*, 16.

6 Mary Chesnut, who gave us so many wonderful pen pictures of Confederate higher-ups, noted that Johnston's power to draw men to his support was "magnetic." (*Chesnut's Civil War*, 483. See also 633). At the same time, however, he was "a good hater" who "hates not wisely but too well." Campbell Brown (*Brown's Civil War*, 49-50), who served on Johnston's staff early in 1863 and who knew the general for many years, wrote soon after the war of Johnston's "power of attaching his subordinates & his troops devotedly to himself. . . . [but] he unfortunately falls short . . . in that . . . temper which alone could mould [President] Davis [his commander-in-chief] to his purpose." As we shall see Johnston's power failed in 1864 in four crucial instances. See Chapter Four ("Ole Joe in the Vipers' Pit"), in Book Three, Volume 2 of this work.

received from the War Department in Richmond, and settled back in his chair to study an account of the military legislation enacted during the just-closed session of the Confederate Congress.

IN February 1861 delegates from the seven seceded States assembled in Montgomery, Alabama, to organize the general government of their new nation. The need to make military preparations to defend their recently proclaimed independence obviously took precedence over almost everything else. Once the new government had been formed and at least the top executive officers installed, the delegates took up a series of bills providing for the raising of an army and spelling out the details of its organization.

When the legislators completed their task, they had created the legal framework for the Confederacy's basic military structure. The lawmakers had provided for what amounted to two armies. An act approved on February 28 authorized formation of the "Provisional Army of the Confederate States"; a March 6 law brought into being the "Confederate Regular Army."

The former was to be a large temporary force made up of troops raised and organized as regiments and battalions by the separate States and then taken into national (Confederate) service to wage the impending war for Southern independence. That goal achieved, the Provisional Army would disband and the troops would return to their individual States and to civilian life. All but a small handful of the approximately one million men who fought for the Confederacy did so as members of the Rebels' Provisional Army. The much smaller Regular Army, on the other hand, was to be raised directly by the Confederate Government and would remain in existence after independence had been won. It would become the Confederate version of a permanent, standing, professional military force.

The president was to appoint, with the consent of the Congress (later only of the Senate), such officers as Congress had authorized by law to command the Regular Army units and general officers to command the Provisional units above the regimental level. A May 21, 1861, act authorized the Chief Executive to give temporary commissions to RACS officers for service with PACS ("volunteer") troops. During the approaching war the two armies would function as a single organization, much in the way that in modern times a National Guard or Reserve unit called to active duty in Federal service becomes a part of a larger force that includes Regular, permanent United States Army units.

The bulk of the 1861 military legislation dealt with routine matters authorizing the transfer of some of the pre-existing State units to the new Confederate Provisional Army, spelling out details of the armies' size and organization, setting the pay level for soldiers of various grades, and so on. These laws also provided for creation of the different staff branches of the Regular Army—Adjutant and Inspector General's Department, Corps of Engineers, Ordnance Department, Quartermaster and Subsistence (Commissary) departments, and so on.

Section 8 of the March 6 law provided for the appointment in the Regular Army of four "brigadier generals, who shall be assigned to such commands and duties as the President may specially direct." On March 14 Congress increased the number of brigadier generals to five. In May 1861, Lee and Johnston received their appointments as brigadier generals in the Confederate Regular Army under the provisions of these laws.[7]

AS the Secessionists went about perfecting and implementing their army organization, they found a potentially serious problem with the grade structure of their military force. Each of the Confederate States had seceded and theoretically had been an independent republic before joining the Confederacy. As a sovereign country, each of the Rebel States had organized its own army under the command of one of its own officers who usually held the grade of major general in that State's military force. Upon resigning from the United States Army, Robert E. Lee had been named (by Virginia authorities) as the State major general to command the Old Dominion's State army. Jefferson Davis, prior to his election as Confederate president, had served as the State major general in command of the Mississippi State army.

When the Rebels organized the Confederacy's military force, they formed its Provisional Army by calling upon each State to raise its quota of troops and, once organized as regiments and battalions, turn them over to the Confederate government for national ("volunteer") service in the Provisional Army. The individual State armies themselves (minus the units turned over to the Confederacy) remained in existence as an army or as part of the State militia. They were independent of the national (Confederate) military establishment just as in modern times a National Guard unit not in Federal service is a state force.

Should a Confederate State be invaded, the governor could send its army into the field to reinforce and to operate in conjunction with the Confederate

---

7 These laws are in United States War Department, comp., *The War of the Rebellion: Official Records of the Union and Confederate Armies*, Series IV, Volume I, 117, 126-131, 163, 326, and 341. Hereafter this compilation will be cited as *OR*. Unless otherwise noted, all references are to volumes in Series I. Citations to volumes in Series I will be volume number, *OR*, part number (if applicable), and page. Examples: 8 *OR*, 74; 38 *OR* pt. 4, 116, 134.

government's own forces. In such a case could—or should—a State major general (a "two-star" grade) exercise command over a Confederate brigadier general ("one-star")? Could a State brigadier who was senior to his Confederate counterpart order the latter about? Would Alabama troops in the Confederate Provisional Army be willing to serve under the command of a general of the Georgia State army?[8]

To deal with this problem, as well as with several lesser matters, the Confederate Congress on May 16 passed an act amending the law of March 6. Section 2 of the May 16 law declared that the five Regular Army brigadier generals whose appointments were authorized by earlier legislation would be re-designated "general . . . which shall be the highest military grade known to the Confederate States." These "full" or "four-star" Confederate generals would outrank any State officer.[9]

The May 16 law solved the problem of whether a State general would exercise command over a Confederate army. Later Congress would tinker with the army's organization and make various changes, but for our present purposes the acts summarized above created the relevant grade structure.

In the late summer of 1861, however, another problem arose. This one concerned only General Joseph E. Johnston. It involved the matter of rank within a grade, and it grew out of a provision in the March 14 law. This problem set the tone for the remainder of Johnston's Confederate career. In many ways it set the tone for the remainder of his life. It was to have a profound effect on the history of the Confederate States of America and therefore on the history of the United States.

CAREER soldiers have always taken great interest in promotion and rank. At isolated antebellum army posts officers spent hours poring over whatever documents came their way to learn who had died, retired, or been promoted or transferred, possibly opening slots into which they themselves might move. Frequently arguments, sometimes bitter, raged over who outranked whom.[10]

---

8 The status of all Confederate general officers was, in fact, indicated by three stars surrounded by a wreath. In some cases such as these sentences, I have used modern terms for clarity.

9 1 *OR*, Series IV, 249, 267, 326-327. See also Weinert, *Confederate Regular Army*, Chapter I. Late in 1862 Congress created the grade of lieutenant general ("three stars").

10 One Confederate general explained to a civilian official early in the war that "The jealousy with which professional soldiers look upon military rank is second only, my dear sir, to that of honor." Braxton Bragg to Judah P. Benjamin, Sep. 25, 1861, 6 *OR*, 744.

In the March 14 Confederate law that increased the number of brigadier generals from four to five, the Rebel Congress undertook to deal with the hypersensitive question of "rank" among officers of the same grade in the new Southern army. Section 5 of that law read:

> Be it further enacted, that in all cases of officers who have resigned, or who may within six months tender their resignations from the Army of the United States, and who have been or may be appointed to original vacancies in the Army of the Confederate States, the [Confederate] commissions issued shall bear one and the same date, so that the relative rank of the officers of each grade shall be determined by their former commissions in the U. S. Army, held anterior to the secession of these Confederate States from the United States.

The intent of the passage of this legislation is clear enough: The Southern Congress did not want a Confederate officer to be outranked by another Confederate officer of the same grade whom he had outranked in the antebellum United States Army.[11]

WE do not know when Joseph E. Johnston first became aware of the several Confederate statutes and their provisions regarding grade and rank in the Rebel army. He may have known of at least some of the legislation even before he resigned from the United States Army on April 22 to join first the Virginia State forces and then the Confederate Army. More likely, it seems, he would have learned of the law in May 1861 when he was in the then-Confederate capital of Montgomery, Alabama, at the time of his appointment as a brigadier general in the new nation's Regular Army.

Whenever the laws came to Johnston's attention, the section regarding rank doubtless pleased him greatly. He, after all, had been a brigadier general in the United States Army, and he believed himself to be the highest-ranking officer to leave the old service and to join the new Confederate Army. Johnston, therefore, naturally concluded that under the provisions of the March 14 law, he would be the

---

11 Some of the seceded States had earlier adopted similar legislation with regard to their forces. See, for example, Georgia's Jan. 25 stipulation on the subject (1 *OR*, Series IV, 79 and 167); *Virginia's policy* (ibid., 738); and South Carolina's problems with the question (ibid., 189, 190, and 202-203).

highest-ranking Confederate officer—and rank was crucial to Joseph E. Johnston. The desire (need?) for it consumed him.[12]

UNTIL the great reforms it underwent in the late nineteenth and early twentieth centuries, the United States Army employed a complex grade/rank structure. The army divided its officer corps into "line officers" and "staff officers." The former commanded troops, the latter performed specialized tasks for a commander but could not in their own names exercise command over troops. Although an individual could sometimes switch from line to staff or vice versa, ill-feelings and jealousies often flared up between the two groups. (Douglas Southall Freeman entitled one chapter of his great book *R. E. Lee* "The Ancient War of Staff and Line.")[13]

Every United States line officer below the grade of brigadier general received a commission into a regiment; every staff officer, including general officers, into a staff branch. Promotion up through the grade of colonel was within the regiment or staff branch and went strictly by seniority. Thus, no matter how capable an officer proved himself, or how brilliant his performance in a given assignment, or how brave his conduct on the battlefield, he had to await a vacancy above him in his

---

12 See also the comments in Newton, *Johnston*, 99-100. Historian Steven Woodworth (*Davis and Lee*, 53, 55, and 56) writes of Johnston's "never-ending lust for high rank." Johnston was clearly wrong in the matter of being the highest-ranking United States Army officer to join the Confederacy. David Emanuel Twiggs of Georgia, a brigadier general since the late 1840s, held that distinction. Twiggs, however, was old (born 1790), not a graduate of the Military Academy, in bad health in 1861, and had quarreled with Jefferson Davis in the 1850s. He served for a few months as a Confederate major general—outranking, per the law, all other Confederate major generals—and died in 1862. An interesting sidelight in his case is the fact that he did not resign from the United States Army in 1861. President James Buchanan dismissed him "for treachery" in March 1861. Would that fact have altered his Confederate status? (See the wording of the law quoted in the text.) The matter never came up.

13 Freeman, *Lee*, I, 111-128 (Chapter VII). The theme of staff-line conflict in the nineteenth-century United States Army runs through the pages of Daniel Beaver's *Modernizing the War Department*. See the same provision in Confederate law (*1 OR*, Series IV, 115). The Rebels did, however, permit the assignment of staff officers to line duty by special direction of the President. For some examples of staff-line conflict in the Confederacy, see Goff, *Confederate Supply*, 66-67 and 75-88. In *Manassas to Appomattox* (112), James Longstreet wrote, "officers of the line are not apt to look to the staff in choosing leaders of soldiers, either in tactics or strategy." He probably intended this as a swipe at Lee, whom he criticized in the postwar decades.

regiment or staff branch before he could move up in the military hierarchy. His place in the regiment or staff branch was his "permanent grade."[14]

The army then had no "up or out" rule or mandatory retirement age. It was not unusual, therefore, for an officer to find himself "stuck in grade" for long periods. Robert E. Lee, for example, spent seventeen years (1838-1855) in his "permanent" status as a captain of engineers. Ironically, his third cousin, Samuel Phillips Lee, who was to become a distinguished Union naval officer in the Civil War, also found himself "stuck in grade" as a navy lieutenant at almost the same time (1837-1855).[15]

TO get around the many morale problems inevitably generated by this system, the army—borrowing from British practice—developed a second grade/rank structure running parallel to its "permanent" system. This "brevet" system fulfilled three functions. First, and most often, it served to allow promotion of an officer outside the army's permanent structure. Thus, outstanding service could be quickly acknowledged with a "brevet" promotion. In effect, while promotion within the permanent structure of the army was based solely on seniority, in the brevet structure it could be based on merit.

For this reason, a captain who distinguished himself in a battle but who could not receive a permanent promotion because no vacancy then existed in his regiment, could be awarded a brevet majority. When he left the regiment—to go on leave, say, or to sit as a member of a military court at another post—he did so as a major. Under these circumstances he was entitled to wear a major's uniform, to be addressed as "Major," and to rank as a major. In some cases, he could also draw a major's pay. Upon returning to duty with his regiment, he reverted to his permanent status as captain. Thomas J. Jackson, for example, graduated from the Military Academy in 1846 and received a commission as second lieutenant in the 3rd Artillery Regiment. He quickly proved such a terror on the battlefields of

---

14 Historian Wayne Wei-Siang Hsieh (*West Pointers*, 145) writes of the *antebellum* army's "profound respect for seniority" and of "the army's iron-clad respect for seniority." Jefferson Davis's biographer William J. Cooper observed that in the "old army" "seniority dominated all else." (*Davis*, 246).

15 A study conducted in 1836 found that an officer who entered the army that year as a second lieutenant and spent the average time in each grade could expect promotion to colonel in 1894—after fifty-eight years of service. One officer who joined the army in 1799 died on active duty as a colonel in 1857 at the age of ninety-three. The monetary cost of a retirement system seems to have been a key factor in the decision not to establish one. Coffman, *Old Army*, 49, 99.

Mexico that fourteen months later he was "First Lieutenant and Brevet Major Jackson."[16]

The brevet system also permitted the President and the War Department to detach an officer from his unit or staff branch and order him to temporary duty in his brevet status. An officer could, therefore, receive an assignment in his brevet grade to some specialized task for which he was unusually well qualified even in cases in which the law, army regulations, or practice mandated that the task be performed by an officer holding a higher grade than his permanent one.

Captain Robert E. Lee of the Corps of Engineers received three brevets for his brilliant service in the Mexican War and, therefore became "Captain and Brevet Colonel Lee" in 1847. In September of 1852, Captain Lee, by order of the War Department, put aside his normal engineering duties and "[Brevet] Colonel Lee" became superintendent of the Military Academy—a post he filled for three years. The secretary of war then selected him for assignment to the newly organized 2nd Cavalry Regiment, transferred him from staff to line, and promoted him to the permanent status of lieutenant colonel in that unit. He, therefore, became "Lieutenant Colonel and Brevet Colonel Lee." His March 1861 promotion to colonel of the 1st Cavalry Regiment rendered his brevet status irrelevant.

Third, the brevet system gave the army a place to put (i. e. administratively to account for) surplus officers. On occasion a Military Academy graduate found himself commissioned "brevet second lieutenant" when he left the school. Although formally commissioned into a unit or staff branch, he had no permanent grade because no vacancy then existed in his unit or branch into which he could be placed.

As a brevet second lieutenant, the new officer reported to his unit or branch and performed whatever tasks could be found for him. (The technical term for his status was "supernumerary.") Brevet Second Lieutenant Jefferson Davis spent three years in that status with the 1st Infantry Regiment. When a second lieutenant's slot finally opened, he received a permanent promotion to second lieutenant to fill it, with his date of rank set back to his 1828 graduation day from the Military Academy. Since his "permanent" and "brevet" grades were then the same, the latter lost all meaning.

---

16 It was for this reason that after Lieutenant Thomas Jackson resigned from the army in 1851 and began teaching at the Virginia Military Institute he was "Major Jackson" although, of course, he no longer held any commission in the United States Army. VMI faculty held commissions in the Virginia militia. They still do, although it is now officially "the Virginia Militia unorganized." Irreverent cadets call it "The Virginia Militia disorganized."

As if to complicate matters even more, the army implemented what amounted to a third grade/rank system by designating staff officers' grades as such. In 1860, when Joseph E. Johnston became the new Quartermaster General of the army, the War Department transferred him to that staff branch from his line unit, the 1st Cavalry Regiment, in which he then held the permanent grade of lieutenant colonel and the brevet grade of colonel. As a result of this transfer, he received a promotion to the grade of "brigadier general, staff." He thereupon lost his permanent status as a line officer along with his permanent grade of lieutenant colonel, and his brevet grade lost its meaning.

IN summary, an officer could hold different permanent and brevet grades simultaneously. He could not, however, hold both line and staff grades. His active grade depended upon where and in which capacity he served at any given time—line, permanent, brevet, or staff. So, too, did his rank relative to other officers. Officer A might outrank Officer B in their permanent grade, but not in their brevet status. Which was the higher-ranking man at any given time depended upon what the active status of each then was.[17]

Such a grade/rank structure could (and frequently did) produce endless hyper-byzantine bureaucratic bickering. It could also greatly complicate application of the March 14, 1861, Confederate law, which stipulated that an officer's rank in the new Rebel army derived from his rank in the old Federal army.

TO President Jefferson Davis fell the task of selecting the men to nominate for the general officer posts created in the Confederate Provisional and Regular armies by the early 1861 legislation. Although Davis had involved himself in the detailed work of drawing up the laws to create the new Southern military force, he did not immediately act to select its top Regular Army generals.[18]

We have no record of the reason for Davis's delay in naming the men he wanted to head the Confederate armies. It seems a reasonable speculation, however, that he had several excellent possible selections (or possible selections that he thought were excellent) in mind, but did not know for some time which men would be available. After all, when Congress enacted the initial military legislation, the Confederacy comprised only the seven states from South Carolina

---

17 Many thanks to the late, great Dick Sommers for crucial help in puzzling out the complicated subject of "rank" in the *antebellum* United States Army.

18 Cooper, *Davis*, 335.

JEFFERSON DAVIS,
president of the Confederacy.
LOC

west to Texas. Those states, as Davis well knew, could boast of few really distinguished high-ranking military men, and it was possible that not all those officers would opt to join the Confederacy.

From his own long experience—at West Point (1824-1828), as an antebellum army officer (1828-1835), as a regimental commander in the Mexican War (1846-1848), as secretary of war (1853-1857), and as chairman of the Senate Military Affairs Committee (1857-1861)—Davis had gained extensive personal knowledge about many of the professional military men of the small antebellum United States Army. He doubtless knew all too well that the most distinguished Southerners in that army hailed from States that had not joined the Confederacy at the time the Southern Congress enacted the first laws organizing the Rebel forces. Probably for that reason Davis did not immediately rush to submit to Congress formal nominations for the Regular Army generals' slots. Instead, he elected to wait to see if future events would bring him more and better options.

VIRGINIA was one of the keys. The Old Dominion boasted a long martial tradition and as of 1861 had sent far more of her sons to the national Military Academy and into the United States Army than had any other Southern state. On February 15, 1861, the Atlanta *Gate City Guardian* published a study of the 1,132 commissioned officers then serving in the United States Army. Of the 413 from the fifteen slave states, only 96 hailed from the first seven states to join the Confederacy. Another 198 came from the four states that joined the Rebels after the war began—and 127 of those were Virginians.[19]

In the secession winter of 1860-1861 Virginia claimed five of the chief officers of the national army along with scores of younger men whose records indicated promising careers in the future. Should the Old Dominion join the Confederacy, Davis could hope to have in the Secessionist army such distinguished Virginians as Major General Winfield Scott, commanding general of the army;[20] Brigadier General Joseph E. Johnston, the army's quartermaster general; Colonel Samuel

---

19 Freeman, (*Lee's Lieutenants*, I, 709) calculated that by the time of the Civil War Virginia had 104 living graduates of the Academy (not all of them then in active service). The other ten Confederate states combined had only 184.

20 Davis and Scott had quarreled bitterly (and usually foolishly) in the 1850s. For that reason, the President may not have wanted him in the Confederacy. See W. Davis, *Davis*, 245-246 and 252-254.

Cooper, adjutant general of the army;[21] Lieutenant Colonel Robert E. Lee of the 2nd Cavalry Regiment—Colonel of the 1st Cavalry Regiment as of March 16; and Major George H. Thomas of the 2nd Cavalry. In March 1861, in fact, the Rebel government had contacted some of these officers to inquire about their accepting appointments in the Secessionist forces although their State had not then declared herself out of the Union and they still served in the Federal army.[22]

EVEN more than the Virginians, as distinguished and highly regarded as they were, Davis desperately wanted the man whom he and a great many others judged the most renowned of living American soldiers. In the spring of 1861 Colonel and Brevet Brigadier General Albert Sidney Johnston (no kin to Joseph E. Johnston) commanded the far-off Department of the Pacific from his headquarters in San Francisco. Born in Kentucky, Sidney Johnston had long since associated himself with Texas. He had served as a general in the army of, and then as secretary of war for, the Lone Star Republic when it was an independent nation. Would he follow his adopted State into the Confederacy?[23]

IN mid-April, when Virginia declared herself out of the Union, Scott and Thomas elected to remain loyal to the Federal government. Cooper had joined the Confederacy several weeks prior to his State's secession and had received an appointment as a Regular Army brigadier general from President Davis. When Lee and Joseph E. Johnston chose to follow their State, Davis quickly named them brigadier generals in the Confederacy's Regular Army. Once the May 16 law took

21 Born in and appointed to the Military Academy from New York, Cooper had married into a prominent Virginia family and become an adopted son of the Old Dominion. Many sources list New Jersey as his native state. The Military Academy *Register* (205) gives New York as his birthplace, as does Heitman's *Register* (I, 326). See also the errata sheet for Warner's *Generals in Gray.*

22 The state of Virginia had also initiated such contacts. See 51 *OR*, pt. 2, 22 and 37; 1 *OR*, Series IV, 165-166, 738, 956; Govan and Livingood, *Different Valor*, 27; Freeman, *Lee*, I, 434; and J. Davis, *Papers*, Vol. 7, 115.

23 Jefferson Davis later labeled Sidney Johnston "that truly great and good man, . . . one of the greatest and best characters I have ever known" (quoted in V. Davis, *J. Davis*, I, 36-37). On Sep. 2, 1861, the Richmond *Daily Dispatch* commented that Sidney Johnston was "a star of the first magnitude in the military world." Five days later the Macon *Daily Telegraph* noted that he and Lee were regarded by all as very highly qualified for military command. On Sep. 8 another Southern newspaper correspondent reported that A. S. Johnston "is generally conceded to be the finest field officer in the Confederate States, if not on this continent." Alexander, *Writing & Fighting*, 39.

effect, Cooper, Lee, and J. E. Johnston automatically became full generals. Davis, however, did not then formally nominate any of them for Congressional confirmation. It seems likely that he had chosen to wait to learn what Albert Sidney Johnston would decide to do.

NEWS of the secession of Texas did not reach San Francisco until April 9. That same day Sidney Johnston dispatched a letter to the War Department in Washington relinquishing his commission in the United States Army, and on May 6 the authorities accepted his resignation. Hoping that a North-South conflict could be averted, Johnston moved to Los Angeles after he left the Federal service.

A few weeks later Johnston concluded that duty compelled him to fight for Texas and the Confederacy. On June 16 he rode out of Los Angeles in the company of a small party of men going east to join the Rebels. After an arduous trek across the deserts of what are now the states of Arizona and New Mexico, he and his party reached the western boundary of Texas. In mid-August he arrived in Houston. On the sixth of September he reached Richmond. Overjoyed at Sidney Johnston's coming, President Davis, then ill in bed, quickly named him a full general in the Confederate Regular Army and assigned him to command Secessionist forces in the Kentucky-Tennessee-Arkansas-Missouri area.[24]

Already on August 31, with Sidney Johnston safely inside the boundaries of the Confederacy and soon to be in Richmond, Davis had sent the names of the nominees for the Confederacy's five highest generals' slots to Congress for confirmation. The lawmakers quickly gave their approval and then adjourned.

Joseph E. Johnston found an account of the August 31 Congressional action confirming Davis's full general nominees in his Manassas, Virginia, headquarters mail packet early in September—about the time Sidney Johnston reached the capital.

---

24 Roland, *Johnston*, 246-260; Richmond *Daily Dispatch*, Sep. 6, 1861; P. W. A. letter, Sep. 8, 1861 (published Sep. 15), Alexander, *Writing & Fighting*, 38.

PART II

> "Your strictures upon my order . . .
> imply strong disapproval—I suppose that of General Lee."
> — Joseph E. Johnston, June 26, 1861

THE packet from the War Department reached Joseph E. Johnston's Manassas headquarters sometime between September 3 and 10, inclusive.[25] An aide placed the packet on the general's desk, and Johnston found it there when he sat down to go through the day's mail. Once the general opened the packet and examined its contents, his attention focused on an account of the recent Congressional proceedings when the lawmakers had confirmed President Davis's nominees for the five full general slots authorized for the Regular Confederate Army by the law of May 16, 1861.

Johnston's anger rose as he read down the short list of appointments. The President had not only nominated the five officers to be confirmed as full generals, but he had also assigned to each a different date of rank. In so doing he had bestowed upon them their relative status in the Confederate army based upon the hallowed practice of seniority.

IN first place among the Confederacy's full generals with a May 16 date of rank stood Samuel Cooper. As "colonel, staff," Cooper had been the antebellum Adjutant General of the United States Army, and Davis had named him Adjutant and Inspector General of the new Confederate Army.[26] Johnston doubtless knew that Davis and Cooper had been allies in several political and bureaucratic battles in

---

25 On September 3, 1861, Johnston ended a letter to Davis with the warm "your friend & obt servt"—a closing he would not have used once he learned how Davis had ranked the generals. Johnston completed his written protest of the rankings on or before September 10. A date of about September 5 or 6, therefore, seems reasonable as the time of Johnston's receiving the packet. See J. Davis, *Papers*, vol. 7, 322.

26 A provision of the March 14 law (as amended by the law of May 16) stipulated that the President could assign one of the Regular Army full generals as the Adjutant and Inspector General—the army's chief administrative officer.

the 1850s.[27] Second place on the seniority list went to the recently arrived Albert Sidney Johnston, whose date of rank Davis had set at May 30.

Joseph E. Johnston did not even stand third on the roster. Robert E. Lee occupied that position with a June 14 date of rank. Johnston probably found Lee's superior rank especially galling. Although the two had been friends since the first days of their cadetships at the Military Academy thirty-six years earlier, they had also been—at least in Johnston's easily-agitated mind—serious professional rivals.[28] Until the summer of 1860 when Johnston's selection as Quartermaster General had brought him promotion to "brigadier general, staff," Lee had always been a step or two in the lead. Now, Johnston, whose date of rank Davis had set at July 4, found himself once again outranked by his long-time friend and (as he thought) rival.[29]

Fifth place among the generals went to Pierre G. T. Beauregard, upon whom Davis had bestowed the date of rank July 21. Beauregard's status also upset the hyper-sensitive Johnston, but not because of that officer's elevation from brigadier general Provisional Army to full general in the Regular Army. Johnston himself, in fact, had recommended Beauregard's promotion to his new grade. Now Johnston took offense with the symbolism of Beauregard's date of rank.

On July 21, with Beauregard as second in command, Johnston had been at the head of the army that had won the Battle of Manassas, the war's first significant engagement. In the weeks after that battle the public had come to credit the flamboyant Beauregard with the victory. As early as July 22, for example, journalist Peter W. Alexander reported that in the previous day's battle Johnston had carried out Beauregard's plan and that Beauregard "was really the officer and hero of the day." As a result of the public acclaim for his subordinate, Johnston had more or less faded into the background, his crucial role in the overall management of the battle almost ignored. Now, the date of rank that Davis assigned to Beauregard seemed to Johnston's impassioned mind to reinforce that tendency.[30]

---

27 In her "memoir" of her husband, Varina Davis (*Davis*, I, 563) called Cooper the president's "dear friend and coadjutor."

28 This subject will be discussed in Book Two, Chapter Two, Part II.

29 See, for example, Glatthaar, *Lee's Army*, 46.

30 Alexander's reports first appeared in the Savannah *Republican* on Jul. 20 and 27, respectively. See also Alexander, *Writing & Fighting*, 18 and 20. After the war Johnston and Beauregard would clash in their accounts of the battle. See Book Six, Chapter One, Part I, in Volume II. Johnston had his own newspaper advocate. In early August, a letter from "a prominent officer,

Believing that he rightfully and lawfully held the post of highest-ranking general in the Confederate Army, and deeply wounded by what he easily convinced himself was a clear and intentional violation of the law and a gross act of injustice on the part of the President, Johnston sat down sometime about September 6 or 7 to compose a letter protesting the position assigned him by Davis.[31]

JOHNSTON'S September protest was not the first manifestation of the general's extreme, often unwise, sometimes intemperate, usually petty and childish, and always foolish hypersensitivity with regard to his status and reputation in the Confederate military establishment. His initial touchiness regarding the matter surfaced in June 1861, a mere twenty-three days after he arrived at his first Confederate duty station at Harpers Ferry, Virginia.

Johnston reached his post at the confluence of the Shenandoah and Potomac rivers a little after noon on May 23 and assumed command the following day. Almost from the moment he saw Harpers Ferry, Johnston was unhappy with his situation. Indeed, he came to the post with "preconceived ideas" that it was untenable. "A complete reconnaissance of the area," he reported, confirmed this belief and led him to the conclusion (realization?) that Harpers Ferry was a trap and simply could not be defended. Even to try to hold it, he feared, would tie down the defending Confederates while allowing an enemy force "unrestricted" movement.

The town sat in a bowl in the acute angle formed by the two rivers, with high ground all around. Johnston did not have enough troops to defend it, and most of those he had were raw, undisciplined, and untrained. His men, he moaned, lacked weapons, ammunition, and equipment of all sorts. Of one of his units he wrote, "It is much to be regretted, I think, that the Tennessee regiment was admitted into the service. It is without accoutrements, instruction, or subordination." "Most of the reinforcements that have joined since my arrival," he complained on July 9, "have

---

who bore an honorable part in the battle" appeared in the Richmond *Dispatch*. The author wrote to dispel the widespread idea that Beauregard had fought the battle. "It is due to Gen. Johnston to say," wrote the prominent officer, "*that he planned the battle . . .* no one can now dare to dispute the sagacity which planned all the [army's] movements" (quoted from *Dispatch*, n. d., in Macon *Daily Telegraph*, Aug. 12, 1861). This was not the last time that newspaper criticism of Johnston was quickly followed by articles defending and praising the general. See Book Two, Chapter Eleven, and Book Three, Chapter Eleven (the latter in Volume II). At an unknown date Mrs. Chesnut noted that Johnston had many good writers on his staff (*Chesnut's Civil War*, 608).

31 In his postwar *Narrative* (71) Johnston wrote: "This [Davis's action] was illegal and contrary to all the laws enacted to regulate the rank of the class of officers concerned."

incompetent officers, and are therefore uninstructed." In a pattern he was to repeat with slight variations on several other occasions, Johnston began to bombard Confederate authorities with reasons why he could not successfully defend his post and how risky it would be for him even to try to do so.

At Harpers Ferry in the late spring of 1861 Johnston found himself confronted for the first time by what his biographer Craig Symonds called "the ambiguities of high command." If he made the wrong decision, he could bring a major—perhaps a mortal—defeat to the Confederacy and severely damage if not destroy his own carefully burnished reputation.[32]

CONFEDERATE leaders wanted to hold Harpers Ferry, if possible, but they realized that circumstances might well force the Rebels to evacuate the place once Federal troops pushed southward from Pennsylvania and Maryland. Johnston, commanding on the ground, must decide if and when the time had come to withdraw from the town.

For almost three weeks after reaching Harpers Ferry, Johnston agonized over his situation. Unable to devise any way that he could improve things, he constantly moaned about his plight. In reply he received repeated assurances that the government relied upon his judgment. Twice on June 1, for example, General Lee, writing for the Confederate authorities, told Johnston that he should move out of Harpers Ferry if threatened by a force he could not resist—a message that Lee repeated on June 7.

As Symonds points out, Johnston feared that abandoning the town might tarnish his honor and besmirch his reputation. If, however, he could induce the authorities to order him to withdraw, he would preserve his carefully guarded prestige.

BY mid-June, with a large Union army only a few miles north of the Potomac and bearing down on the entrance to the Shenandoah Valley, Johnston pulled his army out of Harpers Ferry and marched for Winchester. While en route, he received a letter from Adjutant and Inspector General Samuel Cooper. Dated June 13, the document was the government's latest response to Johnston's incessant whining about his plight at Harpers Ferry. It read in part:

---

32 Symonds, *Johnston*, 103-109. See Johnston's comments in May and June, 2 *OR*, *passim*.

You had been heretofore instructed to exercise your discretion as to retiring from your position at Harper's Ferry. . . . It is to be inferred that you have considered the authority given as not equal to the necessity of the case. . . . In all the directions which have been given to you[,] you will not have failed to perceive that, relying equally on your sound judgment and soldierly qualifications, it was intended that you should judge of the necessities of your condition and of the means best adapted to answer the general purpose of the campaign. As the movements of the enemy could not be foreseen, so it was impossible to give you specific directions, and the cause of the country could only be confided to one who, like yourself, was deemed entirely competent to decide upon events as they arose.

As you seem to desire, however, that the responsibility of your retirement be assumed here [in Richmond], and as no reluctance is felt to bear any burden which the public interests require, you will consider yourself authorized, whenever the position of the enemy shall convince you that he is about to turn your position and thus deprive the country of the use of yourself and the troops under your command, to destroy everything at Harper's Ferry . . . . and retire upon the railroad towards Winchester [my emphasis].

. . . . It has been with reluctance that any attempt was made to give you specific instructions, and you will accept *assurances of the readiness with which the freest exercise of discretion* on your part will be sustained [my emphasis].

Immediately upon receipt of this letter Johnston fired off a telegram in response: "I am confident that nothing in my correspondence with my military superiors makes me obnoxious to the charge of desiring that responsibility for my official acts should be borne by any other person than myself." (Johnston used "obnoxious" in the old sense of liable or deserving censure.)

Back from Cooper came the reply, dated June 18:

In the letter to you of the . . . [13th], if the instructions seemed to you specific, be assured it was only intended to respond to the desire manifested . . . by you, and both then and theretofore and now the fullest reliance was placed in your zeal and discretion and *you are expected to act as circumstances may require* only keeping in view the general purpose to resist invasion as far as may be practicable, and seek to repel the invaders whenever and however it may be done. In order that all disposition may be made to meet your wants *it is necessary that you should write frequently and fully as to your position and the movements which may be contemplated by you* [my emphasis].

. . . I would enforce upon you the necessity of *communicating promptly* all reliable information which you may obtain in relation to the enemy [my emphasis].

With General Cooper's June 18 letter the correspondence on the subject came to an end. Johnston was obviously correct about the impossibility of holding Harpers Ferry with a force too small to occupy the surrounding high ground and to block the Potomac River crossings above and below the place, as well as with regard to tying down a garrison in what could only have been a hopeless attempt to hold the town itself simply by occupying it. The general, however, had clearly shied away from the responsibility of deciding to evacuate his post and had left it only when events had forced his hand. Cooper's June 18 letter seems to have been a clumsy attempt to close out the matter and to salve Johnston's very fragile ego.

The incident, nevertheless, had clearly "irritated" Confederate authorities (to use biographer Symonds's word). It had created the strong impression that Johnston placed his own reputation above more important matters.[33]

THREE sentences from this small flurry of correspondence stand out as adumbrations of what was to come. Two of them are quoted above: Cooper's pleas that "In order that all disposition may be made to meet your wants it is necessary that you should write frequently and fully as to your position . . . ," and "I would enforce upon you the necessity of communicating promptly. . . ."

A third prophetic sentence appeared in Johnston's June 15 telegram but is not quoted above: "*I know myself to be a careless writer*, and will not, therefore, pretend to have expressed clearly the opinion I wished to have put before the government [my emphasis]."

Four days after Cooper penned his June 18 letter President Davis himself would plead with Johnston, "I wish you would write whenever your convenience will permit, and give me fully both information and suggestions . . . I am sure you cannot feel hesitation in writing to me freely and trust your engagements will permit you to do so frequently."

These messages were but the first of multiple such exchanges. The following four years would see many similar pleas from Richmond and numerous instances of missed and misunderstood communications.[34]

LESS than a week after the question of Johnston's willingness (or unwillingness) to assume responsibility for the evacuation of Harpers Ferry died

---

33 Symonds, *Johnston*, 109.

34 All this correspondence is in 2 *OR*, 881-945, where the documents are arranged chronologically. For an example of Davis asking Johnston to communicate see his Aug. 1, 1861, message (5 *OR*, 766-767). Johnston's biographer Symonds ("Fatal Relationship," 14-15) noted that a lack of full and free communication was "the single greatest failing in the Davis-Johnston relationship" and was "primarily Johnston's fault." He also commented on Johnston's "deliberate" failure to cultivate Davis's support. See also ibid., 14-15, 20, and 25-26.

down, another brouhaha flared up when the prickly general convinced himself that he had again been censured by the Confederate authorities in Richmond. Even worse to Johnston's excitable mind, the authority in this case was none other than his old rival Robert E. Lee.

On June 21 Johnston directed (State) Brigadier General Gilbert S. Meem, commanding a local brigade of Virginia militia, to activate two additional regiments to help support Johnston's Confederate army near Winchester. When the state's governor learned of the order a few days later he inquired through channels if the report was correct. The query went to the Richmond office of Robert E. Lee, who still functioned as commander of the State forces and directed the activities of both Virginia and Confederate troops in the Old Dominion.

Lee had Lieutenant Colonel George Deas, his assistant adjutant general, write Johnston on his behalf to ask about the matter. The note, dated June 24, also included some advice for Johnston:

> If certain allegations in respect to the general's [Meem's] habits and daily condition, which have been made to General Lee are correct, he certainly would not be a fit person for this responsible duty. In addition to this, also, it is believed that the population from which these [militia] regiments would be taken is by no means loyal to the cause of Virginia.

Two days later Johnston replied to Deas, correctly pointing out that as a Confederate general he could not pick and choose officers of the State forces and that the allegation (of too much drinking by Meem) should be handled by the Virginia authorities. Then his well-honed desire to guard his reputation flared up:

> Your strictures upon my order to General Meem imply strong disapproval—*I suppose that of General Lee.* If I am correct in so understanding you, would it not be well to countermand the order in question at headquarters [my emphasis]?

Deas, again writing for Lee, replied on July 1:

> The general desires me to say that it was far from his intention to cast any strictures upon you. . . . The matter coming from the governor in the form of an inquiry was submitted to you for reply, as none could be given from this office. . . . The latter part of my letter was simply to convey to you certain information of a nature which might influence you if found correct.

In his first month commanding a Confederate force in the field Johnston had twice reacted explosively to what he clearly perceived as severe official censure of his professional actions. In both cases the comments that provoked him had come from officers he had outranked in the "old army" and whom he then believed he still outranked in Confederate service. Johnston's first field command as a general officer had not begun auspiciously.[35]

FOR the first two-and-one-half weeks of July Johnston's force hovered about Winchester, drilling and occasionally skirmishing with small parties of the enemy striking southward into the Shenandoah Valley. Some fifty miles to the southeast another Confederate army under Beauregard defended the crucial rail junction at Manassas. Should either Johnston or Beauregard find himself threatened by a superior force, the Rebels' best chance to meet the danger would be to unite their two armies.

Johnston received the order at 1:00 a.m. on July 18. "General Beauregard is attacked," Cooper telegraphed. "To strike the enemy a decisive blow a junction of all your effective force will be needed. If practicable, make the movement, sending your sick and baggage to Culpeper Court-House. . . . In all arrangements exercise your discretion."

Disengaging from the Federals near Winchester and leaving some cavalry and the local militia (Meem and all) to protect the area, Johnston had his troops on the way by 12:00 M. The Confederates were able to utilize a railroad for part of their movement, and Johnston's leading units reached Manassas during the afternoon of July 19. Johnston himself arrived the following day, but the last of his men did not get to the area until the afternoon of the twenty-first.

WHILE en route, Johnston realized that a problem might erupt over command of the united forces. Doubtless he knew by then that he was or would be a full general by virtue of the law of May 16. As of yet, however, he had not been nominated for and confirmed in that grade. Might he still be a brigadier general? If so, did Beauregard, who had held that grade in the Provisional Army since March 1, outrank him? (Johnston, in fact, sometimes continued to sign documents "J. E. Johnston, Brigadier General" at least as late as July 23.)[36]

Unlike so many of Johnston's spats with the government, this was a legitimate matter of concern. Uncertain lines of authority and doubts about who outranked and commanded whom could produce chaos and defeat on the battlefield. To

---

35 2 *OR*, 948, 956, and 962; 5 *OR*, 808, 810, and 826.

36 2 *OR*, 995.

clarify matters, the general paused on the march to Manassas to dispatch an inquiry to Richmond. His telegram has been lost, so we do not know how he worded the question. Davis's July 20 reply read:

> You are a general in the Confederate Army possessed of the power attaching to that rank [grade].
>
> You will know how to make the exact knowledge of Brig. Gen. Beauregard, as well of the ground as of the troops and preparation, available for the success of the object in which you co-operate. The zeal of both assures me of harmonious action.

Three things about this short presidential dispatch merit comment. First, Davis did not give a clear and direct answer to Johnston's question—a practice he was to repeat on other occasions and one which sometimes must have frustrated those to whom he addressed his messages. Second, did the President expect the two generals to "co-operate," or was Johnston as the senior officer higher in grade and rank to command? Third, the telegram's last sentence is especially revealing. As will be discussed several times throughout this work, the President held consistently to a naive conviction that every Confederate would put aside personal considerations and grievances stemming from past events and cheerfully cooperate in the Secessionist cause. No experience to the contrary could shake this belief.

It did not affect this case, but it constituted one of Davis's major weaknesses as a wartime leader. On several occasions it contributed to defeats and massive disasters for the Rebels when the Chief Executive was not clear in his directives and simply would not enforce necessary subordination and obedience on some of his headstrong generals.[37]

ONCE arrived at Manassas, Johnston assumed command of the combined Southern forces. On July 21, with Johnston managing the overall battlefield and directing the movement of troops into the action and with Beauregard exercising tactical command, the Confederates won a convincing victory. After the battle Johnston and most of his troops from the Shenandoah Valley remained in the Manassas area, and he took overall command of the defense of northern Virginia. Almost immediately the previous pattern of his relations with the authorities in Richmond reemerged.

37 2 OR, 895; J. Davis, Papers, vol. 7, 254; Johnson, Memoir of Johnston, 49; Woodworth, Davis and Lee, xii; Cooper, Davis, 3, and 15-16.

On July 23, Lieutenant Colonel Dabney H. Maury reported to Johnston with orders from Lee assigning him to duty as Johnston's adjutant general. Johnston professed delight at seeing his old friend, but when he read Maury's orders, he exploded. "This is an outrage!" Maury remembered him exclaiming, "I outrank General Lee, and he has no right to order officers into my army." Johnston soon calmed down enough to assure Maury that he would like to have him serve on the staff, but he had already named another officer to the post and could not allow his inferior in rank (Lee) to assign officers within his command. The next day, while an embarrassed Maury returned to Richmond to seek another assignment, Johnston protested to Cooper about the order.

Lee had been using paper with the letterhead "Headquarters of the Virginia Forces" printed at the top of the page. When he began to exercise some authorized but ill-defined authority over Confederate troops as well as those of the State, clerks or staff officers lined out the word "Virginia." The altered stationery also provoked Johnston.

"I rank Genl. Lee," Johnston maintained to Cooper, ". . . and can admit the power of no officer of the Army to annul my order nor can I admit the claim of any officer to the command of 'the forces,' being myself the ranking General of the Confederate Army." When President Davis read this protest, he wrote one word on it: "Insubordinate." On July 29 Johnston again addressed a letter to Cooper:

> I had the honor to write you on the 24th instant on the subject of my rank compared with that of other officers of the C. S. Army. Since then I have received daily orders purporting to come from the 'Headquarters of the Forces,' some of them in relation to the internal affairs of this army. Such orders I cannot regard because they are illegal.
>
> Permit me to suggest that orders to me should come from your office [because, as Adjutant and Inspector General, Cooper communicated with troop commanders on behalf of the President and the secretary of war].

Davis also scrawled the word "Insubordinate" on this letter.[38]

---

38 J. Davis, *Papers*, vol. 7, 335n3; 2 *OR*, 1007; Maury, *Recollections*, 143-146; Symonds, *Johnston*, 126. Symonds commented that Johnston "went out of his way to make the point that he did not consider himself within the command structure in Virginia presided over by . . . Lee." A few years after the war, Johnston declared that he had been the ranking Confederate general and that he "would not have obeyed his [Lee's] order, but would have insisted on his seniority." Entry (date unknown, but 1870s) in diary of Susan H. Mims, Atlanta *Constitution*, Feb. 1, 1914. Maury also quotes Johnston as saying that for him to accept Lee's order would be to acquiesce "in so unlawful an assignment of rank of the Confederate generals as has been made." The

AUGUST passed relatively quietly. Lee had left Richmond on July 28 to command troops in western Virginia, so no more communications from him or from the "Headquarters of the Forces" arrived to upset the touchy general at Manassas. Events elsewhere, notably in Missouri and along the Outer Banks of North Carolina, drew attention away from northern Virginia where the hostile armies remained quiet.

Most of the August communications between Johnston and the government dealt with humdrum matters of army organization, weapons, the use and misuse of railroad freight cars, the quantity and quality of food issued to the troops, medical care for the soldiers, and so on. The tone of Johnston's correspondence with President Davis himself remained friendly—indeed, some of it could be called sycophantic.

On August 23, for example, Johnston ended a letter to Davis, most of which he had devoted to a discussion of rations, soldiers' health, and army organization, with "leave for two months the drudgery of you[r] civil duties. Command the army leaving the burden of administration to Generals—Occupy yourself merely with the [military] Campaign itself—& win the high glory of achieving the independence of our country. Your friend & obt servt."

So friendly had the summer's Davis-Johnston correspondence become that on July 13 the President wrote to the general, "Mrs. Johnson [sic] bears up very well under all her [medical] troubles, but frequently exhibits the anxiety which is common with the rest of us but even more intensely she feels for your safety." Two days later Johnston replied, "The kindness of your tone Gave this pleasure [of receiving your letter]."[39]

---

assignment of rank of the Confederate generals was something that Johnston could not have known at the time if, for no other reason than that no such assignment of rank of the Confederate generals had yet been made. The quotation doubtless reflects Maury's knowledge of later events at the time he penned his *Recollections*. Nor would Johnston's August correspondence with the Chief Executive have been as friendly as it was had he then known of the rankings. For examples of this correspondence, see 5 *OR*, 777 and 779, and the next section of this chapter. Confederate grade/rank structure could be as complex as that of the Union. Maury then held three grades: as a colonel in the Virginia State Army, as a captain in the Confederate Regular Army, and as a lieutenant colonel in the Confederate Provisional Army. His meeting with Johnston is often dated Jul. 24 (the date of Johnston's protest). Maury's account, however, shows that he reached Manassas on Jul. 23, the day President Davis returned to Richmond from a visit to the army.

39 J. Davis, *Papers*, vol. 7, 305-306. For other examples, see 5 *OR, passim*.

THE thirty-first of August—the day Congress confirmed the President's ranking of the full generals—marked Joseph E. Johnston's one hundredth day as commander of a Confederate field army. His disputes with the authorities during that period concerned his official status and had been with Cooper and Lee—his juniors in rank, as he then believed.

As the calendar turned over into September, Johnston was about to take his quarrels with the Richmond government to what psychologically, linguistically, and bureaucratically would be a whole different level.

PART III

". . . the wrong which I conceive has been done me."
— Joseph E. Johnston, September 12, 1861

JOHNSTON probably labored for several days on his letter to President Davis protesting his rank among the Confederate generals. It seems unlikely that he consulted anyone else. If he did, no record of such consultations is known to survive.

The first version of his letter ran to about 2,300 words, but Johnston quickly realized that parts of it were too harsh even for him. He therefore cut it by about fifteen percent, deleting many of the most caustic passages. The normal day-to-day hassles of army command doubtless interrupted work on the protest from time to time, but the general completed the document sometime on September 10. When satisfied with what he had written, Johnston put the letter in final form and set it aside to give himself a couple of days to collect his thoughts.[40]

---

40 If Johnston did in fact discuss the matter with anyone else, it was probably with his brother Beverley (spelled "Beverly" in some records), who on occasion visited him at Manassas. See Newton, *Johnston*, 221 n15. The passage Johnston excised is available, ibid., 213-214. See also Johnston's *Narrative*, 72-73. The manuscript version of the letter ran to nine pages. See Johnston, "Responsibilities of the First Bull Run." The general's draft of the letter can be found in the Hughes Papers.

WHILE the protest smoldered in his desk drawer, Johnston, on September 10, took up his pen to write to President Davis about another matter. A week had passed since his last communication to the Chief Executive—a crucial week for the Confederacy during which Johnston had learned of Davis's ranking of the generals—and the tone of his correspondence had changed.

The September 10 letter dealt with criticism that Johnston had heard had been directed at himself "by the two persons in Richmond highest in military rank." The "two persons" (obviously Cooper and Lee—Sidney Johnston had not been in Richmond more than a few days and had departed for his command in the West, and it is possible that Johnston did not even know that he had been there) were reported to have "censured" Johnston (his word) for the way he administered his army. This failure on his part, they allegedly charged, had produced "inconvenience" to the service.

Specifically, the supposed complaint was that Johnston had not "assumed command of the army." By this allegation the complainants seem to have meant that Johnston had failed to unite into one army the two Confederate forces that had joined to wage the July 21 Battle of Manassas. Rather, Johnston was said to have continued the original divided arrangement under which he commanded one army and General Beauregard commanded the other. (Beauregard, it must be said, fueled this charge by frequently corresponding directly with governmental authorities, sometimes on matters that far transcended the limits of his old command.)

This accusation, Johnston asserted to President Davis, was "untrue." He treated Beauregard, he wrote, as a colleague in his position should be treated and "not in the manner usual from a United States colonel to his next in rank." (Cooper and Lee, of course, were former colonels in the *antebellum* United States Army.) Then, Johnston sneered, "the inconveniences perceived in the army have been thought by it to have been produced in Richmond."

The general admitted that he "may have written carelessly" about some matters. He then pointedly referred to himself as "being by our laws *next in military rank* to yourself [Johnston's emphasis]." He closed with the formal "Most respectfully your obedient servant." His letter of a week earlier (before he had learned of the ranking of the generals) had ended with the warm "your friend and obt[.] servt."[41]

---

41 J. Davis, *Papers*, vol. 7, 322, 333-334; 5 *OR*, 850-851. I have found no specific information on whatever the incident or report was that ignited Johnston's protest. See, however, Alexander, *Writing & Fighting*, 38-39, for what seems to have been a similar complaint.

Davis replied to this letter on September 13, assuring Johnston that he did not believe that "any disposition has existed on the part of the gentlemen to whom you refer to criticize, still less to detract from you." Any complaints about Johnston and Beauregard, the President wrote, had come not from "the two officers highest in military rank in Richmond," but from uninformed persons who simply lacked any understanding of military affairs.

The President closed his letter with an important comment: "The laws of the Confederacy in relation to [full] generals have provisions which are new and untested by [bureaucratic] decisions. Their position is special, and the attention of Congress was called to what might be regarded as *a conflict of laws.* Their [Congress'] action was confined to fixing the dates [of rank] for the [full] generals of the C. S. Army [my emphasis]." Davis signed the letter "Your friend," but his failure (refusal?) to address the matter raised by Johnston's assertions about his rank seems an attempt to dodge the issue. His implication that Congress had fixed, with its hint that the legislators had determined, rather than merely confirmed, the generals' dates of rank as set by the President was at best misleading.[42]

EVEN as Davis wrote the September 13 letter, Johnston's protest about his rank was on its way to Richmond. On the twelfth, the general had taken the letter out of his desk drawer, read it over, and concluded that it was not an improper communication for a general to send to his civilian commander-in-chief. After dating and signing the letter, Johnston sealed it and put it in the mail. Davis received it on the fourteenth.

The document the President opened and read that day must stand as the most unusual communication that an American general in active service has ever written to his commander-in-chief. The action of the Chief Executive and Congress in ranking the generals, Johnston wrote, had produced surprise and *mortification . . .* in my mind." Then, he went on:

> I am deeply impressed with the conviction that these proceedings are *in violation of my rights as an officer*, of the plighted faith of the Confederacy, and of the Constitution and laws of the land. . . . [L]est my silence be deemed significant of acquiescence, it is a duty as well as a right on my part at once to enter my earnest protest against *the wrong which I conceive has been done me.* I now and here declare my claim, that notwithstanding these nominations by the

42 J. Davis, *Papers*, vol. 7, 314; 5 *OR*, 850-851. Note that Davis did not specify what Johnston's rank was, correct the general's assertions, or explain the rankings. For the importance of the words "conflict of laws," see the third following section of this chapter below.

President and their confirmation by Congress, I *still* rightfully hold the rank of first general in the armies of the Southern Confederacy [my emphasis]."

Johnston thereafter launched into a detailed discussion of the laws of May 6 and 16, quoting several passages from the legislation. Under the provisions of these laws, he asserted, he—a brigadier general in the antebellum Federal service—clearly outranked the three pre-war colonels whom Davis had placed senior to him in Confederate service. Then Johnston hurled a very serious accusation at the President:

The effect of the course pursued [by Davis] is this: *It transfers me* from the position of first in rank to that of fourth. The relative rank of the others amongst themselves is unaltered. It is plain then that *this is a blow aimed at me only*. It reduces my rank in the grade I hold. This has never been done heretofore in the regular service in America but by the sentence of a court-martial, as *a punishment and a disgrace* for some military offense. *It seeks to tarnish my fair fame as a soldier and a man*, earned by more than thirty years of laborious and perilous service. I had but this, the scars of many wounds, all honestly taken in my front and in the front of battle, and my father's Revolutionary [War] sword. It was delivered to me from his venerated hand, *without a stain of dishonor. Its blade is still unblemished* as when it passed from his venerated hand to mine. . . . [The rankings constitute] a studied indignity offered me. . . . If the action against which I have protested be legal, it is not for me to question the expediency of *degrading* one who has served laboriously from the commencement of the war on this frontier and borne a prominent part in the only great event of that war [the Battle of Manassas on 21 July] for the benefit of persons neither of whom has yet struck a blow for this Confederacy [my emphasis].

Johnston signed the letter with the formal "Your obedient servant." The president's reply came swiftly:

I have just received and read your letter of the 12th inst. Its language is, as you say, unusual; its arguments and statements utterly one-sided; and its insinuations as unfounded as they are unbecoming. I am &c.,

Jeffn. Davis.

This telegram closed the official wartime correspondence between the two men about the subject. Neither would take up the matter again until his postwar writings.[43]

WHAT are we to make of this episode?

Easy things first. On several occasions during the quarter of a century that he lived after the war, Johnston wrote at some length to make the argument that legally he had been the highest-ranking Confederate general.[44] The President's action, he charged, had marked the beginning of an effort by the Chief Executive and others in the administration to disgrace him and to force him to leave the army. (Why he thought that Davis wanted to do this he never stated.) Davis made a few postwar attempts to present his side of the case, but he usually chose to ignore the matter (as well as many other wartime intramural Confederate spats) in order to present an after-the-fact façade of wartime white Southern unity.[45]

On one occasion, for example, Davis pointed out that Lee and Johnston had entered Confederate service from the Virginia State Army, not from the antebellum United States Army, and that in State service Lee had outranked Johnston. At another time, Davis apologists claimed that the President had ranked the generals in the order of their graduation from the Military Academy: Cooper (1815), Sidney Johnston (1826), Lee (1829, standing second in the class), Joseph E. Johnston (1829, standing thirteenth), and Beauregard (1838). In truth, this coincidence simply reflects the fact that those who have been in a hierarchical organization longest will usually be older than and stand above those who join later. Someday, no doubt, a desperate graduate student will uncover convincing evidence that Davis ranked his generals by height and weight.[46] In fact, the Rebel Chief

---

43 1 *OR*, Series IV, 605-608; J. Davis, *Papers*, vol. 7, 340. Johnston, of course, was not the only Civil War officer to resent and protest his ranking among his colleagues. For a couple of other examples, see William S. Rosecrans to Henry W. Halleck, Sept. 26, 1862 (17 *OR* pt. 2, 239) and Col. R. R. Garland of the 6th Texas Infantry Regiment (17 *OR* pt. 1, 788). The others, however, were almost all professional matters. As discussed below, Johnston's was also deeply personal.

44 In addition to Johnston's *Narrative* (as discussed below), see his "Responsibilities of the First Bull Run."

45 As we shall see, Davis's private postwar correspondence was another matter. These writings will be discussed in Book Six in Volume II.

46 See Cooper, *Davis*, 363; Symonds, *Johnston*, 127; V. Davis, *Davis*, I, 57; and Johnston, *Narrative*, 71-73.

Executive ranked his generals in what seems to have been the order intended by Confederate law.

To protest his standing, Johnston cited and quoted Section 5 of the March 14 law, which stipulated that a Confederate officer's rank within his grade would be determined by his *antebellum* ranking in the United States Army. When he did so, Johnston was either unaware of or chose to ignore Section 29 of the March 6 law, which specified *how* rank in Confederate service would be determined.

Section 29 seems to have been an effort by Rebel officials to deal with the problems that inevitably would arise in applying the complex grade/rank structure of the United States Army (described in Part I of this chapter) to the new Confederate forces. President Davis himself may have been responsible for inserting this provision into the law. (Who else in the Confederacy's February-March 1861 government had the knowledge of, and the experience with, the numerous problems growing out of the United States Army's pre-war rank and grade structure that Davis had acquired during his years as an officer, as secretary of war, and as chairman of the Senate Military Affairs Committee?)

Section 29 of the March 6 law provided for adoption of the "Rules and Articles of War" of the United States Army by the Secessionist army with two alterations. First, wherever in the Articles the words "United States" appeared, the words "Confederate States" would replace them—a simple administrative and legal change.

Second, Section 29 spelled out the rules for using *antebellum* United States brevet and staff status in the Confederate Army. These new rules stipulated that an officer's old brevet status would not be used in the Secessionist army except in certain narrow cases when an officer was assigned to duty as a member of a military court or of a board of officers. In all other circumstances Section 29 stipulated that a Confederate officer would "*do duty and take rank . . . according to the commission he held in his own corps* [my emphasis]."[47]

---

47 *OR*, Series IV, I, 131. My guess is that the provision regarding the use of brevet grades was intended to deal with the problems that sometimes would arise under Confederate law in assembling enough officers of appropriate grades for a court or board. A captain, for example, should not serve on a board if the regulations stipulated that the board consist of majors or officers of higher grades. If enough such officers were not available and the captain had held a brevet colonelcy in the *antebellum* United States Army, he could join the board in that capacity. The Confederate Army did not award any brevet grades, although one occasionally finds Rebel officers so designated—especially in the early months of the war. On July 17, 1861, for example, the Huntsville (AL) *Democrat* referred to Colonel Francis S. Bartow as a brevet brigadier general. Most such careless usage seems to have occurred when an officer was acting

It was probably the potential discrepancy ("the conflict of laws") between Section 29 (rank in one's corps) and Section 5 (rank based upon rank in the pre-war army) to which Davis referred in his September 13 letter quoted above.

As Davis interpreted and applied the law, the awkwardly worded Section 29 meant that a staff officer from the old army who became a Confederate staff officer would rank according to his old staff status, a line officer as a line officer. A line officer in the Confederate Army who had been a staff officer prior to secession would rank in the Rebel army according to whatever line status he may once have held in the old Federal army, or if he previously had held no line rank, according to whatever Confederate rank as a line officer the Southern President bestowed upon him in the new Rebel army.

For this reason, Joseph E. Johnston, who went from quartermaster general and brigadier general, staff, to the Confederate post of a general commanding troops, reverted for the purpose of determining his Confederate rank to his former Federal (permanent) line status of lieutenant colonel, 1st Cavalry Regiment. As such, Johnston was outranked by Samuel Cooper (a colonel as of 1852), who held a staff post in both armies and therefore ranked as a Rebel staff officer, as well as by Albert Sidney Johnston (who was a colonel of the line as of 1855) and Robert E. Lee (who was a line colonel as of March 1861), both of whom served as line officers in both the United States and Confederate armies.[48]

---

temporarily in a higher slot than his actual grade. Bartow then commanded a brigade, normally a brigadier general's post. The term "corps" had several meanings. It designated a large unit made up of two or more divisions ("IV Corps"). It was also used to refer collectively to an army's officers ("officer corps"), to the student body of a military school ("corps of cadets"), and sometimes to designate a pre-war militia company. On Jan. 23, 1861, the Huntsville (AL) *Democrat* referred to the Madison Rifles as "this handsome corps." A short time later that "handsome corps" became Company D of the 7th Alabama Infantry Regiment. On Aug. 21, 1861, the New Orleans *Bee* described the Watson Light Artillery as "this crack corps of Creole gentlemen." In the case under discussion here, "corps" meant a branch of the army such as "Corps of Engineers" or "Artillery Corps," and as such it also meant staff or line. For an extreme example of how the term "corps" could be used, see the section entitled "Enrollment and Disposition of Recruits," in General Orders 30, Adjutant and Inspector General's Office, Richmond, 28 Apr 1862, 1, *OR*, Series IV, 1097-1099.

48 Since Section 29 had been enacted some six weeks before Virginia seceded and Joseph E. Johnston joined the Confederacy, it clearly was not aimed at him. So far as I know, Steven Newton (*Johnston*, 5-9) was the first to call attention to Section 29 and thus to resolve this long-debated matter.

WE simply do not know why Davis did not explain all of this to Johnston at the time. Part of the reason may have stemmed from the resentment that the President almost certainly felt at the general's petty and incessant carping and whining about his rank and status throughout the preceding four months (detailed in the previous part of this chapter) as well as at the childish and intemperate language in Johnston's September 12 letter. Davis's wretched health may also have contributed to the President's curt reaction. He was ill for much of the month and, in fact, had mentioned his condition in several pre-September 12 communications to Johnston.[49]

Had Johnston written a courteous and respectful letter simply inquiring about the matter rather than one filled with foolish whining about his father's Revolutionary War sword and about his treatment by, and wild accusations against, the government; or had Davis had the sense to put the general's letter aside for a few days before replying; or had Lee been in Richmond to advise presidential patience and restraint, the Chief Executive might have handled the whole episode differently.[50]

Would Davis have been a big enough man and a great enough president to have deflected Johnston's inflammatory charges and calmly to have explained the law to his outraged general? Would Johnston have been appeased by knowledge of Section 29? In such a case could harmony and cooperation have been restored and maintained between Johnston and Davis? If so, what would have been the impact on the war and hence on American history? We can never know.

A second crucial matter concerns the effect of the rankings and of Johnston's letter on the personal and professional relationship between the President and the general. In his *Narrative of Military Operations Directed During the Late War Between the States* (published in 1874), Johnston wrote,

> It is said it [the September 12 letter] irritated him [Davis] greatly, and that his irritation was freely expressed. The animosity against me that he is known to have entertained *ever since*

---

49 Davis never offered an explanation as to why he ignored the law's provision that Confederate appointments be as of the same date. By assigning different dates of rank, however, he precluded all dispute over the generals' status and ensured that Cooper, who as Adjutant and Inspector General spoke for him, would clearly outrank all the others.

50 Johnston's sympathetic biographer Craig Symonds (*Johnston*, 128) calls the general's letter "fatuous verbiage," "ill-judged and foolish," "self-indulgent and deliberately confrontational," and "the single worst decision of his professional career." And all this on one page!

was attributed, by my acquaintances in public life in Richmond *at the time* to this letter [my emphasis].[51]

Most historians and biographers of the two men have agreed with Johnston and maintained that the letter opened a gulf between the President and the general that never closed and, in fact, widened as the war went on. Biographer Symonds discussed the matter in a chapter entitled "Genesis of a Feud" and concluded:

> Johnston never forgave Davis for the ranking, and Davis never forgave Johnston for his outburst. The seeds of a lifelong feud would flourish in the ensuing years until that feud defined their whole attitude toward one another . . . . The two men would never again be able to exchange full and frank ideas about strategy, logistics, or any other subject. Nor would either man subscribe any of his letters to the other 'Your friend.'

Davis's biographer William Cooper agrees: "This incident fundamentally altered the relationship between president and general . . . neither man ever again trusted the other."

The major exception to the view that the September 12 letter immediately poisoned the Davis-Johnston relationship is historian Steven Newton. He questions how quickly the letter affected the "working relationship" between the two men. Instead, Newton maintains, neither man brought the matter up again during the war, and each conducted himself professionally over the following months. In the weeks after mid-September, Newton points out, Davis turned most of the routine day-to-day War Department business over to his new secretary of war, Judah P. Benjamin, who assumed the office on September 17, only three days after Davis received Johnston's letter.

Benjamin and Johnston soon began to squabble bitterly over a whole series of issues, and, argues Newton, Johnston "became more contentious with the president because he believed that Davis had condoned Secretary Benjamin and the rest of the military bureaucracy in Richmond in meddling with his legitimate prerogatives of command throughout the winter and spring [of 1861-1862]."[52]

---

51 Johnston, *Narrative*, 91.

52 Symonds, *Johnston*, 125, 128-129; Cooper, *Davis*, 364; Newton, *Johnston*, 5-9; Govan and Livingood, *Different Valor*, 69; and Woodworth, *Davis & Lee*, 345 n71. See also Symonds's "Fatal Relationship," and Brown, *Brown's Civil War*, 50. Most of Johnston's 1861-1862 correspondence with Benjamin can be found in 5 OR.

In fact, whatever differences exist among biographers and historians about the extent to which the September 12 letter damaged relations between Davis and Johnston involve matters of degree and timing, not of kind. All agree that the dispute over rank contributed much to the inability (unwillingness?) of the two to work together.

The bitter difference over rank as reflected in the exchange of communications quoted above came quickly on the heels of Johnston's spring and summer complaints and was followed almost immediately by disputes over several other matters, many of which involved Benjamin. The various issues stand too close to each other in time to permit us to spell out with any degree of certainty the extent to which the latter disputes proved more or less damaging than did the question of rank. No doubt exists that relations between the President and the general cooled very rapidly after the late summer of 1861 even though both men, in public at least, continued to observe most of the official proprieties of military etiquette.[53]

TO what extent might the dispute over rank have affected Davis as an individual (as differentiated from whatever effect it had on his official and personal relations with Johnston)?

Davis's biographer William Cooper understands the Rebel chief far better than does anyone else. He maintains that the President "could not countenance the human flaws of pride and ambition" that Johnston displayed in the September 12 letter. The document showed Davis that the general "cared more about rank than [about] the cause," and to the President "the Confederate purpose was far too serious to permit indulgence in such luxuries."

Here again, it becomes a question of the influence of the protest over rank as distinguished from the degree to which Davis's attitude was shaped by earlier and later matters. While the issue of rank certainly would have been more significant in this regard than the earlier spats and many of the later ones—and for Johnston, at least, was clearly more personal—it is simply impossible to separate the different influences of the various issues.[54]

MUCH more relevant to this essay is a fourth question concerning the effect on Johnston himself as distinguished from its influence on Davis and on the

---

53 "The entire winter was spent in quarrels of one kind or another." James, "Johnston," 350.

54 Cooper, *Davis*, 3, 352, 362-365, 389, 399, 412, 434, and 462. See also Cooper's *Davis and the Civil War Era*, 15-17, 50, 54, and 76-77.

general's relationship with the President. Here, I think, we can be a bit more definite in our conclusions, although the evidence is not as strong as I would like.

Johnston's September 12 letter was clearly penned by a deeply wounded man. Consider his language: "mortification," "violation of my rights as an officer," "the wrong which I conceive has been done me," "a blow aimed at me only," "it reduces my rank," "a punishment and a disgrace," "tarnish my fair fame as a soldier and a man," (an especially revealing assertion), "I had but this" (top rank), "a studied indignity offered me," and "disgracing one who has served laboriously."

The section that Johnston cut from the letter offers further insights into his wounded feelings. In July, he wrote, he had marched to reinforce Beauregard's army at Manassas

and against immense odds won a victory which in the minds of all men and nations established the glory and independence of the Confederate States, and crowns the army and its generals with the highest honor to which they could aspire. The applauding acclamation of the country, the Thanks of Congress, voted unanimously. Such is the first result presented to our view. What is the next reaped by the victorious general? What next? The General was already first in the highest grade known to the service. He could not be advanced. Something should be done—so he was degraded. Three officers, his inferiors in grade and in [Confederate] service, for neither of them had fought or won a battle for the Republic, were placed above him.... His commission is made to bear such a date that *his once inferiors in the service of the United States and of the Confederate States shall be above him* [my emphasis].

IN Johnston's mind, the President had done more than simply misinterpret the law or deny him the status to which he had concluded he was entitled by statute. Davis, Johnston had convinced himself, had unlawfully taken away the status the general had legally held prior to the August 31 action of the Congress confirming the generals' dates of rank. Consider Johnston's consistent assertions quoted in Part II of this chapter [the emphasis is mine]:

On July 23 to Maury: *"I outrank General Lee, and he has no right to order officers into my army."*

On July 24 to Cooper: *"I rank Genl. Lee . . .*and can admit the power of no officer of the Army to annul my orders . . . *being myself the ranking General of the Confederate Army."*

On September 10 to Davis: "being by our laws *next in rank to yourself."*

On September 12 to Davis: "not withstanding these nominations by the President and their Confirmation by Congress *I still hold the rank of first general* in the Armies of the Southern Confederacy."

In September in the excised part of the letter to Davis: "His [Johnston's own] commission is made to bear such a date that *his once inferiors in the service of the United States and of the Confederate States shall be above him.*"

In illegally stripping Johnston of his rank, the President had violated the general's "rights as an officer," done "wrong" to Johnston, punished and disgraced Johnston, "tarnished" the general's "fair fame as a soldier and a man," dishonored him and degraded him.

CLEARLY Johnston felt the matter of rank to be absolutely crucial. A few days after he mailed his September 12 letter of protest to Davis, Ida Powell Dulany, the niece of Lavinia Beverley Turner Fauntleroy, a friend of Johnston and possibly a relative, made an entry in her diary. Her aunt, she recorded, had received a letter from Johnston indicating that "a serious misunderstanding had arisen between the General and the President with regard to the Genl's rank."

On October 10 Archibald H. Cole, Inspector of transportation on Johnston's staff ("Archie," in some of Johnston's private correspondence) lamented his general's treatment at the hands of the Davis Administration. He bemoaned "the way our new Government proposes to reward their officers for hard fought battles and victories they are pleased to call glorious."

Both these comments from people close to Johnston—especially Dulany's which may have referred to a Johnston letter written before Benjamin took office—came so soon after the new secretary of war assumed his post and before he had clashed with Johnston that they can be taken as clearly reflecting the general's view of his treatment by Davis, not Benjamin.

In the last months of Johnston's life, Robert M. Hughes, the general's kinsman by marriage and first serious biographer, talked with him about Davis's 1861 denial of Johnston's claims to rank. Hughes summed up the results of the interview:

It is clear that in this matter Mr. Davis wronged General Johnston. The latter *always* felt it and to the day of his death looked upon it as second only to the greater wrong inflicted by his removal [from command of the army] in front of Atlanta [in July 1864] at the very juncture when he was preparing to reap the fruits of his strategy [my emphasis].[55]

Not long after Johnston's death in 1891, his friend and former subordinate Bradley T. Johnson wrote that the protest over rank "gives the key to his [Johnston's] character, and [to] his conduct of the war between the States."[56]

Unable to alter the President's decision, Johnston "resumed the role of military stoic" suffering persecution. The general, wrote his biographer Symonds, "brooded about [the matter] for the rest of the war—indeed, for the rest of his life," and he "internalized his disappointment, allowing the memory of that wound to embitter him for the rest of his life." Historian Gary Gallagher commented that relegation to a "position junior to three other Confederate officers sent Johnston into a fury that poisoned his entire Confederate service."[57]

A final and in many ways the most crucial question raised by these episodes (all of which, we must remember, arose in the first four months of Johnston's Confederate service) is why the general reacted as he did to what he clearly perceived as injustices inflicted upon him by President Davis and others in the government.

Why was he so quick to challenge Cooper's June 13 comment about his supposed unwillingness to bear responsibility for the evacuation of Harpers Ferry? Why had he jumped to the conclusion that Lee had censured him in the matter of General Meem? Why did he react so explosively to Lee's order assigning Maury to

---

55 Hughes, *Johnston*, 90. (Hughes accepted without reservation Johnston's interpretation of the law. See 78-79 and 87-89.) and Johnson, *Memoir of Johnston*, 2 and 64-68. See also Chesnut, *Chesnut's Civil War*, 608.

56 Dulany, *Journal*, 28. Dulany noted this under date of Sept. 24. She did not give the date of Johnston's letter to Fauntleroy ("Aunt Bena"). Cole quoted in Govan and Livingood, *Different Valor*, 71. Johnston to wife, Nov. 13, 1861, in McLean-Fisher Papers, Maryland Historical Society (collection cited hereafter as Johnston Letters, MHS). Hughes, *Johnston*, 90. (Hughes accepted without reservation Johnston's interpretation of the law. See 78-79 and 87-89), and Johnson, *Memoir of Johnston*, 2 and 64-68. See also Chesnut, *Chesnut's Civil War*, 608. In his important 1927 article "Johnston," (350) Alfred P. James quoted (although not by name) "one who was present" when Johnston learned of the ranking of the generals. Johnston, that person stated, was "enraged" at Davis's act.

57 Symonds, *Johnston*, 128-129); Gallagher, "Blue and Gray," 18. Johnston's role in the 1864 Georgia Campaign will be covered in Book Three, Volume II.

his staff? Why did he so resent the role of Cooper and Lee in his dealings with the President?

Why was Johnston so deeply hurt by his ranking among the generals and so quick to believe that the Davis Administration in general and the President in particular had set out to punish and disgrace him? Perhaps most significant of all, why did the denial of—stripping of—highest rank "tarnish . . . [his] fair fame as a soldier and a man"?

Speculation—and it can never be more than that—about the root causes of Johnston's cravings for rank and status and his pain, anger, and resentment when he believed himself unjustly and illegally deprived of them must await further examination of other facets of his life, especially of his background, of his Civil War military operations, and of his decades-long relationship with Jefferson Davis and Robert E. Lee ("Jeff, Bob, and Joe").

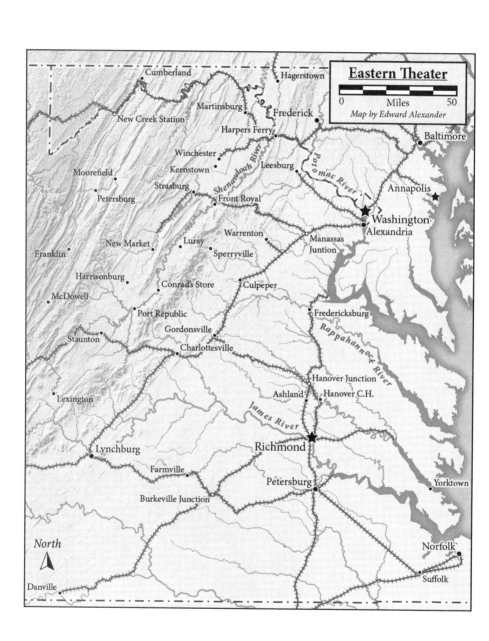

Eastern Theater

0   Miles   50

Map by Edward Alexander

Cumberland
Hagerstown
Martinsburg
Frederick
New Creek Station
Harpers Ferry
Baltimore
Winchester
Leesburg
Moorefield
Kernstown
Petersburg
Strasburg
Front Royal
Annapolis
Washington
Alexandria
New Market
Warrenton
Luray
Manassas
Juntion
Franklin
Sperryville
Harrisonburg
Conrad's Store
Culpeper
McDowell
Port Republic
Fredericksburg
Gordonsville
Charlottesville
Staunton
Hanover Junction
Ashland
Hanover C.H.
Lexington
Lynchburg
Richmond
Farmville
Petersburg
Yorktown
Burkeville Junction
North
Norfolk
Danville
Suffolk

Shenandoah River
Potomac River
Rappahannock River
James River

Chapter Two

Springtime of Despair

"... disaster has followed disaster till our cause,
to the despondent seems almost hopeless."
— Ida Powell Dulany, February 13, 1862

SOME time on Saturday, the seventh day of June 1862, General Robert E. Lee sat down at his desk in "High Meadow," a house belonging to Mary C. Dabbs that stood on the Nine Mile Road about one-and-one-half miles beyond the city limits of Richmond. The house then served as the general's headquarters.[1]

Lee's immediate task was to answer a more-or-less routine administrative communication he had received the previous evening from President Jefferson Davis. The general, however, also had a much larger objective in mind. This simple, ordinary piece of correspondence offered him the opportunity to create an atmosphere of trust and cooperation between the Confederate government in the nearby capital and the headquarters of the untested general to whom Davis only six days earlier had entrusted command of the endangered city's defending army.

THE general's appointment to head the force that was soon to become known as "Lee's Army of Northern Virginia"[2] came at the end of a five-month period of virtually unbroken calamities for the Confederates—a "catalogue of disasters," one Rebel official called it.[3]

---

1 Mrs. Dabbs, a widow, then lived elsewhere. Today the house (3812 Nine Mile Road), altered from its wartime appearance, is a visitors' center and museum.

2 Many modern white professional Southerners would prefer to call the force "Lee's poor, ragged, barefoot, starving, outnumbered Army of Northern Virginia."

3 J. B. Jones, *Diary*, I, 110.

New Year's Day 1862 had found the Secessionists in possession of almost all their own territory in the eleven States that had declared themselves out of the Union. (The unimportant exceptions being some fragments of northern and western Virginia and a few tiny enclaves along the Atlantic and Gulf coasts.)

At the beginning of the year the Rebels had also held significant parts of Kentucky and Missouri (in both of which rump factions of secession sympathizers claimed to have taken their States out of the Union and into the Confederacy) and of the Indian Territory (now Oklahoma). In addition, they laid claim to the southern part of the modern states of New Mexico and Arizona, a region then known to the Secessionists as the Territory of Arizona.

On that first day of January 1862 the great Mississippi River had rolled southward through Confederate-held territory along both of its banks from a point a short distance below its junction with the Ohio River at Cairo, Illinois, for almost 1,000 miles before emptying into the Gulf of Mexico. Virtually no Confederate soil had then felt the tread of an invading foe.

SOON after the new year began the Rebels' fortunes had turned sharply downward. By the time Lee assumed command of Richmond's defending army five months later, the military situation had deteriorated to an extent that alarmed all supporters of Confederate independence. As of late spring Yankee troops occupied even more points along the Rebel coast, notably in eastern North Carolina only a short distance southeast of Richmond. From their new coastal bases in the Old North State the Federals threatened to move inland and cut some of the Confederate capital's vital rail connections with the Deep South.

The Secessionists had also seen their armies driven out of Kentucky, Missouri, and West and much of Middle Tennessee. In addition, they had lost some important chunks of Arkansas, Louisiana, Mississippi, and Alabama. New Orleans, the Rebels' one true metropolis, had fallen to the invaders as had Pensacola with its harbor—the finest on the Gulf of Mexico and, arguably, in the Confederacy. Federal troops had occupied Baton Rouge, Memphis, and Nashville. The Yankees had also severed the crucial Memphis & Charleston Railroad, the South's only continuous east-west line of rail communication between the Atlantic Coast and the valley of the Mississippi ("the very backbone of the Confederacy," a Rebel general called that rail line in February 1862).

Only the short stretch of the Mississippi River (some 240 miles) between Port Hudson, Louisiana, and Vicksburg, Mississippi, remained in Rebel hands, and Yankee warships sometimes ventured into those waters. Even along the far-off Rio Grande a defeated Southern army had limped back downriver from New Mexico to seek safety in Texas. As early as February 13 Ida Powell Dulany, who lived in Fauquier County, Virginia, had noted in her diary, "disaster has followed disaster till our cause to the despondent seems almost hopeless."[4]

IN Virginia, too, the Secessionists found their cause greatly endangered that spring. A massive Union army commanded by Major General George B. McClellan had moved by ship to the southeastern tip of the peninsula between the James and York rivers and then inched its way overland northwest toward Richmond.

By late May McClellan's horde had gotten so close to the Confederate capital that the Yankee troops could hear the city's church bells. Warships of the United States Navy, meanwhile, threatened to push up the James River and, if they could get past the downriver fortifications, level Richmond with their heavy guns. Confederate authorities began planning for the evacuation of their capital, and President Davis's wife and children sought refuge in Raleigh, North Carolina.

On February 14, the day after Ida Dulany penned the sad diary entry quoted above, the *New York Times* prophesied that the end of the war "certainly cannot be postponed. The monster is already clutched and in his death struggle." A week later on February 21, the Clarksburg *National Telegraph*, published in pro-Union western Virginia, speculated that "the back bone of the rebellion is broken. The war, unless some unforeseen event occurs to embolden the rebels, is bound to close in a few weeks." In early April, when a bureaucratic mix-up led the Federal War Department to close (temporarily) its recruiting offices, much of the Northern public took the action as a sign of the approaching end of the war.[5]

ONLY in the Shenandoah Valley, off in west-central Virginia, did the spring's military operations offer even a flicker of hope to the embattled Secessionists. There, a small Rebel army commanded by the eccentric Major General Thomas J. "Stonewall" Jackson marched and marched and fought and fought, baffling and defeating larger Union forces and throwing Federal military operations over much

---

4 52 OR pt. 2, 273; Dulany, *Journal*, 62, 79. For some provocative thoughts on the early 1862 reversal of Rebel fortunes, see Harsh, *Confederate Tide*, especially the early chapters. I date the turning point four months earlier than does Harsh. In early September 1861, the Confederates threw away whatever chance they may have had to add Kentucky to their collection of States. See my *Fourth Battle of Winchester*. Confederate military history for the rest of the war was an increasingly unsuccessful effort to reverse (or at least halt) the spread of the damage that began with that act.

5 See Nevins, *Ordeal of the Union*, VI, 29 and 63-64.

of the Old Dominion into turmoil. Despite Jackson's exploits, however, the Confederacy appeared to be tottering on its last legs as May came to its end.

ON the final day of the month General Joseph E. Johnston, commanding the forces defending Richmond, lunged at the Yankee army east of the capital in an attempt to drive back the invading horde. In two days of confused fighting—known both as the Battle of Seven Pines and as the Battle of Fair Oaks—neither side gained any significant advantage.

The engagement left more than 11,000 men dead, wounded, or missing—6,134 of them Confederates. Among the wounded Rebels was General Johnston, hit late on May 31 by both a musket ball and fragments of an artillery shell. With its commanding general seriously wounded and certain to be out of action for some time, the army passed under the control of the bumbling Major General Gustavus Woodson Smith, the officer next in rank. The day after assuming command, Smith found himself debilitated by some sort of nervous breakdown, a malady that, it seems, often afflicted him when he found himself in a stressful situation.[6]

Sometime during the night of May 31-June 1, as he and Lee rode back to the capital from the battlefield, Davis came to a momentous decision: Robert E. Lee, rather than Smith, would replace the wounded Johnston. Davis's choice turned out to be one of the most consequential decisions in American history. It prolonged the Civil War for almost three years, and in so doing it ensured that the conflict would evolve in new directions and change the United States to a far greater degree than otherwise would have been the case or than anyone could then have foreseen.[7]

The next morning Lee announced to the army that, "In pursuance to the orders of the President," he had assumed command of the forces defending Richmond. The War Department did not get around to issuing the official orders assigning him to the post until the second.[8]

---

6 Smith, noted his biographer Leonne M. Hudson (*Smith*, 116-118), "suffered a mental or physical breakdown brought on by the strain of the fighting" on May 31. "Responsibility and uncertainty ... wrecked his nerves and shattered his confidence" and brought on "an apoplectic condition."

7 See Steven Newton's comments in "The Ten Greatest Successes of the Civil War," 13. Gary Gallagher ("Great General," 10) comments that owing to the wounding of Johnston, the battle "ranked with the most important engagements of the war."

8 Lee, *Papers*, 181-182; 11 *OR* pt. 1, 992, 993; 11 *OR* pt. 3, 568-569, 571.

UP until the time he took command of the army outside Richmond, Lee had played but a slight and inconspicuous role in the Confederacy's struggle for national independence. One of the most distinguished officers of the antebellum United States Army, Lee, in April 1861, had followed his native Virginia into the Confederacy.[9] For several weeks in that first spring of the war Lee had served as commander of the Old Dominion's (as differentiated from the Confederacy's) armed forces. In that capacity he had borne responsibility in the early days of the war for the crucial behind the scenes work of raising, organizing, equipping, and deploying the first troops committed to the defense of the state. Then, in the late spring and summer of 1861 Lee, by then a general in the Confederate Army, had labored skillfully at a desk in Richmond to raise, organize, equip, and deploy troops and supplies across the Old Dominion, Confederate as well as Virginia forces.

Late in July 1861, after most of the State troops had passed into Confederate control, Lee found himself sent off to the mountains of western Virginia (now West Virginia) on what turned out to be a frustratingly unsuccessful effort to hold that region for the Secessionists. He had spent the last part of 1861 and the early months of 1862 working at the unspectacular but vital task of defending the Rebels' South Atlantic coast. Early in March 1862, Davis had summoned him back to Richmond to serve again as the President's chief military adviser. Lee held that post until Davis decided that he should succeed the bumbling Smith.

FEW generals have taken command of an army in circumstances as daunting as those facing the fifty-five-year-old Lee on June 1, 1862, when responsibility for the defense of his state's and his nation's capital fell onto his shoulders. The massive Northern army of some 100,000 men under McClellan then hovering not far beyond Richmond's city limits was the obvious danger, clearly visible to all. The Federal forces pushing forward in Arkansas, Louisiana, Tennessee, and Mississippi constituted a more distant but no less real threat to Rebel independence.[10]

9 See J. B. Jones, *Diary*, I, 96, entry for 2 Dec. 1861, praising Lee. On Jun. 30, 1862, the Lynchburg *Daily Virginian* called Lee "Unquestionably the greatest soldier in the South, if not on the whole continent." This was when he was under heavy criticism for his failed efforts in western Virginia and just beginning the series of battles that would bring him worldwide fame.

10 One situation, eerily similar to that of Lee in 1862, did arise two years later when General John Bell Hood assumed command of another Confederate army that had backed up to the outskirts of the city it was supposed to defend (Atlanta). Hood then replaced General Joseph E. Johnston, who had been relieved from command. This subject is covered in Volume II.

ROBERT E. LEE,
commander of the Army of Northern Virginia.
LOC

Lee, however, discerned another, closer and less apparent but potentially very serious problem that, if left unresolved, could eat away at the Confederacy's very ability to continue the war in Virginia beyond June 1862. This danger threatened to nullify every effort the Secessionists might make to deal with the more obvious peril to their capital city and to their national sovereignty.

OVER the nine months preceding Lee's assignment to command the Army of Northern Virginia, a relationship marked, if not characterized by, misunderstanding, suspicion, resentment, bitterness, distrust, and even paranoia that sometimes spilled over into barely concealed hostility had developed between the government in Richmond and the headquarters of General Joseph E. Johnston, who commanded the army during that period. The protagonists in this debilitating situation were President Davis and General Johnston.

Modern historians debate the origins of the differences between the two men. More accurately, they debate which of several factors loomed most significantly in causing and exacerbating the Davis-Johnston quarrels. Over the years students of the Confederate war effort have squandered paper, time, ink, and physical energy (and now electricity as well) in fruitless attempts to demonstrate that one or the other of the protagonists had been "right" in the positions he took regarding the various particulars around which the quarrels swirled.

In truth, Davis had the better of the argument with regard to some matters; Johnston with regard to others. In many cases, however, their differences came down to issues about which it is simply not possible to reach a definitive conclusion owing either to the lack of reliable (contemporary) evidence or to the nature of the matter at issue. Many of the squabbles revolved around such unanswerable questions as what should the Confederates have done but did not do, and what the result would have been had they done it.[11]

The feud's origins do not concern us here. For our present purposes it suffices to note that by the spring of 1862, both personal and official relations between

11 Writing in the early 1920s, Davis's biographer H. J. Eckenrode (*Davis*, 264) concluded, "The fault was at least as much Johnston's as Davis's." Some writers have traced the bitter feelings between the two men back to their days together at West Point (1825-1828) when they allegedly competed for the attentions of a local belle and are supposed to have settled the matter in a fist fight. (Johnston is said to have prevailed.) Most authorities discount the story. See, however, the Feb. 25, 1910, letter from James A. Bethune to Robert M. Hughes, and Hughes to Alfred P. James, Apr. 21, 1925, both in Hughes Papers. For background in addition to the standard biographies, see Newton, *Johnston*; Glatthaar, *Partners in Command*, 95-134; and McMurry, "Ole Joe in Virginia" and "The *Enemy* at Richmond."

President Davis's administration in Richmond and General Johnston's head-quarters just outside the city had deteriorated to an alarming extent. So heated did the differences become that in late April or early May, a frustrated and angry Johnston offered his resignation, but Davis refused to accept it.[12]

BY the late spring of 1862 any knowledgeable observer of Confederate military affairs could see that the differences likely to arise from this web of distrust would, unless the underlying problems were dealt with, pose a serious obstacle to the successful conduct of future military operations by Johnston, Smith, Lee, or anyone else who might hold command of the Rebel army in Virginia. This, in turn, would almost certainly lead to the loss of Richmond and put a quick end to the Southern effort to establish the Confederacy as a separate nation.

In the spring of 1862, there was no more intelligent and knowledgeable an observer of Rebel military affairs than Robert E. Lee. Nor was there anyone better suited and better placed to see and to understand the deleterious effects that the Davis-Johnston quarrel had already had and was likely to have again in the future.

SUCH were the stakes when Robert E. Lee on that seventh day of June 1862 settled into his chair in the Dabbs House, possibly took a sip of what in the Confederacy in the second spring of the war passed for coffee, placed a clean sheet of paper on his headquarters desk, and reached for his pen—possibly after taking a deep breath.

---

12 In his various writings Davis at least twice went out of his way to declare that Johnston "did not ask to be relieved" from command during the time covered by this narrative. The text is based on a May 4, 1862, statement by William A. Jackson, a literate Richmond slave and "extremely intelligent man" rented by Davis to work as a coachman. He escaped and revealed to his interrogator (Major General Irvin McDowell) information about the Davis-Johnston feud he had overheard while driving the President and Mrs. Davis about Richmond, and from conversations between Davis and visitors to the Executive Mansion. I see no reason to doubt this account. It is not the type of story a slave would have made up, and neither Jackson nor McDowell had reason to fabricate it. My guess is the incident occurred after Davis wrote a March 15 letter stating that Johnston had not asked to be relieved from command. The incident may have taken place in the immediate aftermath of a mid-April conference in which Davis had decided against Johnston after a long discussion of strategy. Gustavus Smith remembered the meeting as "protracted and at times very heated." Davis may have forgotten the incident when he wrote his postwar account, or he may have been trying to paper over wartime differences among Confederate leaders to present a façade of unity. See 51 *OR* pt. 1, 597-598; *OR* Series IV, Vol. 1, 999; "Jeff[.] Davis's Coachman," *Harper's Weekly*, VI, No. 284 (Jun. 7, 1862), 363, 365; J. Davis, *Papers*, Vol. 8, 101; Smith, *War Papers*, 42; and J. Davis, *Confederate Government*, II, 71.

Chapter Three

Davis, Lee, and Johnston

PART I

"Personality plays a tremendous part in war."
— General George S. Patton, 1944

BY JUNE 1, 1862, when he assumed command of Richmond's defending army, Robert E. Lee had known both Jefferson Davis and Joseph E. Johnston for more than thirty-five years. The three were almost the same age. Lee and Johnston had been born early in 1807, the former on January 19, the latter fifteen days later. Davis had been born on June 3, probably in the year 1808.[1]

The three were sons of men who had fought for the American cause in the War for Independence. Lieutenant Peter Johnston had served in the cavalry unit commanded by Lieutenant Colonel (later Major General) Henry "Light Horse Harry" Lee, while Captain Samuel Davis had joined the Patriot forces in Georgia and South Carolina. The sons had first met at the Military Academy in the summer of 1825. Davis, although the youngest of the three, had entered the school in 1824; Lee and Johnston had arrived the following year.[2]

In June 1835, Lieutenant Davis resigned from the army to become a planter in Mississippi. He returned to military service as the colonel of a regiment of Mississippi volunteer infantry during the Mexican War (1846-1848). On February 23, 1847, he gained considerable renown for his heroic conduct in the Battle of Buena Vista during which he took a painful wound to his right foot. Meanwhile,

---

1 Davis long believed the year of his birth to have been 1807. Later, he said, his mother told him that he had been born in 1808. If she didn't know, who did? In either case he was younger than Lee and Johnston.

2 The large number of appointees from Virginia compelled Lee to wait a year after his spring 1824 appointment to enter the Academy. Johnston received his appointment early in 1825.

through the 1830s, 1840s, and 1850s, Lee and Johnston had slowly moved up in the army's officer hierarchy, each gradually gaining wide recognition as unusually competent in the military profession.

ON a few occasions during the three decades after their 1829 graduation from the Academy, Lee and Johnston had been together at various army posts. For a while early in the Mexican War both served on the staff of Major General Winfield Scott. On one well-known occasion in March of 1847, they and several other famous and soon-to-be-famous officers came under hostile fire while in a small boat reconnoitering the Mexican position at Vera Cruz.

After the city surrendered several days later, Scott selected Lee and Johnston as his commissioners to arrange the terms of capitulation. "This selection gave great satisfaction throughout the army," remembered then-Lieutenant Dabney H. Maury many years later. "In rich uniforms, superbly mounted, they were the most soldierly, as they were the ablest, men in the army. We young Virginians were proud that day to see them."[3]

It is possible that Lee or Johnston or both of them encountered Davis on one occasion or another during their first two decades of army service. Any such contacts, however, would have been brief, and there is no known record of them.

In the late 1840s and throughout the 1850s Lee and Johnston doubtless followed Davis's ascending political career through the press. Certainly they would have taken great interest in his outstanding service as President Franklin Pierce's secretary of war from 1853 to 1857, and in his work as chairman of the Senate Military Affairs Committee from 1857 to 1861.

As the country's war minister, Davis in 1855 disapproved a controversial application for a brevet promotion to colonel submitted by Joseph E. Johnston. Davis's successor as secretary of war, John B. Floyd, related to Johnston by marriage, overturned Davis's ruling and approved the promotion. In 1860, Floyd selected Johnston (over Lee and others) to be the army's new Quartermaster General, a coveted post that carried with it promotion to the staff grade of brigadier general.[4]

Davis and Lee worked together on several military projects in the last dozen antebellum years. Lee, for example, served as superintendent of the Military

---

3 Maury, *Recollections*, 34-35.

4 These controversial promotions are covered in some detail in Book Two, Chapter Two, Part II.

Academy for part of Davis's tenure as secretary of war.[5] In the mid-1850s Davis had selected Johnston and Lee for choice assignments in the army's elite new cavalry regiments. Both became lieutenant colonels—Johnston of the 1st Cavalry Regiment, Lee of the 2nd.

THE three men found themselves drawn into the Confederacy in 1861 when their States declared themselves out of the Union. Mississippi seceded in January of that year, and in the following month Davis—almost universally regarded as the South's foremost living political and military figure—was elected president of the newly organized Confederate States of America, which at that time comprised only the seven Deep South "Cotton States" from South Carolina to Texas.

When Virginia left the Union in mid-April after the war began, Lee and Johnston resigned from the United States Army and offered their services in defense of the Old Dominion and, after their state joined the Confederacy, of the South. Davis, along with almost everyone knowledgeable about American military matters, regarded the two as among the men best qualified by intelligence, education, training, ability, and experience to command the Secessionist armies.

To Johnston went an early posting as head of the main Rebel force defending Virginia. From that assignment flowed the bitter quarrels that developed between that general and the President from June 1861 until Johnston fell wounded at Seven Pines at the end of May 1862. (See Chapter One.)

DAVIS and Johnston were intelligent, sensitive, thin-skinned men with frail but hyper-active egos. Each kept constantly on guard against any slight and watched for any infringement—real or imagined—on his official, and often his personal prerogatives and status. Both could carry a grudge for a long time. Neither had much inclination to explain his decisions, actions, reasons, or ideas to anyone else. Johnston, especially, proved insecure, very guarded, and loathe to communicate freely with others. He almost always insisted upon a rigid adherence to the proper and formal rules of military etiquette—at least as far as his superiors' treatment of himself was concerned. Decades later one historian would write of Johnston's "sense of official dignity—of which he had perhaps too much."[6]

---

5 See Freeman, *Lee*, I, 327.

6 Horn, *Army of Tennessee*, 310.

THESE traits would have hampered communication, understanding, and trust between President Davis and General Johnston under the best of circumstances. Some of their fellow Confederates inadvertently made matters many times worse during the winter of 1861-1862. Judah P. Benjamin was a Louisiana planter, lawyer, and politician; at first serving as President Davis's attorney general, then briefly his acting secretary of war, and later as the Rebels' secretary of state. Arguably he was the Chief Executive's closest political ally. Benjamin often differed with Johnston about military matters, and he frequently treated the general as an adversary at the bar.[7]

Most of the issues that arose between Secretary of War Benjamin and General Johnston were, in and of themselves, relatively minor administrative matters. The secretary, for example, had the habit of sometimes granting furloughs directly to individual soldiers in Johnston's army without even sending the paperwork through Johnston's headquarters—a grave violation of military protocol. On a more serious level, Benjamin on occasion issued orders directly to some of Johnston's subordinate commanders. This unorthodox practice could have produced most unfortunate results for the Confederates should one of the secretary's directives have disrupted some military operation being planned or conducted by Johnston.

Such happenings, coming after what Johnston regarded as the President's illegal act in reducing him in rank, exacerbated the general's growing feeling of alienation from and even hostility toward the government in general and Benjamin in particular. As historian Steven H. Newton commented, to Johnston it must have appeared that "the entire civil-military bureaucracy in Richmond seemed consciously determined to undermine him."[8]

On December 27, 1861, the general, writing to his wife, called Benjamin "an impertinent Jew, thro' whom the administration has its correspondence with me." On February 13, 1862, he complained to her of "that miserable little Jew" and opined that "if [he] is retained in his place our country will never be able to defend itself." On March 5, he wrote to her that "the interference of the Secretary of War in its [the army's] administration & discipline" had produced a serious deterioration

---

7 Johnston was not the only Confederate general to have such problems with Benjamin. Under date of Jan. 3, 1862, an official in the War Department noted "there is no *entente cordiale* between Mr. Benjamin and any of our best generals." J. B. Jones, *Diary*, I, 103.

8 Newton, *Johnston*, 19. See also 20-24. Lee experienced similar problems in the summer of 1862 and protested politely, drawing from the secretary of war a promise that the War Department had ceased such practices except in "urgent cases." 11 OR, pt. 3, 638 and 640.

in the quality of the force he commanded. Meanwhile, in Richmond, in February or March 1862 Johnston, at a dinner party, foolishly (and publicly) declared in response to a direct question his belief that the Confederacy could not win its independence with Benjamin as its secretary of war.[9]

Several of Johnston's friends, associates, and subordinates (not always separate groups) helped widen the gulf between army headquarters and the Davis government. Brigadier General William Henry Chase Whiting, one of Johnston's favorite younger officers whom Johnston was later to call "the most devoted of my friends," stood prominent among these people.[10]

On December 19, 1861, Whiting wrote a letter criticizing a presidential plan to reorganize the army. He sent the letter through channels to Adjutant and Inspector General Cooper with the request that it be laid before the Chief Executive. Whiting's letter has been lost, but we can get some idea of its tone and contents from another letter he had written two months earlier to another general on the

9 Johnston letters, MHS. Some authorities have expressed doubt about Johnston's making the statement referred to in the text (Newton, *Johnston*, 37-38). See, however, the Mar. 25, 1862, entry in J. B. Jones, *Diary*, II, 116. Readers should be aware that the dating of entries in this section of Jones's diary presents a problem. Under dates of Mar. 31 and Apr. 1 (117 and 118), Jones refers to the death of Albert S. Johnston, who did not die until Apr. 6. These were probably "catch-up" entries written some time later. So far as Joseph E. Johnston's relations with the government are concerned, the fact that people heard the story and believed that the general had made the anti-Benjamin remarks and circulated reports to that effect was more important than whether he, in fact, did so. Certainly, as his private letters show, the sentiment of the statement reflected his personal views.

10 Johnston to his wife, Mar. 27, 1865, Johnston Letters, MHS. Robert M. Hughes, Johnston's kinsman and biographer, talked with Johnston in the last years of the general's life in preparation for the book he was then writing. On Jul. 29, 1924, Hughes wrote fellow historian T. R. Hay (letter in Hughes Papers) that Johnston had been fond of Whiting as well as of Mansfield Lovell, who as a Confederate general was to play a small but significant role in Johnston's Civil War career, because they had been West Point classmates and close friends of the childless general's orphaned nephew John Preston Johnstone (as his branch of the family spelled the name). Preston, "who was like a son to [Joseph E.] Johnstone," was killed in the Mexican War. News of Preston's death was carried across the battlefield to Joseph E. Johnston by a sorrowful Robert E. Lee. Johnston arranged to have his nephew's body sent to Baltimore for burial. Maury, *Recollections*, 41. Either Johnston or Hughes was mistaken about Johnstone, Lovell, and Whiting. Johnstone (Class of 1843), Lovell (1842), and Whiting (1845) were together at the Academy for two or three years, but they were not classmates. On Mar. 23, 1839, Johnston asked his nephew to think of him as a brother, rather than as an uncle. (Letter in Johnston Papers, W&M.) On the spelling of the name, see Hughes, *Johnston*, 2-8 and 28 n. The nephew's name is spelled "Johnstone" in the West Point Alumni Foundation's *Register of Graduates and Former Cadets* (320). Thanks to Larry Reaume for providing a copy of this publication. Heitman, *Register* (I, 579) also spells it with the "e."

same subject. In that document Whiting fumed that Davis's plan was "a policy as suicidal as foolish . . . inconceivable folly . . . devised solely for the advancement of log-rolling, humbugging politicians—and I will not do it." Not only was the proposal a presidential policy and the President a politician, but to make the matter even more inflammatory, the troops involved in the proposed reorganization hailed from Davis's (and Whiting's) home state of Mississippi.

Johnston, who privately agreed with Whiting, foolishly forwarded his subordinate's letter to the War Department. While the document, doubtless, was less virulent and bitter than Whiting's October rantings quoted above, it was, nevertheless, so intemperate that Davis read it with "grave displeasure" and found it "very insubordinate" and "having a tendency to excite a mutinous and disorganizing spirit in the army." The incendiary letter ignited an angry reaction that singed Johnston and came close to costing Whiting his career.[11]

IN the spring and summer of 1861 and again in the spring of 1862, Robert E. Lee served in Richmond in a capacity that placed him in a position where he had almost daily contact with Davis as well as frequent written communications with and occasional visits to Johnston. Over time Lee's close association with Davis greatly strengthened the ties between the Chief Executive and himself. Biographer Cooper describes "a rapport, even a trust," that developed between the two men. By May 1862 Davis had come to realize that many of his basic strategic ideas as to how the Confederacy should conduct its military operations were in essential harmony with Lee's, and the President had come to place great trust in the courtly Virginian.[12]

Duty in Richmond in the spring of 1862 also put Lee in the perfect place from which to observe the many ongoing quarrels between the Davis Administration and Johnston. By then the numerous differences between the government and

---

11 5 *OR*, 1011-1012. See also, ibid., 1015.

12 Cooper, *Davis*, 354-355, 380-381, 391-393, 397, and 453. See also Gallagher and Glatthaar, *Leaders of the Lost Cause*, 25-26. Steven Woodworth ("I Give You the Material," 1-2) speculates that Lee's close association with Davis's pre-war bureaucratic enemy Winfield Scott may have led the President initially to rate Lee's abilities below some of the other Rebel generals. In addition, almost all of Lee's antebellum service had been as a staff officer, and that fact may have lessened Davis's early appreciation of Lee's ability as a field commander. Woodworth suggests that for these reasons Davis bestowed command of the key armies on Johnston and Beauregard while at first keeping Lee in a position as an adviser to the Chief Executive. After Johnston's wounding on May 31, Lee was simply the only officer available to take command of the army.

army headquarters had metastasized to the point that collectively they had become a gigantic obstacle to cooperation and effective action. Indeed, by then they constituted a massive threat to the Confederacy's very survival.

The War Department files offered Lee the opportunity to familiarize himself with details of the differences between the President and Johnston (although I know of no evidence that he ever seriously studied the earlier correspondence between the general and the government). In addition, Lee certainly would have heard from others in the government and in Richmond society (more-or-less) accurate reports of the raging, semi-public Davis-Johnston differences. More important, Lee's decades-long acquaintance with the two men gave him invaluable insights into their temperaments, and—above all—their personalities. "Personality," General George S. Patton once observed, "plays a tremendous part in war."[13]

ROBERT E. Lee was a born politician—not in the sense that he ever sought, lusted after, or even wanted public office, but in the fact that he possessed unusually great "people skills." He almost always got along well with others. His biographer Douglas Southall Freeman noted that "it was easy for him to win and hold the friendship of other people. . . . He made friends readily and held them steadfastly. . . . He was a diplomat among engineers." Lee was, as all such people are, a careful observer of those around him and usually an astute judge of men's abilities. These gifts combined to give him an uncanny ability to read other people.[14]

Like many a successful politician—Abraham Lincoln, Dwight Eisenhower, and Ronald Reagan come to mind—Lee had the self-confidence, personal security, sense of humor, wisdom, patience, and willingness to overlook personality clashes, personal slights, and even insults if, by so doing, he could harness a man's ability to the cause and use the man to further a larger object. His temperament, wrote Freeman, "was not one to indulge in vendettas."

Late in 1861, when Lee commanded on the South Atlantic coast, Brigadier General Roswell S. Ripley served as one of his subordinates. For now unknown reasons Ripley ("a good General but not a gentleman," in the opinion of one young Confederate) took an intense dislike to Lee. Lee ignored the slights, slurs, and

---

13 Patton quoted in Ricks, *The Generals*, 9. Freeman. *Lee*, II, 6, mentions "a brief study of the tangled records of the adjutant general's office" by Lee.

14 Freeman, *Lee*, I, 450-451 and 456.

insults from Ripley, who, at least, possessed some military knowledge, training, and experience. Lee thereby managed to make the best possible use of his subordinate's abilities. Lee also got along well with such touchy politicians as Governor Francis W. Pickens of South Carolina. As historian Stephen Newton noted, "In the necessary aspects of civil diplomacy required of a senior military officer in a republic . . . Lee was patently gifted."[15]

BLESSED with these traits, Lee almost always worked well with his colleagues, both civilian and military; won and held the trust, respect, and even admiration of others; and often succeeded in accomplishing his goals without drawing much attention to himself, stirring up great bitterness, or creating disruptive turmoil among his fellow Confederates.

Even later in the war, when he determined to rid his army of an officer who did not measure up to his standards and to replace him with someone he considered better, Lee usually managed to do so with little fuss. The unsatisfactory officer simply disappeared from Lee's command. Often, he popped up later in some other Confederate army, there to bedevil some other general less skillful than Lee in the bureaucratic aspects of military command. Such a fate befell Benjamin Huger, Theophilus H. Holmes, W. H. C. Whiting, and Daniel Harvey Hill, to name but four high-ranking examples. It was, of course, President Davis who transferred such difficult officers to other commands. Lee's quite proper concern was to rid his own army of them.[16]

---

15 Ibid., 117, 617, and 630; Newton, *Johnston*, 212. Gary Gallagher (*Leaders of the Lost Cause*, 25-26) called Lee "a master military politician." In 1865, P. G. T. Beauregard described Roswell Ripley as "active, energetic, intelligent, ambitious, cunning, and fault-finding. He complains of every commanding officer he has served under and has quarreled (or had difficulties) with almost every one of his immediate subordinate commanders. . ." (47 *OR* pt. 2, 1031).

16 Many writers have alleged that Lee often proved too courteous toward others and have argued that such a "weakness" greatly reduced his effectiveness in dealing with obstinate subordinates. Even Freeman called Lee's "kindly sentiments and consideration for the feeling of others . . . [a] serious weakness" in a general who as a commander failed to exert his will on his subordinates. A few pages after this comment, however, Freeman wrote that Lee's "patient diplomacy" was having an effect and that the difficult subordinate (Major General William W. Loring in this case) "began to show himself more amenable" (*Lee*, I, 552 and 560). In any case, Loring soon found himself in Mississippi. Brian Holden Reid (*Lee*, 81) wrote: "Lee's gentlemanly bearing disguised a ruthlessness in sizing up subordinates and replacing those unable to live up to his high expectations." In fact, Joseph E. Johnston proved far more unwilling to deal with—or to try to deal with or even to name—unsatisfactory and sometimes

With Lee, it is often necessary to try to infer what he thought from what he did. He was a very private man, and he kept his cards close to his chest. Mary Chesnut once asked, "Can anybody say they know . . . Robert E. Lee? He looks so cold and quiet and grand." One of Lee's own staff officers wrote to President Davis in July of 1862, of "General Lee, whose caution about expressing opinions involving others it is unnecessary to recall to your recollection." His biographer Emory Thomas once observed that "To understand Robert E. Lee it was often important to look beyond his words and watch what he did rather than listen to or read what he said. Lee's actions often modified his words and sometimes the deeds contradicted the words."[17]

No records exist concerning the matter—I suspect that Lee took care to leave as faint a paper trail as possible—but the general's actions in June 1862, just after he took his place as head of the army outside Richmond, indicate that he came to his new command assignment with a full and clear understanding of the massive political-military problem he and his army then faced with regard to the relations between army headquarters and the Davis Administration.

THE great distrust that had grown up between Davis and Johnston had hampered the Confederate cause in the first year of the war, and it had the potential to inflict even more serious damage in the future. Somehow Lee had to close that gap or he would be most unlikely to achieve success in his effort to defend Richmond and win Confederate independence.

The short letter that Lee penned on June 7, 1862, in response to Davis's message of the previous day offered him an early—and so far as the records show—the first opportunity to close the gap between army headquarters and the government that he had inherited from Johnston.

In one sense the effort that Lee began at his desk in the Dabbs House that Saturday marked the opening of his most crucial Civil War campaign—and his most successful. The brief document he composed that day was one of the most important of his official wartime communications and of Confederate (and American) military history. Had he neglected to make the effort embodied in that

---

incompetent and/or disobedient subordinates than did Lee. See, for example, the discussion of Johnston's relations with Lieutenant General John C. Pemberton below, in Book Two.

17 Chesnut, *Chesnut's Civil War*, 116; J. Davis, *Papers*, vol. 8, 297; Thomas, *Lee*, 413. Freeman wrote (*Lee*, I, 573) of Lee's letters: "Sometimes they are so difficult to interpret that one gets the impression Lee was deliberately reticent to the point of leaving the essential facts obscured."

short letter, or had his effort proved less successful, it seems very doubtful that he would have been able to achieve many of his famous successes on the battlefield.

PART II

"Every man wants to be at the head of affairs himself."
— Mary Chesnut, 1861

MR. JEFFERSON DAVIS, while characterized by a great many admirable traits, was not an easy man to get to know, or to like, or to work for or with. Getting to know, liking, or working for or with President Jefferson Davis often proved a trying, difficult, and frustrating experience. The Rebel Chief Executive impressed many of those with whom he came in contact as a rigid man who would break but not bend. He had little time for the amenities and small pleasures of life. He did not suffer fools, or those whom he (often with good reason) regarded as fools, gladly.

The Confederate President was obviously a very intelligent, well-educated, very well-read, usually formal and courteous, always hard-working, and often ill man (one of his biographers noted that he "could seem like a hospital ward all by himself"). Although never a "fire-eating" radical Secessionist, he had committed completely to the Confederate effort, and no one could ever doubt his total dedication to the cause of Southern independence. Indeed, he proved far more steadfast in his devotion to the Cause than did many of the men whose shrill demands for secession had brought on the war.[18]

Almost from the beginning of his service as Confederate President in February 1861, Davis demonstrated several counterproductive work habits (to be described below) and provoked fierce criticism. He became the lightning rod for carping and complaints by hot-headed Southern politicians and newspaper editors. Davis sometimes displayed a great inability to ignore such eruptions. On occasion the

18 In the 1850s radical "Southern rights" spokesmen had often criticized Davis (sometimes severely) for not being strongly committed to defending their region. See, for example, Cooper, *Davis*, 293-296, 433, and 434.

President's visceral need to defend himself against such fulminations and posturing led him into unbecoming, prolonged public or semi-public quarrels, many of them over relative minutiae. These squabbles consumed a lot of his time, drained his psychic and physical energy, undermined his fragile health, and quickly made him a divisive force in Confederate political and military affairs.[19]

TO some degree this state of affairs grew from old antagonisms lingering on into the 1860s from various antebellum bureaucratic and political battles. In Montgomery, Alabama, the Confederacy's first capital, Mary Chesnut observed as early as February 28, 1861 (only ten days after Davis's inauguration as president of the new Southern nation), that "these men [Confederate politicians] have brought old hatreds & grudges & spites from the old Union. Already we see that they will willingly injure our cause to hurt Jeff Davis." Four months later she recorded a South Carolina politician's assertion that Davis was "a failure," and by the fall she was writing of "the senseless abuse heaped upon Jeff Davis." Almost two decades after the establishment of the Confederacy, James Lyons, a former member of the Rebel Congress, recalled the "jealousy, selfish ambition, and consequent discord [that] prevailed from the commencement" of the war.[20]

In part this development also evolved out of the always malignant mixture of human nature and the characteristics of politics, bureaucracy, and government. On February 16, 1861, before Davis took the oath of office, Thomas R. R. Cobb, a Georgia delegate to the convention that organized the new government, wrote from Montgomery to his wife bemoaning "the daily manifestations of selfishness, intrigue, low cunning, and meanness among those who should have an eye to the protection of their people and the preservation of their government."[21]

Members of the Rebel Congress and state governors, for example, sometimes found it to their political advantage to criticize the Davis Administration and its policies in order to deflect complaints that otherwise—and often more justly—might have been directed at themselves. They, after all, would have to face the voters in future elections. The Confederate Constitution limited the Chief

---

19 See, for instance, W. Davis, *Davis*, 112. In *Ike the Soldier* (171) Merle Miller observed of the ultra-successful President Dwight D. Eisenhower "the last thing he allowed a congressman to find out was what he thought of him."

20 Chesnut, *Private Mary Chesnut*, 17 and 84-85; Chesnut, *Chesnut's Civil War*, 204; Lyons to W. T. Walthall, July 31, 1878, (began letter on July 10) in Rowland, *Davis Constitutionalist*, VIII, 214.

21 Quoted, Escott, *After Secession*, 273.

Executive to a single six-year term and therefore barred Davis from seeking the presidency in the national election scheduled for the fall of 1867.

HONEST differences of opinion can arise over almost any issue, policy, or plan. If those differences remain unresolved—especially if they also become entangled with individual psyches and personalities—they can intensify and fester on and on until they produce great, indeed, often fatal wounds to the group or nation in which they develop.

The personality, attitudes, and personal habits of Jefferson Davis greatly exacerbated this situation in the Confederate government. So, too, did the violently clashing ambitions and personalities of numerous Southern politicians, many of whom served as governors or members of the Secessionist Congress and none of whom owed his office to President Davis. Each of these officials easily managed to convince himself that he would make a far better Chief Executive than was the man who had actually been elected to the office. "Every man wants to be at the head of affairs himself," wrote Mary Chesnut of the early period of Confederate history. This kind of situation is not unknown in other times and in other governments, but it rarely rises to the level that it reached in the Confederacy.[22]

Early in the war several prominent generals concluded that major fallacies existed in President Davis's management of the Confederate war effort and that serious errors characterized the general military policies he sought to implement.[23] From that point each of these officers naturally reasoned that he was much better qualified to direct the Secessionist armies than was the man who under the Constitution held the post of "commander-in-chief." Many prominent newspaper

---

22 Chesnut, *Chesnut's Civil War*, 76. See also her *Private Mary Chesnut*, 84; and Cooper, *Davis*, 361-362.

23 Writers often depict Davis and Johnston as being at odds over whether the Rebels should seek to hold various areas of Confederate territory or abandon them in order to preserve the manpower of their armies. Davis stressed the policy of holding Rebel territory and therefore advocated the necessity of fighting invading Federal armies at or near the border of the Confederacy. Johnston, in order to preserve the strength of the Southern armies, wanted to avoid battles except under highly favorable circumstances even if doing so involved evacuating large sections of Rebeldom. Although the two never debated the specific matter, this difference formed the background for several of their arguments and led them to clashing grand strategies. In a purely military sense, Johnston's approach was the correct one. What Johnston never seemed to understand, however, was the larger and more important issue of waging war as opposed to undertaking a campaign or fighting a battle. Davis, beyond doubt, was correct with regard to the larger issue. See Chapter One of Book Two, and the conclusions in Volume II of this work.

editors gleefully jumped into this cauldron, each fantasizing that he could do a far better job as president and in directing the Rebel war effort than Davis was doing.

The conflict had not long been underway before some of these criticizing, posturing politicians found fellow travelers in one or more of the disgruntled generals and carping editors. From this situation quickly evolved a kaleidoscopic set of clashing blocs that supported this or that politician or general; that urged adoption of this or that general strategy; or that wanted to implement this or that policy. Many of these groups lashed out at the beleaguered President when his armies lost a battle or abandoned some territory to the enemy, as they frequently did in the first five months of 1862. The fact that Davis's critics were never able to derail any of his major efforts in 1862 or later, served only to intensify the bitterness and zeal with which they assailed the Chief Executive.

There is a name for this phenomenon. It is called "politics"—and it does not cease to trouble nations in wartime.[24]

SIMILAR problems in one form or another almost always beset those who hold high public office, especially executive office, in any government. Certainly, Davis's opposite number, Abraham Lincoln, faced the same problems to a greater or lesser degree in the United States. The Northern president, however, proved able to work around such difficulties and almost always vanquished his political critics. Lincoln's common sense; intelligence; personality; sense of humor; patience; self-confidence; keen political skills; sense of timing; and—above all—his great ability to reach out to, communicate with, and win and retain the sympathy and support of the common folk of the Union states all combined to enable him to deal more or less successfully with such problems as they arose.[25]

Lincoln also enjoyed the enormous advantage of having the massive human, financial, industrial, agricultural, and material resources of the North, so that to a far greater extent than did Davis, he found himself free from the always politically tricky, difficult, and disagreeable task of having to deny requests from powerful governors and legislators. He, therefore, did not have to divide very limited resources so that everybody got something, but nobody got enough to accomplish

---

24 Presidents inevitably become what T. Harry Williams (*Lincoln and the Radicals*, 94) called "the center of a tug for power between various groups," and they are "bound to disappoint most of the people who voted for them." Williams wrote with regard to Lincoln, but his observation applies at least as much to Davis. See the next section of this chapter.

25 See, for examples, W. Davis, *Lincoln's Men*; Manning, *Cruel War*; and Burlingame, *Lincoln and the Civil War*, 4, 76, and *passim*.

anything. The fact that few areas of the loyal states ever faced threats from Rebel armies, and that Union civilians largely escaped direct wartime suffering even as their section experienced great economic growth and prosperity, meant that such demands on Lincoln occurred much less frequently and proved far less intense than did those on Davis.[26] (In the Confederate case, as we shall see, this situation often resulted in the scattering of small bodies of troops about the country to calm local fears and quiet local politicians. Then, when an enemy advance came, no area had a force adequate for its protection; each often sought to hold on to what it had rather than send help to the threatened point. Davis—for reasons to be discussed in Book Two—found it very difficult to move troops from one area to another to meet a potential or even an actual threat.)

Then, too, from the beginning of his term the Northern President had the great advantage of heading an established government with its functioning military and civilian bureaucracies, its financial and revenue systems, its army and navy, and its established diplomatic recognition by and trade with foreign powers. Lincoln also benefitted from heading a pre-existing political party through which his friends could work to support him, and which gave him a convenient and potent means—appointment to government office—to reward his followers and to rally men to his banner—a means that he proved quite willing to employ and employed quite skillfully.[27]

MANY historians have pointed out that Jefferson Davis stood in sharp contrast to the Northern President. Davis's personality, his sometimes extreme sensitivity to criticism, his general attitude, and his frequently abrupt manner of conducting business all combined to make it most unlikely that he would be able to overcome many of the political, military, personal, and personnel problems that he faced as President. The most characteristic example, several writers have noted, was the Rebel chief's long-standing conviction that once he had considered an issue, evaluated the options, and arrived at a conclusion, the matter was settled.

26 For short but excellent accounts of the "great boom" in the North during the war, see Nevins, *Ordeal of the Union*, VI, Chapter 19 (483-511) and VII, Chapter 7 (212-270, especially 254), and Chapter 18 (271-331). For contrast with the situation in the Confederacy, see ibid., Chapter 9 (332-373). The contrasting situations described in these chapters lend strong support to what I believe was Lee's view of the proper policy for the Confederacy to follow in 1863. See Chapter Eight of Book Two.

27 For fascinating examples of Lincoln's use of patronage, see Etulain, *Lincoln Looks West*.

Many of those who hold this view of the Confederate leader are fond of quoting Varina Howell, who observed in 1843 upon first meeting Jefferson Davis that he had the habit of "taking for granted that everybody agrees with him when he expresses an opinion." Forty-five years later (and after forty-three years of marriage to him) she saw no reason to change her mind. Her husband, she wrote in 1888, was "a man who sees but one side because he is so freely persuaded by his own mind that he cannot understand anyone not accepting his opinions." Students of Davis's life also make much of the fact that he once declared to his spouse, "I cannot bear to be suspected or complained of or misconstrued after explanation by you."

President Davis, so the conventional argument goes, simply believed that no fair-minded person who examined the evidence could honestly differ with him. Those who disagreed with and opposed his announced decisions and policies were, almost by definition, not conducting themselves fairly. Such differences constituted personal attacks on Davis, cover for the schemes of ambitious men seeking to advance their own fortunes, or (perhaps unintentional) efforts to undermine the Confederate government.[28]

JEFFERSON Davis's approach to the job of president, along with the physical and psychological strains to which he subjected himself during the war, as well as the pressures naturally inherent in his office, added greatly to his difficulties in working with others. His post as President of the Confederacy burdened him with four constitutionally mandated duties and with one extralegal but very important function. He served simultaneously as the head of state, the head of government, the nation's chief executive, and as commander-in-chief of the Rebel armed forces.

Although Davis would never have acknowledged the role or admitted that he often fulfilled it, he also occupied an extraconstitutional position in the Rebel government. This position necessitated that he function as the leader of what amounted to a political party.

In their naïveté the Confederates liked to fantasize that their virtuous young republic stood united against the enemy. It had been cleansed and freed of the normal filth, rot, stench, and corruption of party politics. In fact, of course, both a

---

28 J. Davis, *Papers*, vol. 2, 52 and 92; vol. 3, 302-303; V. Davis, *Memoir of Davis*, I, 97, 102, 120, 169, 171, and 198-199. Biographer William Cooper (*Davis*, 16; see also 162) noted that the Rebel President "too often confused agreement with him with devotion to duty."

pro-Davis Administration faction and several anti-Davis Administration factions quickly emerged in the Secessionist political firmament. In reality, if not in name, these blocs soon evolved into embryonic political parties. Davis, whether he desired to be or not, or was even aware of it or not, was the head of one of them simply by virtue of his place in the government.[29]

Because the Confederates did not regard these factions as would-be political parties and organize and conduct them accordingly, they found themselves in the worst of both worlds—the slime of "politics" without the party structure and discipline to whip men into line through an organized patronage system.

ALL five of Davis's presidential duties were part and parcel of serving as the chief executive of a republic. By themselves they would have overwhelmed most human beings. Davis, however, made his already crushing responsibilities much greater by taking onto his heavily laden shoulders two additional and very burdensome tasks.

The Rebel chief chose to function as the Confederacy's secretary of war. Davis had, in fact, frequently been mentioned for the war minister's post prior to his election as president. Beyond any question he was far better qualified for that office than were at least three (and probably four or five) of the six men who held it during the war. (The one certain exception, I think, was John C. Breckinridge, the last man to occupy the post.)[30]

As matters turned out, President Davis usually denied his war ministers any real authority; kept the reins in his own hands; made the major and many of the minor decisions; and micro-managed the administrative work of the War Department. "He wanted all major and myriad minor [military] decisions cleared with him," commented biographer William Cooper. In summary, he expected his secretaries of war to act more or less as clerks whose main task was to implement the decisions he made.[31]

---

29 On the day he arrived in Montgomery for his inauguration as president, Davis proclaimed that at home the Confederacy "shall have homogeneity." See Rowland, *Davis Constitutionalist*, V, 48-49, and Cooper, *Davis*, 329, 331, 342, and 352.

30 For a couple of examples of newspapers suggesting Davis for the post of Confederate secretary of war, see the Augusta *Dispatch*, n. d. (quoted in the Columbus, Ga. *Daily Sun*, Jan. 10, 1861), and the Americus *Georgian*, n. d. (quoted in the Macon *Daily Telegraph*, Jan. 16, 1861). Davis, Breckinridge, and Johnston will be discussed in Book Four, Volume II.

31 Cooper, *Davis*, 414. Frederick Maurice (*Statesmen and Soldiers*, 12 and 17) wrote that Davis "was tempted to rely unduly upon . . . [his military] experience and to take too much upon

Finally, Davis took his constitutional role as commander-in-chief so literally that he refused to countenance creation of the post of commanding general or even that of chief of staff of the Confederate Army. The immense burdens of those offices he also took upon himself, although in 1861 and again in the spring of 1862 he did use Lee, then his military adviser, to carry out some of the lesser duties that a commanding general or a chief of staff should handle. For several months in early 1864 Davis employed General Braxton Bragg in a similar capacity.[32]

IN part because he assumed these additional tasks on top of his immense constitutional duties, Davis frequently found himself both stressed out and bogged down in numerous minor matters that should have been dealt with by his secretary of war, a general-in-chief, a chief of staff, the Adjutant and Inspector General, or even by a lowly War Department clerk. The President's adamant refusal to delegate meaningful authority to his war minister or to a commanding general or chief of staff meant that he spent much of his time and energy laboring over details that should have fallen to others. (I suspect that this situation became even worse once officials in the bureaucracy realized that they could evade responsibility by passing up to the President matters that they should have handled.) The Rebel leader became "[preoccupied] with detail . . . [and] consumed with minutiae . . . . He looked," wrote one of his biographers, "at almost every piece of paper addressed to the president; his personal comments appeared on them all, whether important or trivial."

A clerk in the Rebel War Department noted in his diary as early as May 1861 that the President "was overwhelmed with papers." Seven months later the same clerk wrote of Davis's "multiplicity of employments." In April 1864, Davis's friend Brigadier General William Nelson Pendleton cautioned the President about his tendency to overwork and to get bogged down in details.

---

himself—a not uncommon failing with [government] ministers who have some expert knowledge of the department over which they preside." Davis had "a tendency to rely too much on his small military experience, which caused him to concern himself with minor details." This trait had surfaced in Davis's *antebellum* years even before he held public office. On August 27, 1838, for example, his older brother Joseph wrote to him, "I will . . . Caution you against an error . . . which you I think are Some what liable to an attempt at too much." J. Davis, *Papers*, vol. 1, 450. See also Cooper, *Davis*, 250-253.

32 Cooper, *Davis*, 354-356. Early in 1865 pressure from the Rebel Congress finally forced Davis to acquiesce in creation of the office of commanding general, and the President named Lee to the post. See Book Four, Chapter Two in Volume II.

On February 18, 1862, for instance, Davis took the time to read and endorse over to the Secretary of War for reply, an inquiry from a sixteen-year-old Louisiana boy asking if at five feet-one-and-one-half inches he was tall enough to enlist in the army. A year later the President complained to the Secretary of War that the names on a list of officers nominated for appointments as assistant adjutants general were in such disorder that "it is not possible for me to learn . . . whether the nominations are legal or proper"—a determination that officials at a much lower level should have made long before the paperwork reached Davis for his signature.

The resulting overwork, tension, and strain which these practices created sometimes proved almost debilitating.[33]

THE fact that Davis denied his secretaries of war any meaningful authority and the Confederacy had no commanding general meant that only the President could make important decisions regarding major military matters. Frequently, however, Davis would not decide such matters. He would hold meetings, discuss various topics for hours, defer decisions, or limit himself to making suggestions to his cabinet secretaries and generals, and issue no orders or instructions. At other times he would take so long to arrive at a decision that the Rebels lost promising opportunities—even when the decision itself was clearly the correct one.

As a result, the President often left decisions about the matter in question to the commanders of the Confederacy's separate field armies. At best, such practices resulted in long delays in situations that frequently demanded timely decisions, and at worst they could produce catastrophic disasters. As will be seen in subsequent chapters, Davis's practices (policies?) often created a situation in which each individual general appeared to be—and, in fact was—waging his own war in his own limited sphere of action for his own limited objectives. There was no overall direction to the Rebel war effort and hence no overall push toward a common goal.

After the war Colonel Charles Marshall, who had served as one of General Lee's staff officers, remarked, "I have heard the General say, after an interview of several hours duration with the President that he had lost a good deal of time in fruitless talk." As early as 1868 Alexander Y. P. Garnett, a Richmond doctor who had been the Davis family's wartime physician, remarked to one of Joseph E. Johnston's former staff officers that Davis usually made the correct decision but took so long to do so that the delay cost the Confederates all chance to benefit from it.[34]

To make matters worse, Davis sometimes found himself so tangled up in bureaucratic procedures and regulations that he seemed (came?) to regard them as ends in themselves rather than as guides and methods intended to facilitate achievement of the Confederacy's objective. In some cases this legalistic approach produced a state of governmental paralysis in which he and his administration could not act. It was as though the President were attempting to fit facts and events into a theory rather than trying to derive valid ideas from the facts and circumstances and to devise effective policies to deal with them.[35]

In many cases Davis's absorption in War Department minutiae created a situation in which no one did the President's work. A great vacuum then existed at the top of the Confederate government and the Rebel military command structure. The harmful effects of this state of affairs hampered both the army and many of the non-military facets of the government's war effort. With the President mired down in War Department trivia, such vital matters as diplomacy, the production and transportation of food and other vital necessities, and the public finances ("the Confederacy's increasingly catastrophic financial situation," in the words of one of Davis's biographers) suffered from a lack of overall direction.[36]

---

34 Marshall, *Aide-de-Camp*,7; Brown, *Brown's Civil War*, 141-142. See also Vandiver, *Rebel Brass*, *passim*, especially 19-21 and 114; and Kean, *Diary*, 101.

35 In this practice Davis came to resemble Charles Dickens's "constables and Bow Street men who ran their heads very hard against wrong ideas and persisted in trying to fit the circumstances to the ideas, instead of trying to extract ideas from the circumstances." (*Great Expectations*, 118). See J. Davis, *Papers*, vol. 8, 52, and vol. 9, 63; and J. B. Jones, *Diary*, I, 36 and 97. For some other examples, see Cooper, *Davis*, 332, 333, 354, 425-427, and 520-521. Davis's practice was a continuation, on a higher level and with a much larger military establishment, of the absorption in detail that had characterized his tenure as U. S. secretary of war (1853-1857). See Cooper, *Davis*, 249-253. Like Lee, Joseph E. Johnston often became frustrated with Davis's practices. Unlike Lee, however, he let the frustration get the better of him.

36 William C. Davis (*Davis*, 119-120 and 133) suggested that the Chief Executive's refusal to make "a distinction between matters great or small" is indicative of "an insecure administrator." Steven Woodworth (*Davis and Lee*, xii) wrote that President Davis "suffered severely from indecisiveness." See also Woodworth's comments on 19 and 24. At many places in his book he presents examples of this trait and offers valuable insights into the Rebel leader's behavior. He also (108) refers to Davis's "failure to take quick and decisive action to remedy a bad situation." Brian Reid (*Lee*, 72) writes of "Davis's interminable and often fruitless conferences." Bill Repp, who served as president of the Organization and Development Group and who wrote extensively on personnel matters, commented that many "fence sitters" prefer to put off decisions because of their insecurity, especially in dealing with those whom they

DAVIS, to be sure, faced a most difficult task, one unique to him among American political leaders. He had to birth a nation in the face of many kinds of very serious—and many of them potentially fatal—challenges. He had to realize that goal against the strong opposition of a far more powerful government immediately on his country's national borders, a government headed by the most able of American political leaders.[37]

To a great degree Davis's nation found itself cut off from the rest of the world. Close to one half if not an outright majority of the people in the Confederacy opposed that government's very existence (virtually all the slaves—who are usually ignored when people talk and write about "Southerners"— plus a large minority of anti-secession whites in every Rebel state). Many of these people—white and black—resisted the Confederate war effort either actively or passively from the very beginning of the conflict, and their numbers grew and their resistance intensified as the war went on and civilian suffering increased.[38]

---

cannot trust. See his "Getting Commitments," *Wall Street Journal*, Dec. 24, 2004. "The failure to decide has been a guarantee of failure," noted Daniel Benjamin, a member of the National Security Council in the late 1990s. See his "The Ditherer," Washington *Post*, National Weekly Edition, July 14-20, 2008. Mark Neely (*Lincoln and the Triumph of the Nation*, 146) summed up Davis's weakness very well: "The task of the commander in chief was not to dwell on matters of tactics and proximate threats. . . . He was to think in matters of grand strategy and a whole war and a whole nation for a long time to come." Other examples of Davis's practices as they affected Joseph E. Johnston in particular circumstances are given below in the text.

37 Allan Nevins (*Ordeal of the Union*, VII, 391 and 395) noted, "Never did a country have to cope with so many vicious economic crises as [did] the Confederacy. . . . Without question . . . [Davis's] was one of the most difficult, nigh impossible, tasks any American political leader ever attempted."

38 Stephanie McCurry (see her interview by Keith Poulter, "Confederate Reckoning") speaks of the Rebels' "crisis of legitimacy" resulting from the fact that most Southern whites had no role in the decision to secede. She also described the internal "political incoherence" in the Confederacy as it played out in the struggle between planters and slaves over labor (a long ongoing tussle dating back to the earliest days of slavery), that between planters and the Davis government over the use of slaves to perform military labor, and that between the government and poor white citizens who suffered the most as the economy deteriorated under the pressures of war. Paul Escott (*After Secession*, 23-24) calculates that in at least four states (Alabama, Georgia, Louisiana, and North Carolina) a clear majority of the voters did not favor secession. In addition, large sections of other states (eastern Tennessee and western Virginia, for example) also opposed leaving the Union. Escott based his conclusion on the voting in the 1860 election when the more conservative candidates' combined votes produced an absolute majority in several states. He considered only opposition to secession by Southern whites. See also his Chapter 4, "The Quiet Rebellion of the Common People" (94-138, 151, and 165). Beginning in 1862, for example, "peace societies" sprang up in several states (Alabama, Georgia, Mississippi,

From every side President Davis found himself and his country beset with problems of finance, shortages of almost everything, hordes of civilian refugees, the breakdown of civil government and society, massive logistical problems, difficulties in replacing the thousands of soldiers who fell in battle or who died or were disabled as a result of sickness, the deaths of relatives and friends (including in 1864 a young son killed when he fell from a balcony), and the looming specter of defeat. Every day, and it seemed in every way, the Confederate plight grew worse and worse. Critics did not hesitate to place the blame on the President, and as the war went on and the Confederacy's situation grew increasingly desperate, their attacks became more and more vicious.

It is no wonder that under the strain of trying to do too much of the work of managing the Confederacy's war effort Davis often suffered from bad health; or that he sometimes became irritable, short-tempered, and defensive; or that he came to harbor great bitterness toward those who would put what he saw (often correctly) as petty matters above the Cause. Through it all, however, he persisted,

---

North Carolina, Tennessee, southwestern Virginia, and, perhaps, Florida). These groups soon elected men to local and state offices and even to the Confederate Congress (194). In fact, it seems that an honest vote count in some key Confederate states would have yielded a majority against secession in 1861. See, for example, David Williams, "Bitterly Divided," especially 19-22 and 44). In *Georgia: A Brief History*, Chapter 5, Christopher C. Myers and Williams present such a catalog of dissatisfaction with the Confederacy that I finished the book wondering if *anybody* in the state had supported the war effort. For more details, see the account of the brutal struggle to bring about the secession of Tennessee in Dollar, et al., *Sister States,* 47-64. Escott (*After Secession*, 135) also notes that "with stunning rapidity the Civil War visited mass poverty upon the South." (See also 136-139, 156-159, and 165.) Allan Nevins (*Ordeal of the Union*, VII, 390) pointed out that "by 1863 the [Confederate civilian] population was becoming restive under the interminable exactions laid upon them" by the Rebel government. Book Two, Chapter Two, Part III, of this work gives some examples from Arkansas. Stephen Engle (*Struggle*, 61) pointed out that as early as February 1862, when Union gunboats broke through Confederate defenses on the Tennessee River and ventured far upstream, they were greeted joyfully by large numbers of citizens. "Old grey-headed men wept like children" at the welcome sight of the United States flag, wrote a sailor on one of the Federal vessels (quoted in Smith, *Timberclads*, 232). Such opposition to secession and widespread suffering by so many Southern civilians were key reasons why the Confederacy could not have sustained a long war. The Confederate governments (national and state) were never able to deal with the problems these developments presented. This situation was caused and/or exacerbated by military defeats. As discussed in Chapter Eight of Book Two of this work, I believe the realization of this fact formed a crucial element in Robert E. Lee's overall view of the war and was a major factor in the position he took in the great spring 1863 debate among Confederate leaders over the strategy they should pursue in the crisis they then faced. It was also an important reason why Joseph E. Johnston's approach to the war almost certainly would have proved unsuccessful. This last thesis will be discussed at several points below, and especially in Volume II.

drove himself onward—often by sheer willpower—and remained doggedly committed to the Cause of Confederate independence.[39]

CONTRARY to what many said about him during the war and later, however, Jefferson Davis was not so stupid as always to reject advice, or to adhere to a fixed opinion, or to resent those whose ideas differed from his. He held firm convictions about various matters—especially military matters and arguably more so about the necessity of following rigid bureaucratic procedures. Often, he would vigorously defend his views, opinions, positions, and policies; and, as noted above, he would frequently hesitate to make a decision—or would altogether avoid doing so.

Davis would, however, and on a few occasions did, change his policies radically if events clearly proved him wrong. The best example came in February 1862 when he completely revised at least the theoretical framework of his grand geopolitical military strategy a few days after unexpected disasters in Kentucky and Tennessee made it clear that his earlier policy had failed. (See Book Two, Chapter One.)

It would be more accurate to say that Davis could be stubborn—very stubborn—and that he was not very good at foreseeing problems before they arose; or at learning from experience; or that harsh criticism sometimes blinded him to the need to change course, or to step outside the routine bureaucratic procedures, or to replace some of the men whom he had charged with carrying out his policies (especially if they were his long-time friends and associates).

In fact, Davis proved quite willing to listen to advice and carefully consider differing viewpoints—if those differing viewpoints were presented in a respectful, respectable, and private manner—if he believed that he could trust the advocates of those viewpoints not to have ulterior motives, and if he felt assured that he could depend upon their cooperation and complete devotion to the Southern Cause whatever his decision in the matter.

FOUR steps then were necessary for those who hoped to influence and work constructively with the Rebels' Chief Executive. First, and perhaps most important, one had to keep the President informed about what was happening in the area of one's responsibility. This proved especially the case when the area of

---

39 In addition to the biographies by Cooper and W. Davis, see Wiley's "Reluctant Helmsman." Despite its age, Wiley's essay remains arguably the best brief summary of Davis's Confederate career.

one's responsibility involved the army, for the Confederacy's very existence depended upon the country's military forces, and the President, understandably, was especially interested in that facet of his administration.

Second, one also had to avoid all but the most formal, necessary, and official association and even communication with the President's political critics and enemies in Congress and in the State governments and to avoid talking with or complaining to the press.[40] Third, one had to present the Chief Executive a strongly reasoned argument supported by detailed facts and evidence. Finally, one had to present that argument in a way that showed dedication to the Cause of Confederate independence and that did not challenge the President's prerogatives or constitutional position (*as Davis interpreted those matters*) or arouse any personal antagonism. Davis craved information, especially about military matters. Often, he asked—and sometimes begged—his generals for it. He would listen carefully to those whom he trusted and weigh fairly their opinions and advice. Once convinced, he would devote his great energy and harness his considerable intelligence and abilities to further the common effort.

If, on the other hand, Davis felt that he could not rely on a person's dedication to the Confederate Cause, or if a person supported the Chief Executive's political or journalistic critics, or if a person offered an affront to the President (especially a public affront), communication and cooperation between the two would break down almost completely. When such matters involved great public interest, a national disaster could result.[41]

NOT the least of Robert E. Lee's many gifts was his ability to see, understand, and appreciate the numerous strengths and the true nature of President Jefferson Davis. Lee quickly realized what a great asset presidential support and cooperation would be to an army commander who enjoyed the Chief Executive's trust and who had his full confidence and support.[42]

---

40 Responding to an official letter from a Davis critic who was a governor or member of Congress inquiring about one of his state's military units serving under a general's command, for example, would be proper. Complaining to a member of Congress or a journalist about an administration policy or strategy would not be.

41 Such statements cannot be documented precisely (no "smoking gun"). My conclusions are based on the President-general relationships of Davis and Lee (positive) on the one hand and of Davis and Johnston (negative) on the other. Examples of both will be given below.

42 See Gallagher, *Lee and His Army*, 191.

Lee's most important task in the first weeks of June 1862 was to keep the personal trust he had developed with Davis over the preceding year and to expand it to benefit the army he had recently come to command. By so doing he would secure the President's understanding of and support for his efforts. To succeed in his new assignment, Lee simply could not allow a situation to arise that would open between himself and President Davis the sort of chasm that Johnston and Davis had created between themselves in the first year of the war.

When he sat down at his desk in the Dabbs House on that seventh day of June 1862 to pen his response to Davis's note of the previous day, Lee began an effort toward that purpose that he continued until the end of the war.

Chapter Four

State Brigades

PART I

"... our exalted acquaintance ... is full of Malice—& hates me ..."
— Joseph E. Johnston, January 15, 1862

BACK in the spring and summer of 1861 the Secessionists had found themselves faced with the urgent necessity of organizing as quickly as possible an army to defend their newly proclaimed independence. As each seceding State declared itself out of the Union, it undertook to raise troops by calling for "volunteers" to form a State army to defend against possible invasion.

Initially these volunteers entered State service in one of the locally organized "companies," often under the command of some prominent citizen who served as its captain. Some of the companies were pre-existing units that had been antebellum social clubs as well as military outfits. Each company numbered about one hundred men. Once formed, the company chose its officers and non-commissioned officers (usually by election) and began to learn the manual of arms and close order drill under the tutelage of some local veteran or, perhaps, of a military school cadet or alumnus who lived in the community.[1]

Early in the organizing process the company also chose a name. A unit from the Magnolia State, for example, styled itself "the Mississippi Yankee Hunters," while a Virginia company chose as its *nom de guerre* "the Pig River Invincibles." Then, its organization complete and its training well under way, the company

---

1 Although the individual members of these volunteer companies were also members of the militia, the companies themselves were separate from the militia. The states may have made this distinction because the militia included by law all white males eighteen to thirty-five and, therefore, many men who opposed secession and who could elect opponents of secession as officers. Thanks to Jim Ogden for pointing this out to me.

offered its services to the State through the governor, the State's adjutant general, or some especially constituted State "military board."

Upon accepting the company, State authorities ordered it to report to a "camp of instruction." There, the camp commander combined it with nine other companies to form a "regiment." On occasion the camp commander did not have enough companies to create a regiment and would combine the companies he had to form a "battalion."

In the process of forming the regiments and battalions the companies lost much of their colorful individual identities and acquired a simple letter designation in a regiment or battalion that, in turn, was denominated by number, type, and state name. In this way the Mississippi Yankee Hunters became Company K of the 1st Mississippi Infantry Regiment, and the Pig River Invincibles Company C of the 46th Virginia Infantry Regiment. Each regiment was commanded by a colonel; each battalion by a lieutenant colonel or major (depending on its size). These officers were elected (usually by the unit's company commanders) or appointed by the governor. Up to this time the regiment or battalion was under State control.

MEANWHILE, the Secessionists had created their national government and Confederate authorities began the process of organizing a national army (the Provisional Army). When the War Department called upon the individual States for troops, the States used the regiments and battalions they had formed to fill their quotas of men for national (Confederate) service. The regiments and battalions carried their State designations into the Confederate Provisional Army.

Once a regiment or battalion had passed from State to Confederate control, Rebel authorities directed it to proceed to the "seat of war" or the "scene of action." In the earliest months of the conflict that usually meant to Virginia, where most observers expected the crucial battles to take place. As units from other states arrived in the Old Dominion, Confederate officials dispatched them to various threatened points. At their duty stations the newly arrived units came under the control of local Confederate commanders who combined two or more of them into a "brigade." Each brigade was commanded by a brigadier general named to the post by the President. If no brigadier general had been assigned to command a brigade, the senior (as determined by his grade and date of rank) regimental commander serving with the brigade exercised command of it.

WHENEVER possible, most local commanders seem from the outset to have followed the practice of brigading together troops from the same State. Thus, for example, at Harpers Ferry, Virginia (now in West Virginia), four infantry regiments from the Old Dominion—the 2nd, 4th, 5th, and 27th, with the 33rd Virginia added a short time later—were united to create a brigade commanded by Brigadier General Thomas J. Jackson, a Virginian.

In some cases, however, the local commander did not have enough regiments and battalions from one State to form an homogeneous brigade. In such cases he had no choice but to place units from two or more States into a brigade as those units reported to him. For that reason, Jackson's fellow brigade commander at Harpers Ferry, Brigadier General Barnard E. Bee of South Carolina, found himself at the head of a "mixed" brigade made up of an Alabama regiment, two Mississippi regiments, and a regiment from Tennessee.

The army that won the Confederacy's first major victory at Manassas not far outside Washington on July 21, 1861, consisted of ten brigades (plus several units not then assigned to any brigade). Nine of those brigades were mixed outfits with troops from two or more States. Jackson's all-Virginia brigade, which became the "Stonewall Brigade" that day, was the exception.[2]

NOT long after the Battle of Manassas (which the following year became known as the First Battle of Manassas), some complaints arose about the organization of the army's brigades. Many of the troops, their officers, their friends and families at home, local newspapers, and—not surprisingly—the politicians, favored and urged a policy of uniting regiments and battalions with other units from the same State.

Such homogenous State brigades, many thought, would serve several purposes. They would enhance morale by bringing together men with much in common, appeal to State pride (both in the army and on the home front), and ensure that men from one State would not suffer discrimination or unfair treatment at the hands of strangers should their unit find itself assigned to a brigade commanded by an officer from another State.[3]

---

2 2 *OR*, 469-470.

3 For the same reasons Virginia sought to carry this policy even further. On April 27, 1861, Robert E. Lee wrote to Jackson at Harpers Ferry that he should form regiments or battalions "uniting as far as possible companies from the same section of the State" (2 *OR*, 784-785). During the next few weeks Lee sent similar instructions to other post commanders (ibid., 799, 803, 806, 813-814, 824, 856, and 858). Lee probably sent these directives at the order of State authorities. If he sent the instructions on his own, he soon changed his mind. See Part II of this chapter for more on this subject.

State brigades would also reflect the spirit and facilitate implementation of Confederate military law which stipulated that general officers should "be appointed [so] as to make a joint apportionment among the states furnishing the troops." Finally, and unofficially, such brigades would offer ambitious commanders who fancied a postwar political career a golden opportunity to garner favor with the troops, most of whom were or, if they survived the war, soon would be voters.[4]

EXAMPLES of this desire for homogenous State brigades are widespread and run all through Confederate military and political history. As early as May 17, 1861, an officer wrote, "it is very desirable that all the Maryland men should be together." On August 6, 1861, Governor Henry T. Clark of North Carolina wrote to remind President Davis that his State "has some claim to have her regiments commanded by her own sons." In the following spring an aide-de-camp to General Albert Sidney Johnston noted that some Arkansas soldiers "came here [Corinth, MS] with the inducement held out to them that they would be thrown with troops from their own state. The general desires to gratify them."

In May 1862, two prominent Alabama politicians complained to Davis that their State had suffered "an actual tho not designed injustice" because on many battlefields "our troops . . . were led by Brigadiers from other States." A year later

---

4 See J. Davis, *Papers*, vol. 10, 71 (Davis to Cooper, Nov. 14, 1863). The *antebellum* United States Army had a long history of attempting to give each state a proportionate number of military appointments. Coffman (*Old Army*, 12) traces the practice back to the Jefferson Administration in the first decade of the nineteenth century. (The Jeffersonians were concerned with the number of Republicans and Federalists who held military appointments and what they saw as a potential threat to the republic if too many of the latter party had command positions in the army.) In the post-Civil War decades, a law required that Regular Army officers commissioned directly into the Army from civil life be apportioned among the states and territories in a ratio that reflected the number of volunteers from each state in the Civil War (ibid., 219). The practice by which members of Congress appointed boys to the Military Academy created a similar distribution of officer appointments among graduates of that school. See also J. Davis, *Confederate Government*, I, 21; and V. Davis, *Memoir of Davis*, I, 520. In 1901, when Congress enlarged the Army, the lawmakers specified that quotas for officers' commissions be assigned to each State. Under this provision of the law, future five-star general and World War II chief of staff George C. Marshall received a second lieutenant's commission as part of the quota for his home State of Pennsylvania. See Pogue, *Marshall*, 65. In 1861, Joseph E. Johnston must have been aware of the long-standing practice of tying politics to military matters. He seems, however, not to have appreciated its importance in relations between generals and elected officials. If he did understand the practice, his failure to realize its importance and his refusal to cooperate with the Davis government in the matter is yet another example of his obtuseness concerning matters of high-level military command.

Robert E. Lee wrote of a situation in which "The brigade is composed of 2 North Carolina and 3 Virginia regiments. The former have complained of being commanded by a Virginia brigadier, & I presume the latter would complain if commanded by a North Carolinian." Always wise, General Lee resolved the matter in a truly Solomonic way. He named to the post a brigadier general from Maryland who, "being of the old [*antebellum* regular United States] army, no one has a right to complain."

This feeling of State loyalty remained strong throughout the conflict. In February 1864, after almost three years of "the nationalizing influence of war," some Texas troops then serving in East Tennessee picked up a rumor that their unit might be consolidated with one from another State. Brigadier General John Gregg, commanding the Texans, wrote that he thought "the horror of consolidation among the troops arises from fear of consolidation with troops of other States."

As late as March 1865, Brigadier General Francis M. Cockrell was engaged, he reported, in "preserving and maintaining intact the separate State identity of the Missouri Brigade east of the Mississippi River. . . . [so as to] preserve and maintain during the entire struggle its separate State organization and name, of which every Missourian feels most proud."[5]

IN the first autumn of the war, as public and political interest in the organization of State brigades intensified, the subject naturally drew the attention of President Davis and other political figures. On September 2, Adjutant and Inspector General Samuel Cooper wrote to General Joseph E. Johnston on behalf of the President requesting a report showing how the brigades of Johnston's army were organized and who commanded them.[6]

As additional regiments reached northern Virginia in the late summer and early fall, the army—either in response to this presidential interest or by coincidence—

---

5 Cooper, *Davis*, 352; J. Davis, *Confederate Government*, I, 381-386; J. Davis, *Papers*, vol. 7, 277-278, and vol. 8, 34, 165, and 258; "The Fatal Memo Not Carried Out," *B&G*, XXII, No. 6 (Winter 2006), 24; 2 *OR*, 856; 31 *OR*, pt. 2, 779; 49 *OR*, pt. 2, 1117. See also C. C. Clay and W. L. Yancey to Davis, Apr. 21, 1862, J. Davis, *Papers*, vol. 8, 150; 2 *OR*, 591-592, 671-672, 698-699, 704, 716, and 729; and 20 *OR*, pt. 2, 418. For an example of troops from one State complaining of their treatment by an officer from another State, see A. K. Allison to Jefferson Davis, Apr. 21, 1865, Governor's Letter Book, Series 32, Vol. 7, 191-192, Florida Department of Archives and History, Tallahassee (quoted in part in J. Davis, *Papers*, vol. 11, 532-533). Of course, not all Confederates favored homogeneous brigades.

6 5 *OR*, 826-827.

was evolving toward an organization in which more and more of its brigades consisted of troops from only one State. Still, however, several mixed brigades remained.[7]

President Davis paid a visit to the army September 30 - October 4, and the organization of State brigades was among the subjects he discussed with Johnston and his leading subordinates. After the Chief Executive returned to Richmond, the matter became a frequent subject of correspondence between the government and army headquarters. On October 7 Secretary of War Judah P. Benjamin wrote to Johnston about the President's desire to brigade regiments and battalions by States "as far as possible . . . so as to gratify the natural State pride of the men and keep up that healthful and valuable emulation which forms so important an element in military affairs."[8]

Ten days later the President addressed a similar letter to General Pierre G. T. Beauregard, then Johnston's second in command at Manassas. Organization of State brigades, the Chief Executive opined, would improve morale. "They [the troops] will be stimulated by extraordinary efforts, when so organized that the fame of their State will be in their keeping. . . . In the hours of waiting for spring," he added, "men from the same region will best console and relieve each other."[9]

BY the fall Confederate authorities had divided Johnston's force into three area commands or "districts." The center Potomac District was by far the largest of the Rebels' northern Virginia commands. Johnston maintained his headquarters with that part of his overall force. On October 22 the War Department issued an order directing organization of the troops of the Potomac District into four "divisions." One of these divisions was to comprise three infantry brigades, one four, and the last two five each.

Under this projected reorganization, all but three of the district's seventeen infantry brigades were to consist of regiments from only one State. The exceptions

---

7 See the organizational tables for Johnston's northern Virginia forces on various 1861-1862 dates in 2 *OR*, 469-470, 558, 565, 943-944, and 999-1000; and in 5 *OR*, 825 and 1029-1030. In his authorized biography (Roman, *Beauregard*, I, 120) General Beauregard claimed to have anticipated the policy and to have formed his force into eight single state brigades. The table of organization he presented (ibid., 471-472) shows only six such brigades along with two mixed ones.

8 Smith, *War Papers*, 34; 5 *OR*, 892, 903-904, and 907.

9 5 *OR*, 903-904. In J. Davis, *Papers*, vol. 7, 358 this letter is dated Oct. 16. See also 5 *OR*, 894-895.

involved units from States that did not then have enough troops in the Manassas area to form a separate brigade. For example, the authorities put the army's one Maryland regiment (a unit made up of Confederate sympathizers from that non-seceding slave State) into a brigade with three Georgia regiments. Johnston was to designate the specific units that would make up each brigade. "The arrangements will be gradually carried into effect," the order stipulated, "as soon as, in the judgment of the commanding general, it can be safely done under present exigencies."[10]

ABOUT a month before the War Department issued the October 22 order Johnston himself faced an organizational problem involving State pride. A proposal arose to assign an officer from Maryland to the 1st Virginia Cavalry Regiment. Johnston objected to the proposed assignment. "State pride," he wrote, "excites a generous emulation in the Army, which is of inappreciable value in its effect on the spirit of the troops." For that reason, he hoped, the regiment would be allowed to remain "exclusively Virginian" and the officer would be assigned to a Maryland unit.[11]

Johnston's appreciation of the value of State pride among the soldiers, however, seems not to have extended to troops above the regimental level—or perhaps not to non-Virginia units. He could see no good military reason to reorganize his existing brigades, especially when doing so involved breaking up long-established mixed brigades to create new homogeneous units.[12] Unconcerned with either civilian politics or usually even with military matters above the level of his own command, he simply had little understanding—or at least never exhibited much awareness—of his civilian superiors' worries about the all-important larger logistical, diplomatic, psychological, and political aspects of warfare, let alone their deep concerns about their personal political careers. He seems to have been largely

---

10 5 *OR*, 3, 913-914. The authorities soon modified the organization (see ibid., 960-961). The changes simply added another brigade to one of the divisions. Under the original order the authorities assigned the army's cavalry brigade to one of the divisions. Johnston objected on the grounds that the mounted arm should be under the army commander's direct control. He had a very strong case, and on Oct. 25 wrote a short but well-reasoned letter explaining his views. The War Department agreed and changed the organization as Johnston wished (ibid., 922, 930, and 934-935). Johnston, as was to prove typical of him, learned nothing from this episode and rarely sent such communications to the government in the future.

11 5 *OR*, 181.

12 See the comments in Hughes, *Johnston*, 97-98.

oblivious to President Davis's problems in dealing with headstrong State governors and members of Congress.

In addition, several of Johnston's chief subordinates opposed the State brigade scheme, and their opinions carried great weight with their commander. General Whiting, whose mixed brigade would be broken up under the proposed reorganization and some of whose caustic comments about the plan were quoted in the preceding chapter, was especially averse to the change. Rather than obeying the President's directive, Johnston chose, in the words of historian Steven Newton, to resist "the process, both actively and passively at every step."[13]

"It is scarcely practicable to make such a change now," Johnston protested to Secretary Benjamin eleven days before the War Department issued the October 22 order for the new organization of his force. "It would be dangerous, I think, to make such a rearrangement in the presence of the enemy while we are liable to attack at any moment. I beg you and the President to consider this and to permit the postponement of the reorganization of our troops until a time when we may have better opportunity to make it."[14]

Some of Johnston's subordinates expressed similar objections—albeit in more polite and mature terms than did Whiting. Under the proposed new organization, one pointed out, casualties might fall disproportionally on one state. "We are hourly expecting an attack from an enemy 3 or 4 times our numbers & far better equipped in every respect than we are," he explained. "The consequences of such a change at this time might be most disastrous to our cause & to our Country."[15]

---

13 Newton, *Johnston*, 23.

14 51 *OR*, pt. 2, 340. Could Johnston's fears have been the reason for the wording of the October 22 order giving him the authority to implement the change when he felt it safe to do so?

15 J. Davis, *Papers*, vol. 7, 357, 368-370, and 424. Davis did admit that there were disadvantages to forming State brigades, but he thought that the benefits of doing so outweighed them (5 *OR*, 907. See also 930 and 934-935). We should acknowledge the validity of the argument regarding casualties falling disproportionately on one state. As early as February 13, 1862, Mary Chesnut noted that North Carolina newspapers complained that President Davis thought of the state only when he wanted more troops (*Chesnut's Civil War*, 290). Glatthaar (*Lee's Army*, 255-256, 302, and 314) points out that about thirty percent of the North Carolinians in the army were casualties at Chancellorsville in May 1863. Two months later a staggering 46.4 percent of Lee's Tar Heels fell at Gettysburg. The seven regiments that suffered the highest losses in killed and wounded at Chancellorsville were all from North Carolina. At Gettysburg the top four and six of the top seven Confederate regiments with the highest casualties hailed from the Old North State. Was it pure coincidence that there was so much dissatisfaction with the Davis government in North Carolina? See also ibid., 517 n40, and Escott, *After Secession*, 132-133.

By late November Johnston had found an additional reason to delay the ordered reorganization of his army. The weather had turned bad with the approach of winter, and the roads were in such wretched condition, he argued, that his troops would find it difficult to move from their established posts to the camps of their new brigades.[16]

AS 1861 neared its end, Davis's major concern so far as the matter of State brigades went, obviously had come to center on the status of the nine Mississippi regiments then in Johnston's command. Mississippi was the President's home State, and he wanted her troops serving with Johnston's army united in two brigades, he wanted each of those brigades to be commanded by a Mississippi brigadier general, and he wanted them in a division commanded by a major general from Mississippi. In December 1862, Davis admitted his special concern for the Magnolia State's regiments. Speaking to the state legislature in Jackson, he pointed out that, as President, he had to serve the entire Confederacy, but, he then confessed, "I have looked on Mississippi soldiers with a pride and emotion such as no others inspired."[17]

On September 4, 1861, the War Department ordered Brigadier General Charles Clark, a Mississippi politician, to duty with Johnston's army in northern Virginia. The government clearly intended for Clark to command a brigade of troops from his State. Five weeks later Davis complained to Johnston that Clark had been assigned to direct a post and supply depot rather than to command a brigade of Mississippians. In November, when Clark received a transfer to the West, Brigadier General Richard Griffith took his place. Griffith had served as Davis's adjutant during the Mexican War and later became one of the President's political allies. Griffith did receive command of a four-regiment brigade of Mississippians—not, however, the four regiments that Davis wanted in his brigade. The President planned to have W. H. C. Whiting command another brigade

16 In justice to Johnston, we should note that on October 24, 1861, one of his South Carolina soldiers wrote his "Deer brothers and sisters" that "tha ar talk of figting her. I don't think tha will be iney more figting her this winter for the rods is giting so bad that ole Abe can't com. The rods is the worst I ever saw. It rains ever weak." Some Rebel officers seconded this opinion. On November 24, 1861, and again on March 21, 1862, one of Johnston's subordinates wrote that the roads were then in very bad condition and that the hauling of supplies during the winter had "greatly weakened" his unit's teams. Keith, *Boys of Diamond Hill*, 26; 5 *OR*, 529 and 970.

17 J. Davis, *Papers*, vol. 8, 566. See also 578 and 5 *OR*, 894-895 and 935. Johnston was in the audience when Davis made this remark. See Book Two, Chapter Three below.

comprising five of the army's Mississippi regiments. Both were slated for a division to be commanded by Major General Earl Van Dorn, also a Mississippian.[18]

By early December Davis clearly had become fed up with Johnston's stalling. On the third, Adjutant and Inspector General Samuel Cooper sent a blunt message to Johnston: "The President directs the immediate assignment of the Mississippi regiments as follows: To First Brigade under General W. H. C. Whiting . . . [the 2nd, 11th, 13th, 17th, and 18th regiments]. To Second Brigade under General R. Griffith . . . [the 12th, 16th, 19th, and 21st regiments]." "The above regiments," the directive read, "will join their respective brigades without delay."[19]

At that time Griffith's Brigade occupied Leesburg, some thirty miles northwest of Manassas and contained the 13th, 17th, 18th, and 21st Mississippi regiments. The 12th, 16th, and 19th regiments belonged to separate brigades. The 2nd and 11th served in Whiting's Brigade, then spread along the Potomac River below Washington, D.C.[20]

BY the simple step of switching the 4th Alabama Regiment and the 12th Mississippi Johnston could have created an all-Alabama brigade and brought three of his Mississippi regiments together. Another simple exchange of the 1st Tennessee for the 19th Mississippi would have brought another Magnolia State regiment to join the 2nd, 11th, and 12th and put what was then the army's only Tennessee unit into a brigade with Alabama troops. A swap of the 16th Mississippi for the 6th North Carolina would have given Whiting an all-Mississippi brigade and united two Tar Heel regiments in another brigade. By that time, however, Johnston found nothing that involved Jefferson Davis to be simple.[21]

Three days after Benjamin dispatched the December 3 directive to Johnston, the general wrote "urgently" requesting suspension of the order. Implementation

18 J. Davis, *Papers*, vol. 7, 357, 368-370, and 424.

19 5 *OR*, 979; 51 *OR*, pt. 2, 402. Cooper specified the regiments by the name of the commanding officers. I have used the numerical designations for simplicity. My guess is that Davis took the seniority of the commanders into consideration and therefore put particular regiments together.

20 See Davis to Major General G. W. Smith, Oct. 10, 1861, 5 *OR*, 895. In the Confederate Army brigades, divisions, and corps were designated by the name of their commanding officer. Therefore, "Whiting's Brigade" (but not "General Whiting's brigade") is a proper noun and is capitalized accordingly. Union brigades, divisions, and corps were numbered. Hence "Jones's brigade" in the Federal army is not a proper noun.

21 See 5 *OR*, 1029-1030.

of the President's wishes, he stated, would necessitate withdrawing the nine Mississippi regiments from the field for five or six days to move them to the camps of their new brigades and to get them distributed as Davis wanted. "The subtraction of so considerable a force even for one day, at this crisis, would of itself be attended with extreme peril." An enemy attack at such a time, "by no means improbable," could, he warned, produce disaster. He then believed "an attack from the enemy to be imminent at any moment and at any point." Apparently, the cunning Yankees had found some way to move their legions over the wretched northern Virginia roads that were too much for Johnston's troops to negotiate. The Federals could, therefore, strike the Rebels at a time and place of their own choosing while the Southerners were mired in their own muddy positions or stuck on the march while in transit from one camp to another. It appears not to have occurred to Johnston that he could have obviated much of the problem by moving the Mississippi regiments one at a time or even one company at a time.[22]

DESPITE the directive from the War Department, Johnston took no action. A week into the new year Benjamin wrote the general, "The delay in organizing your army . . . [as ordered] has embarrassed me in providing brigadier generals appropriate to its several brigades in accordance with the act of Congress directing that they should be assigned as far as possible according to States."[23]

Even after this direct admonition from the secretary of war, Johnston did nothing to implement the Chief Executive's wishes. On January 14 he wrote to Secretary Benjamin of his "regret . . . that the President is dissatisfied with the manner in which I have exercised the discretion with which he invested me" as to the reorganization of the army. "There has been no time since those orders were given," he went on, "when I did not believe it utterly unsafe to attempt such reorganization and no time when I was not, as now, anxious to carry out his wishes." However, he claimed, the mid-January weather had inflicted even more damage on the northern Virginia roads, the teams that would haul the regiments' baggage should they move to the camps of their new brigades were weak, and such changes were "physically impracticable now." Besides, he argued, such changes would also be "impracticable because unsafe" while the destination of a Union

22 5 *OR*, 985, 987-988, and 993-994.

23 Ibid., 1023.

naval expedition then reported to be fitting out to strike somewhere on the Rebel coast remained unknown. (It eventually struck at eastern North Carolina.)[24]

HAD Johnston not been so insensitive in such matters, he long since would have become aware of the President's rising anger and frustration. The Chief Executive and the general were then under great pressure, and each deserved some slack that, it seemed, the other was unwilling to grant.[25]

Both Davis and Johnston faced major problems and great difficulties on a scale far beyond anything that any American politician or soldier had ever experienced prior to 1861. Even as the matter of State brigades greatly exacerbated the ill-feelings between the government and army headquarters, Davis and the administration on the one hand and Johnston on the other found themselves entangled in numerous convoluted spats, quarrels, mutual misunderstandings, and disagreements over many other matters large and small. These issues included the War Department's sometimes sending orders directly to some of Johnston's subordinates, logistics, personnel, army administration, the use and reported misuse of railroad cars, the careless destruction and waste of property and supplies, the granting of furloughs, housing for the troops, Johnston's refusal (not failure) to communicate meaningfully and fully with the government, and—most bitterly of

---

24 5 *OR*, 1028. There can be no doubt that Johnston's fears were sincere and not just excuses. The Rebels expected daily to learn of an advance by the large Federal army based in the Washington area. See the letters of Edmund Kirby Smith to his wife for the following 1861 dates: Oct. 29, Oct. 30, Nov. 5 ("the long-expected battle"), Nov. 11, Dec. 5 ("good assurances that the enemy is about to advance"), Dec. 8, Dec. 11, and Dec. 14 (Johnston "expects every day to receive news" of the Yankees' advance). At that time Smith served at Johnston's headquarters. On Jan. 3, 1862, Johnston wrote his wife that he was "afraid to go more then a mile or two from my headquarters" until he learned the fleet's destination (Johnston Letters, MHS).

25 For the pressure on Davis, see his October 10, 1861, letter to G. W. Smith, 5 *OR*, 895. Some idea of the pressure Johnston and his entourage felt can be gleaned from Edmund Kirby Smith's letters, which doubtless reflected Johnston's attitude (see preceding note). "I feel the fate of our Country, our very independence & existence hangs upon the fate of this army" and "the present state of uncertainty & anxiety" (Oct. 28, 1861); "we will have great odds to contend against" (Nov. 1, 1861), both in E. K. Smith Letters. President Davis did not help to ease the pressure on Johnston. On September 5, he wrote the general that "To permit the enemy to gain a success over any portion of . . . [your army] would be a sad disaster." He then added that he had done all he could to strengthen Johnston's force. Three days later the Chief Executive informed the general that "The cause of the Confederacy is staked upon your army" (5 *OR*, 829-830 and 834).

all—the question of Johnston's rank among Confederate generals. (See Chapter One of this study.)[26]

None of these other matters festered on for so long and so openly as did the question of the Mississippi regiments. Even more important, none of the other matters in dispute caused similar political headaches for Davis and Benjamin.

As these quarrels dragged on, they intensified the bitterness between Johnston and the administration. In the winter of 1861-1862, perhaps even in the fall of 1861, clear signs began to emerge that the general was becoming alienated from his government and at least a bit paranoid about the President's attitude toward him. As Johnston's feelings of alienation grew, he began to see himself as a victim or martyr. He was trapped in a predicament where he faced an almost impossible situation, caught between an overwhelmingly strong enemy army in his front and his own uncaring, unsympathetic, even hostile government in his rear. Under such circumstances his usually pessimistic view grew stronger and gloomier.[27]

By January 15, 1862, Johnston was writing his wife Lydia that he had proof about the "feeling of our exalted acquaintance toward me. He is full of Malice—& hates me more than any man in the army except Beauregard." Two weeks later Johnston, then feeling especially sorry for himself, wrote his spouse that he had "big cares upon my mind & heart always such as few generals have ever had inflicted upon them." Without divine intervention, he added, "there is little ground for hope."[28]

---

26 Most of the correspondence regarding these matters is in 5 *OR*. Steven Newton (*Johnston, passim*) maintains that historians have consistently understated the volume of Johnston's communications with the government and that many of the reports and information that he sent were in enclosures to pieces of routine correspondence.

27 One historian called Johnston "a pessimist of the first order." Black, *Railroads of the Confederacy*, 222. Most of Johnston's unhappy correspondence with Benjamin is in 5 *OR*. See also the comments in Newton, *Johnston*, 24, 38, and 212.

28 Johnston Letters, MHS. Back on October 27, 1861, Johnston had written to his long-time friend and future chief of staff William Whann Mackall that the problems he faced at Manassas had caused him "deep and incessant anxiety." Letter in Mackall Papers, SHC. What became a long-running feud between Davis and Beauregard began when the President and his advisers (including Robert E. Lee) rejected an impractical plan submitted by Beauregard prior to the Battle of Manassas. It worsened when the general's report of that battle appeared without government authorization in the Richmond newspapers, and Beauregard expressed criticism of the Davis Administration to members of Congress. It soon expanded to include several other matters. See Williams, *Beauregard, passim*. Johnston and Beauregard had their own falling out during the postwar period. See Book Six, Chapter One, Volume II of this work.

IN the late spring, after Johnston had moved his army from the Manassas area first back to Fredericksburg on the Rappahannock River and then on to the peninsula between the James and York rivers southeast of Richmond, the subject of brigade organization again arose. On April 30 members of the 16th Mississippi Infantry Regiment petitioned the President to reassign their unit to a Mississippi brigade. A week later Davis endorsed the document to his adviser Lee, noting that "the feeling that they were discriminated against, in not being as the troops of other States associated together, has been injurious. . . . Reiterate the order [to Johnston]."

On May 11, as Johnston led his army back toward Richmond from Yorktown near the tip of the peninsula, Davis—doubtless with the recently received petition from the 16th Mississippi in mind—again wrote to Johnston. "I have been much harassed and the public interest has suffered by the delay to place the Regts. of some of the States in Brigades together," wrote the President, "it being deemed unjust discrimination was made against them . . . some have expressed surprise at my patience when orders to you were not observed. . . . The reasons formerly offered [for not carrying out the orders] have one after another disappeared and I hope you will, as you can, proceed to organize your troops as heretofore instructed."

Two-and-one-half weeks later, not long before Johnston's ill-fated May 31 attack on the Yankees at Seven Pines, the President sent yet one more plea to his general about the troops from his home state. "I have been further urged to have the Missi. Regts thrown together without delay," he wrote. "The wish is that it should be done before the impending battle and I would be glad that it should be complied with."

Johnston, as Davis must have anticipated, replied that he had been unable to restructure his brigades because he feared the consequences should he disrupt the army's organization in the presence of the enemy.[29]

THE general, it seemed, could not execute the presidential directive in good weather because the Yankees might then attack. He could not carry out the instructions in bad weather because, even if the Yankees did not strike then, his own troops would find it too difficult to move along the wretched roads to join their new brigades. He could not reorganize the army when it was in camp (fall

---

29 J. Davis, *Papers*, vol. 8, 158, 170–171, and 202. See also Symonds, *Johnston*, 157–158. Davis also brought the matter up during a visit to the army, likely on May 20. Smith, *War Papers*, 58.

1861, winter 1861-1862) or when it was on the move (spring 1862). He could not do so when the enemy was distant (late winter 1861-1862 when the army was posted along the Rappahannock River) or when the enemy was close by (May 1862 near Richmond). He found it impossible to obey Davis's orders before, during, or after the period of uncertainty about the objective of the Union naval expedition.

We may forgive Davis if he wondered just when Johnston might think it feasible to obey the oft-repeated order. Perhaps the general could find the occasion to do so during the summer or fall of 1862—nine to fourteen months after the first directive on the subject.

Then, on May 31 Johnston fell wounded at Seven Pines, and Robert E. Lee took command of the army.

PART II

"But as it is your wish. . . ."

— Robert E. Lee to Jefferson Davis, June 7, 1862

A heavy rain fell across the Richmond area during the morning of Friday, June 6, 1862. In the afternoon, when the downpour had ceased, General Lee rode out to visit some part of his army. For that reason he was absent from his Dabbs House headquarters when the messenger brought the letter from the President. Upon returning that evening Lee opened and read the document. The next morning he sat down at his desk to answer it.

Davis's letter, dated the sixth, has been lost, but its contents can easily be reconstructed from Lee's reply. The Chief Executive wrote to inquire about four matters. He was considering the promotion of Brigadier General Richard H. Anderson of South Carolina to major general. The President, however, expressed doubts about such a promotion because of reports that Anderson drank too much and even had been intoxicated while on duty the previous January. Lee replied that he knew only "little of Genl[.] A. personally," but that Major General James Longstreet ("a capital soldier") had a high opinion of the brigadier who "I am told is now under a pledge of abstinence, which I hope will protect him from the vice he fell into." The difficulty, Lee added, was that the army had no vacancy for a major general. Longstreet's recommendation, as transmitted by Lee, satisfied Davis. When a position opened up several weeks later Anderson received the promotion.

The President found himself under pressure from the Alabama congressional delegation to promote Colonel Evander M. Law to brigadier general to command a brigade. He had also received a petition from some officers of Whiting's Brigade (which Law then commanded) to the same effect. He therefore wrote Lee to inquire about the matter. Patiently, Lee again explained that the army currently had no position into which Law could be promoted because Whiting's absence from the brigade was temporary. Four months later, when casualties and transfers had created an opening, Law received a well-deserved brigadier's appointment.

With regard to the President's third query, Lee wrote that he would call "the other matters to which you allude" to the attention of division and brigade commanders. These unspecified subjects probably involved more or less routine administrative and perhaps disciplinary matters, and they likely reflected Davis's penchant for involving himself in details that rightly belonged to the secretary of war or some other subordinate administrative official.

The fourth matter that Davis raised concerned the long-festering question of organizing State brigades. In response to the President's letter Lee wrote:

> I have . . . sent a circular to Division commanders to see what can be done as to reorganizing brigades by states. I fear the result nor do I think it the best organization. I would rather command a brigade composed of regts[.] from different states. I think it could be better controulled, more emulation would be excited, there would be less combination against authority. I can understand why officers looking to political preferment would prefer it, & it may be more agreeable to the men. The latter consideration has much weight with me[.] But as it is your wish [and] may be in conformity to the spirit of the law, I will attempt what can be done. It must necessarily be slow & will require much time. All new brigades I will endeavor so to arrange.[30]

LEE'S LETTER MUST have surprised and pleased President Davis for several reasons. For one thing, the general had already taken action with regard to the matter of state brigades—without, we should note, prompting from Davis: "I have . . . sent a circular to Division commanders to see what can be done." Second, never, so far as the record shows, had Johnston been so open and so honest in

---

30 The subject of State brigades was, in fact, the second topic Lee covered in his reply to Davis. I have placed it last because it alone among the letter's subjects relates to the central thesis of this essay and is treated in some detail. It makes sense, therefore, to list it last. Lee's reply is in J. Davis, *Papers*, vol. 8, 229-230. See also ibid., 227 and, on Law, 145. For examples of Lee's implementation of Davis's wishes see 11 *OR*, pt. 3, 591, 620, and 654.

communicating with regard to the Chief Executive's cherished scheme of brigade organization (or anything else). Never had Johnston presented any reasoned objections to the State brigade plan. He had simply refused to do anything to implement the reorganization while professing his earnest desire to do so as soon as possible even as he presented one excuse after another as to why he could do nothing about the matter until some indefinite—and, apparently, constantly receding—date in the unknown future. By taking this passive-aggressive stance, he seems, in fact, to have hoped that the whole matter simply would fade away.[31]

Third, although Lee strongly disagreed with the President's policy of forming homogenous state brigades, he had stated his reasons honestly, openly, rationally, and respectfully. His language differed completely from Whiting's fulminations, some version of which Johnston had sent to the government the previous winter. In substance, Lee agreed completely with Whiting and Johnston. (See Part I of this chapter.)

Fourth, Davis must especially have appreciated the pledge with which Lee followed his objections to the President's plan—"*But as it is your wish* I will attempt what can be done" [my emphasis]. Finally, the general had also been candid enough to caution Davis that implementation of the change would require "much time." In this prediction Lee turned out to be completely wrong.

So far as the extant record shows, President Davis made only one additional reference to the subject of all-Mississippi brigades in the Army of Northern Virginia. On June 12, probably in what he intended as a comment on Lee's letter of the seventh, the President reminded his general that the second all-Mississippi brigade "remains yet unorganized." After that, as things turned out, the President had no more cause to complain about the subject of homogenous State brigades in Lee's army.[32]

---

31 These sentences have to be qualified because some of the 1861-1862 Davis-Johnston correspondence has been lost (see, for example, 5 OR, 892, for reference to a now-missing document that dealt with army organization and possibly—although probably not judging from the context of this reference—state brigades.) In addition, Johnston could have expressed his reservations verbally during Davis's fall 1861 visit to the army or at one of their early 1862 meetings.

32 J. Davis, *Papers*, vol. 8, 238. The President's July 25, 1862, correspondence concerning some Louisiana troops grew from the concerns of others who talked with Davis, not from any worries on the Chief Executive's part. The same is true of Lee's letter of that date regarding the 2nd and 11th Mississippi regiments (ibid., 301). On the Louisiana units, see 12 OR, pt. 3, 917-918.

THROUGHOUT the early weeks of June, his first month as the army's commander, Lee constantly kept busy. He devoted long hours to conferences with his staff and his generals and to working out a plan by which he would attempt to drive the massive Yankee army away from Richmond and destroy it. He put his soldiers to work building extensive lines of fortifications to shield the city. He sought to improve the discipline of his army and to provide more for the men in the way of food, shoes, and clothing. He undertook a partial reorganization of his force to prepare it for what was to come. He kept open lines of communication from his headquarters to the President's office and to the War Department in Richmond. In this way Davis and other civilian authorities would know what he was doing, what problems he faced, and what he hoped to accomplish. They would also be more likely to know what they could do to help Lee achieve his goals.

Somehow, Lee also found the time that hectic month to deal with the vexing question of the President's beloved Mississippi regiments.[33]

BY that time Lee had another Magnolia State unit to add to his concerns. When he assumed command of the army, Lee found the nine Mississippi regiments that had been with Johnston in northern Virginia still distributed throughout the army as described in the first part of this chapter (four in Griffith's all-Mississippi brigade; two in Whiting's Brigade, then temporarily under Law; the other three scattered in three different brigades). In April, when Johnston had taken the army onto the peninsula below Richmond, it absorbed the small Confederate force already in the Yorktown area. Among those additional units was the 2nd Mississippi Infantry Battalion. On June 1, when Lee superseded Gustavus Smith, the battalion served in a brigade commanded by Brigadier General Samuel Garland.

Garland's Brigade was one of the most diverse outfits in the army, if not in the entire Confederacy. Garland, a Virginian, headed a brigade composed of the 2nd Florida Regiment, the 5th and 23rd North Carolina Regiments, and the 38th Virginia Regiment—in addition to the 2nd Mississippi Battalion. At the same time Brigadier General Winfield Scott Featherston, a Mississippian, found himself commanding an almost equally mixed brigade comprising the 27th and 28th Georgia regiments, the 4th North Carolina Regiment, and the 49th Virginia Regiment.

---

33 Glatthaar, "Profiles in Leadership," covers Lee's June efforts to improve the army but does not deal with the matter of State brigades.

On June 12, the very day that Davis wrote to remind Lee that the second all-Mississippi brigade yet remained unorganized, the process of forming that unit got underway. A new brigade officially came into existence, and Lee transferred Featherston, recovered from a recent illness, from his old post to command it. Lee also reassigned the 12th and 19th Mississippi regiments from their respective old brigades to form the nucleus of Featherston's new command. Twelve days later the 2nd Mississippi Battalion joined the brigade. Sometime that month the 16th Mississippi transferred from its old command to Featherston's Brigade.

Lee had managed to form a second all-Mississippi brigade and had so arranged his army that eight of his ten Magnolia State units were in brigades composed solely of troops from the State and were commanded by two of the State's brigadier generals. What Johnston had been unable—or unwilling—to do, or even to attempt, for eight months, Lee had brought about in a couple of weeks. Douglas Southall Freeman marveled that "a cautious commander would not have dared to change his organization with the enemy in his front."[34]

For the moment Lee could do nothing about his two remaining Mississippi regiments, the 2nd and 11th. Both were in Whiting's Brigade, and that unit had been among the troops Lee sent away from the Richmond area in June to reinforce Thomas "Stonewall" Jackson in west-central Virginia.[35]

EVEN as Lee went about creating his second all-Mississippi brigade, he was implementing his plan to drive the Yankees away from Richmond. As part of this effort, Jackson's force from the Shenandoah Valley, augmented by Whiting's Brigade and other troops, moved eastward into the Richmond area. From June 26 through July 1 Lee's army hammered the Federals east of the capital, slowly pushing them back down the James River to Harrison's Landing, some twenty miles below the city. The Confederate troops followed but could find no opportunity to strike a blow against the new Yankee camp which stood on easily defensible ground and under the protection of the big guns on the Federal naval

---

34 In January 1863, the 2nd Mississippi Battalion was enlarged and became the 48th Mississippi Infantry Regiment. See Bearss, "Featherston," in W. Davis (ed.), *Confederate General*, II, 119; Sifakis, *Compendium: Mississippi*, 70-71, 92, 99, and 105; B. Hewett, et. al. (eds.), *Supplement to the Official Records*, vol. 46, 345. (This source will be cited hereafter as *ORS*. Citations will be volume number, *ORS*, and page number. This citation would be 46 *ORS*, 345.) Freeman's comment is in his edition of *Lee's Dispatches*, xxix.

35 See Lee to Davis, July 25, 1862, Lee, *Papers*, 236-237.

vessels in the river. On July 9 Lee pulled most of his troops back to their old camps around Richmond.

The Seven Days' Battles produced more than 20,000 casualties in Lee's army, some 16,000 of them wounded men. For days details scoured the battlefields to retrieve the dead and wounded, and long lines of ambulances, farm wagons, and other conveyances crawled into Richmond bringing their suffering cargoes of injured men. Citizens and government officials turned their attention to burying the dead and caring for the wounded. Lee, however, had to keep his mind focused on the fast-developing military situation in the state.

On July 12 came word that Federal authorities had organized a new army in northern Virginia and that force was pushing southward toward Culpeper and Gordonsville only some sixty miles northwest of Richmond. It threatened the crucial Virginia Central Railroad. On the thirteenth Lee began shifting parts of his army to meet the new danger. For several weeks, however, the two Mississippi brigades remained with the force he left near the capital to keep watch on the Yankees at Harrison's Landing lest they renew their effort to capture Richmond.

NO more pressure came from the President to put his home State's units in the Army of Northern Virginia into all-Mississippi brigades. For one thing, as of mid-June eighty percent of them already served in such brigades, although there was not, and never would be a single division in the army that united therein all the Mississippi troops in Virginia. For another thing, Griffith had been killed in the recent battles for Richmond, and whatever plans Davis may have had for his political ally's military career died with him. Colonel (later Brigadier General) William Barksdale of the 13th Mississippi took Griffith's place at the head of one of the Magnolia State brigades. Finally, the necessity for quick action to meet the new Yankee threat that had materialized in northern Virginia precluded any immediate further changes in the army.[36]

Lee found his attention almost completely absorbed by the military operations of late July, August, and September—the battles of Cedar Mountain, Second Manassas, Chantilly, South Mountain, Sharpsburg (Antietam), and Shepherds-

36 This last sounds like one of the excuses Johnston had used to avoid implementing the presidential order. The crucial difference is that Lee had already obeyed the order to a large extent and then was clearly engaged in active operations. Johnston had only expressed his fear that some action might become necessary at some unknown future date to meet some possible Union advance that had not yet begun.

town. Not until October did Lee have the opportunity to undertake a thorough reorganization of his army.

THAT fall President Davis decided to promote his nephew Colonel Joseph R. Davis, then an aide on the presidential staff, to brigadier general and assign him to command a brigade. After some complaints of nepotism and one rejection of the nomination by the Senate, the new general, his promotion finally confirmed, found himself in the spring of 1863 at the head of a new brigade comprising the 2nd and 11th Mississippi regiments from Whiting's old brigade; the 42nd Mississippi, which had reached Virginia after the Seven Days' Battles and been held in the Richmond area for some time; and the 55th North Carolina Regiment. For several months after its activation Davis's Brigade served in southeastern Virginia and eastern North Carolina. It joined Lee's army in the summer of 1863 for the Gettysburg Campaign and remained with that army until the end of the war.[37]

Early in 1864 the 26th Mississippi Regiment reached Virginia. That unit and the 1st Confederate Battalion (the latter an outfit comprising unregimented Alabama and Georgia companies) became part of Davis's Brigade. Early in 1865 Lee transferred the 55th North Carolina Regiment from Davis's Brigade to a unit made up of troops from the Old North State.

When the Army of Northern Virginia surrendered at Appomattox Court House on April 9, 1865, it included the remnants of two all-Mississippi brigades and of a third brigade comprising four Mississippi regiments and the 1st Confederate Battalion. Thirty-four of the army's other thirty-six infantry brigades then consisted of troops from only one State. The exceptions were the Texas Brigade which included Lee's only Arkansas regiment (in fact, an all-Trans-Mississippi brigade) and the Tennessee brigade, which contained the army's lone Maryland unit.[38]

FOR all practical purposes, creation of the second all-Mississippi brigade in June 1862 brought to its end the long-simmering problem of State brigades in Lee's army. Lee, however, remained acutely sensitive to the importance of State ties in Confederate political and military circles. On numerous occasions throughout the remainder of the war he stressed the matter of State connections in the army and

37 At Gettysburg thirty-three of Lee's thirty-seven infantry brigades were single-state units.

38 46 OR, pt. 1, 1267-1275. In a Confederate (or at least an Army of Northern Virginia context), "Texas Brigade" is a proper noun; "Tennessee brigade" is not.

the (political) importance of having troops commanded up through the brigade level by officers from their own State.

On July 29, 1863, two weeks after Lee had gotten his battered army back across the Potomac River following the defeat at Gettysburg, the general addressed President Davis on the subject of reorganizing his force in light of its recent heavy casualties. Several of his especially hard-hit units Lee consolidated. One he discussed in some detail:

> As regards General [Joseph R.] Davis's [Mississippi] brigade, I think it will be better to attach the three Mississippi regiments [2nd, 11th, and 42nd] to [Brigadier General Carnot] Posey's [originally Featherston's Mississippi] brigade in [Major] General [Richard H.] Anderson's division, where I hope they will soon be increased in number. The [55th] North Carolina regiment of this [Davis's] brigade I suggest be attached to [Brigadier General J. Johnston] Pettigrew's old [North Carolina] brigade.

> The only objection to this plan is that it breaks up General Davis's command, but if his indisposition will detain him long from the field, it will be best to do it for the present at least.[39]

On February 8, 1864, Lee wrote to the War Department concerning the official interpretation of an 1862 law that the department had construed to mean that a soldier could receive a promotion for valor and skill (a "battlefield promotion" to use a term from a later war) only if a vacancy in the higher grade existed in his company. This policy, Lee pointed out, put severe limits on such well-deserved promotions. He suggested a change in the law (or the interpretation of it) "so as to permit promotions on this account *to any company or regiment from the same State*," or at least to a vacancy in any company in the deserving man's regiment [my emphasis].[40]

Almost four months later, on May 30, 1864, in the midst of the terrible Overland Campaign against the far stronger forces of Ulysses S. Grant and at a time when he was under great stress, in very poor health, and nearing physical exhaustion, Lee sought reinforcements for his weakened army. Since he was then operating close to Richmond, he wrote to Davis:

39 Lee, *Papers*, 563. General Davis had contracted a fever that kept him from active service until the spring of 1864. Lee probably hoped that President Davis's nephew was gone from the army for good, but was too politically savvy to say so.

40 Ibid., 669.

It has occurred to me that . . . [it may now be] possible to spare with safety some of the garrison troops in Richmond or its defenses [to serve with the army in the field]. *It is immaterial to what State the troops may belong, as I can put them in brigades from the same*, and even if they be few in numbers, they will add something to our strength [my emphasis].[41]

Only a general extremely well-attuned to his civilian commander-in-chief's political needs would have thought of such a matter at such a time.[42]

NOR did Lee neglect to appeal to (humor? flatter?) Davis's desire to have a major voice in military matters that normally should not have concerned a head of state or even a commander-in-chief. The general's numerous 1862-1865 letters and telegrams to Davis and the War Department are filled with information, suggestions, comments, and questions. These all indicated how well Lee read Jefferson Davis's personality, that he was aware of the President's desire (need?) to be kept informed, and that he was sensitive to the Chief Executive's legitimate concerns about the Confederacy's military affairs during a war for the nation's very existence.

In truth, many of Lee's communications also catered to the President's need (vanity?) to see himself as a military commander and to be kept informed about army matters that ideally he should have left to others. Contrary to frequent allegations, however, Davis did not attempt to micro-manage the field operations of the Rebel armies. As discussed at several points in this book, he almost always made it clear that any specific suggestions in his correspondence with field commanders concerning such operations were only suggestions and not orders. Indeed, it was Davis's refusal to give (or delay in giving) orders that, on several occasions, played a major role in bringing about the defeat of one of his armies or turning that defeat into a disaster.

A Confederate general who kept the President informed and who refrained from cooperation with the Chief Executive's opponents and critics in political, military, and journalistic circles would have no cause to complain about presidential interference in his field operations.

FINALLY, Lee's letters and telegrams also contain scores, if not hundreds, of examples of what one well-known student of human and professional relations

---

41 Lee, *Dispatches*, 290. See also Lee, *Papers*, 725.

42 For some other examples, see Lee, *Dispatches*, 63, 115-117, 119-122, and 127-129.

called "the little kindnesses and courtesies so important to a deep relationship." Such expressions as Lee used, trivial in themselves, can do a great deal to create, build, and maintain trust and to foster cooperation and good will.[43]

Consider the following examples from some of Lee's 1862-1863 correspondence with the President and the War Department:

August 14, 1862, to Davis: "What do you think of the propriety of . . . [followed by reasons to do so]?" "Unless I hear from you to the contrary I shall . . . [followed by reasons to do so]." "I will keep you informed of everything of importance that transpires. When you do not hear from me, you may feel sure that I do not think it necessary to trouble you." "I shall feel obliged to you for any directions you may think proper to give." "Wishing you every happiness & prosperity, I am with high esteem, your obt servant."

August 17 to Davis: "I beg you will excuse my troubling you with my opinions, and especially these details, but your kindness has led you to receive them without objection so often that I know I am tempted to trespass."

August 24, reporting troop movements to Davis: "Should you not agree with me in the propriety of this step please countermand the order & let me know." (This after Lee had explained the reason for the movement.)

September 4 to Davis: "I shall proceed to make the movement at once, unless you should signify your disapprobation. . . . I propose . . . unless you should deem it inadvisable on political or other grounds."

November 24 to Davis: "I propose . . . [but] I do not wish to undertake it without due consideration, and should you think it preferable to concentrate the troops nearer to Richmond, I should be glad if you would advise me . . . how glad I should be if your convenience would permit you to visit the army that I might have the benefit of your views and directions."

December 6 to Davis: "I hope your Excellency will cause me to be advised when in your judgment it may become necessary for this army to move nearer Richmond."

January 19, 1863, to Davis: "I have . . . suspended the march of the brigades ordered to North Carolina until I can ascertain something more definitely. If in your opinion the necessity there is more urgent than here, I will dispatch them immediately."

---

43 Covey, *7 Habits*, 55. See also Chapter Five of this book.

February 5, 1863, to Davis: ". . . in case of necessity troops from this army can be sent to Richmond, and if you think the exigencies of the [area to] the South more pressing than here I will send them at once."

February 26 to Davis: "I was very glad to learn from your letter of the 18th that your health had been reestablished & that you were again able to take the open air. I hope that you will soon regain your strength & be long preserved to the Republic."

April 9 to the secretary of war: "I must therefore submit . . . [the] proposition to the determination of yourself & the President."

April 16 to Adjutant and Inspector General Samuel Cooper: "The President from his position being able to survey all the fields of action, can better decide than anyone else, and I recommend that he follow the dictates of his good judgment. I am anxious for our success, and will cheerfully concur in any arrangement which may be decided upon."

April 16 to Davis: "I therefore submit the matter to your Excellency for consideration."

May 20 to Davis: "If therefore you think . . . I submit to your better judgment whether . . ."

May 30 to Davis: "I have given Your Excellency all the facts in my possession to enable you to form an opinion as what is best to be done."[44]

MANY—doubtless including Joseph E. Johnston had he ever read this correspondence—would have accused Lee of sycophancy. Some of those critics, again doubtless including Johnston, would have added the observation that many of Lee's remarks were inappropriate. They were irrelevant and cluttered up official military correspondence. Lee and the President had more important things to do than composing and reading such inappropriate and insignificant comments. Davis, the critics might well have added, simply should not have been involved in many of the matters mentioned in Lee's correspondence with him.

Such critics would have been absolutely correct in all these observations—and they also would have been just as wrong as they possibly could have been in the circumstances that faced a Confederate army commander. Davis wanted to involve himself in such matters. He wished to be consulted, to exchange thoughts on

---

44 Lee, *Papers*, 245, 258, 259, 263, 294, 345-346, 353, 388, 392, 399, 408-409, 430, 435, 488, 496. Lee seems also to have had another unexpressed (but very real) point in some of these comments. See Book Two, Chapter Eight.

military subjects with his generals, and to be kept informed. He was the President, the commander-in-chief. It was the duty of his generals to carry out his plans, or at least his policies, and to honor (humor?) his desire to be kept informed about military matters. The President did not have the responsibility of accommodating the whims of his generals (although a greater man and a better President than Davis might well have done so in order to humor the generals and to get them to perform up to their potential.)[45]

Knowledge of such matters as Lee covered in his correspondence kept Davis informed as to the condition of the army. It also showed the Chief Executive that his general possessed a real and sophisticated understanding of the Confederacy's overall situation; appreciated the administration's economic, strategic, political, diplomatic, and logistical concerns; and was—or seemed to be—following the government's policies. All of this stood in marked contrast to the conduct of many other Confederate generals—including Joseph E. Johnston.

Davis never had any political problems that arose from Lee's actions and conduct. Lee had earned and kept the President's trust. The short paragraph concerning State brigades that he wrote to Davis in his letter of June 7, 1862, inaugurated an effort that paid huge dividends to Lee and to his army and on several occasions brought the Confederacy close to independence.

SO successful did Lee's efforts prove that as early as July 5, 1862 (in the immediate aftermath of Lee's recent success in driving the Yankees away from Richmond) Davis wrote to his new Virginia commander, "The entire confidence reposed in you would suffice to secure my sanction of your view.... I would not be regarded as interfering with the free exercise of your discretion." That fall Davis wrote to a friend that his general "will, I am sure, cordially sustain and boldly execute my wishes to the full extent of his power."[46]

Almost a year and a half later Davis sent a most remarkable letter to Lee that in itself belies the assertion that he interfered with his generals' plans and operations.

---

45 One might contrast Davis's dealings with Joseph E. Johnston with Lincoln's deft handling of Johnston's friend and protégé Major General George B. McClellan. For starters see Waugh, *Lincoln and McClellan*.

46 Could it have been that Lee gained too much influence over Davis in the absence of effective counterweights to Lee's ideas and proposals? Did Davis, in fact, come to accept Lee's views in the belief that they were his own? Biographers of the two men should explore this topic in depth.

After discussing the situation facing the Confederates in Virginia and some possible actions they might take, the President informed Lee:

> I am willing, as heretofore, to leave the matter to your decision. You are better informed than any other can be of the necessities of your position . . . *and I cannot do better than to leave your judgment to reach its own conclusions* [my emphasis].

Nineteen months later Davis penned an indorsement on a memorandum from Beauregard:

> Lee is best informed of his situation, and his ability is too well established to incline me To adopt the opinion of anyone at a distance as to . . . [his maneuvers].[47]

WOULD—could—Jefferson Davis ever have written such letters to and about Joseph E. Johnston?

---

47 11 *OR*, pt. 3, 633; Cooper, *Davis*, 397; 36 *OR*, 50; J. Davis, *Papers*, vol. 8, 287; vol. 10, 423 and 426. Such expressions of confidence in generals who did not challenge the administration or cooperate with the President's political and journalistic opponents and whom the President trusted were not limited to Lee. On December 22, 1861, Secretary of War Judah P. Benjamin wrote to Joseph E. Johnston's Western counterpart Albert Sidney Johnston: "We know that whatever can be done will be done by you, and rest content" (7 *OR*, 784).

Chapter Five

The Habits of a Highly Effective General

"What matters most is how we *respond* to what we experience in life."
— Stephen R. Covey, 1989

Stephen R. Covey was a late-twentieth/early-twenty-first century scholar who specialized in the study of leadership, organizations, management, and human behavior. The president, explained Covey,

> . . . had a very dictatorial style of management. He tended to treat people like 'gofers,' as if they didn't have any judgment. His manner of speaking to those who worked in the organization was 'Go for this . . . go for that . . . now do this . . . now do that—I'll make the decisions.' The net effect was that he alienated . . . [many of those] surrounding him. But one of [his subordinates] . . . took the initiative—he anticipated, he empathized, he read the situation. He was not blind to the president's weaknesses; but instead of criticizing them, he would compensate for them. Where the president was weak . . . he'd try to make such weaknesses irrelevant. And he'd work with the president's strengths—his vision, talent, creativity.
>
> This man . . . was treated like a gofer also. But he would do more than was expected. He anticipated the president's need. He read with empathy the president's underlying concern, so that when he presented information, he also gave his analysis and recommendations. . . .
>
> [O]ne day . . . the president said, . . . 'I just can't believe what this man has done. He's not only given me the information I requested, but he's [also] provided additional information that's exactly what we needed. He even gave me his analysis of it in terms of my deepest concern, and list of recommendations.
>
> 'The recommendations are consistent with the analysis, and the analysis is consistent with the data. He's remarkable! What a relief not to have to worry about this part of the business.' At the next meeting, it was 'go for this' and 'go for that' to all . . . [those present] but one. To this man it was 'What's your opinion?'
>
> . . . [T]he president did not feel threatened because this man's strength complemented his strength and compensated for his weakness. So he had the strength of two people. . . . This man's success was not dependent on his circumstances. Many others

were in the same situation. *It was his chosen response to those circumstances that made the difference* [my emphasis].[1]

ROBERT E. Lee died in 1870.

Covey frequently consulted with businesses and governments about their personnel, organizational, and management problems. One hundred and nineteen years after Lee's death Covey published *The 7 Habits of Highly Effective People*. The book quickly became a bestseller, and its admiring readership soon made Covey into what the June 25, 2003, issue of *U. S. News & World Report* called "America's leading management guru." In 2004, Covey added *The 8th Habit: From Effectiveness to Greatness*.

In offering advice as to how people can become "effective" (not, we must note, "efficient," which is something altogether different) and achieve "greatness," Covey placed much emphasis on "personal character." "The primary greatness of 'character,'" he maintained, is the foundation for the successful application of his ideas. Character, in turn, is the product of living in accord with what Covey termed "correct principles." These principles—fair play, personal integrity, honesty, truth, and so on—"are natural laws, and . . . God, the Creator and Father of us all, is the source of them." These principles are embodied in all major religions. People who choose to live in accord with these principles position themselves, Covey wrote, to release the "divine endowments within . . . [their] nature."

What Covey called "right living" thus bestows upon those who choose to practice it an internal "changeless core" of guiding values and hence the psychological security; personal peace, strength, and freedom; moral standing; integrity; patience; and wisdom that are necessary if those people are to become truly effective. People characterized by these traits acquire the power and personal strength to free themselves from the old paradigm (or framework) of the organization of which they are a part.

These people, therefore, find themselves able to rise above the existing—and often petty, dysfunctional, and counter-productive—state of things in which they find themselves and to think in terms of (to envision) what might be rather than what is. They see (or sense) the potential of people and the possibilities of their circumstances rather than focusing narrowly on their actual behavior and the existing, possibly messy, situation.

---

1 Covey, *7 Habits*, 86-88.

Individuals who internalize and live by these principles position themselves to develop and apply the "Habits" that Covey described and analyzed. These Habits, Covey asserted, "represent a *complete* framework of universal *timeless* principles of character and human effectiveness." As people develop and internalize the Habits, they are led to practices that, when applied to specific situations, can produce great results.

Through the Habits the practitioners can win the trust of others in the organization; enhance cooperation with them; and tap their enthusiasm, energy, and the output of their minds and hearts—not just of their hands. They thereby harness their colleagues' full potential for the common good, and in so doing they change the very nature of the organization itself. The result carries the organization beyond routine functioning and efficiency to "effectiveness" and on to "greatness."[2]

COVEY'S approach can be understood on two levels. On one it is a philosophical or moral, indeed, almost a religious plea for a return to what Covey labeled the "Character Ethic." This approach (paradigm), which, he thought, dominated American "success literature" until about 1920, rested on the eternal "basic principles of effective living." In more recent times this framework has been superseded by the "Personality Ethic," which stresses that "success" is the product of image, public relations, and manipulation of what is often called "spin." This unfortunate development, Covey lamented, "has drawn us away from the very roots that nourish true success and happiness."[3]

On the second or lower level—and the one far more relevant to this essay—Covey's approach describes (and prescribes) a number of surprisingly effective actions by which those working in large organizations can improve the chances of achieving their goals and bringing greater success to the entire organization. Such actions often enable the effective person to transform an unworkable,

---

2 These themes run through Covey's books. For specifics as quoted in the text, see: *7 Habits*, 15, 30, 43, 74, 104, 108-109, 110, 117, 306, and 319; and *8th Habit*, 4, 72, 146-149, 153-154, and 161-162.

3 Covey, *7 Habits*, 18-19, and 30. "Generalship is . . . largely built on character and personality," wrote General J. F. C. Fuller (*Grant and Lee*, 6). Fuller did not have a high opinion of Lee ("one of the most incapable Generals-in-Chief in history," ibid., 8). Lee, we must note, served as a "General-in-Chief" for only a few weeks in 1865. Fuller also failed to consider the peculiar circumstances that faced Jeffferson Davis's generals. The important point to be stressed here, however, is the emphasis on "character."

dysfunctional organization or relationship into one that performs well and achieves—indeed, often exceeds—its objectives.

THE first 7 Habits are:

1: Be proactive ("the first and most basic habit of highly effective people"). The proactive person realizes that, while he cannot control what happens or what others do, he can always control himself. He, therefore, can choose to respond to events and to the actions of others in ways that will produce positive results. He focuses on those matters that he can influence. The reactive person, by contrast, blames others for the unpleasant, frustrating situations in which he finds himself, chooses to do little or nothing about the basic problem (which, essentially, is often himself), complains about everything, sinks deeper into bitterness, and comes to see himself as a helpless victim.[4]

2: Begin with the End in Mind ("so that the steps you take are always in the right direction"). Effective people constantly ask themselves what will matter most at the end of the day/career/life—or, in the case of the Confederacy, the war? Visualizing and focusing on that goal, they expend their time and energy on what is important if they are to achieve their objective. "The main thing," wrote Covey, "is to keep the main thing the main thing." In the case of the Confederacy the "main thing" was to achieve national independence.[5]

3: Put First Things First ("effective self-government"). Long-term objectives must be filtered down to the few things that have to be done immediately toward realizing the ultimate goal. This Habit often involves dealing with people rather than with things; building trust and "helpful personal relationships"; preventing a crisis from arising; scheduling priorities rather than prioritizing the schedule; concentrating on the important, not the urgent.[6]

4: Think Win/Win ("most of life is not competition"). Competition within relationships is undesirable and can often hamper accomplishment of the organization's mission. The effective person seeks mutual respect, trust,

---

4 *7 Habits,* 65-94. "The only way you can begin to improve the situation is to realize there's something going on with you too," Robert J. Flower, a student of organizational systems, in an interview with Virginia Anderson, in Atlanta *Journal-Constitution*, Oct. 1, 2006. See also Flower's *Potential: Pathways to Understanding, passim.*

5 *7 Habits*, 8, 95-104, and 160.

6 Ibid., 145-182.

cooperation, and mutual benefits. "There is no way to maintain . . . [a Win/Win situation] without personal integrity and a relationship of trust."[7]

5: Seek First to Understand and Then to be Understood ("the single most important principle in the field of interpersonal communications"). Effective people see the situation from within the other's framework or, as Covey remarked, "we must learn to listen." From a mutual viewpoint effective people can offer their own ideas in the context of a real understanding and appreciation of the others' thoughts and concerns.[8]

6: Synergize ("the essence of principle-centered living"). The effective person thinks of finding a better way (a synthesis)—"not my way; not your way; but our way." Through such creative cooperation people become interdependent and can therefore accomplish much more than they can if each acts alone. The whole thus becomes greater than the sum of its parts. For such a situation to come about, however, there must be a very high level of trust between and among the people involved.[9]

7: Sharpen the Saw ("balanced renewal"). The effective person strives for "continuous improvement" in all four areas of his being—physical, spiritual, mental, and social/emotional.[10]

Covey's *8th Habit* grew from his conclusion that near the end of the twentieth century mankind entered a new age. Covey called this new period "the Knowledge Worker Age" and contrasted it with the old "Industrial Age." To thrive in this brave new world where the most important work is done with the brain, not the muscles, people must unleash "the higher reaches of human genius and motivation"—both their own and those of others. Covey called this Habit "Find Your Voice and Inspire Others to Find Theirs."[11]

ROBERT Edward Lee's name does not appear anywhere in either of Covey's books. Yet Covey would have had to have searched long, far, and wide to find a better example of a person who by nature and instinct, if not by conscious thought,

7   Ibid., 136, 204-234; *8th Habit*, 136.

8   *7 Habits*, 37, and 235-260; *8th Habit*, 192. Abraham Lincoln once said, "I always try to understand both sides and begin by putting myself into the shoes of the party against whom I feel a prejudice." Quoted in Burlingame, *Lincoln and the Civil War*, 76.

9   *7 Habits*, 261-284.

10   Ibid., 289-307.

11   *8th Habit*, 20, 25, 75, 103-105.

practiced most of the Habits of effectiveness and to some degree even that of greatness more assiduously, consistently, and with greater success than did Lee.

Of course, not all of Covey's ideas are fully applicable to Lee who, after all, served as a Confederate general for only four years and as commander of a major army for only three and who died half a century before the dominance of the "Personality Ethic" and more than a century prior to the advent of the "Knowledge Worker Age." Some of the Habits, especially the Seventh, are not really relevant to Lee's wartime situation—unless one wishes to classify Lee's constant efforts to build and maintain his good relationship with President Davis and to improve the quality of his army as variants of "Sharpening the Saw." Nor did Lee follow the "development process" of the Habits consciously (so far as we can tell) or in the sequence that Covey prescribed (in the sequential order listed above). Lee, in fact, may well not even have thought through the full range of his acts and what their cumulative impact might lead to.

LIKE most prescriptions for improving one's situation and with jargon stripped away, Covey's *7 Habits* boil down to common sense if one views them in the overall context of human relations. It is not surprising, therefore, that a man of Lee's background, education, confidence, training, intelligence, and experience would at least have sensed that *choosing* to follow certain practices rather than others would be more likely to enhance cooperation among the Confederates and especially between his army and the government and between himself and President Davis. By *making these choices* and following the practices he did, Lee would thereby enhance the Secessionists' chance to win their independence. Thus, I suspect, Lee was led more by instinct than by conscious thought to practices that Covey would describe and analyze a century and a quarter later.

LEE'S practice of the Habits of effectiveness dates from very early in the war and probably—at least in part—from his family background in Virginia's Tidewater aristocracy. The Davis-Johnston squabbles he observed during his 1861 and 1862 stints as the President's military adviser almost certainly did not serve as the initial or sole catalyst for his behavior.

In April 1861, for example, Lee, then a major general in the Virginia State Army and commander of the Old Dominion's military forces, was asked by Vice President Alexander H. Stephens if he would recognize the authority of a lower-ranking Confederate brigadier general (at that time the highest grade in the Rebels' national army). Certainly, replied Lee, who clearly understood that his personal status was of no real importance, that close cooperation between State and Confederate officials was essential for the successful conduct of military operations, and that the Secessionists' national government must direct the national war effort. He simply would not allow his personal situation to hamper the far larger cause of Confederate independence.

Thus, Lee literally began his Confederate career with the end (Confederate independence) in mind and demonstrated that he would put first things first. Nor did he ever change this attitude. To one general he wrote early in the war, "we must endure everything in the cause we maintain." A few days later when that same officer claimed that he had been insulted, Lee advised him to "let that pass till the enemy is driven back." On June 11, 1863, Lee wrote, "We have a great work to accomplish, which requires the cordial and united strength of all." "When a necessity arises," Lee wrote that day, "every consideration must yield to the public interest." Ten months later he commented, "We have now but one thing to do; to establish our independence. We have no time for anything else, & nothing of doubtful bearing on this subject should be risked."[12]

SOMETIME in 1862 Lee began to develop another idea that dovetailed nicely with his realization that the Confederates' objective of national independence must take precedence over all else. On what might be called the "operational level" of proactivity, he came to understand that the Rebels simply could not afford to sit around complaining about their situation—or even just to sit around. Time, Lee increasingly came to understand, worked against them. What the Confederates could not change—the greater strength of the Federal government, for example—they must accept, and they must act quickly within the parameters created by those unchangeable conditions. "The key question," observed Covey in a sentence that neatly describes Lee's approach to his and the Confederacy's situation, is "what is the best thing I can do under these circumstances?"[13]

To sit; to complain about existing conditions that could not be changed; to wish for perfect or even for more favorable circumstances that did not exist and could not be brought into being; to whine about one's status or petty troubles; and to wait passively while the Federal government organized its armies, massed its overwhelming strength, perfected its plans, and selected the point it would strike

---

12 Schott, *Stephens*, 337; 5 *OR*, 842 and 868; 11 *OR*, pt. 3, 582; Lee, *Papers*, 512; Lee, *Dispatches*, 161. See also Gallagher, *Lee and His Army*, 163-166.

13 *8th Habit*, 133. See also Freeman, *Lee*, I, 188.

would be to doom the Confederacy to eventual defeat. Such a policy would guarantee failure of the Secessionists' bid for independence.[14]

On April 17, 1862, Lee wrote to an officer, "The more active the troops on the Rappahannock [River] the more on the defensive will the enemy be kept." A few weeks later he commented to "Stonewall" Jackson that "now is the time to concentrate on any [enemy force] that may be exposed within our reach. . . . The blow, wherever struck, must to be successful, be sudden and heavy. Should an opportunity occur for striking the enemy a successful blow do not let it escape you." In sending reinforcements to Jackson a few days later, Lee wrote that "the object is to enable you to crush the forces opposed to you." On the same day he informed another general, "If it be impossible to drive the enemy from his present position, I desire you to lose no effort to keep him confined to the smallest possible margin." In early June he directed Jackson to give his troops a rest after their recent strenuous campaign, "but not to omit to strike the enemy if it can be done successfully."

"We must decide," Lee wrote on June 8, 1863, "between the positive loss of inactivity and the risk of action." A few weeks later he commented to President Davis, "So strong is my conviction *of the necessity of activity* on our part that you will excuse my adverting to the subject again [my emphasis]." In the following month he urged a general to take advantage of any opportunity "to shake him [the enemy] in his position." He instructed another to "take command of the [Shenandoah] Valley District and so dispose your troops to operate as to the best advantage . . . damaging the enemy all in your power."[15]

These concepts of the best steps the Rebels could take seem to have grown in Lee's mind during the first eight or nine months of 1862. By the winter of 1862-1863 they had come to dominate his thinking. (These developments are covered in some detail in Book Two, Chapter Eight below.)

THE best example—by far—of Lee's practice of the Habits of effectiveness, however, came on the highest level of Confederate military activity: his realization that he had the *power to choose* to enhance the trust between himself and President Davis. By so doing, Lee clearly realized, he would put the Confederacy in a much better position to win its independence. This Habit is best seen in Lee's successful,

---

14 See Freeman's comments in *Lee*, II, 3, 17, 42, and 249; and 12 *OR*, pt. 3, 866 and 908. For Lee's approach in applying these basic principles, see Chapter Eight, Book Two below.

15 Lee, *Papers*, 504, 532, 547, and 556; 12 *OR*, pt. 3, 652, 866, 867,907, 908, and 910.

proactive June 1862 effort described in the preceding chapter to keep and expand Davis's trust and support. The matter of forming homogenous State brigades fell into Lee's lap (or onto his desk) as the perfect vehicle with which to apply this Habit. He did not waste the opportunity.

LEE could no more control President Davis's actions than could Joseph E. Johnston. Like Johnston, however, *Lee could control his own reactions* to what Davis did. Unlike Johnston, Lee *chose* to react to Davis's message about placing the army's Mississippi units in homogenous brigades by promising to do so *and by acting to achieve that end*—even as he politely, professionally, and respectfully expressed to the Chief Executive his strong doubts about the wisdom of the idea— doubts that, to repeat, largely duplicated those of Johnston.[16]

Johnston, by contrast, had freely chosen to react to Davis's policy in a negative, destructive, passive-aggressive way (or "oppositional" approach). Johnston's choice only widened the gap between himself and the President and increased the suspicion with which the Richmond authorities would view his future communications and actions—or lack of communications and actions. "What matters most," Covey wrote, "is how we respond to what we experience in life."[17]

Lee's proactive record, his practice to a greater or lesser degree of the other Habits, and his guiding realization that time worked against the Confederates and that passive inactivity would lead ultimately and inevitably to Confederate failure all stand in sharp contrast to the conduct of a great many of his fellow Rebel commanders, not just in contrast to the conduct of Joseph E. Johnston. Often other Southern generals *chose* to spend much of their time and energy complaining about and feuding with each other, President Davis, the secretary of war, and/or the War Department bureaucracy. Many of them also chose to cooperate with the administration's critics and political enemies in Congress, the press, and the State governments.

On a lower level, those generals often also *chose* to sit and wait for the enemy to act. Then they would react in some (often ineffective) way to whatever the Yankees did. Often such reactions took the form of abandoning some valuable area of the Confederacy and retreating to await the invaders' next move. Under such

---

16 Lee's practice is sometimes called "managing up"—"a crucial political skill in every organization," wrote Marie McIntyre. See her "Your Office Coach," Atlanta *Journal-Constitution*, Apr. 1, 2007.

17 *7 Habits*, 75.

conditions, as Lee seems to have come to realize during 1862, if not earlier, it would be only a matter of time until the Federals mustered their full strength and found and exploited one or more of the many weaknesses of the Confederacy.[18]

IF Robert E. Lee's Confederate career can serve as the near-perfect model for Covey's thesis, that of Lee's old friend, classmate, colleague, and professional rival Joseph E. Johnston stands as the complete template for a future book to be entitled *The Seven* (or *Eight*) *Habits of Highly Ineffective People*. For some reason or reasons (about which I shall speculate later in this work) *Johnston chose* to react to President Davis's instructions about the Mississippi troops and other matters in a counterproductive, indeed, often a destructive manner. He consistently displayed what Covey called the "old patterns of self-defeating behavior."[19]

Lee on the other hand *chose* to accept the reality of the Confederate political-military structure and to make the best of his situation within that framework which, he realized, he could not change. Unlike Johnston, he *chose* not to waste time and psychic energy complaining uselessly to his spouse, the press, members of his staff, his favorite subordinates, and the President's political rivals about a situation that neither he nor they could alter. "*Our chosen response*," observed Covey, "is the key determiner in our life [my emphasis]."[20]

JOHNSTON'S chosen response was to haunt and to hamper both his own career and the military fortunes of the Confederacy. We, of course, can never know what the outcome would have been had Johnston chosen a different path in the circumstances in which he found himself in 1861 and early 1862 and specifically in his chosen responses to Davis's ranking of the generals and to the presidential plan to form State brigades. We know only what stemmed from the actions that Johnston *chose* to take (or not to take in the case of the Mississippi regiments).

---

18 See Freeman's comments in *Lee*, II, 42, 53, and 359. See also Frederick Maurice's comments (*Statesmen and Soldiers*, 41) concerning Lee's frame of mind. For some fascinating observations on Lee's application of his proactive approach to waging war, see Rafuse, *Lee*, 17, 22-23, 136-137, and 200-202. One might, although Rafuse does not, classify those examples of Lee's proactive approach as the tactical level of the Habits. For Lee's view that the Confederates had to act, see Book Two, Chapter Eight below. See Lowe, "Battle of Chickamauga," for a study applying Covey's thesis to a lower level of Civil War military activity.

19 *7 Habits*, 61. Dan Seligman, an editor at *Forbes Magazine*, called this "a thinking pattern that leads to poor outcomes." "Bookshelf," *Wall Street Journal*, Nov. 30, 2005.

20 *8th Habit*, 179.

Nor can we ever know what, if any, success Johnston would have won in the field had he enjoyed the full support and trust of the President and the government. As it was, Johnston's 1861-1864 periods of command were marked by failure and disaster.[21]

Lee chose another course in the hope that doing so would lead to better results for him and his (and Davis's and Johnston's) Cause—and on several occasions it came close to doing so.

---

21 As will be seen in many of the chapters in both this and the second volume, Johnston's performance as commander of a field army suffered from factors in addition to those stemming from his self-inflicted difficulties with Davis.

The Civil Wars of
General Joseph E. Johnston

Book Two

Jefferson Davis, Joseph E. Johnston,
and the Mess in the West,
1862-1863

Chapter One

A New Strategy

PART I

"We . . . must find our security in the
concentration and rapid movement of troops."
— Jefferson Davis, December 21, 1862

IN the spring and summer of 1861, President Jefferson Davis committed the
Confederacy's military forces to the defense of the far-flung frontiers of
the would-be Southern nation. Rebel army units took up static defensive positions
all along the Atlantic and Gulf coasts as well as on the long land border between the
seceded and the loyal states. They even pushed forward into the southern parts of
Kentucky, Missouri, and what are now Oklahoma, New Mexico, and Arizona. (The
Secessionists claimed these four last-named areas as parts of the Confederacy.)
Considerations of politics, diplomacy, and—above all—logistics, compelled the
Rebel government to adopt this geopolitical military grand strategy and to push its
armies as far forward as possible.[1]

---

1 One can make a respectable case that the Confederacy never had what in a modern sense
would be labeled a "strategy." Today's theorists and students of warfare draw distinctions
among national policy, grand strategy, strategy, operations, and tactics (and sometimes
subdivide those categories into "grand tactics" and so on). Most Civil War-era officials and
generals would have understood tactics as the handling of troops on the battlefield in the
presence of the enemy. They would have agreed with the fictitious Lieutenant Tom Jenkins of
Howard Bahr's novel *The Black Flower*, who said that tactics was where you studied how to
"whup the other fellow's ass," 15. It is in this Civil War-era sense that I use the term in this
work. See D. Stokes, *Grand Design*, 3-9 and *passim*; Young, "Perhaps a . . . Strategy"; and
[Poulter], "Did the Confederacy Have a Coherent Strategy?" On the offensive nature of overall
Confederate policy in 1861 and early 1862, see Harsh, *Confederate Tide*, Chapter One, especially
11-21.

Tennessee and Virginia, for example, on the Confederacy's northern frontier, were in the late spring and summer of 1861 clearly the two most important of the Rebel states. Each, however, contained a large percentage of anti-secession, anti-Confederate Southerners among its inhabitants, and many of those dissidents opposed the new Southern nation either actively or passively from the beginning of the war.

Pro-Confederate citizens of Tennessee and Virginia, who had just waged titanic political battles to bring about their States' secession, would be very displeased and greatly demoralized should their new national government quickly decide not to defend them from a Yankee invasion or not to protect them from an internal rebellion by those remaining loyal to the Union. The two states' governors and their large Congressional delegations echoed their constituents' demand for protection. So, too, did each state's newspapers. Rebel efforts to win diplomatic recognition from European governments—never very promising—would face even more serious obstacles should the Davis government quickly give up such major parts of Confederate territory as Tennessee and Virginia.

Loss of the farms, raw material, and industries of the Volunteer State and of the Old Dominion would deal a major blow to the Confederacy's ability to carry on a protracted war. The Tredegar Iron Works in Richmond, for example, turned out thirty-seven percent of the Confederacy's entire 1861 iron production. At the beginning of the war Tredegar possessed what was then the only steam hammer (necessary for really heavy iron work) available to the Secessionists. (Later the Rebels were able to use Tredegar's facilities to manufacture a second steam hammer for the great munitions/industrial complex they created at Selma, Alabama.)

At the war's beginning, the Nashville area contained the South's only functional gunpowder facility. In the Tennessee capital stood a factory capable of turning out one million percussion caps a week and other facilities that produced saddles, bridles, shot, shell, and artillery gun carriages. Historian Richard Goff observed, "a march southward of 150 miles through Virginia and Tennessee would carry Union troops to nearly all of the significant [in 1861] iron mills, coal mines, flour mills, grain fields, and slaughterhouses in the Confederacy."

President Davis also had to defend Confederate territory in order to keep Union armies from disrupting the very fragile institution of slavery. Slavery, after all, was the *raison d' etre* of the Confederacy, and to permit enemy forces to disrupt it at the beginning of the war would undermine the very cornerstone of the new

Southern nation. As historian Robert Tanner observed, only a vigorous forward defense could have protected slavery.[2]

Davis, in truth, found himself locked into defending Rebeldom's far frontiers because so much of the Confederacy's most economically, logistically, diplomatically, and politically crucial territory lay on or very near the nation's periphery. So too did many of the South's most important railroad routes.

In summary, Davis and the Confederates had no choice. They simply had to defend all those areas—especially Tennessee, Virginia, and several coastal cities through which passed essential railroad lines. Even a brief occupation of an area by a Federal force would render it virtually worthless to the Confederates even if the Rebels managed to regain the region.[3]

---

2 While slavery provided the Confederates with an essential labor force, it proved also a major source of weakness. Slaves often gave valuable information to invading Union forces and served as guides. In addition, the need to protect the institution hamstrung Rebel military operations. After the war Charles Marshall, a former member of Robert E. Lee's staff, observed (*Aide-de-Camp*, 65) "the mere existence of slavery gave the Federal government a great advantage in the prosecution of the war and imposed additional cares and responsibilities upon those charged with the conduct of military operations in the South. It imparted consequences to movements of the enemy otherwise trivial, and enabled a small [invading] force to excite apprehension along the whole sensitive border of the South."

3 See Connelly, *Army of the Heartland*, 1-12; Newton, *Johnston*, 33; Goff, *Confederate Supply*, 5 and *passim*; A. Jones, *Confederate Strategy*, 20-21; Cooper, *Davis*, 352-353; and "Up and Doing," Nashville *Daily Gazette*, Aug. 24, 1861 (reprinted from Memphis *Avalanche*, n. d.); Woodworth, *Davis and Generals*, 18-19, offers several valuable comments on Davis's reasons for the cordon defense. Davis expressed his view most clearly in a Nov. 19, 1863, letter to Lieutenant General E. Kirby Smith, 22 *OR*, pt. 2, 1072. The Confederate President has received much criticism for his policy of attempting to defend all Rebel territory. Robert Tanner, *Retreat to Victory*, shows beyond any question how rational and necessary Davis's policy was. Robert E. Lee seems from the first to have understood this basic fact of Confederate existence. Joseph E. Johnston—among others, then and now—seems never to have grasped it. For Tanner's comment regarding slavery, see 111-112. See also D. Stokes, *Grand Design, passim*, especially 12 and 26-27. On Johnston's attitude, see, for example, Govan and Livingood, *Different Valor*, 76-77, and James, "Johnston," 353-354. In addition, as Harsh (*Confederate Tide*, 13-14) pointed out, Federal forces threatened Rebeldom at virtually every point on the long land border between the seceded and loyal states, while the Union navy could land troops at almost any place on the coast or even move up many rivers to penetrate the interior. Where should the Secessionists concentrate? To do so at one point would leave other places in danger unless the Rebels could gain some great success that would compel the Federals to give up their efforts elsewhere. All these factors combined to present the Confederates with a strategic dilemma that they never resolved. Eventually, they developed three general approaches. Joseph E. Johnston advocated an immediate concentration to fight the decisive battle. Lee favored maneuvering to put the enemy at a disadvantage, then a quick concentration to strike a decisive blow. Davis fell somewhere in between—never willing to take the great risk that Lee's approach necessitated,

THUS it came about that by the fall of 1861 the Confederate government had committed its armies to a "cordon defense" all around the nation's perimeter. This strategy represented, in the words of Steven Newton, "a desperate but calculated gamble" by Davis. The President realized that (for the reasons listed above) the Confederacy simply had to maintain possession of almost all its territory even though it did not then have enough cannon, individual firearms, ammunition, and other equipment and supplies for its armies.

Davis adopted this policy in the hope that the "audacity" of his cordon geo-political/military grand strategy "could disguise abject weakness" long enough for the Rebels to manufacture, import, and capture sufficient weapons and equipment to outfit and arm the tens of thousands of eager volunteers who wished to enlist but who then lacked the items they needed to enter active service. Once those needs had been met, the Confederate armies could fight with a reasonable hope of success. They could even take the offensive and wage war to solidify Secessionist control over Kentucky, Missouri, and other Rebel-claimed territory. The Southern Congress, be it noted, had committed the Confederacy to such a policy. Confident Rebel legislators even pledged to ensure that voters in the slave state of Maryland would be able to hold a free election to determine if their state would join the new Southern nation.[4]

Davis's daring bluff worked through 1861. The major Union armies stood mostly inactive in the face of what their commanders erroneously believed to be an imminent Confederate offensive.[5]

IN large part the Rebels' 1861 grand strategy depended on enemy forces remaining quiescent at least until the Secessionists could organize their own armies and acquire weapons and other equipment for them. Should the Yankees not cooperate and mount a major offensive of their own, the Confederates would find

---

but unhappy with Johnston's unceasing demands for "more" and his passive approach once concentration had been effected. Lee's active defense involved risk; Johnston's passive approach yielded the initiative to the enemy. These differences will be discussed on several cases below in this book and in Book Three (the latter in Volume II).

4 See Harsh, *Confederate Tide*, 9-10.

5 For an example of how a Confederate commander, Albert Sidney Johnston in this case, managed to bluff his opponent, see Roland, *Johnston*, 271-272. For examples of the Rebels' longstanding desire to wage offensive war in the enemy's territory, see Settles, *Magruder*, 119-124; Davis to J. Foster Marshall, July 11, 1862, J. Davis, *Papers*, vol. 8, 287; Newton, *Johnston*, 27-28; and Wade Hampton to his sister, May 21, 1862, quoted in Cisco, *Hampton*, 84.

themselves in a desperate situation for the Rebels had no reserves to reinforce an endangered point. "We have no second line of defense," wrote an apprehensive Jefferson Davis in the fall of 1861, "and cannot now provide one."[6]

If the Federals broke through anywhere along the advanced Southern line, almost nothing other than geographical obstacles and the Union commander's hesitancy would prevent the invading foe from striking deep into the vitals of the Confederacy. Steven Newton has compared the Secessionists' 1861-early 1862 strategic situation to an "eggshell"—if the shell cracked anywhere a large part of Rebeldom would lie at the mercy of the invading Federal army. On February 12, 1862, a member of the 11th Virginia Infantry Regiment noted in his diary that this strategy "imposes on us the necessity of being successful everywhere—the inherent weakness of Defense."[7]

THE Confederate eggshell cracked early in 1862, and the crack came in the vast area between the Appalachian Mountains on the east and the Mississippi River on the west. In the language of the day this large region was known simply as "the West."

In the first weeks of the new year five columns of Union troops began southward thrusts from an east-west line that roughly traced the Ohio and Missouri Rivers. One of these columns pushed into southern Missouri and northern Arkansas. A second, supported by Union gunboats, started down the Mississippi River from Illinois and eastern Missouri. Three other columns moved south from the Ohio River through Kentucky toward Tennessee.

On January 19 the easternmost of these forces won a smashing victory in the Battle of Mill Springs. In so doing the Yankees crushed the right-center of the Confederate line across southern Kentucky. A few weeks later the Federal column pushing southward up the Tennessee and Cumberland rivers captured the Rebel defenses on those waterways (Forts Henry and Donelson, just south of the Kentucky-Tennessee border), along with some 13,000 troops who garrisoned them. This success ripped apart the left-center of the Secessionists' Kentucky line. It also opened those rivers to Union forces from their mouths up to their heads of navigation (for large boats)—Nashville on the Cumberland and the "Shoals" in the Florence-Tuscumbia area of northwestern Alabama in the case of the Tennessee.

6 5 OR, 834.

7 Newton, *Johnston*, 27-28; Kean, *Diary*, 25. See also Davis to William M. Brooks, Mar. 15, 1862, J. Davis, *Papers*, vol. 8, 100-102.

Meanwhile, another column of Yankees moved southward along the Louisville & Nashville Railroad, seized Bowling Green, Kentucky, in the center of the Confederate line and continued along the railroad to occupy Nashville, the first Rebel state capital to fall to the invaders.

This string of disasters compelled General Albert Sidney Johnston, commanding Confederate forces in the Kentucky-Tennessee-Arkansas-Missouri area to abandon all his positions in the Bluegrass State and most of those in West and Middle Tennessee. All through late February and on into March long columns of dispirited and demoralized Rebel troops tramped southward seeking the safety they would gain only after they crossed the broad Tennessee River in northern Alabama. By late March Johnston was across the river and shifting his forces westward to concentrate them at Corinth in northeastern Mississippi.[8]

THE early 1862 collapse of the Rebel position in the West—and therefore of Jefferson Davis's geopolitical/military grand strategy of the cordon defense— set in motion a string of events that, if not reversed or at least halted, would lead inevitably to Confederate defeat and destroy the dream of an independent Southern nation. In response to this clear danger President Davis had to rethink his overall approach to defending the Confederacy. Writing on November 19, 1863, Davis summed up the Confederacy's dilemma. He admitted that concentration increased an army's power, but "The evacuation of any portion of territory involves not only the loss of supplies but in eve[ry] instance has been attended by greater or less loss of troops." It was, he stated, "a complex problem to solve."

On February 25, 1862, only nine days after Fort Donelson on the Cumberland River had surrendered, Davis sent his annual "Information on the State of the Confederacy" message to Congress. "I have to communicate," he sadly acknowledged, "that since my message to the last session of the . . . Congress, events have demonstrated that the Government had attempted more than it had power successfully to achieve. Hence, in the effort to protect by our arms the whole of the territory of the Confederate States, Sea-board and inland, we have been so exposed as recently to encounter serious disaster."[9]

Very quickly the Chief Executive realized that since the Secessionists could no longer afford to think in terms of passively defending all their territory, he would have to adopt some new general method of waging the war. Unfortunately for the

8 See T. B. Smith, *Grant Invades Tennessee.*

9 J. Davis, *Papers*, vol. 8, 58; vol. 10, p. 81.

Rebels, the method he chose, the way he tried to implement it, the generals he put in crucial command positions, Davis's ineptitude as a president, and Johnston's quirks as a commander, combined to exacerbate greatly the rift between the Chief Executive and Joseph E. Johnston.

ALTHOUGH Davis did not explicitly so state—and may not even have realized the fact—the new approach he adopted to defend Rebeldom in truth implied that for at least the foreseeable future the Confederates would have to abandon less important areas and concentrate their strength to make a defense of those places (such as industrial and rail centers) without which the Southern nation could not hope to survive.[10]

To implement his new grand strategy Davis more-or-less abandoned the Atlantic and Gulf coasts except for Norfolk, Wilmington, Charleston, Savannah, and Mobile. Norfolk was the site of the South's chief navy yard. The four last-named heavily fortified cities had to be held, for their political importance, their industries, as ports for blockade runners bringing supplies and weapons to the Confederates, and—even more important—because the crucial rail routes passing through them were essential if the Confederates were to hold their country together and supply their armies. Davis also stripped New Orleans of most of her defending force. Military units from Arkansas and Missouri started eastward to cross the Mississippi River. These troops joined others at Corinth, Mississippi, where they formed a mobile field army that could maneuver to strike the enemy in the President's new "offensive-defensive" grand strategy.[11]

10 Robert E. Lee had realized this on a smaller scale in 1861 when he commanded on the South Atlantic coast and saw how easily the Federal navy overwhelmed Rebel fortifications at Port Royal Sound in South Carolina. Lee, therefore, had pulled his forces back from most coastal areas to get them beyond the reach of the big guns on the Yankee warships. In mid-Feb. 1862, General P. G. T. Beauregard had urged the same overall policy in western Kentucky and Tennessee. On Feb. 15, 1862, General Braxton Bragg had advised the government to concentrate to defend vital points. See also Lee to Governor Henry T. Clark of North Carolina, Aug. 8, 1862, 9 *OR*, 478.

11 J. Davis, *Papers*, vol. 8, 58; and Newton, *Johnston*, 26-34 and 175. New Orleans was, of course, a very important city for the Rebels, but they incorrectly assumed that the downriver Forts Jackson and St. Philip would protect it from enemy forces trying to move up the Mississippi. A Union fleet coming from the Gulf of Mexico ran by the forts in late April and forced the Confederates to evacuate New Orleans, the Secessionists' largest and arguably most important city. D. Stokes, *Grand Design*, 10 and *passim*, maintains that the offensive-defensive was a tactical, not a strategic concept. Most historians have regarded it as a strategy—at least in the Civil War-era sense. See also A. Jones, *Confederate Strategy* and his "Jomini and Strategy."

ON a larger stage than the March-April Corinth concentration, Davis envisioned a new grand strategy of having Confederate military units moving about from point to point and uniting to defeat invading enemy armies. The Rebels could also draw inactive troops from different, unthreatened areas and use them to launch their own offensive campaigns. "We can not hope at all points to meet the enemy with a force equal to his own, and must find our security in the concentration and rapid movement of troops," the President was to write a few months later in explaining the new policy.[12]

In theory, and on rare occasions in practice, this scheme could be implemented all across the Confederacy. In fact, however, geographical, political, and logistical considerations almost always meant that the President's new strategy would take the form of three separate "offensive-defensive" systems. The Rebels would implement one of these systems in each of the three great geographical areas into which the Appalachian Mountains and the Mississippi River divided the Confederacy: the East (Virginia and the Atlantic Coast); the West or Central (between the mountains and the Mississippi River); and the Trans-Mississippi. For the rest of the war Confederate authorities would seek to apply Davis's early 1862 strategic vision in each of these areas or "theaters."

THE Davis government sought to apply its new grand strategy by using the existing administrative/territorial "military departments" into which the authorities, following common military practice, had earlier divided the Confederacy. Each of these departments operated under the direction of an army officer who bore responsibility for its defense and commanded most of the military personnel serving within it.

In most cases each of these departments was administratively and logistically separate from adjoining departments and usually reported directly to, and received orders directly from, the authorities in Richmond. Most of the time only one military authority operated in Richmond—President Davis himself, who often dealt personally and directly with the commanders of the larger and more important departments. (As mentioned in Book One, Chapter Three, Davis chose to function not only as the Confederacy's chief executive but also as its commanding general and its chief of staff.)

On occasion, however, the Confederate President placed two or more departments under the (usually partial, temporary, and vaguely defined) control of

---

12 J. Davis, *Papers*, vol. 8, 562.

one officer. In Davis's new 1862 grand strategy, troops based in unthreatened areas would reinforce a department that found itself under attack. Such troops could also unite with other Rebel forces to launch an offensive at some point chosen by the Confederates.

WHETHER or not he had thought the matter through completely enough to realize it, Davis had based his new policy on seven crucial assumptions. The Yankees, the President firmly believed, had but two major military objectives: the capture of Richmond in the East and securing control of the Mississippi River in the West.[13] Even with their great strength, Davis thought, the Federals could mount but one large-scale offensive in the West at a time. Thus, the Chief Executive believed, only one Western Confederate department would face serious danger at any given moment. To mount such a major operation, believed Davis, the Federals would transfer troops from other areas to strengthen their army at the point they had chosen to attack. Fourth, Rebel intelligence, Davis assumed, would be able to ascertain the point at which the Unionists planned to make their great effort before the danger became serious.

Once the enemy objective had become clear, thought the President, he had only to notify his generals in unthreatened areas and they would rush reinforcements to the department menaced by the enemy. The telegraph would enable Davis himself to direct all these movements from Richmond, and the Southerners' "interior lines" of transportation—especially the railroads—would enable the Rebels to move troops about quickly. After the Confederates had defeated the invading Union army in a major battle (a Rebel victory was Davis's sixth assumption), the reinforcements would return to their previous posts and await the next enemy advance. Then the whole process would be repeated.

13 Davis's neglect of the crucial importance of Tennessee surfaced more than once during the war's early years and is simply inexplicable. The Rebel government, explained historian Peter Cozzens (*Stones River*, x), "acted as though Tennessee were a strategic backwater rather than the key to the Confederate heartland." On more than one occasion in 1863 this matter became a major difference between Davis and Johnston. The President's focus on Mississippi and his relative neglect of Tennessee may have owed something to his background. Davis had lived most of his life in the Mississippi Valley, had spent much of his time as a U.S. Army officer there in the early 1830s, and had a plantation on the Mississippi River a short distance below Vicksburg.

Eventually, the President concluded, the Yankees would realize that they could not overcome the Confederacy and would acquiesce in Southern independence.[14]

The offensive side of Davis's new strategy involved a modification of this scheme. After defeating the Yankees, the Confederates could launch an aggressive campaign of their own with their reinforced army at the point of their recent victory or at another place of their choosing. Troops from two or more departments could unite to seize the initiative and undertake the offensive, striking the Federals before they began their own campaign.[15]

14 The defensive side of this strategy is sometimes called "win by not losing." It therefore stands to reason that if the Rebels lost the battles, Davis's strategy—at least the defensive side of it—was not working. See comments in the Preface above concerning the reasons for Confederate failure. Then, too, how long could a society as fragile as that of the Confederacy sustain a major war? See, for example, 32 *OR*, pt. 3, 625, and 634-635, as well as Chapter Three of Book One above, and Chapter Two, Part III, and Chapter Eight of this Book.

15 My guess is that Davis devised at least the basics of this scheme on his own, drawing on common nineteenth century military thought that stressed the use of "interior lines" by which a weaker power could meet multiple threats on its borders. With Lee absent on the South Atlantic coast until March 1862, there would have been no high-ranking general in Richmond with whom Davis could have discussed the revised strategy in any detail. General Samuel Cooper was an aged administrative officer. Neither he nor Benjamin, who served as secretary of war until late March, would have been likely to have raised serious questions about Davis's new concept even if the President had consulted with them. Serious critiques of the new strategy such as Lee or Joseph E. Johnston might have raised could have led to discussions and modifications that might have lessened many of the problems discussed below in the text. Frederick Maurice (*Statesmen and Soldiers*, 41-42, 47, and 50) commented that the real weakness of the Confederacy was the lack of good military advice available to Davis. (Maurice was writing with specific reference to the post-May 1862 months when Lee had gone from the capital to command an individual field army. The observation, in, fact, was valid for any time that Lee was not in Richmond.)

PART II

"The biggest part of a President's job is to make decisions."
— Harry S. Truman

THE President's new strategy carried with it serious risk, and it faced many potential difficulties. On the highest level of warfare, a major long-range problem would quickly develop as soon as the Confederates put their new scheme into effect.

If, contrary to Davis's assumptions, the Federals advanced at two points in the West—West Tennessee and Middle Tennessee, for example—and the Rebels chose to withdraw troops from one to concentrate at the other, the weakened area would face increased danger. Should it be lost, its resources would be added to the already overwhelming Federal strength as soon as the advancing Yankees moved in to replace the departed Secessionists. To make the matter worse, many of the most valuable regions of the Confederacy were, as noted above, along the country's northern periphery in the very areas most likely to be targeted by Union offensives.

Thousands of pro-Confederate refugees would stream southward ahead of the withdrawing Secessionist army. In so doing, they would increase the strain on the now diminished resources of Rebeldom. If this situation continued, it would "snowball" until Confederate society and the South's economy simply collapsed under the increased burden of feeding, sheltering, and caring for the refugees. The slaves in the evacuated area, if left behind, were likely to run off with the invading Yankees, and their labor would be lost to the Confederacy. If taken along with the refugeeing whites, they would have to be fed, clothed, sheltered, provided with medical care, and guarded lest they escape. They would thus become a burden that did not provide labor to offset the cost of holding them.

In late February 1862, however, Jefferson Davis and the Confederates did not have the luxury of thinking long term. The President's initial strategy (the cordon defense) had failed, and Davis had to adopt and implement a new plan (the offensive-defensive) immediately to deal with the massive military crisis then threatening the very existence of his nation. (See Book One, Chapter Two, above.)

HUMAN nature and its reflection in Confederate life and politics clearly posed another, if intermediate term, high-level obstacle to the success of Davis's new concept of how the Rebels should conduct their struggle for national existence. Virtually all Secessionists might well agree with the wisdom of not squandering limited resources in foredoomed efforts to hold every less important or indefensible point and with the need to concentrate their strength to defend vital areas. Inevitably, however, they would differ over which points were unimportant and which were vital.

What Rebel governor would acknowledge that his state, or any significant part of it, was not crucial? Which members of Congress would calmly accept abandonment without a fight of the areas and people (or, at least voters) they represented? What Confederate general would think his force so strong and his position so secure that he would agree to release large numbers of his troops to reinforce some other commander? Nor would such questions be limited to the higher echelons of the Confederate political-military structure. Would troops from Georgia, North Carolina, or Mississippi serving in Virginia lose heart and desert if Yankee armies occupied their home areas and their families were caught behind Union lines or cast adrift in the shrinking Confederacy? How would Confederate planters react if their slaves ran off to seek freedom with the approaching Yankee armies?[16]

When the Rebels decided to take the offensive similar problems would arise over where they should strike. Did Virginia or Tennessee offer the better opportunity to attack the enemy? Eventually differences over these questions would give rise to competing blocs of politicians, generals, and newspaper editors. Each such group convinced itself that its favored approach offered the Confederates their only hope for success.

The politics of implementing Davis's new grand strategy would necessitate much delicate work by the President to win and sustain popular and political support for it and to secure and retain the cooperation of Congress, state officials, and Rebel generals. Conversely, if Davis failed to persuade local political leaders and military commanders of the wisdom of his decisions as to what points should be weakened—and, to repeat, no one else could make such a decision—would he prove skilled and ruthless enough to implement his policy over their objections? Confronted with such objections, would Davis himself stick to his own strategy in the face of opposition from those whose ideas differed from his? Doing so, after all, would require him to make decisions and assume responsibility, actions no

---

16 For some examples, see Manning, *Cruel War*, 167; 52 OR, pt. 2, 463 and 471; and Escott, *After Secession*, 56-57.

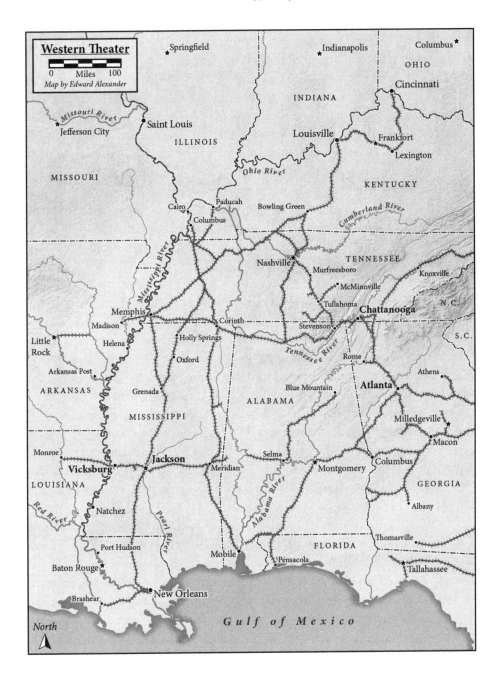

politician likes to take if they are likely to prove unpopular. Failure to do so would, in fact, be simply a resumption of the cordon defense.

The key to the success of this new policy was, obviously, quick success in battle. If the President's new plan produced good results before the public lost patience, such problems as those mentioned above would be much less significant—indeed, they would evaporate. Victories that enabled Southern forces to regain the areas from which they had withdrawn, or to return to those positions before the enemy seized them, would show citizens the clear benefits of the new strategy and all would be well. If, on the other hand, the Secessionist armies could not defeat the invaders and reoccupy endangered or abandoned areas, the new policy would fail on a massive scale. Both civilians and soldiers would lose heart, and the strains on Confederate society would intensify. Every hour would then bring disintegration and defeat closer.[17]

OTHER, more immediate difficulties also loomed large in the face of Davis's new plan. The most obvious, clearly visible on any map of North America, was the avenue of invasion that the great rivers of the Confederate West offered to the Federal army and navy. The Mississippi, the Tennessee, and the Cumberland, along with their numerous navigable (for at least part of the year) tributaries opened large parts of western Rebeldom to the national forces. Although the Secessionists on occasion managed to sink or even to capture a Federal vessel on those waterways and could always harass the boats from the rivers' banks, they simply had no way permanently to block the movement of the Yankees' powerful ironclad gunboats along those streams on the Mississippi and the great ocean-going warships that sometimes ventured far up that river after capturing New Orleans in late April 1862.[18]

Even as they brought invading forces into the western Confederacy, some of these rivers constituted major obstacles to the Rebels' ability to implement Davis's new policy. The Mississippi and the lower Tennessee (flowing north to south and south to north on parallel courses only about one hundred miles apart) presented formidable barriers to the east-west movements of defending or advancing

---

17 For an excellent example of how a Confederate far more skilled in handling such matters than Davis dealt with the problem of local concerns, see Lee to Governor Henry T. Clark of North Carolina, Aug. 8, 1862, 9 *OR,* 478.

18 Warren Grabau (*98 Days,* 29) called the rivers of the West "the highways of Federal military Power." Most of these lesser waterways are no longer navigable. See Bearss, *Campaign for Vicksburg,* II, xiii.

Confederate troops in western Tennessee. No bridge spanned that portion of the Mississippi in Confederate territory. While the east-west stretch of the Tennessee across northern Alabama served as a moat protecting most of the state against invasion from the north, it also formed a barrier to a northward advance by Rebel troops and to a degree isolated Middle Tennessee from the rest of the Confederacy. After early 1862 there was no permanent bridge across the Tennessee below Bridgeport in extreme northeastern Alabama (and the span at Bridgeport was out of service for much of that year). "The Tennessee," moaned a Rebel general on November 7, 1862, "is a barrier we cannot overcome." It became even more of a barrier late the next year and in 1864 when the Yankees seized its entire right bank and even began to employ small gunboats above the Shoals to patrol the area between that point and Loudon, about 110 miles above Chattanooga.[19]

In large part the surrender in February 1862 of Fort Henry on the Tennessee and of Fort Donelson on the Cumberland precipitated Davis's abandonment of the initial Rebel strategy of the cordon defense. In the weeks after Davis announced the new strategic concept of the offensive-defensive the Confederates suffered similar defeats at Island Number Ten above Memphis and at Forts Jackson and St. Philip near the mouth of the Mississippi. Later in the war Arkansas Post on the Arkansas River, Vicksburg and Port Hudson on the Mississippi, and Fort DeRussy on the Red River experienced the same fate. In all, the Secessionists would lose some 60,000 to 65,000 men as prisoners plus several thousand others—victims of disease or killed and wounded—in vain efforts to hold these river posts.

STILL other problems inevitably would arise as soon as the Confederates attempted to implement Davis's new scheme. Could the Rebels determine where the enemy intended to strike in time to concentrate before the blow fell? Davis optimistically assumed that men who had access to the same information ("co-intelligence," he usually called it) would agree on interpreting it.[20] As a minimum, such an assumption depended upon full communication among the Secessionist authorities so that they all would share fully whatever knowledge of the enemy the Confederates possessed. The Rebels would also have to overcome the all-too human tendency of each commander to see the military situation only

19 17 *OR*, pt. 2, 744, 756.

20 See, for example, ibid. 726; 52 *OR*, pt. 2, 474; and J. Davis, *Confederate Government*, II, 472 and 482.

from the perspective of his own position. (In the modern military— or, at least in the military when I served in the army, which may no longer be considered modern—this phenomenon is known as "localitis.")

Even if all the Rebels agreed on where the danger lay and if other commanders immediately made reinforcements available, would there be enough of them to do any good? The North's huge overall advantage in population gave the Federal government the capability of forming armies far larger than those the Confederacy could put into the field. For this reason, the Rebels would always find themselves outnumbered in terms of total manpower and almost always in terms of the total number of troops available to opposing theater commanders. On individual battlefields, however, the Southerners could hope to achieve numerical equality or even superiority (as they did several times in the West) by maneuver, an enemy blunder, a sudden concentration of Rebel forces, or by simple blind luck. Could (would?) Confederate generals prove capable of taking advantage of such opportunities and win the battles?

EVEN if other Rebel commanders made enough reinforcements available, could the Confederates move such large bodies of troops to the threatened point in time? This problem loomed as a much greater obstacle west of the Appalachians than it did in the Eastern theater of Rebeldom. Secessionist armies in the East operated in a relatively small area, and they enjoyed what was by Southern standards an excellent rail system across Virginia and with relatively easy connection to the critical points along the coast in the Carolinas and Georgia.

Distances in the western Confederacy, by contrast, were much greater and the Rebel forces operating there faced far more serious obstacles to the rapid movement of troops. Nor did the Secessionists in the West have the use of a well-developed system of railroads. In fact, after early 1862, when the Yankees cut the railroad across northern Alabama, the Secessionists did not even enjoy the advantage of interior lines of transportation in the West.

MOST of the western waterways ran the wrong way to offer much help to the Confederates when it came to moving troops from point to point—or at least to the points where they were most likely to be needed to defend the West. Almost all the rivers in Georgia and Alabama ran to the Atlantic or to the Gulf of Mexico, and they did not provide the east-west routes that defense of the Rebel West required.

The Tennessee, flowing from east to west across northern Alabama, was the major exception to this geographical fact. That river, however, lay so far to the north that after early 1862 it was largely irrelevant for the purpose of moving

Southern troops between Tennessee and Mississippi given the frequent presence of Union forces at many points on its banks and Yankee control of the crucial railroad junction at Corinth, Mississippi.

WHEN the Unionists broke through the Confederate cordon in West and Middle Tennessee in the late winter and spring of 1862 they reached and severed the Memphis & Charleston Railroad in northern Alabama and Mississippi, "the vertebrae of the Confederacy," in the words of a Secessionist general. That rail line was a crucial part of the only continuous rail route connecting the Atlantic coast of the Confederacy with the Mississippi Valley.[21]

After the Federals cut the Memphis & Charleston Railroad, the Confederates found themselves with only one feasible way for their forces in Tennessee and Mississippi to reinforce each other—a roundabout rail journey through Chattanooga, Atlanta, Montgomery, Mobile, and Meridian to Jackson and other points in the Magnolia State. The only rail route that did run (more or less) across western Rebeldom—that through Alabama from Blue Mountain in the northeastern part of the state southwest to Demopolis—had no connection to any other rail line.

Even the long, indirect peripheral route could not be traversed by a single train. The railroad from Atlanta to West Point, Georgia, on the state's border with Alabama, used a track gauge of five feet. At West Point, troops, equipment, and supplies would have to be unloaded and transferred to the railroad to Montgomery, which had track with a four-foot, eight-and-one-half-inch gauge. At Montgomery the troops would have to repeat the process because from there to the northeastern side of Mobile Bay the railroad used track laid with a five-foot gauge. (These movements, in fact, involved five separate railroad companies that would have to coordinate their operations.) Upon reaching the northeastern side of Mobile Bay along the Tensas River, troops, equipment, and supplies would have to be transferred to boats to cross the bay. Once across they would have to be loaded onto rail cars before they could go on. The same problems and delays, of course, would arise in bringing additional supplies to the troops after they had reached their destination.[22]

---

21 7 OR, 889.

22 See the item from the Macon *Confederate*, n. d. (reprinted in the Augusta *Daily Constitutionalist*, July 21, 1864). The end map in Black, *Railroads of the Confederacy* shows the

The Secessionists also had several variations of these routes that they could use—none of which would accelerate their troop movements. Cavalry and artillery units could march overland through Alabama, but they would still have to deal with the obstacle posed by the Tennessee River. Infantrymen could ride trains through Chattanooga to Rome, Georgia, and then make a sixty-one-mile march—at least three days, probably four, and maybe five or more depending on the weather and condition of the roads—to Blue Mountain (near present-day Anniston), Alabama. They would go thence by rail via Selma to Demopolis on the Tombigbee River in western Alabama. Once there, they would transfer to boats to make a four-mile trip downriver because at Demopolis no bridge spanned the river and the railroads, two different lines, reached the stream at two different points on the left and right banks. After getting across the river and climbing onto another train, the troops would go on by rail to Meridian, Jackson, or other points in Mississippi. It seems most unlikely, however, that the Blue Mountain to Demopolis rail line (two different railroads) had sufficient rolling stock to handle expeditiously a major troop movement, and, owing to its isolation, it could not borrow cars and locomotives from other railroads.[23]

Troops could also move by rail as described above from Tennessee to Montgomery, go from there by boat to Selma, and then transfer to the railroad to Demopolis or go on by boat to Mobile. Troops could even travel by boat from Rome or Resaca, Georgia, down the Coosa and Alabama rivers to Selma or Mobile, and then complete their journey by rail. It seems likely, however, that only a few boats would have been available, and their capacity would have been very limited.

WHICHEVER route or routes the Secessionists chose, large-scale troop movements across the western Confederacy would put a severe strain on the Rebel transportation infrastructure in Tennessee, Georgia, Alabama, and Mississippi. Such movements would also produce major disruptions in the Rebels' system of supplying Southern armies in other areas including Virginia, which was coming to draw an increasing part of its food supply from the Deep South. The troop

---

routes, companies, and gauges. In more recent editions of this work, the map is printed in sections on interior pages.

23 In May 1864, a Confederate general then moving a relatively small body of troops along this line commented: "Regret we have not as much rolling-stock as we could use" (38 *OR*, pt. 4, 676). Granted, this was after another year of wear on the rail line and its equipment. Nor do we have much knowledge of the boat part of the trip across the Tombigbee. In Aug. 1863 one soldier recorded that the boat trip had taken four hours. See Dunlap, *Diary*, 93-94.

movements would also disrupt the civilian economy by diverting transportation resources to army use and in so doing inflict hardships on civilians and perhaps weaken their support for the war effort.

By the fall of 1862, eighteen months of war had left Confederate railroads—most of them not very well built to start with—in great need of maintenance, repair, and new ties, rails, and rolling stock. Many locomotives and cars had been worn out, scattered, lost, or damaged in military operations or accidents, and the Rebels could not replace them. Worn track and rolling stock caused numerous derailments and led to reductions in train weight, length, and speed, thereby increasing the time necessary to move troops, equipment, and supplies from point to point.

In November of 1862, the president of the East Tennessee & Georgia Railroad reported to the area's military commander, "My [rolling-]stock is now so far gone that it will be useless before winter is half over." Three months later, on February 14, his counterpart for the Mississippi Central Railroad (which ran north from Jackson) wrote that of his line's five hundred cars, only fifty or sixty were on home rails and in useable condition. A Confederate general reported in early 1862 that the rail line between Vicksburg and Jackson, Mississippi, "is in such bad condition" that troop movements "will be slow." Similar comments applied to other rail routes as well. Each day the railroads deteriorated further, and their capacity to move large numbers of troops decreased as they did.

Could the Rebel infrastructure support Davis's new concept of warfare which was based on the movement of large bodies of troops quickly across the vast distances of the Confederate West? Was the President's new strategy—especially its defensive side—more appropriate for the much smaller, more highly developed and more compact Eastern theater with its better infrastructure?[24]

---

24 20 OR, pt. 2, 407; see also, ibid., 421; 24 OR, pt. 3, 599, 609, 627-628; Black, *Railroads of the Confederacy*, 5, 12-15, 27, 124, 153-159, 162, and 181. See also Jno. Kember's letter of Jan. 5, 1863, to U. S. Secretary of War E. M. Stanton, reporting on the East Tennessee & Virginia Railroad (20 OR, pt. 2, 302-303) and the report of a Federal agent sent in June 1863 to evaluate the condition of Rebel railroads in the West (23 OR, pt. 2, 453-454). Davis's own Feb. 1861 journey from his Mississippi plantation to Montgomery for his inauguration as President should have served to caution him about the difficulties the Secessionists would experience moving troops long distances in the West. Davis had to travel from his plantation up the Mississippi to Vicksburg by steamboat, then by rail east to Jackson and north to Grand Junction, Tennessee (at which point he was outside the then-boundaries of the Confederacy), then east to Chattanooga, from there south through Atlanta and on to Montgomery. The journey consumed four days. Moving a large body of troops with its equipment would take much longer.

ON a lower level Davis's revised grand strategy raised several practical questions. Who, for example, should decide from which areas troops should be removed? When should the Confederates withdraw from an area they did not intend to defend? Some Rebels, of whom Joseph E. Johnston would become the most prominent, usually favored pulling back immediately from outer positions to concentration points to prepare for decisive battle at some crucial place. Others, Robert E. Lee would speak for them, preferred to keep Southern forces dispersed as far forward as possible for as long as possible. This approach, Lee maintained, would preserve Confederate options and protect Rebel resources, including slavery and slaves. It would also compel the enemy to reveal his intentions by massing a significant part of his army on the route he had chosen for his advance. The Secessionists could then make their own concentration to defend the threatened point. By such a strategy, Lee thought, the Rebels could limit the damage to and loss of their resources, keep the enemy as far from important points as possible, maintain the morale of both soldiers and civilians, and gain time to shift their own forces as well as to strengthen their defenses. Once the Unionists' intentions became clear the Southerners could swiftly unite their own forces and quickly assail the enemy before he bought all his own troops together, or the Rebels could mass to strike a counter-blow elsewhere.

This Lee-Johnston difference attained practical importance only once, but it illustrates, perhaps better than anything else, the different attitudes of the two generals. It also shows that the former approached warfare on a far higher level than did the latter. In the spring of 1862, the two men differed over whether to defend Yorktown on the Virginia Peninsula (a matter discussed briefly in Chapter Two, Part II of this book). After May 1862 these two generals served in widely separated areas, so such differences did not affect their relationship or their operations.[25]

FINALLY, the Yankees also posed several obstacles to Davis's new concept of military operations. They, too, would collect and analyze information on their enemy's movements. Once the Federals realized that the Rebels were shifting reinforcements from Point A to Point B, could they simply reverse the Secessionist

---

25 For a discussion of the Napoleonic concept of dispersal as a prelude to concentration, as opposed to reliance on concentration alone, see Connelly and Jones, *Politics of Command*, especially Chapter 1. The above discussion of Rebel strategy, of course, applies mostly to the defensive side of Confederate policy. See Chapter Eight of this book for a discussion of how Lee applied his ideas to the offensive side.

strategy by assuming the defensive in a fortified position at B and striking the weakened Confederate position at A? Would control of the western rivers enable the Unionists to move their own reinforcements by boat to offset Rebel troop transfers by rail? President Lincoln, we should note, saw this possibility early on. In January of 1862 he wrote, "if he [the enemy] . . . weakens one [point] to strengthen the other, forebear to attack the strengthened one, but seize and hold the weakened one, gaining so much."[26]

Very important as things turned out was the question of whether Yankee numerical superiority was great enough to enable the Federals to assume the offensive at two or more points in the West simultaneously—central Tennessee and western Mississippi, for example. Was it so great that no number of reinforcements that the Confederates could possibly send would enable the Secessionists to prevail even if reinforced? Would Rebel political leaders and generals prove skillful and daring enough to deal with such massive and multiple threats that by their very nature would allow the Confederates little time to analyze the situation, develop a plan, move troops to meet the enemy, prepare them to do so, and then act to win a victory?[27]

FOR Davis's new system to succeed, all his assumptions would have to prove valid in every case. The Confederates would have to collect accurate intelligence about the enemy, analyze it perfectly, communicate quickly and fully, reach a common understanding of the situation, and make decisions without delay. All of this would have to be done in a military structure without a commanding general or a chief of staff, and one in which the only man with authority above the departmental level—the President—was given to long and often inconclusive conferences, did not like to make decisions, usually refused to give orders to his field commanders, and frequently issued "directives" that were little more than comments, pleas, requests, or suggestions.[28]

---

26 7 OR, 928-929.

27 In fact, as time went on and Federal strength increased, the Yankees' capability to launch multiple offensives grew rapidly—even as Confederate strength and the ability to deal with such multiple threats decreased.

28 "The greatest part of a president's job is to make decisions—big ones and small ones, dozens of them almost every day," observed President Harry Truman. Quoted in Kenneth T. Walsh, "History's Verdict," *U. S. News & World Report,* vol. 142, no. 4 (Jan. 29/Feb. 5, 2007), 33.

The Rebels would also have to move troops about rapidly, strike immediately upon uniting them (which meant taking the offensive), defeat the enemy in the ensuing battle, and be blessed with a great deal of luck.

WHATEVER problems were to arise with Davis's new scheme, however, lay months in the future when in February 1862, disasters in Kentucky and Tennessee compelled the Rebel Chief Executive to announce his new offensive-defensive concept to his cabinet.

Chapter Two

Latent Problems

PART I

"[Johnston] will cure all discontent
and inspire the army with new life and confidence."
— Leonidas Polk, February 4, 1863

EARLY in April 1862, General Albert Sidney Johnston led his army—augmented by troops gathered from all across the Deep South—out of its camps at Corinth, Mississippi, for a strategic counterstroke that he hoped would undo the year's earlier disasters in Kentucky and northern Tennessee. In the two-day Battle of Shiloh, fought April 6-7 in southern Tennessee about twenty miles northeast of Corinth, the Rebel effort failed and Johnston was killed. After the battle the Secessionist army, then under the command of General P. G. T. Beauregard, retreated to Corinth, which it held until late May. Advancing Union forces compelled the Confederates to evacuate the town and move to Tupelo some fifty miles farther south.

At Tupelo the army got another commander, General Braxton Bragg, who soon shifted most of his force by rail, road, and steamboat to Chattanooga in southeastern Tennessee. From that point Bragg's army marched into Kentucky. Two other Rebel columns joined in this early application of the offensive side of Davis's new offensive-defensive strategy. One, under Major General E. Kirby Smith, came from the Department of East Tennessee; the other, led by Brigadier General Humphrey Marshall, from western Virginia (now West Virginia). Smith, at least in theory, had authority over Marshall.

The three Confederate columns entered Kentucky separately, and President Davis specifically refused to give Bragg any authority over Smith until he and the latter actually joined forces. At that point Bragg's higher status (full general) would automatically put him in command of the united columns. Until then, Davis assumed naively that his generals would cheerfully cooperate.[1]

Owing at least in part to this divided command, the Confederate effort to establish Rebel rule over the Bluegrass State failed. In the early October Battle of Perryville fought in east-central Kentucky, Bragg's outnumbered army more than held its own. However, the heavy losses it sustained in that engagement, along with the Rebels' dwindling supplies and a lack of meaningful support from the people of the state, compelled the Secessionists to abandon the campaign. Bragg retreated through Cumberland Gap to Knoxville. By late November he had shifted his army to Middle Tennessee, where it took up a position just northwest of Murfreesboro some thirty miles from Union-occupied Nashville.

MEANWHILE, the Confederate units that Bragg left in Mississippi to defend that state had coalesced into another Rebel army whose top generals (Earl Van Dorn and Sterling Price) in true Confederate fashion soon began to squabble with each other. Early in October this army failed in an attempt to drive the Yankees out of northeastern Mississippi. Following that unsuccessful effort, these Confederates turned to the defense of Vicksburg and Port Hudson on the Mississippi River. The Confederate government regarded those two points as essential both to maintain communication with the Trans-Mississippi and to block use of the river by the Federals. Late in 1862 President Davis selected the newly promoted Lieutenant General John C. Pemberton to command all Rebel forces in Mississippi and East Louisiana.

THUS by the fall of 1862 two separate major Confederate field armies operated in the West: Bragg's in Middle Tennessee (officially known after November 20 as the Army of Tennessee), and Pemberton's in Mississippi (designated officially as of December 7 as the Army of the Department of Mississippi and East Louisiana, but often called the Army of Vicksburg or the

---

1 In fact, these three columns were part of a massive late summer-early fall 1862 offensive that spontaneously developed along the Confederacy's northern border as nine columns of Secessionist armies moved forward. In addition to Bragg, Smith, and Marshall, the advancing Rebel forces comprised Lee's army moving into Maryland, a thrust into Federally-occupied western Virginia and even Ohio by columns under Major General William W. Loring and Brigadier General Adam ("Stovepipe") Johnson, an advance into northern Mississippi by forces under Major Generals Earl Van Dorn and Sterling Price (eventually consolidated into one column), and an offensive into northern Arkansas by Major General Thomas C. Hindman. See Harsh, *Confederate Tide Rising*, and Leigh, *Confederacy at Flood Tide.*

Army of Mississippi.)[2] The Rebels also maintained a garrison at Mobile, Alabama, a small army in East Tennessee to protect the vital East Tennessee & Virginia Railroad, which linked Chattanooga and the West directly with the Old Dominion, and smaller units at Port Hudson and several other points.

The orders assigning Bragg to command Confederate forces between the Appalachians and the Mississippi River remained in effect. For that reason, Bragg still held at least nominal command of Pemberton's army in Mississippi and of the troops in East Tennessee and of the Mobile garrison.[3]

IN Richmond on November 12, meanwhile, General Joseph E. Johnston, believing himself finally recovered from the wounds he had received in the Battle of Seven Pines nearly six months earlier, reported to the War Department for duty. President Davis, who retained a high opinion of Johnston's reputed ability despite their differences of the previous fall and winter, decided to assign the general to overall command of the Secessionist forces in the West.

Such an assignment would meet several needs. For one thing, it would satisfy a general clamor for an overall commander of the area between the Appalachians and the Mississippi, and in particular for Johnston to be that commander. Even some of the always-squabbling Rebel generals in the West (Braxton Bragg and Leonidas Polk among them) suspended their internecine bickering long enough to recommend to Davis that he place Johnston in command of the entire region. (See the following section of this chapter.)

The President hoped that Johnston, among other things, would coordinate the efforts of the different Rebel forces in the West and order troops from point to point as the need arose. The Confederates could, Davis believed, thereby offset the enemy's overall numerical superiority by massing their own strength quickly at the place where danger threatened. In effect, the Chief Executive expected Johnston to apply the offensive-defensive concept to the western Confederacy.

THE President's decision to assign Johnston to the chief Western post also grew from the obvious need to have some commander closer to the area than were the authorities in Richmond. In addition, Johnston's new assignment would solve Davis's immediate problem of finding a new slot for the Confederacy's third

2 17 OR, pt. 2, 787, 792, and 824.

3 Ibid., 624, 716-718, 726-728; 20 OR, pt. 1, 1; 20 OR, pt. 2, 384-385.

highest-ranking officer and its second highest-ranking field commander.[4] Prior to his Seven Pines wound, Johnston had commanded the principal Rebel army in Virginia, and in late 1862 he wanted to resume that post. By the time he was ready to return to duty, however, Robert E. Lee had more than adequately filled that position and Davis was not about to replace him.

Finally, as 1862 neared its end, it had become painfully obvious that serious personnel and personal problems existed in the Western Rebel military forces—especially in the high echelons of the Army of Tennessee. Bragg and several of his leading subordinate generals had commenced a bitter, disruptive, and semi-public quarrel over responsibility for the failure of their recent campaign into Kentucky. Several of those officers vigorously lobbied the President to remove Bragg from command of the army. The feud between Bragg and his critics—which historian Peter Cozzens called "the Army of Tennessee's dirty laundry"—created what were to become several deep and long-lasting fissures in the army's command structure. These, in turn, led quickly to the emergence of factions within the army's officer corps and created demoralization among the army's rank and file. Not surprisingly, these developments so hampered the Army of Tennessee that it lost much of its combat effectiveness.[5]

In summary, one of the Confederacy's greatest military needs—almost certainly its greatest—in late 1862 was to provide some effective overall command and administrative structure for the defense of the West. Such an arrangement, whatever form it took, might moderate the suicidal squabbling among Rebel generals in the region and enable them to conduct some sort of coordinated defense of that most critical area. Joseph E. Johnston, as an outsider with no preexisting ties either to Bragg or his critics and with his great prestige, high rank, widespread popularity, and exalted reputation, seemed the logical and indeed the only available person to fill the post.[6]

---

4 As noted at several places in this work, J. E. Johnston originally stood fourth among Rebel generals. A. S. Johnston's death at Shiloh moved him up a notch so that only Samuel Cooper and Robert E. Lee outranked him. Cooper did not serve in the field.

5 Cozzens, *No Better Place*, 179. See Connelly and Jones, *Politics of Command*, 62-72. See also "Gen. Bragg and His Generals," *Memphis* (Atlanta) *Daily Appeal*, Feb. 23, 1863 (reprinted from the *Charleston Courier*, n. d.) This division in the high command of the Army of Tennessee as it affected Joseph E. Johnston will be discussed in detail in Book Three, Chapter Four, Volume II.

6 Lieutenant General Leonidas Polk, the ringleader of the anti-Bragg generals in the Army of Tennessee, wrote President Davis on Feb. 4, 1863, that Johnston "will cure all discontent and

ALTHOUGH Johnston's qualifications appeared to make the general the obvious choice to head President Davis's new Western command scheme, the decision to name him to that post was questionable on two broad grounds. One stemmed from the detrimental effect that Johnston's longstanding (and by late 1862 greatly exacerbated) estrangement from the Chief Executive and the administration might have on any command arrangement that depended upon cooperation between the general commanding in the West and the Richmond government. The second potential source of major problems arose from the highly questionable command and administrative structure that the President decreed as the framework for applying the offensive-defensive strategy to the West.

AS pointed out earlier in Book One, the Davis-Johnston relationship, friendly and respectful at the beginning of the war, had deteriorated rapidly under the pressures of the first thirteen months of the conflict. Normal differences arose over several professional military matters. Left unresolved and intensified by the personalities and associates of the two principals and fueled by many quarrels, especially by the question of Johnston's rank and that of State brigades, they grew into distrust and bitter animosity.

Despite this rift, Davis maintained his belief in Johnston's high military competence. The President had hastened to Johnston's side after the general fell wounded at Seven Pines on May 31. A short time later the Chief Executive had offered to have Johnston live in the Presidential Mansion while he recovered. The general, however, had chosen to take up quarters in a private house in Richmond. Within a week or so he accepted an invitation for himself and his wife to stay at the "comfortable" Grace Street house of their friends Senator and Mrs. Louis T. Wigfall of Texas.[7]

Prior to his election to the Confederate Senate, Wigfall had served as a volunteer staff officer and then as a brigadier general and brigade commander in

---

inspire the army with new life and confidence" (20 *OR*, pt. 1, 698). As discussed in Book Three, Chapter Four, in Volume II, Polk's recommendation stemmed more from a loathing of Bragg than an admiration of Johnston.

7 Wright (née Wigfall), *Southern Girl*, 90. Johnston also spent an unknown (and unpleasant) length of time that summer at Amelia Springs about sixty miles from Richmond. From that spa he wrote to Wigfall on July 31 describing the resort as "the meanest of the kind in the world. Kept by three brothers who vie with each other in miserly & unaccommodating spirit & ignorance of ordinary decency." See also Johnston to "My dear Sir" (John L. Manning), July 22, 1862. Letters in collection of Doug Schanz who kindly made copies available to me.

Johnston's army in Virginia. Although initially a supporter of President Davis and his administration (and for a while a member of the President's staff) and always a strong Confederate nationalist, Wigfall as the conflict went on found himself frequently disagreeing with the Chief Executive about various relatively minor military matters. By the second summer of the war Wigfall, fueled on more than one occasion by alcohol, had convinced himself that what he saw as Davis's mismanagement of the war inevitably would result in the defeat of the Confederacy. He had become a prominent and volatile figure in the emerging anti-Davis forces rapidly developing within the Rebel Congress.[8]

The Wigfalls, like the Johnstons, had enjoyed a close friendship with then-Senator and Mrs. Davis in pre-war Washington. Her father, remembered one of Wigfall's daughters, "had loved and esteemed him [Davis] as a friend and admired him as a man" during that time.

In the early days of the Confederacy, however, Mrs. Wigfall and Mrs. Davis had had a falling out of some sort. We do not know the cause of this squabble, but the bickering added another element to their husbands' evolving estrangement. "The females contributed greatly to the quarrel," notes Alvy King, Senator Wigfall's biographer. Lydia Johnston, possibly motivated by her husband's many differences with President Davis, took Charlotte Wigfall's side in this spat with Varina Davis.

Mrs. Davis's biographer wrote that "Mrs. Johnston came to believe that the Davises were deliberately hurting her husband's career, and she began to despise them both. . . . [The Johnstons' friendship with the Wigfalls] only seems to have stoked their shared hostility for the Davises until it became a fixation, despite overtures from the First Lady, including a dinner invitation to the [Confederate] White House."

After the war ended, Mrs. Burton Harrison remembered that "Mrs. Joseph E. Johnston, coming of the distinguished McLane family of Baltimore, had a little court of her own, in later days rather antagonistic to the ruling power of the [Confederate] White House, it was said. . . . People we met said that the Executive's

---

8 Some idea of Wigfall's temperament can be seen in the fact that in a five-month period in 1840 he was involved in a fist fight, three "near duels," two duels, and one shooting. These brawls left one dead and two (including Wigfall) wounded. He seems to have become less rambunctious after his marriage. In May 1862, President Davis told a visitor that he had lost confidence in Wigfall—in part because of the senator's drinking. See King, *Wigfall*, 29, 36-37, 77, and 139.

animus against Johnston was based upon a petty feud between their wives, who had been daily associates and friends in the old Washington days."[9]

Johnston's close friendship with Wigfall—especially his decision to live at the senator's house while completing his recovery from the Seven Pines wounds and after declining a similar invitation from the President—at least created the impression that the popular general sympathized with, even if he had not joined, the anti-administration bloc. In November 1862 Johnston attended what became a famous Richmond champagne breakfast organized by several of Davis's most vociferous political enemies. The general's presence at that gathering, notes his biographer, gave "further evidence that he had become not only a political issue but [also] a political player."[10]

Johnston's perceived flirtation with, if not actual assimilation into, the growing crowd of Davis's political foes should have raised caution flags about his new assignment to so sensitive, important, and prominent a post as overall commander in the West. The President, however, remained blind to experience and held firmly to his belief (his "creed," writes one of his biographers) that, as he put it in 1861, "my co-laborers, *purified and elevated by the sanctity of the cause they defend* [my emphasis], would forget themselves in their zeal for the public welfare[,]" put aside all personal animosity and grudges, and cooperate to advance the Confederacy's bid for independence.[11]

IN the summer of 1862 Johnston's attitude toward Davis seems to have begun to shift (if, indeed, it had not begun to do so earlier) into a new and even more toxic channel. Gradually he came to view President Davis not just as a fellow military colleague with whom he had professional differences, but as the man who had illegally taken away the status (rank) to which, he believed, the law entitled him and who had also become his personal enemy bent on destroying his military reputation and driving him out of the army in disgrace.

---

9 President Davis later denied the reports of the ladies' squabble. See Wright, *Southern Girl*, 26 and 90; King, *Wigfall*, 128, 130, and 134; Cashin, *Davis*, 139-140; Ross, *Davis*, 118, 127, 160, 168, 177, and 187; and Harrison, *Recollections*, 154 and 192.

10 Symonds, *Johnston*, 179-181. In an Oct. 16, 2004, lecture during a symposium at Pamplin Historical Park, Symonds remarked that Johnston's presence in the Wigfall house was "a daily implied criticism" of Davis. My notes of Symonds's talk.

11 Cooper, *Davis*, 352, 362, 364-365, 398-399, and 401-403.

It is not possible to document such a matter precisely, but as he convalesced in the Wigfalls' home, Johnston reflected upon his 1861-1862 experiences, talked daily with his hosts, and followed military and political developments through correspondence, the press, and conversations with visitors. Johnston seems slowly to have begun to believe (he, almost certainly, would have said "to realize") that he was increasingly outside the "Confederate establishment." This group of powerful men—mostly politicians, but also including some generals whose advice the government sought and sometimes followed—and their ladies occupied the top places in the Secessionist political-military-social hierarchy orbiting around President and Mrs. Davis and the administration.[12]

For example, on at least two occasions that summer Johnston visited with Brigadier General William W. Mackall, his longtime friend, his future chief of staff, and then a recently exchanged prisoner-of-war. Like Johnston, Mackall fancied himself a victim of President Davis's wrath. We know nothing of their conversations, but it seems safe to say that very few of their remarks would have been complimentary to the Chief Executive or favorable to the administration. These meetings were not the last occasions that gave the two disgruntled generals the chance to commiserate about what they both saw (or soon came to see) as their persecution at the hands of Jefferson Davis and his minions.[13]

IN part the evolution of Johnston's attitude toward the Davis government grew naturally from the general's 1861-1862 experience in dealing with the President and the War Department, especially with Secretary of War Benjamin. In large part it reflected the deep pain that Johnston clearly felt in and after September 1861 when Davis ruled that he did not rank first among Confederate generals.

---

12 I am defining the term "establishment" to mean the formally organized Confederate government—the men who in law and in fact ran the Rebel war effort. Connelly and Jones (*Politics of Command*, Chapter III) use a different definition. They describe several informal blocs of Davis's critics and depict one of them, the "Western concentration bloc," as possibly "the real power base of the Confederacy." These groups were certainly important, and several of them were powerful and played a crucial role in Confederate history. It seems to me, however, that an "establishment" must be established.

13 See Mackall to his wife Sept. 24, 1862, and n.d. (probably Oct. 1862), Mackall Papers. See also Mackall, *Son's Recollections*, 169-170 and 173-174. Gen. Mackall's brother-in-law, Brigadier General G. Moxley Sorrell (*Recollections*, 202) wrote after the war only that "the Executive at Richmond was not favorably disposed toward him" (General Mackall), and that he could not receive any appointment higher than that of brigadier general "although his rank and attainments qualified him for higher duties" than those assigned to him. Joseph E. Johnston, as we shall see, esteemed him highly.

Then, on April 14, 1862. after months of frustration and alienation in dealing with the administration, Johnston met with Davis, his adviser Lee, and his new secretary of war George W. Randolph. The President had convened the group to determine how the Confederates would counter the enemy advance up the peninsula between the James and York rivers against Richmond. In a long and somewhat heated discussion Johnston urged an immediate withdrawal up the peninsula and a concentration of all available Confederate troops at the capital to fight there the great battle for Confederate independence.[14]

Davis listened to the lengthy discussion and finally overruled Johnston. The President sided with Randolph and Lee, both of whom wanted to play for time by sending Johnston's army to join the Rebel forces at Yorktown near the tip of the peninsula to hold that post for as long as possible. Then, when the Yankees forced him to evacuate the town, Johnston was to fall back toward Richmond as slowly as he could while seeking opportunities to strike at the advancing enemy. Such a policy would give the Confederates additional time to remove valuable equipment and supplies from the great navy yard at Norfolk and to strengthen the defenses of their capital city. Meanwhile, they could raise, organize, and bring to Virginia some of the new army units formed under their recently enacted conscription law.[15]

WHATEVER the origins of Johnston's evolving attitude regarding the administration, the general's interpretation of his position vis-à-vis the government would have clarified to some degree in the summer of 1862 as he lived at the Wigfalls' and recovered from his wounds. So, too, would a new factor that seems to have reared its head about that time. Somewhat to his chagrin, Johnston witnessed the extent to which Robert E. Lee emerged in the summer and fall of that year as the great military figure and hope of the Confederacy while commanding Johnston's army—as the wounded general thought of it.

JOHNSTON held an ambiguous view of Lee. The two had been friends as well as—mostly in Johnston's mind—professional rivals ever since their cadet days at the Military Academy more than three decades earlier. The school's academic

---

14 Douglas Southall Freeman (*Lee's Lieutenants*, II, 16-17) called Johnston "a sworn devotee of concentration."

15 By far the best account of this conference is that in Newton, *Johnston*, Chapter 7. Newton calls the conference "a low point" in the Lee-Johnston relationship. As mentioned in Book One, Chapter Two, I believe that it was in the aftermath of this conference that Johnston offered his resignation and Davis refused to accept it.

and military systems pitted a boy against all other members of his class in constant competition for academic standing and military status within the Corps of Cadets. Driven and ambitious, Johnston soon showed himself very sensitive to his status, and he did not like to lose at any competition. No matter how hard he worked, however, he could not outperform or outshine Lee.

Over their four years at the Academy (1825-1829) Lee proved clearly superior to Johnston and to everyone else who graduated in the Class of 1829. When their time at the school came to its end, Lee stood second academically of forty-six graduates and held the post of adjutant, the highest in the Corps of Cadets. Johnston finished a respectable thirteenth at graduation and then occupied the post of cadet private.[16] Johnston accumulated a total of fifty-five demerits over his four-year cadetship—an excellent record. Lee had none. Jefferson Davis, by contrast, amassed 327 during his last three years at the Academy.[17]

When the class graduated in 1829 Lee's outstanding record sent him into the elite Corps of Engineers; Johnston went into the less prestigious artillery. In 1839 Johnston transferred to the recently created Topographical Engineer Corps, still a notch or two below the Corps of Engineers in status. In the mid-1850s the secretary of war reassigned both Lee and Johnston to the army's new cavalry regiments.

EVERYWHERE that Lee served during his three decades in the United States Army he left behind a trail of admiring relatives, friends, officials, and fellow soldiers. People found themselves greatly impressed by Lee's appearance, ability, competence, bearing, intelligence, personality, and—above all his "character." A cousin thought that he "certainly look[ed] more like a great man than anyone I have ever seen." In April 1861 an observer commented that Lee was "the noblest-looking man I had ever gazed upon . . . handsome beyond all men I had ever seen."

Montgomery C. Meigs, a Georgian who as a young lieutenant had worked with Lee on a Mississippi River engineering project at St. Louis and who in 1861

16 For a while in his final year at the school Johnston was a cadet lieutenant. For now unknown reasons (possibly health) he was reduced to cadet private. See Symonds, *Johnston*, 19-20.

17 Destruction of some records in an 1838 fire makes it impossible to determine Davis's four-year total. See J. Davis, *Papers*, vol. 1, 97-100. Thanks to Suzanne Christoff, archivist at the Academy, for information on the conduct records of Davis, Lee, and Johnston. See also R. K. Krick, "Snarl and Sneer," 166-167; and Symonds, *Johnston*, 5. Symonds notes that for years Johnston displayed traces of "envy and resentment" toward his classmate.

succeeded Joseph E. Johnston as quartermaster general of the United States Army, a post he held during the Civil War, wrote of Lee's "noble and commanding presence and . . . [of his] admirable, graceful, athletic figure." The Virginian, Meigs recorded, was "one with whom nobody ever wished or ventured to take a liberty, though [he was] kind and generous to his subordinates, admired by all women, and respected by all men."

Mayor John F. Darby of St. Louis, with whom Lee worked on several river engineering projects, recorded that Lee "maintained and preserved under all circumstances his dignity and gentlemanly bearing, winning and commanding the esteem, regard[,] and respect of every man under him." Lee had, Darby recalled, "one of the most gifted and cultivated minds I have ever met with, he was as scrupulously conscientious and faithful in the discharge of his duties as he was modest and unpretending. He had none of that coddling, and petty puerile planning and scheming which men of little minds and small intellectual caliber use to make and take care of their fame." Other citizens chimed in with similar praise of Lee and his work at St. Louis.

Significantly, such assignments frequently put Lee in the position of dealing with elected civilian officials—men whom he had to convince because he could not order them about. He also had to learn how to deal with civilian laborers who did most of the actual work on the engineering projects, and had to concern himself with matters of budgets, contracts, and periodic status reports on his engineering work. These assignments also showed him something of the psychology of civilian workers, men who were not very different from volunteer as opposed to career Regular Army enlisted soldiers, which gave him valuable insights into how things get done at the higher levels of government.

Henry J. Hunt, who served with Lee in the 1840s and who, like Meigs, became a Union general in the Civil War and who commanded the Yankee artillery at Gettysburg, described Lee "as fine looking a man as one would wish to see. Quiet and dignified in manner, of cheerful disposition, always pleasant and considerate, he seemed to me the perfect type of gentleman."[18]

18 Freeman, *Lee*, I, 120-121, 181-183, 191-195, 480, and 612; Dowdey, *Lee*, 63 and 65. On this subject see McDonald, "The True Gentleman." Thomas Lawrence Connelly ("Lee and the Western Confederacy" and *The Marble Man*) argued that Lee's reputation was largely the product of post-Civil War myth-making. In response, Albert Castel, ("Historian and General") pointed out that a vast body of evidence from the antebellum years shows that "even before Lee became the South's hero, he consistently impressed almost all who came in contact with him as a man of superior parts and potential greatness." Castel far and away has the better of

On several occasions Lee served as a member of a board of officers appointed to study and make recommendations concerning the Military Academy or sites for coastal fortifications. He also held several antebellum assignments in the War Department in Washington. From time to time he even managed the Corps of Engineers' capital office when his superiors were out of town. On occasion Lee lobbied Congress on behalf of the Corps or of the Military Academy when he served as superintendent of the school in the 1850s.

These duties once again brought Lee into contact with the political figures who made policy and controlled the army's budgetary matters. As was the case with his river work at St. Louis, Lee learned a great deal from these experiences about the importance of working with the government's elected officials, some of whom were prima donnas, and how to go about doing so.

It may have been equally significant that Lee found much of the office work and the dealing with politicians frustrating. His best biographer, Freeman, writes of "his dislike of politicians." He had nevertheless to discipline himself to perform the distasteful duties for the larger good of the army, the Corps of Engineers, or the Academy, and he chose (Covey again) to do so.[19]

THROUGH almost all the antebellum decades Lee kept a step or two ahead of Johnston in what Johnston regarded as the great contest for promotion and status. Lee, for example, became a first lieutenant on September 21, 1836. His date of rank as captain was August 7, 1838—a month after Johnston's as first lieutenant. Johnston did not become a captain until September 21, 1846.[20]

---

this argument. While it is true that postwar white Southerners enhanced Lee's image—some would say they canonized him or even deified him—the evidence against Connelly's position is simply overwhelming. Lee was outstanding as both a man and a soldier, and was widely recognized as such at every stage of his adult life and of his professional career.

19 Freeman, *Lee*, I, 134-135, 178-179, 181-183, 194, and Chapter XIX. One should compare Lee in this regard (as in so many others) to General George C. Marshall, the U. S. Army chief of staff in World War II. Marshall's pre-1939 assignments working with state National Guard units and the New Deal's Civilian Conservation Corps gave him similar insights and experiences. For starters, see Pogue, *Marshall*, 204, 209, 307-312, and 317; Rich, *The Generals, passim*; and Parrish, *Roosevelt and Marshall*, especially 36-38, 80, 125, and 242-243.

20 Johnston's status as 1st lieutenant was complicated by the fact that he was out of the army for about thirteen months seeking work in the civilian sector. He rejoined the army July 7, 1838, as a 1st Lieutenant in the Corps of Topographical Engineers. See R. R. Krick, "Snarl and Sneer," 169-171.

Even in petty matters it must have seemed to Johnston that Lee appeared to lead a charmed life. Late in 1846 Lee and Johnston shared a cabin on the steamer *Massachusetts* as she crossed the Gulf of Mexico. The tossing ship soon made Johnston violently seasick. Lee, of course, was not bothered at all by the rough waves and calmly went about his business while his cabin mate lay moaning in his bunk.[21]

PART II

"There was always envy between him [Johnston] and Lee."
— Lieutenant Oscar Hinrichs, Fall 1864

As noted in the first chapter of this volume, almost all army officers constantly monitored their chances for promotion. With Johnston, however, such concerns were absolutely crucial and went far beyond the normal. Promotion for him was recognition of status, of ability, of success—of honor acknowledged. It vindicated his efforts and validated his self-image. Promotion showed one and all that he stood above his contemporaries. It may also have indicated some deep, perhaps unconscious doubt about whether he deserved such recognition and status.

Some two decades before the Civil War Johnston advised a young kinsman to go into a branch of the army in which promotion would be more likely and rapid than in his own branch (then the Topographical Engineers). Ten years later, on January 6, 1851, he addressed a letter to his brother Edward about the slowness of promotion. In this revealing document Johnston admitted that promotion was "a thing I desire more than [does] any man in the army." However, wrote Johnston, "I think 'twould be indelicate" to seek a position in another branch of the army where

---

21 Symonds, *Johnston*, 55; Govan and Livingood, *Different Valor*, 18; J. W. Jones, *Reminiscences*, 372.

promotion would be more likely. Major General Winfield Scott, the commanding general, "knows the relative fitness of the Military Candidates & they ought not to attempt to sway him by personal application."

Such an idealistic approach, unfortunately, might produce a most undesirable result. "I doubt 'tho," Johnston rationalized, "if any one else, or many others, are governed by such notions." Therefore, "as you [brother Edward] are on intimate terms with him [Scott]. . . . Remind him that I legally hold a B[revet] Colonelcy Senior to any other gained in his army." Johnston closed his letter to his brother with a list of some of his qualifications for promotion and the suggestion that Edward get others to recommend him to Scott. Johnston, it seems, could be quite flexible in applying his principles when a chance to get a coveted promotion presented itself.[22]

THE 1846-1848 war with Mexico brought praise and promotion to both Lee and Johnston, albeit more to the former than to the latter. At the end of the conflict, as at the beginning, both held the permanent grade of captain (of Engineers in Lee's case; of Topographical Engineers in Johnston's). Their status, however, had changed both relatively and absolutely.

Both were members of Major General Winfield Scott's staff in March 1847 when the army landed at Vera Cruz on Mexico's east coast. After a short siege that town surrendered and Scott marched inland, heading for Mexico City. At Cerro Gordo, about thirty-five miles from the coast, Johnston received a severe wound while reconnoitering the enemy position. A short time later Lee found a route that enabled Scott's army to flank and clear away the Mexicans and to continue the march.

When Johnston recovered and returned to duty, he received an assignment as the acting lieutenant colonel of a temporary regiment of light infantry (called "voltigeurs" in the army jargon of the day). He served in that post for the remainder of the war. In September when the army stormed Mexico City, Lee (still an

---

22 Symonds, *Johnston*, 31; letter to Edward in Johnston Papers, W&M. As will be discussed below, the validity of Johnston's brevet colonelcy was highly questionable and was not officially recognized at the time he wrote this letter. Like George C. Marshall (and Joseph E. Johnston), Lee experienced great frustration with the army's slow system of promotion. Like Marshall (but *unlike Johnston*), *Lee did not allow such frustration to dominate his life and career*. For example, see Freeman, *Lee*, I, 136, 182, and 187-188. Connelly, *Marble Man*, greatly overstates his case in arguing that Lee was a frustrated and unhappy man in part because of the slowness of promotion.

engineer on Scott's staff) and Johnston played heroic roles for which each received praise and recognition.

Johnston's "gallant and meritorious conduct" attracted the notice of his division commander who expressed high praise for his "very gallant and accomplished subordinate." Scott himself was reported to have called Johnston "a great soldier."[23]

Lee, owing to his far more visible position as a member of the commanding general's staff (a post that had him working at various times with many different parts of the army), drew much more attention. He won commendation, especially for his actions on August 19-20 at the Pedregal and Contreras outside Mexico City. One division commander praised Lee's "exceedingly valuable services rendered throughout the whole of these operations." Another noted that he wished "to record particularly my admiration of the conduct of Captain Lee. . . . His reconnaissances, though pushed far beyond the bounds of prudence, were conducted with so much skill that their fruits were of the utmost value—the soundness of his judgment and personal daring being equally conspicuous."

A third general wrote of "the valuable services of Captain Lee . . . whose distinguished merit and gallantry deserves the highest praise." A fourth acknowledged his "great obligations to Captain R. E. Lee . . . in whose skill and judgment I had the utmost confidence." Scott wrote that Lee had been "as distinguished for felicitous execution as for science and daring." Later he described Lee's work during the night of August 19-20 at the Pedregal as "the greatest feat of physical and moral courage performed by any individual, in my knowledge, pending the campaign." A decade after the war in Mexico Scott called Lee "the very best soldier that I ever saw in the field." Few American officers have ever received—or merited—such praise.[24]

LEE received three brevet promotions for his performance in Mexico. These honors elevated him from his permanent status as captain of engineers to brevet major, then to brevet lieutenant colonel, and finally to brevet colonel. As of September 13, 1847, he was "Captain and Brevet Colonel Lee."

Johnston's postwar status was less clear. Like Lee, he began the war as a permanent captain, in his case in the Corps of Topographical Engineers. Following distinguished, if brief, service in that capacity and recovery from his rather serious

---

23 Govan and Livingood, *Different Valor*, 20.

24 Freeman, *Lee*, I, 271-272 and 294.

wound he spent the remainder of the war as the acting lieutenant colonel of the temporary regiment of light infantry. For his conspicuous role in that capacity during the storming of Mexico City Johnston received a brevet promotion which, he assumed, made him a brevet colonel. Later, after returning to his permanent status as captain of Topographical Engineers, he received two brevet promotions for his wartime service.

All of this raised questions. Could an officer receive a brevet promotion while serving in an acting capacity in another branch of the army at a grade different from his permanent grade and in a temporary unit? If so, should the brevet be based on his permanent or temporary status? If based on the latter, did it lapse with the deactivation of the temporary unit? What did it mean when he later received brevet promotions from his permanent grade to lower brevet grades? In Johnston's case the matter was even more complicated because his brevet promotion to major was for the same service for which, he thought, he had already been promoted to brevet colonel.

Bureaucrats at the Richmond War Department went to work, poring over volumes of laws and regulations. In due time they issued their ruling: Johnston's brevet promotion to colonel was invalid. He was "Captain and Brevet Lieutenant Colonel Johnston" (the two valid brevets calculated from his permanent grade of captain).

JOHNSTON, to whom such symbols of status were extremely important—indeed, even necessary, for reasons to be speculated upon later—had no difficulty convincing himself that this ruling was both erroneous and unjust. Over the next dozen years he appealed the decision to a succession of secretaries of war, all of whom ruled against him. (One of them was Jefferson Davis.) Even the United States Senate went on record as concurring with the secretaries' ruling.

As the 1840s came to an end, Lee stood several years senior to Johnston in their common permanent grade of captain and one grade above him in brevet status.[25]

THE first half of the 1850s brought no change in Johnston's situation relative to Lee. He continued to perform the routine duties of a "Topog"— mapmaking,

---

25 Symonds, *Johnston*, 88-90; R. K. Krick, "Snarl and Sneer"; "Report on the Claim, Apr. 15, 1858" of Joseph E. Johnston to be brevet colonel, Johnston Papers, W&M. See also Thompson (ed.), *Texas & New Mexico*.

scouting, surveying boundaries, exploring possible railroad routes, inspecting military posts, and so on.

In the mid-1850s Congress expanded the U.S. Army by creating four new regiments, two of them cavalry units. Secretary of War Jefferson Davis selected Lee and Johnston as the lieutenant colonels of the new 1st (Johnston) and 2nd (Lee) Cavalry Regiments. Both men had a date of rank of March 3, 1855, in their new permanent grade. Although these new assignments involved a change of branch and a switch from staff to line (command of troops) duty, Lee still outranked Johnston by virtue of his seniority in their previous permanent grade of captain. Lee remained a brevet colonel. Johnston's brevet status of lieutenant colonel became irrelevant with his new permanent lieutenant colonelcy. Johnston's new regiment served in the Kansas Territory, Lee's in Texas. Both men were sometimes absent from their units for prolonged periods or on detached duty.

JOHNSTON'S fortunes took a decided turn for the better in March 1857 when Secretary of War Jefferson Davis left the War Department at the end of President Franklin Pierce's administration. The new secretary of war in the James Buchanan administration, John B. Floyd, hailed from Johnston's hometown of Abingdon, Virginia, and was related to Johnston by marriage.[26]

Encouraged by this serendipitous development, Johnston renewed his quest for status. He again submitted his claim to a brevet colonelcy. War Department bureaucrats dutifully dusted off their files, reviewed the records of the case, and reported to Floyd that the matter had long since been settled and that Johnston was not, and should not be, a brevet colonel. In March 1860, however, Floyd blithely announced that the rulings of the Senate and those of his predecessors as secretary of war, as well as the findings of the bureaucrats, had been "simply a mistake" and that Johnston was and had been a brevet colonel since September 13, 1847 (the same date of rank as Lee's brevet colonelcy).

Floyd's decision drew a formal protest from two officers to then-Senator Jefferson Davis and stirred several unfavorable (and doubtless other and even more uncomplimentary unofficial) comments. Even Lee, usually loathe to make an unfavorable remark about anyone, was led to believe that his classmate had crossed an ethical line. "I think it must be evident to him," Lee wrote in a family letter, "that it never was the intention of Congress to advance him to the position assigned to

26 Floyd had married one of Johnston's second cousins. See paragraph 10 of Robert Hughes to Alfred P. James, April 21, 1925, Hughes Papers.

him by the Sec'y." Lee also commented that "in proportion to his [Johnston's] services he has been advanced beyond anyone in the army and has thrown more discredit than ever on the system of favoritism and making brevets." Despite the protests, the war secretary's decision stood.[27]

IF Floyd's march 1860 ruling regarding his brevet colonelcy pleased Johnston, he must have been absolutely ecstatic with a decision the secretary rendered a few months later.

On June 10, 1860, the army's Quartermaster General died. As commanding general, Winfield Scott nominated four highly qualified officers for the vacant post: Colonel and Brevet Brigadier General Albert Sidney Johnston, Lieutenant Colonel and Brevet Colonel Joseph E. Johnston, Lieutenant Colonel and Brevet Colonel Robert E. Lee, and Lieutenant Colonel and Brevet Colonel Charles F. Smith. Joseph E. Johnston was the third highest-ranking and arguably the least distinguished of the four nominees—certainly less so than Sidney Johnston and Robert E. Lee. Secretary of War Floyd, nevertheless, quickly selected his relative to fill the vacancy.

Appointment as Quartermaster General was crucial for Johnston's sense of validation. The position carried with it automatic promotion to the grade of "brigadier general, staff." As Quartermaster General, of course, Johnston could not command troops in the field. At long last, however, as of June 28, 1860, he had vaulted ahead of Robert E. Lee! The latter did not even become a full colonel (permanent grade) until March 16, 1861.[28]

BRIGADIER General Johnston had less than a year to enjoy looking down from his exalted new perch upon his now vanquished longtime rival. Nine-and-one-half months after Johnston's appointment as Quartermaster General the state of Virginia declared herself out of the Union and joined the Confederacy.

---

27 Symonds, *Johnston*, 89-90; Newton, *Johnston*, 101; "Report on the claim, April 15, 1858," of Joseph E. Johnston to be a brevet colonel, Johnston Papers, W&M.

28 See Symonds, *Johnston*, 3 and 91. During Floyd's term as secretary of war the Federal government transferred more than 110,000 weapons from Northern sites to storage facilities in the South. Many in the North later accused Floyd of having stocked the future Rebel states with weapons to be used by the Confederate armies once secession had been brought about. In his postwar *Narrative* (426-429), Johnston went out of his way to defend Floyd (who had also become a Confederate general) against these charges. Floyd died in August 1863 from illness.

Lee submitted his resignation to the War Department on April 20 and hastened to Richmond. The state government appointed him a major general on the 23rd and placed him in command of all of Virginia's military forces. Johnston did not resign from the "old army" until April 22. Then he, too, left for Richmond to offer his services to the Old Dominion. On April 25 state authorities, acting on Lee's recommendation, named Johnston a major general of the Virginia forces and assigned him to command all Virginia troops in the Richmond area.

Within a few days state authorities concluded that Virginia needed but one major general and that Lee should hold the post. Offered a brigadier general's appointment in the State army, Johnston declined. Instead, he left for the Confederacy's temporary capital in Montgomery, Alabama. While there he received an appointment as brigadier general (then the highest grade in the Rebel army) and assignment to command at Harpers Ferry in what is now West Virginia.[29]

Davis's 1861 decision regarding the general's rank relegated Johnston permanently to a position subordinate to Lee. In September 1861, when he learned of the President's ranking of the full generals, Johnston was deeply hurt. He had lost the status he had so long coveted and so recently attained, and he had no possibility of ever regaining it. (See Book One, Chapter One.)

WE cannot know to what extent Johnston by late 1862 had come to resent his own loss of status in Confederate service, Lee's higher rank and much greater reputation throughout the Confederacy, and his own recent assignment away from the army in Virginia. From time to time, however, observers commented on what they believed to be Johnston's attitude.

On April 12, 1863, a War Department official informed his diary that Johnston was "full of himself, [and] above all other things eaten up with morbid jealousy of Lee and all his superiors in position, rank[,] or glory." A year and a half later Lieutenant Oscar Hinrichs, an engineer officer who had served with Johnston in 1862 and who then held a similar post with Rebel forces in the Shenandoah Valley, overheard a conversation among several Secessionist officers in which those (unnamed) worthies discussed some of the high-ranking Rebel generals. In summarizing the conversation, Hinrichs wrote:

---

29 Did Johnston resent the state authorities' selection of him rather than Lee for reduction in grade? We simply do not know, but he could well have seen the matter as yet another example of favoritism to benefit his rival—this time by the Old Dominion's establishment in which Lee's family stood very high and Johnston's did not.

There was always envy between him [Johnston] and Lee about their advancement [in state service], and when Lee was nominated Commander in Chief, Johnston got sore and asked for his dismissal, which was accepted, after a commission of three of the first citizens of the State had visited him, telling him, how indispensable his services were for the State. But he was sore, insisted on his dismissal, and offered his services to the Confederate government as soon as his dismissal was granted. . . . his injury during the battle of Seven Pines is considered a lucky happening for the State. The existing enmity between him and the Government seems to have been caused by his vanity and the fact that he did not do anything [in Mississippi in 1863 and Georgia in 1864].

"The quarrel between Joe Johnston and Mr. Davis," explained Mary Chesnut to her journal, "is that General Lee outranks Joe Johnston. Hence these sulks."[30]

THROUGHOUT late 1861 and in 1862 and 1863, indications of an increasing feeling of alienation on the part of the Johnston coterie began to creep into the writings of the general, those of his wife Lydia, some of their friends, political allies, and staff officers. Occasional words, phrases, sentences, and even entire letters and a variety of other documents indicate that over time these people came to share— to a greater or lesser degree—Johnston's growing feeling of having been wronged by, and of estrangement from, those at the head of the Confederate government in Richmond.

Major General Gustavus W. Smith, Johnston's long-time friend, protégé, once second-in-command of his army, and, in early 1862, still "Johnston's most trusted subordinate" (in the words of Smith's biographer), was among the first to give voice to such ideas. Even as early as January 1862 Smith had busied himself preparing a "memorandum for record" of a September 1861 conference he, Johnston, and Beauregard had held with President Davis. Such "cover your derriere" memoranda are common in bureaucracies, but it is a bad sign when people who are supposedly working together in a great cause become suspicious of one another and concerned with collecting records to protect themselves and their

---

30 Kean, *Diary*, 50 and 199; Hinrichs, *Mapmaker*, 197-198; R. K. Krick, "Snarl and Sneer," 187; Chesnut, *Chesnut's Civil War*, 613. See also the comments in Symonds, *Johnston*, 199 and 343-344. The Hinrichs comment is in a "catch-up" journal entry and cannot be precisely dated. Written in the fall of 1864, it refers to events of the Feb.-Mar. 1862 period. R. K. Krick to author, Aug. 23, 2010.

reputation lest their colleagues seek to blame them for decisions that turn out to be wrong.[31]

The following May, Smith clashed with President Davis over whether or not to promote Brigadier General W. H. C. Whiting, another Johnston protégé and the officer who had angered the Davis government with his late 1861 intemperate objections about the President's state brigade scheme. Whiting had, so Davis alleged, advocated overthrowing the Confederate government and installing Johnston as dictator. The Chief Executive had refused to cite a source for this charge, and Smith had defended Whiting.

By mid-summer 1862 Smith had expanded his circle of ire to include Robert E. Lee. Following his collapse on May 31–June 1 at Seven Pines, Smith had gone on medical leave. For some weeks he remained in the Richmond area, "extremely angry," writes his biographer, "because he had been superseded by Lee."[32]

On the afternoon of June 21—three weeks after his collapse at Seven Pines and just a few days before Lee opened the great Seven Days' Battles to save Richmond—Smith paid a call on his successor. The visit did not go well. Lee, who had just held what Smith termed "a long private interview" with President Davis, told his visitor nothing regarding the impending offensive that he was about to launch against the Yankees or even about the division of troops Smith had commanded before Johnston's wounding on May 31 had briefly elevated him to head the army. Should Smith return to duty in the next few days, however, his high rank would put him not only back in command of his former division, but also subordinate only to Lee in the capital's defending army.

Early in July Smith sent word to Lee that his health did not yet permit him to resume duty. "I received yesterday," an offended Smith huffed to Johnston on July 18 from a spa in Montgomery County, "a note from Lee in answer . . . first a layer of sugar, three lines, then two lines telling me to forward a certificate, and then three more lines of sugar. I shall keep him informed from time to time about the

---

31 Eventually Smith became a Johnston critic, but that development did not come until later. Newton, *Johnston*, 119. Smith's memorandum can be found in 15 *OR*, 884-887. See also the comments in Symonds, *Johnston*, 402 n14, and Smith, *War Papers*, 33-34. It was probably in reference to this memorandum that Beauregard claimed in the spring of 1864 that Smith could prove that Davis had lied in his account of the conference (51 *OR*, pt. 2, 843-844). For a discussion of the postwar flap caused by this document, see Hudson, *Smith*, 211-214. Additional quotations and examples of this thesis will be given at appropriate places in the following pages.

32 Hudson, *Smith*, 98-99 and 117.

condition of my health . . . I . . . do not propose supplying General Lee with any more surgeon's certificates beyond that upon which the original leave was granted. He took special pains to tell me that he could not grant me leave except on surgeon's certificate; that was 'his rule,' he said."

Then, after referring contemptuously to Lee's "semi-pious, semi-official, and altogether disagreeable manner," Smith continued,

> 'We will bide our time.' All I want is success to the cause; but there is a limit beyond which forebearance ceases to be a virtue, and if provoked much further I will tear the mask off some who think themselves wonderfully successful in covering up their tracks.[33]

Smith's attitude toward President Davis and Lee did not soften with passing time. Five years later on September 14, 1867, Beverley Johnston wrote his brother Joseph about Smith, with whom he had recently spoken: "His feelings and opinions in regard to Jeff. Davis are not more favorable to his character and capacity than yours. Towards another party (Lee) I also think his feelings and opinions are somewhat akin to yours, only I think there is added something of personal bitterness."[34]

When Smith did return to duty in August of 1862, he received a command in southeastern Virginia and northeastern North Carolina—a post that conspicuously and conveniently kept him away from Lee's army where, by rank, he would have been second in command. That fall seven major generals received promotion to the newly created grade of lieutenant general ("three star"). Smith, conspicuously, was not among them. To make matters even worse from Smith's perspective, six of the new lieutenant generals had been his juniors as major generals, and four of them had once been under his command.

All of this led an angry and frustrated Smith to resign in February 1863. "Since his return to this city," reported the Richmond correspondent of the Charleston *Mercury* that month, "report says he has had an angry colloquy with a high personage." Lee expressed sorrow over the resignation before opining, "No one ought to resign now, from any cause, if able to do duty."[35]

---

33 51 *OR*, pt. 2, 593-594. Smith's threat in the last sentence may have been a reference to his memorandum for record referred to in the text above. See pp.156-157.

34 Letter in Hughes Papers.

35 Hudson, *Smith*, 113 and 149-150; J. Davis, *Papers*, vol. 9, 58; Lee, *Papers*, 408; Kean, *Diary*, p. 38; Mendoza, *Struggle for Command*, 11, 16, 17, and 20-21; Charleston *Mercury*, n.d. (quoted in

Major General James Longstreet and Johnston had developed a very high regard for each other's abilities when they served together from July 1861 through May 1862. During that period Johnston had become something of a mentor to Longstreet. On November 11, 1861, L. Q. C. Lamar, a friend of President Davis and a kinsman by marriage of Longstreet, wrote to his wife, "There is some ill-feeling between the Potomac generals [of Johnston's army] and the President. I feel that Cousin James Longstreet is taking sides against the administration. He will certainly commit a grave error if he does."[36]

Longstreet, like Smith, fed Johnston's growing sense of grievance at losing (being deprived of?) command of the army in Virginia. By the fall of 1862 Longstreet had become Lee's "old war horse" and the highly regarded second in command of the Army of Northern Virginia. On October 5, nevertheless, just days before his promotion made him the senior lieutenant general in the Confederate army, Longstreet wrote to his former commander. The ANV, he assured Johnston, was still in its heart Johnston's army. "I feel you have their [the troops'] heart more decidedly than any other leader can ever have," he wrote. "The men would now go wild at the sight of their old favorite." Johnston, Longstreet hoped, would not go to command in the West when he returned to duty. On November 26, 1862, Johnston, writing to Major General J. E. B. Stuart, commander of the cavalry of Lee's army, added a postscript: "My love to Longstreet."[37]

Brigadier General Wade Hampton, a wealthy pre-war planter from South Carolina whose considerable military talents Johnston had appreciated since the early days of the conflict, also joined the roster of those praising Johnston for his

---

Mobile *Advertiser and Register*, Feb. 19, 1863). The *Advertiser and Register*, the product of an 1861 merger, published in some months as the *Register and Advertiser*. For simplicity's sake, I have cited it throughout this work as *Advertiser and Register*. On Feb. 23, Smith wrote Davis complaining about being passed over for promotion to lieutenant general and claiming that Lee had promised to reform the division he had commanded before and at Seven Pines. The President commented in the margins of Smith's letter "All false," "Lie," and "Not True." J Davis, *Papers*, vol. 9, 72-73.

36 Lamar quoted in Piston, *Longstreet*, 16.

37 Wert, *Longstreet*, 94 and 206; Johnston's letter to Stuart is printed in Pritchard, *Collecting the Confederacy*, 230. Thanks to Keith Bohannon for bringing this document to my attention. The October 5 letter is usually discussed in terms of what it reveals about Longstreet. I wish to raise questions about its possible impact on Johnston's attitude toward the Confederate establishment. See also R. K. Krick, *Smoothbore Volley*, 61-62 and 66-67. After the war Longstreet told a reporter for the *National Tribune* (published Oct. 3, 1895) that Johnston had been "the ablest general the Southern Confederacy had." Many thanks to Bruce Venter for bringing this interview to my attention.

Senator Louis T. Wigfall

LOC

1861-1862 work in Virginia. On January 13, 1863, he wrote to Johnston that the Army of Northern Virginia "[is] the army you formed and which still remembers you so fondly." Should Johnston's new assignment to command in the West carry him near one of Hampton's Mississippi plantations, added Hampton, he should feel free to make use of any of the plantations' resources.[38]

It is probably significant that Smith (Kentucky, New York), Longstreet (South Carolina, Alabama, Georgia), and Hampton (South Carolina) were all outside the Virginia group (clique?) that, some alleged, had come to dominate the major Rebel army in the Old Dominion. Longstreet happened also to be a good friend of Louis T. Wigfall who, at one time, had served on his staff. He was, Longstreet wrote, strongly attached to the Texas senator who, in turn, had become Johnston's foremost political friend and Jefferson Davis's bitter enemy.[39]

JOHNSTON, although holding a high opinion of Lee's intelligence, character, and ability, was reported to have said that "Lee has made them [Davis and the War Department] do for him what they would not do for me"—that is, to concentrate troops at Richmond in late June 1862 to fight the great battle against the Union army that had crept up the peninsula from Yorktown to the outskirts of Richmond. Clearly Johnston never thought to wonder why the government was willing to work closely with Lee and not with himself.[40]

---

38 Letter in Hughes Papers.

39 Symonds, *Johnston*, 18-19, 165, 192, and 199; Govan and Livingood, *Different Valor*, 159.

40 Johnston had urged such a concentration at the April conference with Davis, Lee, Smith, and Secretary of War Randolph. Overruling Johnston, the authorities ordered his army to the Yorktown area with instructions to delay the enemy's advance for as long as he could. The government's later willingness to transfer more troops from the Deep South to the Richmond

On February 21, 1863, Johnston wrote to his friend, former South Carolina governor John L. Manning, referring to his 1861-1862 time in Virginia "when I really commanded an army." Now, he complained, "I have very little authority or occupation [in the Western command]." Several times in the ensuing months Johnston would ask his friend Senator Wigfall to help him regain command of the army in the Old Dominion. "If you can help me out of my present place I shall love you more than ever," he wrote early in 1863.[41]

PART III

"Vicksburg is in danger."

— Joseph E. Johnston, November 1862

JOHNSTON'S personality, along with his evolving attitude toward the Davis Administration and its supporters (including Lee), constituted one major potential obstacle to success in the general's new Western assignment. The command and administrative framework that President Davis decreed on his new Western defensive scheme posed a second major potential difficulty. In addition to being of highly questionable effectiveness, it would over the next several months greatly frustrate Johnston and give him even more reasons to resent the treatment of himself and

---

area in May and June doubtless owed much to the fact that by June summer weather along the coast reduced the likelihood of major military operations there. See McMurry, "Marse Robert and the Fevers." In addition, some of the new units raised under the Rebels' April conscript law had become available.

41 Letter to Manning in Manning Letters; Wigfall in Symonds, *Johnston*, 199. See also King, *Wigfall*, 164 and 169n28. On June 23, 1862, just over three weeks after Johnston's wounding and Davis's appointment of Lee to command the Army of Northern Virginia, John C. Haskell, a young lieutenant who had served at army headquarters the previous winter, wrote to his father. Haskell reported a rumor circulating in Richmond that "the Davis party" was trying to keep Johnston "out of the command of this army [once he recovered from his wounds] and to retain Lee" (K. Stokes, *Everlasting Circle*, 128-129). Haskell makes no mention of such a plot in his *Memoirs*. I have found no further mention of such a scheme, but if the rumor reached the wounded Johnston, it would have intensified (both then and thereafter) the bitterness and resentment he felt toward Davis and the Confederate government and possibly toward Lee.

his friends at the hands of the government. At the same time, Johnston's unwillingness to try to implement several key parts of the President's scheme, his usual failure (refusal?) to communicate fully, his hair-trigger quick reaction to any criticism (real or implied), and his omnipresent concern to safeguard his reputation, gave Davis even more reasons to question the general's commitment to the Cause.

In mid-November, 1862, almost immediately upon learning that Davis had selected him to command Rebel forces between the Appalachian Mountains and the Mississippi River, Johnston developed serious doubts about both the wisdom and the practicability of Davis's new concept of the offensive-defensive, especially as the President intended to apply it to the Confederate West.

The two major Western armies that Johnston was to direct (Bragg's in Tennessee and Pemberton's in Mississippi) were, the general immediately concluded, too far apart to support each other. They operated on different fronts, they faced two separate Federal forces, each was quite inferior in strength to the enemy force it confronted, and each had a mission that almost certainly would keep it from assisting the other except, perhaps, with cavalry forces. To withdraw enough men from Tennessee to enable the Rebels in Mississippi to deal with the Yankees in their front (or vice versa) would so weaken the army from which the reinforcements came that it would have to abandon the area it was supposed to defend. Bragg's force at Murfreesboro was committed to the defense of southern and eastern Tennessee; Pemberton's to the defense of Mississippi and especially to that of the Vicksburg-Port Hudson corridor. In essence, Bragg faced north; Pemberton west.

As described in Book Two, Chapter One above, a broken roundabout rail route via Mobile provided the only viable link between the two Confederate forces. The straight-line distance from Bragg at Murfreesboro to Jackson, Mississippi, was about 320 miles; to Vicksburg about 350.

A direct march from Middle Tennessee to Jackson along that route would take at least two weeks and would bring the marching force into the maw of a 45,000-man Yankee army then operating in northern Mississippi. It would also necessitate a difficult crossing of the broad Tennessee River below the shoals in northwestern Alabama where the troops would have to bridge or ferry the river and where they were likely to be attacked by Union gunboats as they did so. Directing the march eastward to a crossing above the shoals and around the Union army in northern Mississippi would add several days to the time required for the reinforcements to reach their destination. Doing so would also expose the flank of the marching column to the enemy army in northern Mississippi. Nor could such a shift of troop strength be long concealed from the Yankees who, if they did not strike the marching column, could move their own men (in many cases by river) to offset the Rebel troop transfer.

FAR better, Johnston reasoned, to combine Pemberton's army and Rebel troops in Arkansas under one command. Such an arrangement would unite the Confederate forces committed to the defense of the Mississippi Valley. That combination, Johnston believed, would give the Secessionists a much better chance to defeat the Yankees pushing downriver. Those Federals enjoyed a unified command and could, therefore, conduct a coordinated campaign along both sides of the Mississippi. Once the Rebels had defeated the invaders in Mississippi, Johnston thought, the combined Secessionist armies could move to Arkansas and drive the enemy from that state, or they could advance into Tennessee and Kentucky or into Missouri.[42]

Bragg's army, Johnston reasoned, should act in co-operation with Rebel troops in East Tennessee to defend the central part of the Cis-Mississippi Confederacy. The railroad from Chattanooga through Knoxville into Virginia might even enable the Secessionists to conduct some joint operations involving Bragg's army, forces in East Tennessee, and Southern troops in the Old Dominion.

42 Ulysses S. Grant agreed with Johnston about unified command in the Mississippi Valley. On Oct. 26, 1862, he wrote to his own commander, "I would respectfully suggest that both banks of the river be under one command." Three months later he repeated the advice, writing on Jan. 20, 1863, "Both banks of the Mississippi should be under one commander, at least during present operations." President Lincoln agreed and so directed on Jan. 21 (17 *OR*, pt. 2, 297; 24 *OR*, pt. 1, 9). The Unionists, in fact, divided their Mississippi Valley forces, but they did so between those pushing up the river from the Gulf of Mexico and those moving downstream. Those two columns were separated by Pemberton's army and had no speedy means of communicating with each other. The great need for unity of command in the Confederate West was obvious to many. As early as June 20, 1861, Brigadier General Gideon Pillow (of all people) wrote the secretary of war from Memphis, pointing out that having Rebel forces in Arkansas and Tennessee "under the same officer" would enable the Confederates to concentrate against an approaching enemy force and even to advance into Missouri (52 *OR*, pt. 2, 113). On June 23, 1861, Davis assigned Major General Leonidas Polk to command (among other areas) the "river counties" of Arkansas and Mississippi and the "river parishes" of Louisiana north of the Red River (52 *OR*, pt. 2, 115). In September, General A. S. Johnston superceded Polk. As described both earlier and below, the Rebels never managed to overcome six crucial difficulties in the West: a shortage of competent generals, multiple simultaneous Federal offenses, local politics (as expressed in demands for protection), geographical obstacles (especially the rivers), Davis's assumption that he could run the war in the West by telegraphing suggestions to his generals, and his almost utter failure to get his Western generals to act together—or, in many cases, even to act.

ON November 13, only one day after learning of his new assignment, Johnston went to see Secretary of War George W. Randolph to propose such a change in the new Western command. When Johnston presented himself in Randolph's office and began to explain his ideas, the secretary listened politely. As the general spoke, Randolph took out and opened a large letter book. When Johnston paused, Randolph asked him to listen while he read aloud from the papers in his hand.

The secretary first read a copy of an October 27 letter he had written to Lieutenant General Theophilus H. Holmes, commander of Confederate forces in Arkansas. In this letter Randolph had authorized Holmes to cross the Mississippi "when necessary" with "such part of your forces you may select" to aid Pemberton. Randolph then read from a second letter dated November 12—this one to him from President Davis. When he wrote this letter to the secretary, the Chief Executive had just learned of Randolph's October 27 directive to Holmes. The President curtly informed the secretary that, while he hoped that his commanders in the Mississippi Valley would cooperate, share intelligence, and act "conjointly" to defend the area, Holmes himself was not to leave Arkansas.[43]

A few days after this incident Johnston met with Davis. He suggested to the President that Holmes, whom he believed to have 55,000 troops, reinforce Pemberton to oppose the Federals then threatening Vicksburg. Johnston had no more success with the Chief Executive than he had with Randolph. By that time, in fact, Randolph had resigned because of the disrespectful way Davis had treated him.[44]

---

43 J. Davis, *Papers*, vol. 8, 488; Johnston, *Narrative*, 148-149; 13 *OR*, 906-907 and 914-915.

44 13 *OR*, 906 and 914; 20 *OR*, pt. 2, 429; Johnston, *Narrative*, 148-149. The only known record of this Davis-Johnston meeting is a brief mention by Johnston in a Dec. 4, 1862, letter to Wigfall (Wright, *Southern Girl*, 100). Johnston named Generals Samuel Cooper and Gustavus W. Smith as also present at the meeting. He did not mention Randolph as being present—a fact probably indicating that the meeting took place after the secretary's Nov. 15 resignation. If Smith attended in his capacity as interim secretary of war (and there was no other reason for him to have done so), that fact would date the meeting in the Nov. 17-25 period. Davis appointed Randolph's successor, James A. Seddon, on Nov. 20, but the new secretary took several days to arrange his personal affairs and travel to Richmond. Smith acted as secretary of war until he arrived. See Kean, *Diary*, 28-32. Johnston's belief that Holmes commanded 55,000 men was, he wrote (*Narrative*, 148), based on a statement by Cooper who, as Adjutant and Inspector General, handled army administration. Holmes, in fact, had no more than about 18,000 men, most of whom, he wrote, comprised "a crude mass of undisciplined material," many of them unarmed, and others equipped only with shotguns or hunting rifles. Many of his officers, furthermore, were unqualified to hold their commands (13 *OR*, 898-899 and 908).

We know no details about President Davis's response to the general's suggestions. Did Johnston respectfully and fully discuss his concerns about the new Western command structure and offer specific proposals, recommendations, and the reasons behind them? Did he only state briefly that Holmes should reinforce Pemberton and assume that even Davis could see the clear benefits of having him do so? Did Davis patiently explain to his newly designated commander for the West the reasons for the arrangement he had decreed? We shall never know. We do know that it would have been completely out of character for either the President or the general to give a detailed explanation for his ideas and especially of the thinking behind them.

On November 24 Johnston tried again to persuade the government to change its military arrangements in the West. He wrote to Cooper that day urging that Holmes, whose force, Johnston said, "If I have been correctly informed . . . is very much larger than that of the United States" in Arkansas, join Pemberton. The combined armies could then "fall upon Major General [Ulysses S.] Grant." Defeat of Grant's army in northern Mississippi, Johnston asserted, "would enable us to hold the Mississippi [River], and . . . move into Missouri." "As our troops are now

---

Johnston (*Narrative*, 148; "Davis and the Mississippi Campaign," 473) never admitted that he greatly overstated Holmes's strength. His biographer, Craig Symonds, once asserted that the general invented the number of troops he ascribed to Holmes. (Author's notes of Symonds's statement at 2004 Pamplin Historical Park Symposium, Oct. 15, 2004). The misunderstanding about Holmes's numerical strength may well have grown from the complex way that the Confederate Army compiled its numbers. Rebel armies reported their strength in several categories. The number in each was calculated by different criteria and could differ greatly from the total in others. On Mar. 15, 1864, for example, the 8th (Wade's) Confederate Cavalry Regiment reported an "effective strength" of 306, with 404 "present for duty," 434 "aggregate for duty," 434 "aggregate present," 404 "total," 672 "total present and absent," and 717 "aggregate present and absent." Ten of the unit's officers and 56 of its enlisted men were then absent without leave. (Report in "Inspection Reports and Related Records Received by the Transportation Branch in the Confederate Adjutant and Inspector General's Office," National Archives.) See also E. J. Harvie to R. M. Hughes, Nov. 9, 1891, Hughes Papers. We must always keep in mind the fact that Confederate Army administration was slipshod in the extreme. Cooper surely based whatever statement he made on strength returns in his office, which at best would have been those for Nov. 1862. In late 1862 and early 1863, Holmes's command lost some 7,500 men at Prairie Grove and Arkansas Post. My guess is that Cooper mentioned some category—perhaps even what had been reported as total Confederate strength in the Trans-Mississippi—and Johnston either misunderstood or heard what he wanted to hear. Others also misunderstood. The Jackson *Mississippian*, n. d., was quoted in the Mobile *Advertiser and Register* of Dec. 3. 1862, as giving Holmes's strength at 50,000.

distributed," he warned, "Vicksburg is in danger." So far as the record shows, Johnston received no answer to this letter.[45]

DAVIS'S decision not to unite under one command Pemberton's army in Mississippi and Holmes's force in Arkansas owed far more to political factors than to the military considerations that were Johnston's sole concern. By late 1862 chaos threatened to engulf Confederate Arkansas.

In the autumn of 1861 Arkansas's economy and the state's civil society began to disintegrate under the early strains of war. At the same time the state's Secessionist military commanders in its northern regions and in southern Missouri fell into a bitter quarrel. In a belated effort to resolve the matter President Davis, on January 10, 1862, had created the Military District of the Trans-Mississippi and sent Major General Earl Van Dorn from Johnston's army in northern Virginia to command it. Davis hoped that Van Dorn would be able to impose order on the squabbling Confederates in the Arkansas-Missouri area and to hold the region for the Rebels. On March 7-8 Van Dorn's force suffered a stinging defeat at Pea Ridge in northwestern Arkansas.[46]

Soon after the battle, Van Dorn received orders to move his "Army of the West" (then numbering some 22,000 men) across the Mississippi to join the force that Albert Sidney Johnston was assembling at Corinth. Van Dorn's army reached Corinth too late to participate in the Battle of Shiloh, but it did aid in the April-May defense of the rail junction. Van Dorn's command retreated with the Rebel army from Corinth to Tupelo. Later, after Bragg had taken most of the troops at Tupelo off to Chattanooga for the campaign into Kentucky, Van Dorn's men became part of the force left behind to protect Mississippi. By late 1862 Van Dorn's command had become part of Pemberton's army of the Department of Mississippi and East Louisiana (the Army of Vicksburg).

VAN Dorn's spring 1862 departure from the Trans-Mississippi—he took along virtually all of the troops, weapons, ammunition, other military supplies, and government horses in Arkansas—stripped the state (and in so doing Confederate

---

45 20 *OR*, pt. 2, 424. Why Johnston would address this correspondence to Cooper whose responsibilities were purely administrative is not known. He may have done so out of simple frustration or desperation, hoping to get somebody in the administration to think seriously about the situation in the West.

46 Pea Ridge was one of the Western battles in which the Confederates outnumbered their enemies—about 17,000 to 11,000 in this case.

Missouri as well) of the means of defense. In effect, Van Dorn abandoned Arkansas and Missouri to their fate.

Arkansas politicians were soon howling about the plight of their state, and some of them began to hint darkly about possible secession from the Confederacy. Exiled Rebels from Missouri quickly added their voices to the clamor. In response to these protests Rebel authorities dispatched Major General Thomas C. Hindman, a pre-war Arkansas politician, to assume Van Dorn's old post at the head of the Trans-Mississippi District and to rebuild the defenses of Arkansas.

Upon reaching Little Rock in late May, Hindman found Arkansas in a desperate situation. The Union army that had won the battle at Pea Ridge was marching eastward across the northern part of the state, living off the country and plundering and burning both public and private property as it went. Peace societies flourished, especially in northern Arkansas. Local Confederates were resorting to brutality to preserve their grip on the area.

Going to work with a will, Hindman ruthlessly applied the conscription laws, implemented a scorched-earth policy to deny the state's resources to the Yankees, destroyed cotton to keep it out of the hands of the enemy, impressed supplies of all kinds, seized state revenues to pay his soldiers, and even undertook to impose price controls on the civilian economy. He also permitted organization of "partisan ranger" groups and loosed them in a guerrilla war that soon degenerated into what historian Thomas DeBlack has called "a brutal and merciless . . . conflict" characterized by destruction of property, robbery, murder, and personal vendettas.

Hindman's efforts quickly produced a military force that offered some opposition to the invading Yankees, upset what was left of the state's economy, disrupted civil government and society, and set off even more loud protests. All of this soon led to a clamor for a new Confederate commander for the region.

After a few months of the turmoil President Davis sent Holmes to replace Hindman at the head of what the Chief Executive re-designated the Department of the Trans-Mississippi. Hindman found himself commanding a subdivision of the new department, the District of Arkansas, which then included Missouri and the Indian Territory (now Oklahoma). Conditions under Holmes did not improve. By the last months of 1862 smallpox had broken out in some areas of Arkansas and outright starvation threatened people in several parts of the state.[47]

47 Snead, "Conquest of Arkansas"; DeBlack, *Fire and Sword*, 30-31, 57-58, and 73-76; Kean, *Diary*, 38. See also Dougan, *Confederate Arkansas*, 73-74 and 83-102; Johnston, *Narrative*, 147-150; and 13 *OR*, 898-899 and 916.

HOLMES, Johnston believed in late 1862, faced only a small Union force in Arkansas. In urging the government to unite the armies of Holmes and Pemberton into one command to defend the Lower Mississippi Valley, Johnston seems to have assumed that such was Holmes's assigned mission and that most of Arkansas's defending troops were in the Little Rock area. He was wrong on both counts as well as about Rebel strength in Arkansas. Holmes's task was to defend the whole state and, in fact, the entire Trans-Mississippi, although as he confessed, rarely was he able to give attention to areas outside northern Arkansas.[48]

The defense of Arkansas involved more than simply protecting the Mississippi River. Upon reaching Little Rock, Holmes found himself facing two distinct and immediate threats. One, to be sure, was from the Mississippi River along the eastern side of the state. Union gunboats controlled the river as far south as the Arkansas-Louisiana border, indeed, as far south as Vicksburg; the Yankees already had a great base about ninety-five miles east of Little Rock at Helena on the Mississippi which they had occupied in mid-July.

The second great danger to Arkansas loomed up off to the northwest. Federal forces pushing south from Missouri had occupied Fayetteville, about 150 miles from Little Rock, and threatened further penetration of the state. This danger seemed especially serious because Union sentiment ran very high in that region.

Holmes had only about 18,000 men to defend all of Arkansas, not the 55,000 that Johnston believed comprised his force. About half of Holmes's troops were posted to face each of the major dangers to the state. Distance, geography, and the lack of rail and water transportation made it impossible for the Confederates to concentrate against either the threat from Helena or that from Fayetteville. As a result, the Rebels on both Arkansas fronts faced heavy odds and had no realistic hope of getting any reinforcements. The disparity of strength in the Fayetteville area was made even greater by the fact that many of the Confederate troops there were conscripts from pro-Union areas and their chief desire was to go home.

In December 1862, a few days after Johnston assumed his new Tennessee-Mississippi post, the Rebels in northwestern Arkansas, fighting under Hindman's command, suffered a defeat at Prairie Grove some twenty miles south of Fayetteville. Hindman lost about 1,400 men in the engagement which was, commented historian William L. Shea, "another unmitigated disaster" for the Rebels. Many of Hindman's thoroughly demoralized conscripts deserted in the aftermath of the battle. Hundreds of them, in fact, went over to the Yankees.

---

48 22 OR, pt. 2, 797.

In the following March an official in the Rebel War Department noted in his diary, "There are indications that Arkansas is in a state of great irritation and disloyalty. Their delegation in Congress show many indications of dissatisfaction with the Government and complain of neglect of the Trans-Mississippi."

Given the late 1862–early 1863 crisis raging in Arkansas, Davis did not dare weaken Confederate forces there. Only if the state was secure, he thought, should Holmes release any part of his army to aid in the defense of Vicksburg—and Holmes was the only one who, in Davis's judgment, could determine that question.[49]

THE administrative arrangements that Davis imposed on Joseph E. Johnston's new command also proved troublesome and exacerbated the bitter feelings between the general in the field and the government in Richmond.

Prior to his April 1862 death at Shiloh, Albert Sidney Johnston commanded "Department Number Two" (also known as the Western Department). At one time or another that vast area had included all Confederate forces between the Appalachian Mountains and the western boundary of the Indian Territory except the troops along the Gulf Coast. In late June, after Bragg had taken command, Richmond officials lopped off the Trans-Mississippi part of Johnston's old department and added the Gulf Coast (by then, for all practical purposes, limited to Mobile). President Davis himself instructed Bragg on June 20 to "correspond directly with and to receive orders and instructions from the Government in relation to your future operations."[50]

That summer, when Bragg took most of his troops off to Chattanooga and then on into Kentucky, he left Major Generals Earl Van Dorn and Sterling Price in charge of the Rebels remaining in Mississippi. Those two worthies, with Van Dorn commanding by virtue of seniority when their forces were united, were, under Bragg's plan, to push into the northern part of the state and, if possible, on into Tennessee to support the Rebel campaign in Kentucky. Van Dorn and Price soon fell to arguing and botched battles at Iuka and Corinth in mid-September and early October. Bragg, by then in central Kentucky, was distant from and out of

49 See Snead, "Conquest of Arkansas"; Kean, *Diary*, 45; 22 OR, pt. 2, 799; Shea, *Fields of Blood*, especially chapter 1.

50 17 OR, pt. 2, 614 and 624. "Department Number One" comprised Louisiana. After the fall of New Orleans in late April 1862, Rebel authorities placed the part of the Pelican State east of the Mississippi River into Bragg's truncated "Department Number Two." As late as July 22, 1862, Bragg remained uncertain as to what areas were in his command (ibid., 652-656).

communication with his subordinates, did not know their situation, and could not give them orders.

News of the fall 1862 situation in Mississippi came to the attention of President Davis and Secretary of War Randolph. The two civilian leaders, however, realized that they faced a major problem in trying to deal with the Rebels' predicament in the Magnolia State. "I feel some hesitation in giving directions which might conflict with . . . [Bragg's] plans," wrote Randolph on September 9. Ten days later Davis informed Bragg, "I am at a loss to know how to remedy evils without damaging your plans. If . . . [the Confederate commanders in Mississippi] each act for himself disaster to all must be the probable result."[51]

By the end of the month Davis thought he had the solution to the problem. John C. Pemberton, who had become very unpopular at his post in South Carolina, would take command of all Rebel forces in Mississippi, southwestern Tennessee, and East Louisiana. "Until further orders," Randolph instructed Pemberton on September 30, "you will report directly to this [the War] Department." Pemberton's area of responsibility, however, remained a part of Bragg's department, and Pemberton would, therefore, be under Bragg's command. When Joseph E. Johnston assumed overall command of the Western Confederates, these directions to Bragg and Pemberton were not revoked or modified.[52]

Over the next several months Pemberton, especially, would continue to deal directly with the government. This situation made it inevitable that Johnston, as the new Western theater commander, would sometimes lack information about what was happening on one or both of the major fronts of the vast department that, in theory, he commanded. Even worse, it made it inevitable that a subordinate commander would sometimes receive orders (or suggestions carrying the weight of orders, or comments that he understood to be orders) from Richmond that ran contrary to whatever plans Johnston may have made or to whatever orders he had issued. What, for example, should Pemberton do if Johnston ordered him to do one thing and Davis, quite probably without consulting or even informing

51 17 *OR*, pt. 2, 697-698, 707, 716-717, and 752. As will be seen below, awareness of the problems that could result from giving such orders did not always keep Davis from doing so. In fairness to Davis, however, we should note that on more than one occasion what he intended as a comment, or a suggestion, was taken by a field commander as an order.

52 Ibid., 717-718, 726-727, 737, and 752. Govan and Livingood (*Different Valor*, 164) believe that the authorities did not inform Johnston about this arrangement when they assigned him to the West. See also Ballard, *Pemberton*, 115 and 118.

Johnston, directed him to do something else—or, as events turned out, Pemberton thought Davis had directed him to do something else?[53]

WHAT Johnston correctly saw as the ambiguous nature of his status would also prove a major source of annoyance, embarrassment, frustration, and worry over the coming months. It, too, would help widen the gulf between Davis and Johnston. Commanding an army Johnston could understand. Leading troops in the field was an undertaking to which he was accustomed. Participation in a battle was something he had done on several occasions in Florida, Mexico, and Virginia. But what was he to do in the new situation into which Davis sent him in the late fall of 1862?

The President envisioned Johnston at departmental headquarters, shifting troops back and forth between Tennessee and Mississippi as the situation at one point or the other dictated. In effect, Johnston was to allocate the Western Department's manpower and other resources to meet whatever situation arose. Was he also to direct the operations of individual armies in specific local situations? After all, his orders also read the general "will repair in person to any part of said command whenever his presence may for the time be necessary or desirable."[54]

What, Johnston wondered, was he to do when he "repaired" to the army of Bragg or Pemberton? Whenever he showed up there would be two generals at the army's headquarters. That, Johnston firmly and correctly believed, would be one too many. If he arrived on the eve of battle, should he assume command? Doing so might well humiliate Bragg or Pemberton. Even worse, as Johnston saw the matter, if he took command he would find himself in a situation in which he had had no control over the army's pre-battle organization, its logistical and administrative arrangements, or its maneuvers in the days or weeks prior to his arrival. In such a situation he would have to fight a battle in circumstances not of his own making or choosing and with—at best—but limited knowledge of the army he temporarily commanded, the area, and the enemy force in his front. When should Bragg or Pemberton resume command? Victory under such circumstances would be very unlikely.

---

53 See Ballard, *Pemberton*, 135 and 143. Former Vicksburg National Military Park historian Terrence Winschel ("Tragedy of Errors," 40) maintains that this version of divided command became a "principle [sic] cause" of the Confederate failure at Vicksburg.

54 24 *OR*, pt. 2, 213.

Even should Johnston choose to act only in an advisory capacity while with one of the armies, his very presence would create problems and imply that the local commander was incapable of acting on his own. Would any advice Johnston might offer be, in fact, an order? Would his presence inhibit Bragg or Pemberton and cause him to direct the battle with one eye over his shoulder to watch Johnston? Would Bragg or Pemberton resent Johnston's presence? Would Johnston bear responsibility if the army he advised but did not command suffered a defeat?

Bragg's army was Bragg's; Pemberton's army was Pemberton's. In Johnston's mind there was no real service that he could perform in his new post except, perhaps, that of an inspector when he was with one of the armies or to get a rifle and fight in the ranks. The latter obviously would hardly be an appropriate undertaking for any officer, let alone for the Confederacy's third highest-ranking general. The President's directive simply was not clear as to Johnston's function, and, of course, Johnston never did much to try to clarify the matter.[55]

DAVIS seems to have thought of his generals and military units as interchangeable parts. They could be rushed from one point to another, incorporated at once into an existing force upon arrival at their destination, immediately sent into battle as part of that force, and then just as quickly be pulled away and sent some place else or returned to their original duty station.

This practice might sometimes work in the short run—if the reinforcements arrived just before or even during a battle such as First Manassas (July 1861) and Chickamauga (September 1863), when the new units could immediately be thrown into combat. Over even a few days, however, such large scale shifting about of military forces would necessitate major changes (disruptions) in the Rebels' administrative and logistical systems. Officers and men would have to adjust both professionally and personally to a new army commander and his practices. Arriving commanders would have to learn details of the terrain in their new area of operations.

This scheme almost dictated that the Rebels would have to launch an immediate attack whether the situation was favorable or not. Delay would severely strain the reinforced army's supply system and give the Yankees time to bring

---

55 See Johnston's Dec. 27, 1862; Feb 14, Mar. 4, and Mar 9, 1863, letters to Wigfall, quoted in Vandiver, "Davis and Unified Army Command," 31-32.

reinforcements of their own to the area—and those additional Federal troops were quite likely to outnumber the newly arrived Confederates.[56]

Proactive officers of good will who had confidence in themselves, who respected and trusted each other, and who enjoyed the support of their government, their subordinates, and their troops might have been able to make something of the system, or at least to have rendered it less unsatisfactory. Conversely, a commander who proved ruthless in insisting that his orders were orders that had to be obeyed might have salvaged something from the arrangement. As will be seen below, none of these conditions existed in the Confederate West in late 1862 and early 1863—or early 1864 for that matter.[57]

Davis's concept of Johnston's position was highly impracticable at best, and simply impossible at worst. Equally serious, the arrangement offended Joseph E. Johnston's rigid but hyper-delicate sense of military propriety and decorum.

WHY would Davis devise and maintain—in the face of experience, common sense, and Johnston's constant complaints—such obviously flawed administrative and command arrangements? Or, if he insisted on the arrangements, why did he keep Johnston in command?

The clear possibility of politically losing a state by its secession from the Confederacy (not just its occupation by enemy forces) and the political crisis that such a development might well engender explain, if they do not justify, the President's concern for Arkansas and Missouri. This concern also accounts for his unwillingness to place Holmes and Pemberton under one command and to commit the forces of the former to aid in the defense of Vicksburg rather than facing the Yankee threat to northern Arkansas. What assurances could Davis give frightened and angry Trans-Mississippi governors and members of Congress that any of Holmes's men who left Arkansas would get back to help defend the region west of the great river? How would pro-Confederate Missouri politicians, generals,

---

56 See McWhiney, "Davis and the Art of War." Davis greatly admired Zachary Taylor, his first father-in-law, who, as Davis wrote in October 1864, "paused for no regular approaches, but . . . dashed with sword and bayonet on the foe" (quoted ibid., 108-109). This simplistic view almost certainly grew from Davis's own military experience at a very low level of the command structure of an army.

57 General George C. Marshall once observed that the scope of an office can "come not only from written mandates but [also] from what the occupant could make of it." See Parrish, *Roosevelt and Marshall*, 80 and 139. On Johnston's views see his Mar. 8, 1863, letter to Wigfall quoted in Vandiver, "Davis and Unified Command," 32-33.

and common soldiers react to the withdrawal of Rebel troops from northern Arkansas? Would such a withdrawal mean abandonment of all Confederate concern for their State?

Van Dorn, after all, had taken thousands of Arkansas and Missouri troops across the Mississippi early in 1862, and they had not returned. For the rest of the war those soldiers were anxious to get back to protect their Trans-Mississippi homes and to establish Confederate control of Missouri. They and their political and military spokesmen often petitioned the Rebel government to that effect. Other than men on furlough or sent home as disabled or on recruiting duty, none of those troops re-crossed the Mississippi until survivors of Van Dorn's Army of the West straggled home at the war's end.[58]

Under late 1862 circumstances using Holmes's army to help defend Vicksburg could well have involved far more than the permanent loss of Missouri and the (possibly permanent) Yankee occupation of Arkansas. It could well have led to the actual withdrawal of one or both states from the Confederacy. Such an event would have created a great political and probably diplomatic crisis for the Confederacy as well as leading to the mass defection to the enemy of Missouri's and Arkansas's suffering civilian populations.

The Union forces that might well overrun Arkansas in such an event would then be poised to mount a new offensive into northern Louisiana. While logistically a very difficult undertaking, a campaign into the Pelican State from the north could have carried the Yankees to the Red River at Shreveport or Alexandria and outflanked Vicksburg and Port Hudson even if the Rebels managed to maintain possession of those two river fortresses. The Red River was, after all, the only important line of communication between the Cis-Mississippi Confederacy and the Trans-Mississippi part of Rebeldom. A Federal presence at any point on that river would have severed the line of communications that holding Vicksburg and Port Hudson was meant to protect. (In 1864 such a thrust from Arkansas into Louisiana

---

58 See, for examples, 17 *OR*, pt. 2, 759-761 and 794-796; and J. Davis, *Papers*, vol. 9, 74-76. This situation also raised the question of whether Trans-Mississippi troops would have been willing to serve east of the Mississippi River in 1863. As the war went on and early enthusiasm waned, more and more of them became increasingly unwilling to leave their home area. Eventually their commanders came to fear massive desertion if they ordered such a transfer. We simply do not know to what extent that feeling had developed by the first half of 1863. So far as I know, no one communicated such fears to Davis or other high-ranking Rebels in the Cis-Mississippi Confederacy. The chimera of vast bodies of Secessionist troops swarming out of the Trans-Mississippi to reinforce Rebel armies in Mississippi, Tennessee, or Georgia remained an element in Confederate military thought (fantasy?) for the rest of the war.

was part of the Yankees' unsuccessful Red River Campaign.) In this sense Davis could well have argued—but did not, even if he understood the matter in these terms—that the defense of Arkansas constituted a crucial part of the Rebel effort to hold together the eastern and western halves of the Confederacy.

THE president's practice of having (or continuing to have) Bragg and Pemberton communicate directly with Richmond is less clear-cut. In part it almost certainly resulted from precedent and sheer bureaucratic inertia. In late 1862, in all probability, nobody in Richmond thought to revoke or modify the permission—indeed, orders—that had been given to Bragg in June and later to Pemberton to communicate directly with the government.

Randolph's mid-November departure from the War Department removed from the capital the official who had been most deeply involved with the defense of the Mississippi Valley and with the practice of allowing direct communication between subordinate Western commanders and the government. It may well have been that Randolph's successors (Gustavus W. Smith on an interim basis for a week or so and then James A. Seddon) simply remained unaware of the special status that the government officially had conferred upon such communications while Bragg was in Kentucky and out of touch with his distant subordinates.

Doubtless Davis's earlier practices also played a role in creating this faulty administrative system. In April 1862, when Johnston had taken his army to Yorktown, Davis had given him temporary authority over several previously independent forces in southeastern Virginia. "The commanders of the departments [of Norfolk and of the Peninsula] and navy-yards while conforming to his [Johnston's] instructions will make their reports and requisitions, as heretofore, to the proper departments [of the War Department] in Richmond," reads the President's directive.[59]

Military developments soon rendered this arrangement irrelevant. Had it remained in effect for long, it certainly would have created great confusion and numerous administrative problems. Without the regular reports and requisitions from his subordinate units, Johnston would have lacked complete and crucial knowledge of the force he commanded.

In October of 1862, Davis created a similar but even more bizarre and confused (and confusing) command arrangement. Special Orders 255 announced that "With a view to combined operations, the command of General Bragg will

---

59 12 OR, pt. 3, 846.

embrace such portions of the troops belonging to the Department of East Tennessee as circumstances may render necessary and for such time as the exigency of the operation may determine." Adjutant and Inspector General Cooper explained to Bragg that under the order he had the "authority to draw such portions of the troops from the Department of East Tennessee as may be disposable." Then, Cooper added, "The experience of Lieutenant-General [E. K.] Smith [commanding the Department of East Tennessee] will probably enable him to determine the number required" to protect the vital East Tennessee & Virginia Railroad and Cumberland Gap. The number of troops that Smith "probably" determined could not be withdrawn from their posts to join Bragg. In effect the order put Smith under Bragg's command but gave him a veto over orders from his commander.

Special Orders 255 created an arrangement that looked good on a bureaucratic organizational chart. It was probably worded to allow as much flexibility to the generals as possible. It was based on Davis's longstanding assumptions that Confederate generals would always willingly put the Cause ahead of their own concerns, agree in interpreting intelligence reports, and cooperate.

The arrangement, however, was fundamentally flawed. A few days after receiving the order Bragg protested the new command structure. In so doing, he pointed out a basic weakness in Davis's management of the war. The "great importance of unity and promptness in military duty," he wrote, made this new arrangement highly questionable. "I submit," Bragg went on, "whether movements involving so much should be left to the uncertainty of two officers agreeing in their views, however much the Government may confide in them or they in each other."[60]

The Richmond officials (i. e. President Davis) seem never to have realized that a structure whereby a force was subject to a commander's authority for some purposes but not for others, and in which the subordinate had the authority to decide whether to obey or not, was an arrangement certain to create massive problems, especially under stressful conditions. Such a result would be even more likely and the resulting damage more massive when the individual commanders and

---

60 20 *OR*, pt. 2, 384-385. Bragg might have added, but did not, that E. Kirby Smith had joined the cabal among the Rebel generals then opposing Bragg and seeking to bring about his removal from command. Perhaps Bragg intended to hint at the fact and hoped that Richmond would get the message. See Part I of Chapter Four, in Book Three, Volume II.

the government officials did not trust one another and would not communicate fully.[61]

THEN, too, Davis also believed that sometimes decisions had to be made too rapidly to allow for the normal rules of military correspondence flowing through the proper channels.

This observation, of course, leads to the never-asked and never-answered question: If decisions were to be made in Richmond, why did Davis bother with installing Johnston at a "command" level between the Western field armies and the government in the capital? Perchance to get him out of the capital and away from his political allies? Maybe because he had to be put somewhere to appease his Congressional supporters? With Lee firmly in command in Virginia, Johnston could not return to the post he had held prior to his May 1862 wounding. Outside the Old Dominion there were only three possible assignments for a general of Johnston's status: the West, the Trans-Mississippi, and the Atlantic Coast. Beauregard held the last post, and his great engineering skill was most useful in the work of defending port cities like Charleston. Sending Johnston to the Trans-Mississippi would probably have been viewed by Johnston and his friends as exile (and would have been). That left only the Western Department. Perhaps Johnston, removed from close contact with Richmond politicians, might do some good there.[62]

IN part Davis's system of organization, administration, and command must certainly have evolved from the President's longstanding convictions that he alone had to give general direction to the entire war effort, that he could always count on all of his generals to see and interpret intelligence reports in the same way, and that they would all always cheerfully cooperate. The President may also have had some (unknown and unknowable) psychological need to keep all aspects of Rebel military activity under his own eye—even as he usually refused to make crucial decisions and only gave suggestions to his commanders as he pleaded with them to do this or that.

---

61 In August of 1863, the War Department decided that the Department of East Tennessee would be "merged" with Bragg's Department of Tennessee "only for strategic purposes" and would remain "entirely disconnected in administration." Not surprisingly, this situation led to confusion and controversy. See 31 *OR*, pt. 3, 650-668.

62 See Davis's June 17 and July 15 explanations in 24 *OR*, pt. 1, 196 and 203.

BEYOND these factors, however, and to the extent that it was a conscious choice, the Chief Executive's decision to maintain direct communication between Richmond and each of the Western field armies probably stemmed partly from Davis's frustrating experiences dealing with Johnston in Virginia in 1861 and 1862. Could the President depend on Johnston to keep him informed about the situation in Tennessee and Mississippi? Would Johnston carry out the government's policies any better in the West than he had done a year earlier in Virginia—especially in the matter of forming state brigades? Davis, Johnston, and the Confederacy were about to pay a very high price for the lack of trust that the President and the general had chosen (Covey again) to allow to grow up between them.

FINALLY, I find it impossible to avoid the conclusion (but can cite no sources to support my belief) that Davis at least sensed by the winter of 1862-1863 how massive and serious the problems in the West had become, and that he simply did not want to (could not?) face up to them.

As he was soon to demonstrate during a late 1862 whirlwind visit to Tennessee and Mississippi (see following chapters), Davis found it far more congenial to give some (usually vague) instructions (suggestions?) about the messy situation west of the Appalachians, leave his commanders there to sort it all out as best they could (or would), submerge himself in the administrative minutiae of the War Department, and focus his attention on events in Virginia where the Rebels' prospects appeared much brighter and his generals much more cooperative. The West was too complex. The region presented too many formidable problems. With Albert Sidney Johnston in his grave in New Orleans, the President had no one in the West upon whom he felt he could rely. Manifestations of this subconscious attitude would surface in the months after Davis assigned Joseph E. Johnston to the Western command—to the post once held by Sidney Johnston.[63]

ON November 29 Johnston—harboring great doubts about the wisdom and viability of Davis's new Western command structure and at least beginning to suspect that the Davis government had no intention of treating him fairly, indeed,

---

63 Sidney Johnston's body was removed to Austin, Texas, after the war. Historian Michael Ballard (*Pemberton*, 88) writes of Davis responding to one disagreement between two of his generals "as if no problem existed." Almost certainly the Chief Executive believed that none did. In Nov. 1863, a Rebel general was to write of "the harmony and kind feeling which the President desires" in the army (31 *OR*, pt. 3, 668).

that it had determined to destroy his reputation and drive him from the service in disgrace—boarded a train in Richmond and left for Tennessee.

Back in the capital President Davis knew that the general to whom he had entrusted command of the vital central part of the Confederacy disagreed with the whole concept upon which the Chief Executive based his plan to defend that region and favored an entirely different strategic arrangement from that which the President had sent him to implement.

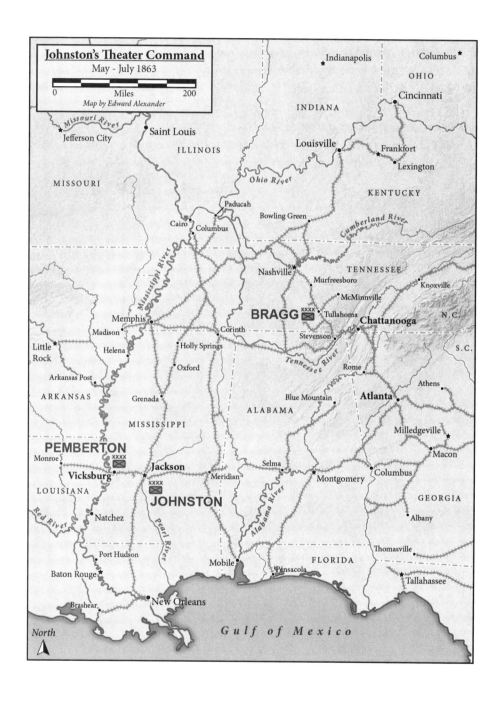

Johnston's Theater Command
May - July 1863

0   Miles   200
Map by Edward Alexander

Missouri River

Jefferson City

Saint Louis

ILLINOIS

MISSOURI

Indianapolis

Columbus

OHIO

Cincinnati

Louisville

Frankfort

Lexington

Ohio River

KENTUCKY

Paducah

Bowling Green

Cumberland River

Cairo

Columbus

Mississippi River

Nashville

Murfreesboro

McMinnville

Knoxville

TENNESSEE

Memphis

Madison

Corinth

BRAGG
XXXX

Tullahoma

Chattanooga

N.C.

Holly Springs

Stevenson

Tennessee River

S.C.

Little
Rock

Helena

Oxford

Rome

Arkansas Post

ARKANSAS

Grenada

Blue Mountain

ALABAMA

Athens

Atlanta

MISSISSIPPI

Milledgeville

Macon

PEMBERTON
Monroe
XXXX

Selma

Columbus

GEORGIA

Vicksburg

Jackson
XXXX

Meridian

Montgomery

LOUISIANA

Alabama River

JOHNSTON

Albany

Red River

Natchez

Pearl River

Thomasville

Port Hudson

Mobile

FLORIDA

Baton Rouge

Pensacola

Tallahassee

Brashear

New Orleans

North

Gulf of Mexico

Chapter Three

Visits to Two Fronts

"Nobody ever assumed a command under more unfavorable circumstances."
— Joseph E. Johnston, December 4, 1862

Joseph E. Johnston's late 1862 rail journey took him west from Richmond, through Lynchburg, Bristol (on the Virginia-Tennessee border), and Knoxville. The general's party included his wife Lydia, the Wigfalls, who left the train at Amelia Springs two or three hours (about sixty miles) out of Richmond, and what Charlotte Wigfall called "quite a numerous staff"—altogether some ten or twelve people.

Civil War historians would give much to know what Johnston and Wigfall discussed in the days prior to and during the trip. Did the Texas senator warn his friend about possible criticisms he might receive from President Davis? Within a few months Wigfall was advising Johnston to keep careful records to protect himself against the machinations of the Davis Administration. By the end of the year Lydia Johnston was complaining that the government was treating her husband "shabbily." Indeed, as early as November she had told the general that Davis "hates you & he has power & he will ruin you."[1]

Three railroad accidents delayed the travelers—experiences that could only have confirmed and strengthened Johnston's already serious reservations about the capability of the Confederate transportation system to move large numbers of troops rapidly from one point to another. The weary Johnstons and their fellow travelers did not reach Chattanooga until shortly after midnight December 3-4. "A

---

1 20 OR, pt. 2, 436; Wright, *Southern Girl*, 98; King, *Wigfall*, 172; Symonds, *Johnston*, 192-193, 220-221 (quoting Mrs. Johnston in an Aug. 2, 1863, letter recounting earlier events), and 226 (quoting Wigfall). Four members of Johnston's staff are listed in SO 275, Nov. 24, 1862. Others joined later.

perilous journey," Johnston called the trip in a letter he wrote to Wigfall later on the fourth.[2]

Some time that day, probably about 12:00 M., a street crowd gathered outside the Johnstons' hotel and called for the general to come out and speak. When Johnston finally appeared (and one suspects he was not very happy at the interruption), he bluntly told his listeners that he "would much prefer to see them in the army"—a statement that may well have shut them up and dispersed the crowd. That day, too, he formally assumed his new position.[3]

JOHNSTON'S new command embraced a vast area. As announced in Special Orders No. 275, issued by the War Department on November 24, its boundary began at the Blue Ridge Mountains in western North Carolina, ran southward along those mountains, and then across northern Georgia to the Western & Atlantic Railroad that connected Chattanooga and Atlanta—a rail route with which Johnston was to become very familiar. The boundary then followed the railroads through Atlanta and southwest to West Point, Georgia, on the Chattahoochee River—the state's border with Alabama. From West Point the line continued down the right bank of the Chattahoochee to the Alabama-Florida border, thence westward along that line to the Choctawhatchee River, and down that stream to Choctawhatchee Bay (near present day Fort Walton Beach) and the Gulf of Mexico.

Johnston commanded all the area between that line and the Mississippi River. Special Orders No. 275 did not specify a northern boundary for the department. That, Confederate authorities probably would have said had anyone asked, would be as far north as Rebel armies could put it.[4]

---

2 Wright, *Southern Girl*, 98-99; Johnston, *Narrative*, 150. The Richmond *Examiner*, Dec. 2, 1862, reported that Johnston had been "taken ill" during the trip and had to see a physician. I have found no other report of such an illness, but the general was in bad health throughout the next several months. Mrs. Johnston wrote Mrs. Wigfall on Dec. 12, 1862 (letter in Wigfall Papers) that her husband "has been very unwell Ever Since we came here, & has spent several days in bed." A few days after Johnston's trip from Richmond to Chattanooga, President Davis made the same journey in only two days. This may indicate that Johnston's illness forced him to spend a day or so *en route* in Bristol or some other town. A short time later Campbell Brown, traveling to join Johnston's staff, was in a train wreck near Bristol (*Brown's Civil War*, 177-178).

3 Macon *Daily Telegraph*, Jan. 6, 1863; 17 *OR*, pt. 2, 4; 20 *OR*, pt. 2, 4; 20 *OR*, pt. 1, 2; 20 *OR*, pt. 2, 430.

4 On Nov. 29, 1862, Atlanta was specifically included in Johnston's department. 17 *OR*, pt. 2, 782; 20 *OR*, pt. 2, 423-424 and 432. Except for some officers and men on duty in such

ONE of the major forces in Johnston's department was Braxton Bragg's 55,000-man Army of Tennessee, then posted about Murfreesboro some 110 miles northwest of Chattanooga and only about thirty miles from a large Union force based in Nashville. At the time Johnston assumed his new post, all seemed quiet on Bragg's front.[5]

The other large force in the department was Pemberton's army in Mississippi. In late November, as Johnston prepared to begin his trip from Richmond, Pemberton faced a threat from the north. A Federal army of about 45,000 men commanded by Major General Ulysses S. Grant was advancing southward along the Mississippi Central Railroad toward the state capital. To meet this danger Pemberton had posted 22,000 of his 34,000 troops along the Tallahatchie River in northern Mississippi.

A few days before Johnston reached Chattanooga, Pemberton learned that another Federal force had come down the Mississippi River and landed at Friar's Point and Delta in the northwestern part of the state. From those places the force threatened the left flank of the Tallahatchie line. To deal with this new danger and to block the Yankee advance from the north, Pemberton, even as Johnston traveled toward Chattanooga, was shifting his force to a new line centered at Grenada on the Yalobusha River. In that position, his left could not be turned. The remainder of Pemberton's force was scattered about, most of it in the garrisons of Vicksburg (about 6,000) and that of Port Hudson, Louisiana (about 5,500).

In early December, even as he faced the two enemy columns moving against his Yalobusha line, Pemberton learned of two more Yankee threats to his command. A Union force under Major General William T. Sherman was reported to be descending the Mississippi to make a direct attack on Vicksburg. At the same time, Major General Nathaniel P. Banks with another Federal column was pushing upriver from New Orleans and Baton Rouge, threatening Port Hudson on the Mississippi just below the Mississippi-Louisiana border.[6]

---

specialized assignments as hospitals, the Ordnance Bureau (munitions), the Subsistence Department (food), and the Quartermaster office (other supplies, pay, and transportation), Johnston commanded all Confederate troops in his area of responsibility.

5 The strength numbers for Bragg's army for this period vary from date to date as men arrived from East Tennessee after the failed campaign in Kentucky. The figure in the text is that of Dec. 10, 1862. See 20 OR, pt. 2, 385, 412-413, 433, and 446.

6 17 OR, pt. 2, 786; 20 OR, pt. 2, 440-441.

Johnston's command area also included about 10,000 men in East Tennessee under Lieutenant General E. Kirby Smith and a 3,000-man garrison at Mobile commanded by Major General Simon B. Buckner. A few other units—mostly cavalry scattered about the department—completed the roster of Johnston's soldiers.

VICKSBURG and Port Hudson (about 250 miles apart by water; some 150 in a straight line) marked the upper and lower boundaries of the Confederate-held section of the Mississippi River. Both towns stood on high bluffs on the river's left bank at points where the Mississippi made a sharp bend. Both enjoyed a rail connection with the rest of the Cis-Mississippi half of Rebeldom (although a gap of about thirty miles separated the inland terminus of the Clinton & Port Hudson Railroad from another rail line).

The east-west corridor anchored by Vicksburg and Port Hudson remained in Confederate hands and was, after the early summer of 1862, the Rebels' only significant route of communication between the halves of their country. The Red River was the only major route out of the Indian Territory, Texas, southwestern Arkansas, and western Louisiana still open to the Secessionists. This stream formed the boundary between Texas and the Indian Territory, cut across the southwestern corner of Arkansas, and then almost bisected Louisiana before emptying into the Mississippi a few miles above Port Hudson. Several tributaries flowed out of Arkansas and Louisiana into the Red. Not all these waterways were navigable all year—and some of them not at all—but collectively they formed an important communication and transportation network.

The only important railroad from the west to the Mississippi was the Vicksburg, Shreveport & Texas. This line stretched eastward for about seventy-five miles from its terminus at Monroe, Louisiana, on the Ouachita River to De Soto Point on the Mississippi opposite Vicksburg. By the late summer of 1862, however, the VS&T operated only over the western half of its line from Monroe to Delhi on Bayou Macon. (Floods and Union raiders had wrecked the line between Delhi and De Soto Point.) The rail line, therefore, could not be used by the Rebels except to move goods west to Monroe whence they could go by boat down the Red River and on to the Mississippi.[7]

Any significant Union force permanently in or along the Red River or in or along the Mississippi between Vicksburg and Port Hudson would sever the

---

7 Estaville, *Confederate Neckties*, 66 and 69.

connection between the halves of Rebeldom. A single Yankee gunboat stationed in the mouth of the Red River, for example, would cut the Confederacy in half and render both Vicksburg and Port Hudson useless to the Secessionists.

In summary, to maintain meaningful communication between the Trans-Mississippi and the Cis-Mississippi parts of the Confederacy, the Rebels had to hold both Vicksburg and Port Hudson and to use the guns on the bluffs at those fortresses to close the river between them to Union vessels. If this were not done, commented the Vicksburg *Whig*, "the river will, while the Federal boats remain in it, be of no use whatever to us. We will hold Vicksburg, but will be unable to control any portion of the river except that fronting the city."[8]

Early in 1863, however, the Federals discovered that their vessels could usually run by the shore batteries at Vicksburg and Port Hudson with little damage. The Yankees' problem was to remain in the section of the river between the two Rebel-held fortified points. Food and water the Federals could procure by sending men ashore to raid local farms, plantations, and towns. Ammunition, however, could not be obtained from those sources, nor could coal, although locally acquired wood could be used temporarily as a substitute fuel for the steam-powered boats. Of course, Confederate troops along the river banks could harass and perhaps capture small parties sent ashore from the boats.

As the commanding general charged with the defense of the vast Western department Johnston faced a daunting task and had only very limited resources with which to try to accomplish it. Always something of a pessimist, he lamented to his friend Wigfall on the day he reached Chattanooga, "Nobody ever assumed a command under more unfortunate circumstances."[9]

BACK in late October, soon after he had taken charge of the Rebel forces in Mississippi, Pemberton had asked the War Department to send some of Theophilus Holmes's troops from Arkansas to aid in the defense of Vicksburg. On November 19, one week after Johnston had informed the department that he could return to duty and ten days before he left Richmond for the West, Adjutant and Inspector General Samuel Cooper had queried Holmes, "*Can* you send troops

---

8 In addition to Estaville's *Confederate Neckties*, see the long item regarding the Vicksburg-Port Hudson corridor in the New Orleans *National Advocate*, Aug. 25, 1862 (reprinted from the Vicksburg *Whig*, n. d., but probably of Aug. 9). See also the comment by Mississippi governor John J. Pettus in 52 *OR*, pt. 2, 368.

9 Wright, *Southern Girl*, 100. See Johnston's quite similar comments during the winter of 1861-1862 concerning his situation in Virginia (Book One, Chapter Four).

from your command—say 10,000—to operate either opposite to Vicksburg or to cross the river [emphasis added]?" That same day Cooper telegraphed Bragg "Pemberton is under your command," and added that he had asked Holmes to send 10,000 men to reinforce Vicksburg *if* he could spare them from the defense of Arkansas. Cooper then dispatched a third telegram, this one to Pemberton: "Holmes has been *ordered* to send 10,000 men to Vicksburg." Three days later a joyful Pemberton informed one of his subordinates, "I am promised 10,000 men from him [Holmes]."[10]

On the day that Pemberton sent to his subordinate the happy news of the 10,000 reinforcements then supposedly en route from Arkansas to Vicksburg, Holmes, in Little Rock, dispatched a message of his own. "I could not get to Vicksburg in less than two weeks," he informed Cooper. "There is nothing to subsist on between here and there [Vicksburg] and the [Union] army at Helena would come to Little Rock before I reached Vicksburg."

By November 27 (with Johnston still in Richmond) Pemberton had learned that Holmes was objecting to sending any of his troops out of Arkansas; Pemberton asked Cooper to reiterate the order to the Trans-Mississippi commander. Two days later, as Johnston left the capital for Chattanooga, Cooper wired Holmes, "Send to Vicksburg without delay the infantry force which you have been twice telegraphed for."

Four days later, after conferring with Davis, Cooper telegraphed a message to Chattanooga to await Johnston, whose train was then rolling through the upper East Tennessee River Valley. "Holmes," Cooper informed the new commander of the West, "has been *peremptorily ordered* to re-enforce him [Pemberton], but his troops may arrive too late [my emphasis]." In the emergency then threatening Mississippi, Cooper concluded, the President urged Johnston to transfer some troops from Bragg's army in Tennessee to help Pemberton in Mississippi.[11]

---

10 Cooper had first made such an inquiry on Nov. 11, 1862 (the day before Johnston had reported his availability for duty) when he informed General Holmes that President Davis said "that if the state of your command will enable you to do so, he thinks it advisable that you should throw re-enforcements, say to the extent of 10,000 men across the river at Vicksburg to aid General Pemberton" for temporary service. "In the meantime, you will not fail to perceive," Cooper added, "that in maintaining the connection of your department with the East it will be rendering you a service than which none can be more important" (13 OR, 914). Note that Davis left the decision up to Holmes.

11 13 OR, 921 and 926; 17 OR, pt. 2, 752-753, 757, 762-763, and 777; 20 OR, pt. 2, 435; Johnston, *Narrative*, 150.

THUS, in early December when he arrived in Chattanooga, Johnston found himself tossed into the rapidly escalating command chaos and confusion that characterized the Confederate war effort in the West all through the conflict.

On the morning of December 4, doubtless after snatching a few hours' sleep, Johnston informed Cooper by letter that Pemberton's recent withdrawal from the Tallahatchie to the Yalobusha had increased the distance between the Confederate force in Tennessee and that in Mississippi while it had shortened the distance between the Rebels in Mississippi and those in Arkansas. (Johnston was then thinking of the overland route between the armies of Bragg and Pemberton.) Since Holmes had been "peremptorily ordered" to send troops to Vicksburg, Johnston pointed out, he could reinforce Pemberton much more quickly than could Bragg. To emphasize his point, Johnston also telegraphed Cooper to the same effect, adding that he would go to Bragg's Murfreesboro headquarters on the following day.[12]

JOHNSTON arrived at the Chattanooga railroad station early in the morning of December 5. He and some of his staff boarded "an elegant car" provided for the general by E. W. Cole, superintendent of the Nashville & Chattanooga Railroad. "A cold, chilling rain" fell as the train got underway at seven o'clock. The car, however, was warm, "kept comfortable by a good fire," noted a reporter who accompanied the party. "The stove," he added, "made it quite pleasant within." Perhaps Johnston nodded off and caught up on his sleep.

The train crawled downriver, ran around the northern end of Lookout Mountain, crossed Will's Valley, and dipped into the northwestern corner of Georgia to labor up the five-mile grade to the 300-foot tunnel through the top of Raccoon Mountain. Descending into the valley of the Tennessee River, the train continued southwest into Alabama for several miles and then crossed the 750-foot bridge over the left channel of the river to Long Island (now Bridgeport Island). After puffing across the island the train came to a stop. The bridge from the island to the river's right bank was out, wrecked by the Confederates the previous summer in the aftermath of the Fort Henry-Fort Donelson fiasco that had led to a temporary occupation of northern Alabama by Union forces.

---

12 Indicative of the confusion, Johnston and the War Department experienced difficulty communicating because the Richmond authorities did not have the cipher Johnston used, and Johnston did not have a signal officer with him. It took several days to get that small mess straightened out. 20 OR, pt. 2, 436-438, 440, and 444-445.

Climbing down from the cars, Johnston and the other passengers boarded a steamboat that ferried them across the 1,300-foot-wide channel. Another train awaited them on the right bank, and at 1:00 p. m. the train stopped in Decherd for dinner. Six hours later, as snow fell silently on the town, the train came to a stop at the station in Murfreesboro.[13]

JOHNSTON spent four or five days with Bragg's army. In one sense, he must have enjoyed his stay in Murfreesboro because he was back in the field with troops and away from the politicians in distant Richmond. In other ways, however, it could not have been a very pleasant time for him. The weather was, as a correspondent put it on December 7, "terribly cold . . . and freezing hard." Johnston also experienced a degree of bad health during the visit, probably a flare up of, or complications from, his Seven Pines wound, perhaps combined with the effects of exposure and exhaustion.[14]

Over the course of his time in Murfreesboro Johnston had the opportunity to consult with Bragg, his corps commanders (Lieutenant Generals Leonidas Polk and William J. Hardee), and other officers as well as to visit with some of the troops. Overall, he was very favorably impressed with the work of Bragg and his officers with regard to the condition, tone, and morale of the army. The Richmond

---

13 "ORA" described the trip in a Dec. 6, 1862, letter to the Mobile *Advertiser and Register*, which published it on Dec. 13. He confused the right and left channels of the river. (They are correctly determined facing downstream.) Since the train crossed the first channel it came to, it was obviously the bridge over the right channel that was out of service. Repairs were then underway. See 20 *OR*, pt. 2, 58 and 417. See also the Nov. 26, 1862, letter from Brigadier General James S. Negley to Major General William S. Rosecrans, 20 *OR*, pt. 2, 99. Apparently there was some problem with the railroad ferry, which Negley mentions, at the time of Johnston's trip. The bridge was back in service by mid-Dec. (17 *OR*, pt. 2, 476). See also the item from the Murfreesboro *Rebel Banner* of Dec. 8 (reprinted in the Atlanta *Southern Confederacy* on Dec 12). "VOLUNTEER," a soldier correspondent who rode on the train, complained that he and about three dozen other soldiers had been evicted from their car and stuffed into another with its original occupants so that the general and his staff could have the car for themselves. "It struck me in my discomfort," he complained, "that thirty entire seats were almost too much for any six men." My guess is that this was the doing of some officious railroad employee, probably before Johnston arrived. The general understood soldier psychology much too well to have ordered or even to have tolerated such an abuse of privilege. He probably did not realize what had been done.

14 See ORA's Dec. 7, 1862, letter in the Mobile *Advertiser and Register* on Dec. 16, and Govan and Livingood, *Different Valor*, 168, along with Lydia Johnston to Charlotte Wigfall, Dec. 12, 1862, Wigfall Papers. In early Dec. Federal commanders had a report from an agent in Murfreesboro that "Joe Johnston . . . is feeble and unable to take the field" (20 *OR*, pt. 2, 19 and 26).

authorities who held a pessimistic view of the quality of the Army of Tennessee were, Johnston concluded, mistaken.

The trip from Chattanooga to Murfreesboro did give Johnston some concrete ideas and reinforced some of those he already held. He learned that Bragg and his officers estimated the Yankee force in Nashville, commanded by Major General William S. Rosecrans, at 65,000 men, with another 35,000 stationed along the railroad between Nashville and Louisville who could quickly be brought forward. At the time, however, the Confederate generals did not anticipate any serious effort by the Federals in Middle Tennessee in the immediate future.[15]

Given the disparity in strength between his forces and the enemy in his front, Bragg resolutely opposed any weakening of his army. Johnston wholeheartedly concurred. To send enough men from Bragg's army to Pemberton to make a significant difference in Mississippi, Johnston wrote in a December 6 letter to Cooper, "would be to give up Tennessee." Even if Bragg could safely spare troops to deal with an emergency in Mississippi, they could not possibly reach Pemberton in time to be of any help. To detach so large a force from the troops at Murfreesboro would, furthermore, "disorganize this army" and allow Rosecrans either to join Grant's Federals in northern Mississippi or to move to Virginia.

So convinced was Johnston of the soundness of this conclusion and of the importance of Tennessee that he flatly declared in a telegram to Cooper on the seventh, "[I] Will not send [troops] south unless ordered [to do so]." On a more hopeful note, Johnston did report that Bragg had dispatched 6,000 cavalrymen to operate against the railroads that supplied the Yankee army then advancing through northern Mississippi toward Pemberton's Yalobusha line.[16]

THE rail trip from Chattanooga to Murfreesboro and back showed Johnston a part of the country that was new to him. All told he would six times (or possibly eight—see the account of Davis's trip below) travel between Chattanooga and Bragg's army in Middle Tennessee. As an experienced soldier, a former quartermaster general with an engineering education and background, and a keen student of military history, Johnston could not have helped noting the fragility of

15 20 OR, pt. 2, 441. Rosecrans commanded the Department and Army of the Cumberland. His strength return for Dec. showed 66,795 officers and men present for duty. The adjacent Department of the Ohio reported 59,829 present for duty, most of them in Kentucky (ibid., 285 and 287).

16 20 OR, pt. 2, 441 and 444; Johnston, *Narrative*, 150.

the rail line that connected the Army of Tennessee with the rest of the Confederacy. There were many bridges, several of them, like the spans at Long Island, major structures that offered tempting targets to raiding enemy cavalry and made Bragg's army, then dangling at the northern end of the rail line, extremely vulnerable.

Should those bridges be damaged and put out of service for an extended period, the army at Murfreesboro could not be supplied and it certainly could not long remain north of the Tennessee River. The reverse would, Johnston would conclude in about eighteen months, also hold true: destruction of the railroad north of Chattanooga would make it impossible, he then came to believe, for a Yankee army to advance southward into Georgia.[17]

After spending several days with Bragg's troops at Murfreesboro, Johnston received a telegram ordering him to return to Chattanooga.

JOHNSTON'S recall to Chattanooga was to enable him to meet with President Davis, who arrived in the Tennessee city on the evening of December 11. Ten days earlier and two days after Johnston had left Richmond, two Mississippians (one of whom was Governor John J. Pettus) had written to Davis. Alarmed at conditions in their state, they pointed out that the President had "often visited the army of Virginia." He had not, however, been in the West since the spring of 1861, and "at this critical juncture could you not visit the army of the west[?] something must be done to inspire confidence[.] a week spent in Mississippi would greatly improve our situation."

When Davis received this plea, probably on December 6 or 7, he promised to "leave immediately." On the eighth he notified General Lee that he was preparing to visit the West "with hope that something may be done to bring out men not heretofore in service, and to arouse all classes to united and desperate resistance."

---

17 Destruction of any of the tunnels on the rail line would, of course, block a movement by an army supplied by the railroad. Such destruction, however, was in almost all cases a major engineering undertaking and far beyond the capability of raiding cavalry. In special cases, however, it could be done. In Aug. of 1862, Rebel cavalry wrecked the Big South Tunnel near Gallatin, TN, by pushing railroad cars into the tunnel and setting them afire. The blaze ignited both the heavy timber supports of the tunnel and seams of coal in the surrounding rocks. As a result, the weakened and porus slate of the tunnel roof collapsed. It took the Federals several weeks to get the passage back into use. Thanks to Paul Childs who many years ago called my attention to the difficulty of wrecking tunnels with Civil War-era equipment, tools, and the relatively weak blasting powder available in the early 1860s. Alfred Nobel did not invent dynamite until after the Civil War.

He hoped, the Chief Executive informed Lee, to be back in Richmond by January 1. Meanwhile, he added, "I shall feel an increasing anxiety to know the events in this quarter, and to have your views in relation to them."

Accompanied by three men—Colonel Joseph R. Davis (the President's nephew, aide, and later the brigadier general who would command the third Mississippi brigade in Virginia), Colonel G. W. C. Lee (also an aide on the President's staff and a future general, and a son of Robert E. Lee), and a slave (whose name is not known)—Davis left Richmond late on December 9. The presidential party reached Chattanooga two days later and Davis conferred with Johnston that night.[18]

THE President, Johnston wrote later, wanted to discuss the feasibility of transferring a significant number of troops from Bragg's army to aid Pemberton's threatened force in the defense of Mississippi. Johnston repeated his standing objections to such a strategy and, "as the expression of my opinion," gave Davis a copy of the December 6 letter he had written to General Cooper from Murfreesboro.

We do not know how long this discussion went on or how vigorously the two men debated the possible troop transfer. In all likelihood the meeting was similar to their November discussion of Western strategy when Johnston unsuccessfully urged the President to unite Holmes's troops with Pemberton's. The Chattanooga discussion probably did not last late into the night. Davis was not feeling well when he left Richmond and must have been exhausted after his journey. Johnston's health was also not very good.

At 6:00 a.m. on the twelfth, with bands playing "The Bonnie Blue Flag" and "Dixie," Davis's train pulled out of the station and headed for Murfreesboro. The President rode in "an elegant new carriage," probably the same coach that had

18 Since Davis went from Chattanooga to Murfreesboro, the question naturally arises as to why he summoned Johnston from the latter city to the former rather than simply joining him at Bragg's headquarters. Any one of three possible explanations may resolve the matter. First, Johnston could have completed his visit to the army and returned to his headquarters before Davis reached Chattanooga. Years later when he wrote his *Narrative* (p. 151) he may have forgotten the circumstances. Second, the telegram may simply have reported that the President would be in Chattanooga and Johnston took it as a directive to meet him there. Third, Davis may not have originally planned to visit the army at Murfreesboro. Then, after meeting with Johnston in Chattanooga and hearing the general's objections to a presidential plan to reinforce Pemberton with troops from the Army of Tennessee, Davis added the Murfreesboro trip to his itinerary to make a personal evaluation of Bragg's situation.

carried Johnston on the first part of his journey a week earlier. In Davis's case, however, a flatboat ferried the car across the right channel of the Tennessee at Long Island, and the Chief Executive was able to make the entire trip in comfort. In Bridgeport, Alabama, just beyond the river, Davis was greeted by a thirteen-gun salute fired by the local artillery company and paid a visit to the commander of the post. After stopping for dinner in Decherd, the President reached Murfreesboro about 6:30 p.m.[19]

DAVIS remained with the Army of Tennessee for only about thirty-six hours. He found the situation in the Murfreesboro area quiet ("the Enemy keep close within their lines about Nashville," he reported) and the Rebel soldiers "in fine spirits and well supplied." He reviewed and spoke to the troops, met with many officers, and conferred with Bragg and probably with other high-ranking generals.

Sometime during the short visit President Davis decided that he would overrule Johnston and Bragg and order reinforcements from Bragg's army to Mississippi where the threat to Vicksburg appeared to be great. The division of Major General Carter L. Stevenson, some 9,000 men recently arrived from East Tennessee, would go. With a brigade sent earlier (also from East Tennessee), the number of troops leaving the Volunteer State for Mississippi would total about 11,000. Bragg objected to the transfer of Stevenson's Division, pointing out that should the Yankees in the Nashville area assume the offensive, the Confederates might well lose all of Middle Tennessee, the area from which Bragg drew the food to supply his army. Davis, who still believed the main Federal efforts were limited to Virginia and the Mississippi Valley, shrugged off the possibility, telling Bragg, "Fight if you can, and fall back beyond the Tennessee River."[20] Then, on the morning of December 14, the President climbed back on board his train and left for Chattanooga.[21]

---

19 Memphis (Atlanta) *Daily Appeal*, Dec. 13, 1862; Chattanooga *Daily Rebel*, Dec. 17, 1862; J. Davis, *Papers*, vol. 8, 548.

20 J. Davis, *Papers*, vol. 8, 548-549; Govan and Livingood, *Different Valor*, 169.Johnston was careful to record that the order for Stevenson's Division "was given in the President's name being his own act" (*Narrative*, 151n).

21 J. Davis, *Papers*, vol. 8, 561-562; 20 *OR*, pt. 2, 416-417, 449-450, and 493. Several accounts state or imply that Johnston accompanied Davis on this trip (e. g. Cooper, *Davis*, 416; Symonds, *Johnston*, 192). Johnston (*Narrative*, 151) does not say one way or the other. In an 1886 article ("Davis and the Mississippi Campaign") he strongly implied that he did not return to Murfreesboro with the President. Govan and Livingood (*Different Valor*, 169) imply that he did

DAVIS spent most of the fifteenth in Chattanooga. Then at 5:00 p.m. he, Johnston, the two presidential aides, the slave, and some of Johnston's staff left by train for Mississippi. The presidential entourage reached Atlanta sometime that night but missed the connection with the train for West Point, Georgia. (Why would the railroad not hold the train for the President?) When the travelers did resume their journey later that morning, they went on to Montgomery where they spent the seventeenth.

Leaving Montgomery, Davis and his party boarded a steamboat to cruise down the Alabama River to Selma. From Selma the travelers went west by rail to the Tombigbee River at Demopolis, where a ferry boat carried them downriver and across the stream. From the boat landing on the right bank, they continued their westward rail journey through Meridian to Jackson. They reached the Mississippi state capital on December 19, "quite unexpectedly," reported a newspaper correspondent, and went on to Vicksburg the next day.[22]

Over two days at Vicksburg Davis and Johnston conferred with the local commander, Major General Martin L. Smith, reviewed troops, and inspected the town's extensive system of fortifications. The party then returned to Jackson and on December 23 headed north to Grenada to see Pemberton and his army along the Yalobusha. On the twenty-sixth, back in Jackson, Davis, by invitation, addressed the state legislature. After the President spoke and in response to calls from the audience, Johnston added a few brief remarks, promising the legislators that, "I shall be watchful, energetic, and indefatigable in your defense."

---

not. I think that Johnston remained in Chattanooga. The general is not mentioned in the newspaper accounts cited in note 19 above. Nor is he mentioned in two telegrams from ORA in the Mobile *Advertiser and Register* of Dec. 18. These messages (dated Dec. 13 and 14) list Bragg, Polk, and Hardee accompanying Davis to review troops, and Davis, along with Generals Polk, John C. Breckinridge, and B. Franklin Cheatham, as speaking to soldiers after a serenade on the evening of Dec. 13. A Federal spy reported from Murfreesboro that Davis had reviewed three divisions on Dec. 13. He mentioned five Rebel generals at the review and involved in various activities. He did not mention Johnston (20 OR, pt. 2, 183 and 192). Nor would Bragg have had to send Johnston an account of his discussion with Davis had Johnston been present (20 OR, pt. 2, 493). My guess is that Johnston remained in Chattanooga owing to his bad health and perhaps to give him time to make arrangements to be away from his headquarters while he accompanied Davis on the rest of the President's trip.

22 Memphis (Atlanta) *Appeal,* Dec. 19, 1862 (quoted in Richmond *Examiner,* Dec. 22, 1862). The *Appeal* and the Mobile *Advertiser and Register* both reported on Dec. 19 that Davis had traveled through Selma. Since he is known also to have passed through Atlanta, the route described in the text is the only way he could have done so. The *Advertiser and Register* promised its readers a presidential visit to Mobile on the return trip.

Davis then returned to Vicksburg for another brief visit. After getting back to Jackson, the President left Johnston there on December 28 and set off for Richmond. He reached the Confederate capital on January 4.[23]

23 On January 5, 1863, the Richmond *Examiner* printed "the chief portions" of Davis's speech and Johnston's remarks. The general's promise "was greeted with tremendous uproarious and prolonged applaudite." Several accounts (e. g., J. Davis, *Papers*, vol. 8, 587) state that Johnston accompanied Davis on the return visit to Vicksburg. I find no evidence that he did, and his Dec. 26-29 correspondence (17 *OR*, pt. 2, 806-809) is datelined Jackson.

Chapter Four

Troubles on Two Fronts

"The lack of a directing hand."
— Frank E. Vandiver, 1956

During the Mississippi leg of the presidential trip the Chief Executive and General Johnston received some encouraging news. On December 20, John C. Pemberton's cavalry under Johnston's one-time Virginia subordinate and afterward the commander in Arkansas, Earl Van Dorn, had captured and wrecked the great Union base at Holly Springs in northern Mississippi. That base supplied the Yankee army threatening Pemberton at Grenada. At the same time part of Bragg's mounted force under Brigadier General Nathan Bedford Forrest tore up railroads in western Tennessee and southwestern Kentucky. Destruction of the Union supply base and rail lines forced the Federals to abandon their effort against Pemberton's Yalobusha position and to withdraw back to Memphis.

More good news soon reached the Confederate leaders. On December 29, the Federal force that had come down the Mississippi assaulted Chickasaw Bluffs (Walnut Hills) on the Yazoo River a short distance north of Vicksburg. Rebel defenders repulsed the attack, inflicting some 1,800 casualties on the enemy while the Confederates lost only about 200 men. Even the attack from the south that threatened Port Hudson fizzled when exaggerated reports of Confederate strength led the Yankees to abandon the effort.

By year's end Pemberton's department was free of any immediate danger. As of that date Pemberton had received no reinforcements from Theophilus Holmes in Arkansas and only a very few of the men President Davis had ordered from Bragg's army in Tennessee had reached the Vicksburg area.

For a brief time it appeared that the Confederates had also improved their situation in Middle Tennessee. Late in December the Federals in Nashville lurched into motion, and by the thirtieth they had deployed in front of Murfreesboro, facing Bragg's army along Stones River. Bragg attacked early on December 31. The

Rebels bent back a part of the Union line in a day of fighting so intense that Bragg felt certain his opponent would abandon the field during the night and retreat to Nashville. His optimistic dispatches reporting a victory in the New Year's Eve battle created the belief in Richmond that the Confederates had won a great triumph.

New Year's Day 1863, however, found the Federals still in front of Bragg's army. When they remained there on the second Bragg launched a poorly conducted assault and suffered heavy losses. The battle casualties, reports of Union reinforcements reaching the area, and a shortage of supplies soon forced Bragg to retreat to Tullahoma some thirty miles to the southeast. The Yankees occupied Murfreesboro but did not pursue the Confederates. Quiet settled over the Tennessee front of Johnston's Western Department for the next six months.

Even west of the Mississippi relative calm reigned, and no large-scale clashes flared up after January 11 when Arkansas Post on the Arkansas River surrendered to a Yankee army-navy expedition and the Federals herded its 5,000-man garrison off to prisoner-of-war camps. The Confederates still held Little Rock and most of the state. The Federals occupied much of the northwestern section and the area along the Mississippi.

THE relative calm that marked the early months of 1863 obscured the fragile state of the Confederate military situation in the West. It could easily have led an observer to erroneous conclusions about the effectiveness of President Davis's strategy for defending the Mississippi Valley.

By the time the Chief Executive left Johnston at Jackson and began his return journey to Richmond, he had, in fact, imposed on the Rebels' Western department a slightly modified version of his earlier (and disastrous) cordon defense in place of his announced offensive-defensive strategy. A year earlier the Western cordon defense had been along an east-west line that stretched across southern Kentucky and Missouri from the border between the Bluegrass State and Virginia (now West Virginia) to the Ozark Mountains. Union military successes in the first months of 1862 had caved in the center of that line so that as of early 1863 it somewhat resembled a gigantic letter U.

The early 1863 Rebel position began to the northwest of Little Rock, ran to the southeast passing through the state capital, and on down the Mississippi River to Vicksburg and Port Hudson. The line then swung to the east to the Selma area, and then bent to the northeast to Montgomery and Atlanta. It ran on to Chattanooga, thence northwest to Tullahoma before turning back and fading off to the northeast in the direction of Knoxville.

A combination of Davis's policies (making an absolute commitment to defend Arkansas), geography (the Western rivers), and the Confederate infrastructure (the railroads in the West) put the Rebels on the outside (convex) side of that U. In this position they found themselves deprived of the interior lines of transportation on which in large part the President had based his strategy for defending the West. Even worse from the Secessionist standpoint, the Yankees were inside (the concave side) of the U, and therefore had the interior lines. In truth, the Federals enjoyed an even greater advantage owing to their ability to use the rivers to transport troops and supplies within the U.

FEW Civil War generals thought much in terms of grand strategy. This was especially true of the Confederates since no Rebel general had any official responsibility for matters beyond the force or area he actually commanded. Few, therefore, would have grasped the seriousness of the danger facing the Confederates in the West in the calm early months of 1863. Their position was strong nowhere and weak everywhere.

It is a tribute to Joseph E. Johnston's ability and intelligence that he seems at least dimly to have perceived (or maybe instinctively to have sensed would put it better) at least part of the problem. It is also a damning comment about his almost completely passive approach to high-level command that he did almost nothing to advise the government about his fears.

Johnston remained most unhappy with the arrangement Davis had decreed for the West. He continued to pine for a return to Virginia. When he turned his attention to his actual situation, he again advocated the transfer of Holmes's troops who (he always professed to believe) numbered some 55,000 across the Mississippi. He also continued to complain to his friend and ally Wigfall about the unhappy situation in which Davis had placed him.

On December 22, while he and Davis were in Vicksburg, Johnston made yet another effort to persuade the President to change his policy. In a letter summarizing his views, he outlined what he believed to be the force the Rebels needed to hold Mississippi. To conduct a successful defense of the state, Johnston wrote, the Confederates needed "an active [field] army of about 40,000 men" plus about 20,000 more to garrison Vicksburg and Port Hudson.

As of the date of the letter, Johnston calculated, the Rebels had about 21,000 men with Pemberton on the Yalobusha, some 9,000 (Stevenson's Division) then en route from Tennessee, 5,900 at Vicksburg, and 5,500 at Port Hudson. "It is supposed," Johnston added, that Holmes had put another 10,000 on the march from Arkansas in obedience to General Samuel Cooper's early December "peremptory" order to do so.

Johnston thus reasoned that Pemberton needed another eight to ten thousand men. These additional soldiers, he wrote, should be drawn from Holmes's force. In fact, he concluded (again), it would be better to combine Holmes's army with Pemberton's and to fight first on one side of the Mississippi and then on the other. That, indeed, was the strategy that the President's offensive-defensive concept would have dictated.

Davis sent Johnston's letter on to Holmes. "It seems to me," the Chief Executive wrote to his Trans-Mississippi commander, "unquestionably best that you should reinforce General Johnston so as to enable him successfully to meet the enemy. . . . Nothing will so certainly conduce to peace as the conclusive exhibition of our power to hold the Mississippi river and nothing so diminish our capacity to defend the Trans-Mississippi States as the loss of communication between the States on the Eastern and Western sides of the river."

Clearly Davis believed that Holmes should send help to Pemberton. In an action (or non-action) altogether characteristic of his conduct of public (and, often, also of private) business, however, Davis would not make a decision and issue the order. Holmes must decide if conditions in Arkansas were such that he could spare troops from that state to aid in the defense of Vicksburg.

The Trans-Mississippi commander did not reply for a week, by which time Davis was on his way back to Richmond. Holmes's forces under Thomas Hindman in northwestern Arkansas were then retreating, he wrote. To send help to Pemberton, he went on, would be to lose Arkansas. If Davis ordered him to reinforce the Confederates in Mississippi, he would obey and do his best; otherwise, he would concentrate on defending Arkansas. On January 28 Davis replied to Holmes, "If you are correct as to the consequences which would follow, you have properly exercised the discretion which was entrusted to you."[1]

This whole episode perfectly illustrates the main problem with Davis's approach to the war—the approach that so frustrated Joseph E. Johnston. The President simply failed to realize that someone with a view of the Confederacy's overall situation had to decide between (in this case) Mississippi and Arkansas. Only one man in the Confederacy had the information and the authority to make

---

1 Johnston commented after the war (*Narrative*, 153) that Holmes "very properly waited for orders."

such a judgment. Only he could make such a decision under the Confederate command system—and he consistently refused to do so.[2]

DAVIS'S western trip had produced only one significant change: the President had transferred a total of about 11,000 troops from Tennessee to Mississippi. Almost all of them had missed the late December fighting at Murfreesboro and that at Chickasaw Bluffs (Walnut Hills), having left Tennessee prior to the former battle and joined Pemberton's force too late for the latter. On January 11 Bragg grumbled that "the unfortunate withdrawal of my troops" had saved the Yankees from destruction at Stones River. "The troops," Johnston commented in a May 7 letter to his brother Beverley, "left Tennessee too soon and reached Mississippi too late."[3]

TWO other serious, if narrower, differences of opinion about the defense of Mississippi also arose during Davis's visit. Typically, they went unresolved.

At Vicksburg the President expressed great satisfaction with the extensive system of strong fortifications the Rebels had built to protect the land side of the town. Johnston, at least silently, bemoaned the fact that a large army-size garrison would be necessary to hold such massive works. Rather than immobilize thousands of men in the city's trenches, he thought, the Confederates should build more modest fortifications that could be held by fewer troops, leaving most of the garrison free to maneuver with the army in the field. Did he express such an opinion to Davis and the local commanders and if so, how strongly? We do not know.

Another—and it was to prove crucial—difference arose at the conference in Grenada. Discussions there revealed that Johnston and Pemberton held mutually exclusive ideas as to how the Rebels should defend Vicksburg itself. Johnston believed that primary reliance should be placed upon a mobile army able to operate in the field against a force that threatened Vicksburg. It followed, therefore, that the city's garrison should be relatively small so as to give the field army as great a

2 20 *OR*, pt. 2, 459-460; J. Davis, *Papers*, vol. 8, 559-562 and 584-587, and vol. 9, 43-44. Note that Davis's approval was conditional: "If you are correct." It also placed the responsibility for the decision upon Holmes's shoulders, and that general knew nothing about the situation in Mississippi and, therefore, lacked the information necessary to decide both if Arkansas was more important to the Confederacy than Mississippi and where the greater danger lay.

3 20 *OR*, pt. 2, 493; Johnston letter in Hughes Papers. The last of Stevenson's troops did not reach Jackson until Jan. 7, 1863 (Johnston, *Narrative*, 154).

strength as possible. Pemberton, on the other hand, wanted to station a strong garrison in the city and provision it to withstand a long siege while it awaited relief by an army from the outside.

Were these differences raised and discussed fully and openly at Grenada? If so, did Davis seriously try to iron them out? Did anyone think to ask how strong such an army of relief would be needed? Where were the troops, supplies, and equipment for it to come from? What field transportation would it require? How much artillery? How was it to be supplied? Who would command it?

We simply do not know if, or how fully and honestly Davis, Johnston, and Pemberton discussed these matters and tried to work them out.[4]

THUS, by year's end, as Davis journeyed back to Richmond, several views had emerged as to how the Confederates should conduct their war for the defense of the West in general, and for the defense of the Mississippi Valley in particular. These views are summarized in the chart on the next page. (Note: some of the ideas shown in the chart have not yet been discussed in the text because the documents illustrating them date from later months than those covered thus far in the narrative. No doubt can exist, however, that the named leader held the views ascribed to him from a very early point in the discussions about strategy.)

The point is not that any of these ideas as to how the Confederates should conduct their defense of the West was necessarily wrong. Nothing foredoomed any of them to failure. Any of them might have produced Rebel success—the goal for which Davis, Johnston, Bragg, Holmes, and Pemberton were all striving. The point is that these ideas were mutually exclusive. Implementation—even partial implementation of, or attempting to implement one—would make it impossible to implement one or more of the others.

---

4 Johnston wrote (*Narrative,* 153) that the differences were discussed at Grenada—how thoroughly, he did not say. In the postwar article "Davis and the Mississippi Campaign" (474), Johnston wrote that at the meeting he and Pemberton "advocated opposite modes of warfare." If so, and if the discussion was full and honest, all three men were guilty of criminal incompetence and negligence in leaving the matter unresolved. We do know that it would have been out of character for Johnston openly to have differed with the President at such a meeting. Michael Ballard (*Pemberton,* 102-104, 113, and 142) speculated that Pemberton's determination to keep his army in Vicksburg resulted, at least in part, from his 1862 experiences in South Carolina when he received harsh criticism for not keeping troops in all parts of the state he was supposed to defend.

Differing Views on How to Defend the West in General, and For the Defense of the Mississippi Valley in Particular				
DAVIS	JOHNSTON	BRAGG	HOLMES	PEMBERTON
Hold Arkansas, Mississippi, and if possible, Tennessee. Union objectives are to capture Richmond and Mississippi Valley. Give up Tennessee if necessary.	Tennessee critical and in danger. Davis should decide clearly between Tennessee and Mississippi.	Tennessee facing very serious threat.	Arkansas in great danger.	Great threat in Mississippi.
Holmes to help with defense of Mississippi only once Arkansas is secured.	Holmes should be ordered to send troops to help defend Vicksburg. Holmes has 55,000 men and is closer to Vicksburg than is Bragg. Regain Arkansas later if Federals occupy state.	Not Applicable.	Only some 18,000 useful troops. Cannot help Vicksburg without losing Arkansas. Will help only if ordered. 3-4 weeks to get troops to Vicksburg.	Davis should order Holmes to support Vicksburg.
Shift troops between Tennessee and Mississippi to meet threats.	Bragg and Pemberton cannot help one another without losing what each is tasked with defending. Railroads unable to move troops as Davis envisions.	Cannot reduce the Army of Tennessee without real danger of losing what is left of the Volunteer State.	Not Applicable.	Not Applicable.
Must hold Vicksburg and Port Hudson to keep communications open with Trans-Mississippi and river closed to enemy vessels.	Would lead to disaster to pin armies down inside fortifications at Vicksburg and Port Hudson. Need field army of 40,000 to operate in Mississippi.	Not Applicable.	Not Applicable.	Reinforce and fortify Vicksburg and Port Hudson to withstand long siege. Organize Army of Relief to raise siege.

In such a situation as the Rebels had created for themselves, massive failure and national disaster would be inevitable unless priorities and policies were clearly set (Davis's responsibility), clearly stated (Davis's responsibility), thoroughly understood by all (everyone's responsibility), the lines of authority unambiguous and observed (primarily Davis's and Johnston's responsibility), and communication full and frequent (everyone's responsibility).

By the time Davis left Mississippi to return to Richmond, none of these conditions had been met. None of them ever would be. The Rebels suffered a self-inflicted fatal wound—something Frank E. Vandiver called the "lack of a directing hand."[5]

DAVIS'S first wartime visit to the Western Theater also highlights several other aspects of his management (mismanagement?) of the Confederate war effort and shows some of his great weaknesses as commander-in-chief of the Rebel armed forces. As mentioned in Book One, Chapter Three of this work, he almost always viewed the conflict from a level more appropriate for a war minister or a commanding general—or even for the commander of an independent field army—than for a president, a head of government, or a head of state.

Davis's late 1862 Western jaunt was a hastily arranged, ad hoc trip. Had the President taken the time to plan it better (and he certainly had the time to do so during the winter), the trip could well have produced some good results for the Rebels.

On his travels Davis visited four crucial Western states: Tennessee, Georgia, Alabama, and Mississippi. So far as the records show, he saw only two of the four governors—Isham G. Harris of Tennessee, then an aide on Bragg's staff with whom he met during the day-and-a-half he spent in Murfreesboro, and John J. Pettus of Mississippi, with whom he held what appears to have been an informal meeting in Jackson. The President probably also saw Governor John Gill Shorter of Alabama when he passed through Montgomery going to and/or returning from Mississippi. Davis appears not to have seen or contacted Governor Joseph E. Brown of Georgia during the trip. (Atlanta was not then the state capital, and Brown would have had to journey from Milledgeville to meet Davis.)[6]

---

5 Vandiver, *Rebel Brass*, 114. Vandiver wrote about staff departments, but his book makes it clear that the remark is equally applicable to the government's entire war effort.

6 Elliott, *Harris*, 129; Dubay, *Pettus*, 152-154. Pettus also attended Davis's Dec. 26, 1862, address to the state legislature. In that speech (J. Davis, *Papers*, vol. 8, 565-584) the President

What can fairly be labeled Davis's neglect of the governors stands as a missed opportunity potentially to strengthen enormously the Confederate cause in the West. Had the President taken the time to plan and organize his trip, he could have assembled the four state executives in, say, Montgomery, for a conference. Were Davis then to explain his concept for defense of the West, the governors might have agreed to commit and coordinate their resources and personnel to expedite the movement of troops between the armies of Bragg and Pemberton in the event of an emergency that threatened them all. State militia, for example, could have been called out and used to move equipment and supplies while Confederate troops rushed ahead as rapidly as possible. Supplies might have been procured and positioned along the railroads for the moving troops.

Such state aid would have been especially valuable in Georgia because the state owned and operated the Western & Atlantic Railroad, the crucial line of track between Chattanooga and Atlanta. If nothing else, involving the governors in such consultations could have enhanced their understanding of the military problems facing the Rebels' national government in the West and, perhaps, lessened the political pressure on Confederate authorities.[7]

NOR did Davis seize the opportunity offered by his trip to deal with one of the major difficulties the Rebels faced in defending the Mississippi Valley—the demands of Trans-Mississippi politicians that their region receive more attention.

So far as the records show, the President did not consult any Trans-Mississippi members of Congress or even Postmaster General John H. Reagan, who hailed from Texas, about the trip. More significantly, Davis made no effort to meet with or even to contact the governors of any of the Trans-Mississippi states to try to iron

---

made no real effort to explain the problems involved in the defense of the Mississippi Valley to a large group of men who could have helped him with the effort. Parks, *Brown* (Chapter XII, 220-252) covers this period. Brown was then tied up with a meeting of the state legislature. The governor was one of those disputatious people who often quarreled with others (frequently over unimportant questions) with no consideration of the detrimental effect the quarrel would have on larger and far more important matters. In 1862, he was carrying on a bitter quarrel with Davis over, among other things, conscription. It would have taken someone far more skilled in human relations than Davis to have worked constructively with him. Davis, in fact, may not have wanted to see him.

7 On July 14, 1863, a month after the Secessionists lost the Mississippi River, Davis did suggest to the Trans-Mississippi commander that he could lessen his difficulties by working with the governors of Missouri, Arkansas, Louisiana, and Texas. See the following section of this chapter and Beringer, et al., *Why the South Lost*, 29-30.

out the political-military problems of defending the Mississippi Valley and holding together the eastern and western halves of the Confederacy.

Had Davis delayed his departure from Richmond for even a few days, he could have sent a request to the governors of Arkansas, Louisiana, Texas, and Missouri (this last state was considered by the Confederates as one of their own and had a state government in exile in Marshall, Texas) to meet or send a representative to meet him in Vicksburg. At such a gathering, perhaps with Johnston present to discuss the military problems and the necessity of holding Vicksburg to maintain contact with the Trans-Mississippi, Davis might have won the governors' consent to move troops to or even across the river, or to give up northern Arkansas to free forces to help hold the Vicksburg-Port Hudson corridor. If nothing else, such a meeting would have demonstrated the distant government's concern for the Trans-Mississippi. Davis could have summoned Holmes to meet with (or to send a representative to meet with) himself and Johnston. Had the President been willing to run a little risk, he even could have crossed the river himself, going to, say, Alexandria, Louisiana, on the Red River to meet Holmes and the Trans-Mississippi governors there.[8]

One of Davis's great weaknesses as a national war leader was his failure to think like a national war leader—to think in terms of waging war as opposed to conducting a specific military operation. He barely conceived of a policy that involved the state or congressional leaders even symbolically in the national defense or of taking public steps to build popular support for the cause in general and for his government's policies in particular.[9]

DAVIS'S great reluctance to make important decisions proved to be another of his crucial weaknesses as an executive—especially one leading a nation in wartime. As described in Chapter Three of Book One, he often convened long meetings with cabinet officers or generals to consider crucial matters. When the meeting broke up—sometimes after many hours of talk—nothing had been

---

8 The risk would have been to the Confederacy as well should Davis have been killed or captured on such a trip. The President certainly would have had no personal fear in facing such a danger. Arthur James Lyon Fremantle (*Diary*, 170) noted on June 17, 1863, while in Richmond, "People speak of any misfortune to him [Davis] as an irreparable evil and too dreadful to contemplate." Vice President Alexander H. Stephens, a man more interested in political theory than in practical governance, was simply unfit to be a national executive leader, especially of a country at war.

9 See Beringer, *et al.*, *Why the South Lost*, 29-30 and *passim*.

decided. On other occasions the Chief Executive abdicated his proper role and allowed (or directed) others to make decisions that only the commander-in-chief should, and under Confederate practice could, make.

In September of 1861, for example, Major General Leonidas Polk violated Davis's policy (and instructions) by sending troops into Kentucky, a crucial border state then trying to remain neutral. Polk wanted to seize the town of Columbus on the Mississippi River. There, Polk thought, Confederate cannon on the high bluffs could close the waterway to Northern boats. Davis assigned General Albert Sidney Johnston to confer with Tennessee political leaders and decide if Polk's forces should remain at Columbus or withdraw from the Bluegrass State. He thus sent a military commander to decide a crucial question that was far more geopolitical than military. In later months Joseph E. Johnston became especially frustrated by the Chief Executive's refusal to make such decisions.[10]

In December of 1862, in the letter quoted above, Davis wrote General Holmes that it seemed "unquestionably best that you should reinforce General Pemberton" and that "*Nothing* will so certainly conduce to peace as the conclusive exhibition of our power to hold the Mississippi river, and *nothing* so diminish our capacity to defend the Trans.-Miss. States as the loss of communication between the States on the Eastern and Western sides of the river" [my emphasis].

Then, after having declared the matter as being of absolute supreme national importance (note the use of "unquestionably" and the two "nothings") Davis turned the whole geopolitical, strategic question of northern Arkansas or Vicksburg—of Confederate grand strategy for the vital Mississippi Valley—over to Holmes and went back to Richmond.

We might well wonder if Joseph E. Johnston, upon learning of this presidential "decision" not to decide, thought back to his own situation of a few weeks earlier. Then Davis had overruled two of his full generals (Johnston and Bragg) and ordered reinforcements from Tennessee to Mississippi. Now, he would not overrule a lieutenant general (Holmes) and order him to reinforce Vicksburg. Did the Chief Executive trust and have confidence in Holmes but not in Johnston and Bragg? Did he think Tennessee of relatively little importance?[11]

Less than three weeks after writing Holmes, Davis would declare that holding the Mississippi was "vital" to the Confederacy, and on June 28 wrote Lee about "the vital importance of holding the Mississippi." The President, however, washed

10 See Woodworth, *Davis and Generals*, 51-54; and McMurry, *Fourth Battle of Winchester*, 91-97.

11 27 *OR*, pt. 1, 32; 52 *OR*, pt. 2, 404.

his hands of the whole matter of deciding how to achieve this "vital" military geopolitical objective.

AS 1862 neared its end, Davis was anxious to return to Richmond, although there was no real need for him to be there. Congress would not even begin its next session until January 12. Lee had won a smashing victory at Fredericksburg in mid-December, and with the Virginia winter closing in, major military action in the Old Dominion during the next several months was very unlikely. Even should the Yankees launch another offensive, Lee was perfectly capable of dealing with it. The telegraph would keep Davis informed on any essential matters that arose, and the telegraph, the mails, and couriers would enable him to prepare for the approaching legislative session.

The President easily could have devoted another week or ten days to the far more serious problems the Confederates faced between the Appalachians and the Mississippi.

DAVIS'S trip to the West had been mostly a wasted effort, and it left matters in the region at least as chaotic, confused, and uncertain as they were when he departed Richmond. Over the next six months after he left Johnston in Jackson on December 28 the mess that the Rebels had chosen to create for themselves in the West (Covey, once more) was to become even worse.

Chapter Five

A Critical Winter

PART I

"Not to decide is to decide."
— Harvey Cox

We can only imagine the thoughts that ran through Joseph E. Johnston's mind on December 28, 1862, as President Davis's train pulled out of the Jackson station and began the first leg of the Chief Executive's long journey back to Richmond. Whatever precise configuration those thoughts took, they must have included large doses of frustration, disappointment, some degree of resentment and self-pity, and at least a dollop of paranoia.

In the spring of 1860, after distinguished service spanning three decades, Johnston had reached the pinnacle of his United States Army career: Quartermaster General and Brigadier General, staff. Even with the suffix attached to his grade, Johnston stood above all of his contemporaries, a goal toward which he had long striven, the measure of his self-worth, and a public acknowledgment and vindication of his outstanding competence and ability in the military profession.

Once he left the "old army" and entered Confederate service, Johnston had found his career—at least in his own mind—spiraling downward. In the Rebel army hierarchy Johnston stood subordinate to three officers whom (he was always to believe) he legally outranked. Jefferson Davis, Johnston convinced himself, had illegally demoted and disgraced him. Even worse, one of the three who now outranked him was his old friend and (in his own mind) long-time professional rival Robert E. Lee.

Johnston had also found his first year as a Confederate general marred by numerous bitter and frustrating quarrels with President Davis and the government about matters other than his rank among Rebel generals. All of these spats as well as his own and Davis's personalities had produced a wide and widening gulf between himself and the Richmond authorities. Then on May 31, 1862, he fell wounded just as (he was to believe for the rest of his long life) he stood on the verge of winning the great victory that might well have secured Confederate independence.

When Johnston returned to duty in November of 1862, President Davis had shunted (exiled?) him off to the West and put him in a military situation in which, Johnston easily convinced himself, success was most unlikely if not downright impossible. Was the President, as Johnston's friend Wigfall warned, placing the general between the government and defeat so that he rather than Davis and the administration would bear responsibility in the all-too-likely event of failure, disaster, and disgrace?

To make a very bad situation even worse, President Davis had rejected Johnston's recommendation to modify his new Western command by separating the army in Tennessee from that in Mississippi and uniting the latter with Rebel forces in the Trans-Mississippi. Then, in December, during his just-concluded visit to the West, the President had overruled Johnston and transferred a large contingent of troops from Tennessee to Mississippi. Finally, to cap it all off, Johnston had discovered that he and Lieutenant General John C. Pemberton, his subordinate commander in Mississippi, held completely irreconcilable views on how to go about defending Vicksburg.

Worst of all, it seems that Johnston's nagging suspicion that the Davis Administration was hostile to him had grown—and was continuing to grow—steadily.

AS matters turned out, Johnston had about three-and-one-half months after President Davis left Mississippi to do what he could, or at least would, to strengthen the defenses of the area entrusted to him. The steps he took, as well as those he did not, during that time reveal much about Johnston and show many of the severe limitations that marked his career as a commander at the highest military levels.

Johnston simply would not accept Davis's scheme for defending the West. If the general had any real understanding of the enormous political pressures that circumscribed the President's geopolitical strategic options, he gave no sign of it then or later. Throughout the winter of 1862 and on into the spring of 1863 Johnston frequently continued to urge his concept of Western defense on the government. On January 6, 1863, for example, the general wrote from Jackson to call Davis's attention to "the impossibility of my knowing [the] condition of things in Tennessee [which] shows that I cannot direct both parts of my command at once."[1]

Two months later, on March 12, he wrote to remind the War Department about what he had said and written several times earlier regarding the impracticability of reinforcing the armies of Bragg and Pemberton from each other. The possibility that the Yankees would move against both simultaneously and the time necessary to shift troops from one army to the other, he stated, rendered such a strategy ineffective. "Our disadvantage in this warfare," he explained, "is that the enemy can transfer an army from Mississippi to Nashville before we can learn that it is in motion, while an equal body of our troops could not make the same movement (the corresponding one rather) in less than six weeks. The infantry of Major General Stevenson's division ordered from here [Tullahoma, TN] to Jackson in December [by Davis, although Johnston did not rub that fact in] was more than three weeks on the way—its wagons & horses more than a month. The rail roads are now in worse condition than they were then."[2]

The President and the War Department officials usually did not reply to such complaints, comments, and observations. Johnston, it must have seemed to them, always complained about whatever situation he happened to find himself in. The closest thing the general got to an acknowledgment of and a response to his concerns was Davis's admission in a January 8 message that "the difficulty arising from the separation of troops in your command is realized but cannot be avoided." When spring came the matter had not been dealt with, and it still festered in Johnston's mind.[3]

JOHNSTON also sought—almost always without much success—to get whatever additional troops he could for the West. Five days after Davis left

---

1 17 *OR*, pt. 2, 827. Could he have *required* Bragg and Pemberton to send him full and frequent reports? See below. Davis seems to have thought of the Western forces as two separate armies; Johnston as one army of two parts. Davis envisioned Johnston as coordinating the two armies, with their actual field operations being directed by Bragg or Pemberton; Johnston of himself as being in actual command of their operations.

2 24 *OR*, pt. 3, 665. Subsequent experience was to show that Johnston's estimate of the time necessary to shift troops between Tennessee and Mississippi was exaggerated. The troops, however, did not move with their full complement of equipment, and that may have been his meaning. Certainly, his conduct in organizing his forces in the following spring so indicates. See Chapter Nine.

3 J. Davis, *Papers*, vol. 9, 18.

Jackson, the general wrote to remind the President that he had given him an estimate that the Confederates would need an additional 20,000 men "to make headway" against the Union forces threatening Mississippi from the north and west.

By then Johnston had abandoned all serious hope of getting any reinforcements from Arkansas, but, he asked, could Lee, who had won a great victory at Fredericksburg three weeks earlier, spare any part of the Army of Northern Virginia to help the Western Confederates during the winter? In March and April Johnston learned that the Federals were transferring to the Mississippi Valley some of their troops who had been serving in western Virginia. He wrote to suggest that the Confederates send to the West their forces from the same area—a plea he repeated on May 1.

The only significant success Johnston enjoyed along these lines was to secure the troops who had been captured at Arkansas Post after their exchange in the late spring. These men, numbering about 4,000, went to join the Army of Tennessee. They replaced some of Bragg's troops whom the authorities had transferred to Mississippi. Even if Davis then saw major threats only to Richmond and the Mississippi Valley, Johnston remained greatly concerned about the Rebels' hold on the Volunteer State.[4]

WITHIN his own command Johnston undertook to arrange matters so that the movement of reinforcements between Pemberton and Bragg would require as little time as possible.[5] Building upon both the scheme used by Bragg the previous summer when he moved his army by rail from Mississippi through Mobile to Tennessee and upon a January 8 suggestion from Davis, Johnston directed Pemberton to station some of his troops at Jackson and others at Meridian. Then, when the need arose to reinforce Bragg from the army in Mississippi, all these men could begin to move immediately. Even the garrison troops at Mobile could become a part of the movement, leaving the Gulf city at once when the order came and being replaced by the units at the rear of the reinforcing column. Meanwhile

---

4 17 *OR*, pt. 2, 823 and 828; 23 *OR*, pt. 2, 256 and 627-628; 24 *OR*, pt. 1, 214 and 239; 24 *OR*, pt. 3, 652 and 665; J. Davis, *Papers*, 125.

5 For an overall account of Johnston's efforts to provide for the defense of the West in early 1863, see A. Jones, "Tennessee and Mississippi." Jones believed (144) that Johnston "undoubtedly did not realize the extent to which this collection of isolated measures [described in his article and to some extent in this text below] had made a comprehensive whole" that would correct or lessen many of the problems of his command.

the intermediate units would be available to defend Mobile should the enemy threaten the city during the movement. The units, of course, could also move in the opposite direction to strengthen various points in Mississippi should the need to do so arise.

Johnston actually activated this "pipeline" concept—troops at all points along the railroad beginning to move simultaneously—in January and again in April. On both occasions, however, renewed Yankee threats against Vicksburg quickly forced him to cancel orders for the transfer and to recall to Mississippi the troops who had already begun to move in accordance with the scheme.

Johnston imposed a similar system on East Tennessee. He rearranged Rebel forces there so that most of the infantry units could reach the railroad in a short time and quickly leave to join Bragg. The Confederates also worked out an arrangement for troops in southwestern Virginia to replace men sent from East to Middle Tennessee.[6]

SHOULD more troops not come to the West from elsewhere to augment Johnston's forces, could some of the Rebels in other areas at least undertake active operations? Such efforts might well draw Yankee troops away from Bragg's and Pemberton's fronts. If Confederates in the Trans-Mississippi could not (or would not) cross the great river, might they assume the offensive into Missouri? Perhaps by doing so they could compel Federal authorities to draw men away from the Union army threatening Vicksburg or Tullahoma to defend, say, St. Louis? Could the Trans-Mississippi Rebels menace New Orleans, Helena, or some other Yankee-held points?

Although the Confederates attempted nothing serious along these lines until the late spring, they did make a few ineffectual efforts throughout the first half of the year. In April, for example, Brigadier General John Sappington Marmaduke convinced a reluctant Holmes that he could conduct a raid from Arkansas into Missouri that would reduce pressure on the Confederates in the Mississippi Valley, encourage Rebel supporters in Missouri, and enable the Secessionists to secure great quantities of supplies.

As was so often the case with Confederate operations in the Trans-Mississippi, Marmaduke's raid quickly degenerated into a fiasco and proved a complete failure.

6 24 OR, pt. 3, 597, 599–600, 602, 665, and 734; J. Davis, *Papers*, vol. 8, 18. Johnston, typically, seems not to have kept the government very well informed about his implementation of this scheme. He, however, might have discussed the matter with Davis during the President's Western trip.

Soon after the raid ended, a Rebel writing from Little Rock called the effort "a grand failure, a farce, . . . a most contemptible burlesque."[7] In June and July, however, the Southerners would again turn to this strategy in an effort to help Pemberton's army. This ploy would lead to battles at Milliken's Bend in Louisiana (June 7), Helena in Arkansas (July 4), and Gettysburg in Pennsylvania (July 1-3).

THERE was yet one more action that Johnston took within his department that, he thought, would strengthen the Confederates' ability to defeat an invading army. He would utilize the one advantage that the Western Rebels then enjoyed over their foe—their superiority in cavalry.

Johnston had been told by, he wrote, "informed gentlemen" and the governor that "until late spring," mounted units could not operate effectively in Mississippi owing to the weather and the bad condition of the roads. He therefore decided to shift most of the horse soldiers in the Magnolia State to Tennessee and unite them with part of Bragg's cavalry. On December 28, the same day Davis departed Jackson, Johnston—who probably had discussed the plan with the President—moved to put his idea into practice. He summoned to Jackson Major General Earl Van Dorn, whose horsemen had recently turned back Grant's invading army in northern Mississippi. Johnston wished to confer with Van Dorn "with regard to future cavalry operations."

A few days later Johnston informed Bragg that he would combine part of the cavalry of the Army of Tennessee with Van Dorn's horsemen taken from Pemberton's command to create a strong mounted unit to be based in the Columbia, Tennessee, area. Such a force operating against Federal communication and supply lines would shield both the northern front of Pemberton's command and the western flank of the Middle Tennessee region whence Bragg drew much of the food for his army.[8]

Although Johnston encountered some problems locating and positioning the units he wanted, he had, when he completed this work in late February, created a cavalry corps commanded by Van Dorn and based in the Columbia-Spring Hill area in south central Tennessee. In effect, Johnston had devised an excellent

---

7 DeBlack, *Fire and Sword*, 85-86; Marshall, *Army Life*, 319 n9; 24 *OR*, pt. 3, 653 and 670; and Chapter Eight of this book. See letter, n. d. or signature, to Mobile *Advertiser and Register* (reprinted in Memphis [Atlanta] *Daily Appeal*, June 8, 1863).

8 The development of this scheme can be followed in scores of the documents in 17 *OR*, pt. 2. See also, 20 *OR*, pt. 2, 475 and 476; 24 *OR*, pt. 1, 210-211 and 247; 24 *OR*, pt. 3, 592, 614, 634, 652, and 685; and J. Davis, *Papers*, vol. 9, 4, 6 n9, and 33.

defense against a replay of the type of overland campaign through northern Mississippi against Vicksburg that Grant's Federals had attempted in late 1862.

As things turned out, Grant too had realized how difficult it was to maintain a rail line of supply in Tennessee and northern Mississippi in the face of Confederate cavalry raids. The next time he moved against Pemberton, he would use the Mississippi River itself as his unbreakable line of supply and he would establish his bases at Helena and Milliken's Bend on the right bank of the river in Arkansas and Louisiana where Johnston's horsemen could not get at them.

Owing to Grant's new approach, Van Dorn and his cavalry (except for a division sent back to Mississippi in the late spring) played no further role in the defense of Pemberton's department. Almost by osmosis Van Dorn and his horsemen slipped out of Pemberton's army and became a part of Bragg's. After Van Dorn died—a jealous husband shot him to death in May—Brigadier General Nathan Bedford Forrest ascended to command the force. In June Forrest was shot by one of his own officers who held a grudge against him. The general then mortally wounded his assailant with a knife. So went what has been called "the comedy" of the Rebels' Western command.[9]

Pemberton, of course, was not happy with the loss of so much of his mounted arm. As early as March 21 he asked Johnston if Van Dorn and his horsemen had been separated from the Mississippi army. "If so," he wrote, "it very much diminishes my ability to defend the northern portion of the State." Johnston replied that the cavalry sent to Tennessee was "absolutely necessary" to enable Bragg to hold the area from which he drew much of the food for his troops. From time to time thereafter Pemberton reminded Johnston that he "ought to have more cavalry, if possible, for northern Mississippi."[10]

By late January Johnston had taken, or at least begun, the steps he could think of to strengthen his command. He decided to pay a visit to Mobile to inspect the defenses there. Afterward he would go on to see Pemberton's army in Mississippi.

---

9 Weinert, *Confederate Regular Army*, 39.

10 24 *OR*, pt. 1, 247; Carter, *Van Dorn*, 129, 163-166, 174, and 179; 17 *OR*, pt. 2, 808-838 (many separate documents). Carter asserts (179) the transfer of Van Dorn's cavalry "sealed the fate of Vicksburg." On May 6, John Cowdery Taylor, a member of Pemberton's staff, complained that a lack of cavalry prevented the Rebels in Mississippi from gathering accurate intelligence about their opponents. He called the transfer of Van Dorn's force "the greatest mistake that was ever made," and commented one might "as well take the arms off a man and expect him to defend himself." See also the entry for June 25. Note: Although classified as a diary, this document contains many obviously non-contemporary sections, and this may well be one of them.

LIEUTENANT GENERAL JOHN C. PEMBERTON,
commander at Vicksburg.
LOC

PART II

"Which is more valuable, Tennessee or Mississippi?"
— Joseph E. Johnston to Jefferson Davis, January 7, 1863

All through the winter Johnston kept complaining about his plight (usually to Wigfall, who, of course, could do nothing to change the situation) and the predicament in which Davis had placed him. The fact, however, is that a confident, proactive officer who trusted his government and kept the authorities informed could have taken several more steps to reshape and strengthen his command and perhaps conducted a successful defense of his area of responsibility. Certainly, such an officer could have so managed the command as to prevent defeat from becoming disaster. Over a few months he might even have won the approval of his government to make some major changes in the whole scheme of Western defense.

As always, Johnston's refusal (not failure!) to communicate meaningfully with the government lay at the heart of his many self-inflicted difficulties. The general often resumed his old practice of asking questions or making only short simple comments or requests without offering any context for the message or explaining why he needed the desired information or why he thought the requested action would benefit his command. In truth, he had learned nothing from his sad 1861-1862 experiences in dealing with Davis or his administration.[11]

On January 7, 1863, Johnston sent a brief (seven short sentences, sixty-eight words), but very important telegram to Davis. The first four sentences were quick statements concerning Bragg's situation in Tennessee. The fifth raised the possibility of returning to Bragg the troops ordered from the Volunteer State to Mississippi by Davis a few weeks earlier. The sixth sentence reported the current location of a Union division.

The last sentence of the telegram dealt with a far larger and much more important subject. Indeed, it concerned the basic dilemma that Johnston and his forces faced during those months, and it raised the crucial question that should have dominated all late 1862 and early 1863 Confederate thinking about, and discussion of, Rebel strategy for the West.

---

11 See A. Jones's comments, "Tennessee and Mississippi," 144-145.

Tacking the sentence on to the end of his telegram, providing no context for the query, without explaining why he desperately needed an answer, and in only eight words, Johnston asked, "Which is the most valuable, Tennessee or Mississippi?" Davis's response came the following day and—as was so often the case—did not provide a direct answer to the question. "To hold the Mississippi," telegraphed the President, "is vital." Note that Johnston asked about states; Davis replied about the river.

A man more sensitive than Davis and a strategist more concerned with the West would have seen Johnston's question for what it was—a desperate plea for guidance. He would then have answered the question directly, taken the time to communicate fully, and explained matters in detail. On the other hand, Johnston could (and should) have made so important a question the subject of a separate communication and of a much more detailed discussion. Even so, the general could have followed up Davis's reply with an immediate and direct request for clarification. Did the President mean that the Rebels should abandon the Volunteer State if necessary to try to hold on to the Mississippi River? Was the Vicksburg-Port Hudson corridor more valuable than the food and raw materials of the Confederate-held areas of Tennessee?[12]

Johnston was absolutely correct to regard (as he did) such questions as political, not military, matters. They could be settled only by the Confederacy's civilian authorities, and that meant only by Jefferson Davis. Would a general who trusted his government have gone back to the President to discuss the matter and seek clarification?[13]

---

12 Later the general did make some half-hearted efforts along these lines. As late as June 15, 1863, he was trying to get the government (the secretary of war in this case) to determine the matter. See his *Narrative*, 511.

13 20 *OR*, pt. 2, 487-488; 24 *OR*, pt. 1, 211-212; 52 *OR*, pt. 2, 404; J. Davis, *Papers*, vol. 9, 7. Davis seems to have been willing to put Tennessee at great risk to have held the Vicksburg-Port Hudson corridor. In addition to the reply to Johnston quoted in the text, consider his Dec. 1862 comment to Bragg to "Fight if you can and fall back [from Tullahoma] behind the Tennessee [River]" (20 *OR*, pt. 2, 493). Consider also his decisions to transfer more than 20,000 troops from Bragg's department to Mississippi during the December 1862 – June 1863 period (to be detailed later in this book). My guess is that Davis either did not (could not?) face the question, or was reluctant to state his decision clearly lest word of the policy reach Tennessee politicians and create even more political problems for him. A president who trusted and had confidence in his general might have sent a confidential message—perhaps conveyed verbally by a trusted aide—to guide his commander. If such a policy were to be revealed to Johnston, would he inform Wigfall? Would Wigfall tell Representative Henry S. Foote of Tennessee? If anything, Foote was more an enemy of Davis than was Wigfall.

WHAT Johnston did not do during the first four months of 1863 also tells us much about the type of man and commander he was and why his record as a Confederate general is almost completely barren of success.

One thing that Johnston chose not to do was to take charge of the area he had been assigned to defend. He did, of course, formally announce on December 4, 1862, that he had assumed command of the Western Department in compliance with the orders of President Davis. He did not, however, specify where his permanent headquarters would be located. (The War Department's orders authorized Johnston to establish departmental headquarters at any point within his command.[14]) Had he selected a central point for his headquarters (arguably, Atlanta would have been the best location), Johnston could have remained there and devoted his time to gaining an in-depth understanding of the West and of its situation and its problems. He then would have been better able to explain his difficulties to the Richmond authorities and, perhaps, to have won greater cooperation from them.

Such a step, however, would have required Johnston to think on a higher level of warfare than he ever did. Doing so, in effect, would have made him an overall chief of the West, but it would have removed him from actual field command. He seems not to have grasped that he could direct without issuing specific orders for field operations—that is, he could assign an objective to a subordinate but not try to give him detailed instructions as to how to accomplish it. This step would also have necessitated that he communicate more fully, forcefully, and openly both with the Davis government and with Generals Bragg and Pemberton than he ever proved willing to do. Equally important, the establishment of a fixed headquarters would have facilitated Johnston's specifically requiring his subordinate commanders to submit regular strength returns, reports, and other correspondence to and through his office.[15]

---

14 The orders actually stated that departmental headquarters were to be in Chattanooga, or such other place in the department that Johnston might select. In his *Narrative* (150), Johnston implied that he had to maintain his headquarters in Chattanooga but then quoted the actual order (231), which made it clear that he was free to move his headquarters to some other place at his discretion.

15 In fairness to Johnston, I should point out, that as far as I have been able to determine, no one in the War Department bureaucracy or the army ever thought about what administrative changes a new post such as that created for Johnston in the West would necessitate. An experienced administrative officer such as Samuel Cooper—or even Davis and Johnston— certainly should have given some thought to the subject. In any case, Johnston could and

Had Johnston not been too passive to take such a step, he would have realized at least two beneficial results. For one thing, he would have had information coming regularly across his desk about the state of the forces in his command. He therefore would know how many men Bragg and Pemberton had available for duty, how well supplied their forces were, where they were stationed, and what was transpiring in their fronts. He would have received constant updates on whatever information the Rebels had about the enemy. He would not have had to send such messages as the three he dispatched to Pemberton on May 6:

> Have heard nothing from you of the previous battle reported on 1st [Port Gibson]. *What is the result, and where is Grant's army* [my emphasis; note this was five days after the battle]?

> Tell me by telegraph, numbers [of cavalry] in cipher, location[,] and strength of your cavalry.

> Let me know the location of your troops, number, and places, in cipher.[16]

Second, had Johnston chosen (Covey once more) to establish and assert his command authority, he almost certainly could have avoided many, if not all, of the difficulties that arose because Pemberton and the Richmond officials frequently communicated directly with each other rather than through him and his headquarters. On February 12, 1863, Johnston whined to Davis, "General Pemberton is not communicative." The President replied, "I am sorry to learn that you have not as full communication from General Pemberton as is desirable." In the previous month (January) Johnston had twice complained to Pemberton about the lack of information coming to him from Mississippi. Would not a commander have simply ordered Pemberton to send to him the desired information and reports?[17]

Pemberton, in turn, seems not fully to have grasped what his relation to Johnston was supposed to be. In April, when Johnston was in Tennessee, Pemberton telegraphed to the Richmond authorities, "I endeavor to keep General

---

should have required Bragg, Pemberton, and other subordinates to keep him informed on a regular basis.

16 24 *OR*, pt. 3, 838 and 839. Pemberton's reply is in ibid., 842. Such a practice might also have led to the elimination of problems with the Rebels' cipher that hampered communications (ibid., 844 and 846; ibid., pt. 1, 198).

17 J. Davis, *Papers*, vol. 9, 59-61; 23 *OR*, pt. 2, 633 and 640-641. We can be forgiven if we wonder whether Davis would have made the same complaint about Johnston.

Johnston informed of any movement [in Mississippi] which may effect *his* army [my emphasis]." This message, Pemberton's biographer states, "indicated . . . [he] did not think of Johnston as his superior in the chain of command." The Mississippi commander still regarded President Davis and the War Department as his superiors. It also indicates that he continued to think in terms of two separate armies (his and Bragg's—or Johnston's) with no overall commander.[18]

FORCEFUL action by Johnston to exercise command (although, of course, not actual field command of operations) through administration might also have prevented the serious trouble that subsequently arose when Davis and the War Department continued to deal directly with Pemberton. Johnston knew of at least some of this correspondence, for on April 30 Davis informed him that Pemberton had telegraphed Richmond that he needed more cavalry.[19]

The problem—like all the Davis-Johnston difficulties from the war's earliest days in 1861—was not new. During Johnston's 1861-1862 service in Virginia the issue had come up several times. Then Secretary of War Judah P. Benjamin had authorized furloughs for some of Johnston's men, he had detailed some individual soldiers for special duty away from their regiments, and he had directed one of Johnston's subordinates to move a part of his force from one point to another, all without consulting or even informing Johnston of his actions.

Upon learning of the secretary's orders, Johnston protested to Davis, but the President justified Benjamin's actions on the grounds that Johnston had not obeyed earlier directives from the government (clearly a reference to the matter of state brigades). Political criticism soon forced Davis to move Benjamin to the State Department, and the matter blew over—but, typically, it was not resolved.[20]

Had Johnston established a real departmental headquarters in the West and required his subordinates to submit regular strength returns and reports and to communicate with the government through channels, or at least to send him copies of their direct correspondence with Richmond, he would have driven home to both Pemberton and the government that the Rebels in Mississippi simply could not have two commanders. Such action, however, would have run contrary to

---

18 On January 5, 1863, Pemberton suggested to Davis that it would be well to define Johnston's authority. J. Davis, *Papers*, vol. 9, 10, 59, and 67; Ballard, *Pemberton*, 135 and 142-143; 24 *OR*, pt. 1, 250.

19 24 *OR*, pt. 3, 805.

20 See Symonds, *Johnston*, 135-138.

Johnston's passive approach to command and to his own tortured relationship with the Davis Administration.[21]

DURING the early months of 1863 Johnston might also have established and maintained a system of regular correspondence with Theophilus Holmes and thereafter with Lieutenant General E. Kirby Smith, who succeeded Holmes on March 7 as commander of the Trans-Mississippi. (After Smith's arrival Holmes took charge of the District of Arkansas.) By taking such an initiative (and sending copies of the correspondence to Richmond) Johnston could have ensured that the Confederate commanders would at least share information (President Davis's "co-intelligence") about the enemy in the Mississippi Valley, and that he and his counterpart west of the Mississippi River would at least understand each other's situation. They might also have stockpiled (or made some other arrangements for) supplies along the route that any troops moving between Little Rock and Vicksburg would use. The Rebel commanders could even have instituted the "pipeline" concept by stationing some units at intermediate points along that route, especially if, as Holmes reported to Davis on April 8, the situation in Arkansas had improved markedly beginning in March.[22]

Johnston made no serious effort to take such actions during the first three-and-one-half months of 1863. Later, when it was much too late to effect anything, he did send a few desperate pleas urging the generals in the Trans-Mississippi to do something to relieve pressure on Vicksburg. Had he and the commanders west of the river acted earlier and displayed more thought and energy (more proactivity, as Covey might have said), the Confederates in Arkansas and Louisiana might have been able to mount a serious threat to the Union bases at Helena and Milliken's Bend or—far more important—the right flank of the column that Grant finally marched down the Louisiana side of the Mississippi to cross the river and operate against Vicksburg from the east and south. If nothing else, such a threat would have slowed Grant's progress and compelled him to keep a division or two west of

---

21 Civil War-era officers were well aware of the danger inherent in divided command. See Davis's remarks quoted in Chapter Two, Part Two, of this book. See also Major General John McClernand's June 10, 1863, comment: "One thing is certain, two generals cannot command this army, issuing independent and direct orders to subordinate officers, and the public service be promoted." 24 *OR*, pt. 3, 19.

22 J. Davis, *Papers*, vol. 9, 131. One wonders why Davis did not then renew his plea for Holmes (or Smith) to send reinforcements to Pemberton—perhaps because no obvious danger then threatened Vicksburg.

the Mississippi to protect what was then his sixty-three-mile overland line of supply and communication.

Finally, and even more important, Johnston could have requested authority to remove subordinate officers in whom he lacked confidence and whom he had come to distrust. As will be mentioned several times below, Pemberton seems from early in Johnston's Western assignment to have been one such officer. (Such a request would have run head-on into both Davis's penchant for army bureaucracy—the regulations, after all, specified the proper, and cumbersome, procedure to remove an officer from his post—and the President's high opinion of Pemberton. It might, however, have driven home to Davis the need to do something about the quality of his generals in the West. This point will come up many times in the pages that follow.)

HAVING taken the steps that he could think of, or at least those that he was willing to take, Johnston traveled to Mobile to make his inspection visit. While there, he received on January 22 a message from President Davis dated the preceding day. "I wish you with the least delay to proceed to the headquarters of General Bragg's army," the Chief Executive telegraphed. "You will find explanatory letter at Chattanooga." Johnston quickly responded that he would leave on the twenty-third.[23]

The general reached Chattanooga on the twenty-fifth. "I find no letter here," he telegraphed Davis that day. The President's reply came on the twenty-seventh. "The letter was mailed on the twenty-second. If not received, proceed as mentioned in the despatch." Doubtless still puzzled by these orders, Johnston went on. He reached Bragg's Tullahoma headquarters on the twenty-eighth or twenty-ninth.[24]

THE letter by Davis of the twenty-second finally caught up with Johnston on January 30. The President found himself troubled by the festering command turmoil in the Army of Tennessee and was besieged by demands from several prominent politicians and generals to name Johnston to replace Bragg. (This latter group included the two infantry corps commanders in Bragg's own army, Lieutenant Generals Leonidas Polk and William J. Hardee.)

23 J. Davis, *Papers*, vol. 9, 35 and 38.

24 Ibid., 40 and 41; 24 *OR*, pt. 3, 602; 52 *OR*, pt. 2, 418.

Unwilling to act without more information (and probably even if he had it), Davis wrote that he wanted Johnston to meet "with General Bragg and others of his command, to decide what the best interests of the service require, and to give me the advice which I need at this juncture." The President closed his letter with a curious sentence: "As that army is part of your command, no order will be necessary to give you authority there, as whether present or absent, you have a right to direct its operations and to do whatever else belongs to the general commanding."[25]

Johnston spent two weeks with the Army of Tennessee. (He was back in Chattanooga on February 13.) During the visit he talked with Bragg and his generals as well as with Tennessee governor Isham G. Harris, and he visited with and inspected the troops. What Johnston learned impressed him very favorably, although he did hear numerous complaints against Bragg.

In reports to Davis dated February 3 and 12, Johnston wrote that the army's "appearance is very encouraging—& gives positive evidence of General Bragg's capacity to command." Morale, he thought, was high. While some generals expressed a lack of confidence in Bragg, Johnston praised that officer's recent operations which, he stated, "seem to have been conducted admirably." Then Johnston gushed on, "I can find no record of more effective fighting in modern battles than that of this army in December, evincing skill in the commanders & courage in the troops." Johnston closed his final report with, "I believe . . . that the interest of the service requires that General Bragg should not be removed" from command of the army.

It is clear that these reports reflected Johnston's honest convictions. In a letter to his friend and ally Wigfall written from Chattanooga on the fourteenth Johnston observed of Bragg's recent operations, "More effective fighting is not to be found in the history of modern battles."[26]

DURING his stay in Tullahoma Johnston learned from Bragg and others more details about the army's fractured high command, including the fact that the corps commanders had become so critical of, if not hostile to, their army leader that they had petitioned the President to replace him with Johnston. The messy situation seems thoroughly to have disgusted the visiting general, who strongly disapproved of such insubordinate conduct. Even worse, were Davis to implement

---

25 J. Davis, *Papers*, vol. 9, 36 and 40. Was Johnston to decide, or only to advise?

26 Ibid., 48-50 and 59-61; Symonds, *Johnston*, 196-199.

such a suggestion after Johnston's report, it might create the impression that the inspecting general had engineered Bragg's removal in order to gain a coveted army command for himself. Such accusations would at least imply that he was guilty of the same type of dishonorable conduct as exhibited by Polk and Hardee.

To forestall such an embarrassing eventuality, Johnston wrote in his February 3, 1863, report, "I respectfully recommend that should it . . . appear to you necessary to remove General Bragg no one in this army, or engaged in this investigation, ought to be his successor." Nine days later he reiterated the point, "I am sure that you will agree with me that the part I have borne in this investigation would render it inconsistent with my personal honor to occupy that position."[27]

IT seems that Davis and Secretary of War James A. Seddon had sent Johnston to Tullahoma hoping (expecting?) that he would recommend Bragg's removal from command of the army. The authorities could then assign Johnston to the post.

Such a development would have permitted the President and the secretary to satisfy Bragg's many critics without, so it would appear, having given in to pressure or soiling their own bureaucratic hands. The change would also placate Johnston and his powerful political friends, especially Wigfall, all of whom had been agitating to change the command arrangements in the West and to put Johnston at the head of a field army. Had this scenario played out, it would have solved several nagging problems and spared Jefferson Davis the always hard and tricky task of making and taking responsibility for a politically very difficult and controversial decision.

THERE WAS YET one more aspect of this possible change of commanders of the Army of Tennessee. Were Johnston to become that army's day-to-day commander, what would happen to Davis's recently created Western command structure? This question must have occurred to Davis and perhaps to Secretary of War Seddon as well.

Should Johnston take Bragg's place as the full-time commander of the army at Tullahoma, he could not realistically be expected to continue in a supervisory role over Confederate forces in Alabama, Mississippi, and East Louisiana. Who, if

27 Note that Johnston in his first report did not offer any reason for suggesting that no officer then with the army succeed Bragg. Polk was the army's senior lieutenant general and second in command. The quoted remark seems to indicate that Johnston had concluded—quite correctly, I think—that neither Polk nor Hardee was suitable for the responsibilities of army command. His opinion of, and relations with, those officers, and theirs of and with him, will be discussed in Book Three, Chapter Four, Volume II.

anyone, would then become the overall Western commander? Only General Lee among Rebel field commanders outranked Johnston, and Davis obviously would not transfer him away from Virginia. Had Johnston and Bragg simply exchanged places, would Bragg have attempted to give orders to his subordinate who outranked him? Had he done so, would the proud Johnston—so touchy on questions of rank—have obeyed them? The same problem would have arisen if P. G. T. Beauregard, the Confederacy's only other available full general, were transferred from Charleston to assume Johnston's old post as overall Western commander. Johnston's preferred solution to the problem would have been for himself and Lee to exchange places. Davis, of course, would never have agreed to such a step, and Lee would have left Virginia only with great reluctance.

President Davis had three other options. He could have put the Army of Tennessee under Johnston's command, separated it from the forces in Mississippi, and brought Beauregard west to command the latter. In such a case he might even have extended Beauregard's authority over Rebel forces in the Trans-Mississippi. From Davis's point of view, however, any such action had two drawbacks. It would place Beauregard in a prominent position—indeed, back into virtually the same position from which Davis had removed him in disgrace only six months earlier. Second, doing so would constitute a clear admission that Johnston had been correct all along in his criticism of Davis's late 1862 scheme for defending the West.

Another option would have been to find some new post for Bragg, give Johnston command of the Army of Tennessee, and not name a new Western commander. Davis would thereby allow the position Johnston had held simply to fade away, and he could hope that the public would forget about it. Such a development would not have much changed the way things were done in practice. Nor would Davis have had to acknowledge the flaws in the command structure he had imposed on the West (over Johnston's objections) but a short time earlier. He would thus be rid of the system without having to admit that his idea had been deeply flawed from the beginning.[28]

Finally, Davis's best option was to face facts (something that he did not do very well or very often) and get rid of Polk and Hardee—or, at least, Polk. As will be discussed in Book Three, however, he would then have faced the problem of finding men to take their places. (Would he have considered some of the promising division commanders then in the Army of Northern Virginia?) Johnston had made

---

28 See 23 *OR*, pt. 2, 640-641.

no such recommendation, and we do not know if Davis ever considered such a step. As will be seen below, it usually took a massive crisis to get Davis to acknowledge that a living Confederate general should be replaced.

WHATEVER the case, Johnston's findings and recommendations prevented such changes. Nor would the general express even privately a desire to have Bragg's place, despite urging from Wigfall and others that he do so, and promises that if he would but indicate a preference the position would be his.

"Telegraph me simply 'You are right' or 'You understand me' or some equivalent expression & I'll understand you and act accordingly," begged Wigfall on February 23. "Make the sacrifice of your honorable delicy [sic] to the importance of the occasion and greatness of our cause," implored Seddon on March 3. Johnston would not budge, and the situation had not yet become so bad that Davis was willing to make such a change without the political cover that only Johnston could provide.[29]

As with so much else when Davis and Johnston were involved, much discussion took place, many letters and telegrams flew back and forth, but nothing was decided upon and nothing was done. "Not to decide," Harvey Cox has observed, "is to decide."[30]

HIS visit to the Army of Tennessee completed, Johnston returned to Chattanooga where he had posted most of his staff officers. Except for a brief trip to Knoxville to check on the East Tennessee region of his command, he remained in Chattanooga until March 9 or 10, 1863. He then journeyed to Mobile to finish the inspection that Davis's January 21 telegram had interrupted. Johnston intended to go on to Mississippi after completing his examination of the troops and fortifications at Mobile and to spend some time with Pemberton's army.

A few days after reaching Mobile, however, Johnston received a telegram ordering him back to Tullahoma and directing him to take command of the Army of Tennessee while Bragg went to Richmond for "consultation" with the government. Johnston left Mobile on the morning of March 14.[31]

29 See Symonds, *Johnston*, 196-200.

30 Laurence J. Peter, *Peter's Quotations: Ideas for our Time*, 297.

31 24 *OR*, pt. 1, 238. Did this order indicate that Davis had finally decided to put Johnston in Bragg's place, using the "consultation" as a blind while he found another assignment for Bragg?

The March journey back to Tullahoma gave Johnston additional evidence that the Confederate railroads could not reliably move troops about the West. Some two or three hours after leaving Montgomery, the passenger car in which Johnston was riding ran off the track and rolled completely over as it tumbled down a ten- or twelve-foot embankment and came to rest on its side. Johnston, who was sitting next to a window, was thrown across the car and landed upon Richard I. Manning, a young South Carolinian who had been sitting beside him and who just recently had become the newest addition to the general's "military family." Both Johnston and Manning landed on an officer who had been sitting across the aisle.

The general suffered a slight cut on his forehead when he hit it against the car's paneling and a bruised right knee when it struck one of the seats. Fortunately, no one received a serious injury. After a twelve-hour delay, during which they "spent the day in the woods pleasantly enough," reported Manning, the travelers were able to resume the journey. Johnston did not get to Chattanooga until late on the sixteenth. He spent a day or two at his headquarters, probably to catch up on work there or, perhaps, to recover from the railroad accident. He reached Tullahoma on the nineteenth.[32]

WHEN he got to Tullahoma, Johnston learned that Mrs. Bragg had contracted typhoid fever and that General Bragg was unwilling to leave her side. Authorizing the distraught Bragg to suspend the trip to Richmond and to remain with his spouse, Johnston quietly assumed de facto command of the army.

By April 10, when Mrs. Bragg had recovered, Johnston himself had fallen ill—probably a flare-up of problems stemming from his old Seven Pines wound, possibly exacerbated by the injuries he sustained in the railroad accident. Whatever the malady, it was serious. Finally, on April 12, the newspapers reported that the general was out of danger (indicating, of course, that he had been in danger).

The illness left Johnston very weak, and he had not fully recovered even late on May 9 when an urgent telegram arrived from Secretary of War Seddon ordering him to hasten to Mississippi to assume "chief command of the forces, giving to them in the field, as far as practicable, the encouragement and benefit of your

---

32 Manning described the trip in a Mar. 17, 1863, letter to his mother. His father was one of Johnston's good friends and shared the general's hatred of President Davis. The younger Manning became a close friend and a valuable aide to the general (he often acted as an amanuensis for him). Manning's extremely valuable letters are an absolute gold mine on what Johnston did and, I believe, thought, during the crucial months of 1863 and 1864.

personal direction." Three thousand "good troops," Seddon added, were to go from Bragg's Army of Tennessee to reinforce the Rebels in Mississippi.[33]

---

33 23 *OR*, pt. 1, 4; 23 *OR*, pt. 2, 825-826; 24 *OR*, pt. 1, 205, 215, 220, and 230; Memphis (Atlanta) *Daily Appeal*, Apr. 22, 1863 (printing an Apr. 12 dispatch). On Apr. 10, Manning noted in a letter to his father, "it is still doubtful—even to Genl. J. whether he is to assume immediate command of the army of Tenn or to remain in command of the whole [Western Department]" (Manning Letters). In a few weeks the question of the extent of Johnston's command would become another subject for an exchange of bitter correspondence between the general and President Davis. See Chapter Eight and Chapter Eleven, Part I, of this book. Of course, Johnston could quickly have resolved the matter with a simple telegraphic inquiry—but, of course, he again proved too passive to do so.

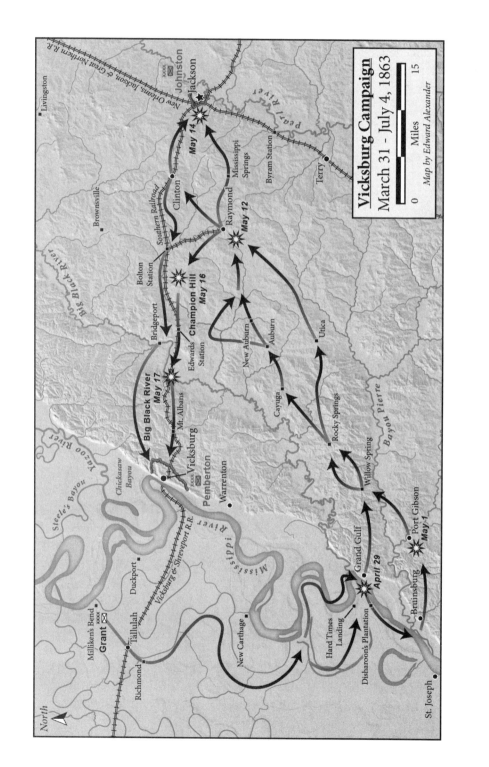

Vicksburg Campaign
March 31 - July 4, 1863

Map by Edward Alexander

0   Miles   15

Chapter Six

Things Fall Apart

"To hold Vicksburg and Port Hudson is necessary
to a communication with [the] Trans-Mississippi."

— Jefferson Davis, May 7, 1863

Secretary James Seddon's telegraphed directive for Johnston to hasten to Mississippi and personally take charge of Rebel forces there had come as the Confederate government's response to a vastly changed situation in the Magnolia State. The crisis that erupted there in the first days of May—"the crisis of April-May 1863" some historians would later call it—confronted Jefferson Davis with a threat to Confederate national existence that would test him, his Western defense scheme, his overall management of the Secessionist war effort, and his Western generals to the utmost.[1]

FOR two months after Johnston left Jackson back in late January, Mississippi's Confederate defenders had seemed to be enjoying a great deal of success. Once Earl Van Dorn's cavalrymen destroyed the Yankee supply base at Holly Springs in December of 1862, Ulysses S. Grant had taken his army back to West Tennessee. Eventually he concentrated his force at Memphis. Soon thereafter he moved most of his troops down the Mississippi to Milliken's Bend and Young's Point on the right (Louisiana) bank of the river only about nine and twenty miles, respectively, above Vicksburg (which sat on the left bank).

Throughout the winter Grant's army tried one scheme after another to get at Vicksburg. All of them failed. Changing water levels in the river frustrated an attempt to divert the Mississippi away from Vicksburg. Hastily constructed Rebel fortifications blocked several efforts to reach the rear of the city by way of the bayous, channels, and streams directly north and northeast of Vicksburg. As spring

---

1 Connelly and Jones, *Politics of Command,* 44.

came to the region in 1863, Confederate Vicksburg on its bluffs appeared to be as securely in Secessionist hands as it had ever been.

In mid-April this situation changed abruptly and drastically. Realizing that he was most unlikely to achieve his objective by renewing an overland campaign along the northern Mississippi railroads, or by attempting to reach the city through the bayous and facing almost certain failure if he launched an assault against Vicksburg directly from the river, Grant determined to try a completely different approach.

The Federal commander decided to move most of his army southward down the Louisiana side of the river to a point below Vicksburg. He would then cross to the left bank. At that time he would have three options. He could strike northward, directly against Vicksburg; he could march east or northeast into the interior; or he could go farther south to join another Union army moving upriver to attack Port Hudson. Meanwhile, a part of his force would remain in the Milliken's Bend-Young's Point area to threaten a renewed effort against Vicksburg from the north. At the same time several columns of cavalry would strike into Mississippi and Alabama from the Mississippi River or from western Tennessee. These efforts, Grant hoped, would divert Rebel attention from the main Union operation and damage the infrastructure—especially the railroads—that supported the army defending Vicksburg.

By early April Grant had his troops at work preparing a route from Milliken's Bend and Young's Point to New Carthage and Hard Times on the Mississippi's right bank about thirty-five miles below Vicksburg. When completed, this route stretched north to south for some sixty-three miles through the water-logged region of eastern Louisiana.

Getting his army down to the New Carthage-Hard Times area, however, was not enough. Grant also needed to get transport boats below Vicksburg to ferry his troops across the river, and gunboats to protect the transports and the downriver base as well as to provide fire support for the land operations once the army crossed to the Mississippi side of the river.

EVEN as Grant put his plan into execution, John Pemberton made arguably the most serious misjudgment committed by a senior military commander on either side during the war.

Throughout the winter and early spring Pemberton remained at his departmental headquarters in Jackson. He was probably exhausted from constant worries about Grant's earlier efforts against Vicksburg and the unceasing labors necessary to counter them. Beyond question he was confused—and certainly distracted—throughout April by the feints and cavalry raids that Grant had launched for that very purpose. An officer on Pemberton's staff noted under the date of April 27 that a Union cavalry force was then raiding through the central part "of the state kicking up a thundering rumpus."[2]

During the winter Johnston had transferred most of Pemberton's cavalry to Tennessee (see preceding chapter). In the spring, therefore, the Rebels' Mississippi commander lacked the means to obtain reliable information or to defend the central and eastern sections of Mississippi against raiding Yankee horsemen who struck from the northwest. Pemberton spent many frustrating April days at his Jackson headquarters using the telegraph to order infantry units about the northern and eastern sections of the state in equally unsuccessful efforts to protect bridges and railroads and to catch and punish the raiders.

Doubting some early April reports of massive Federal activity west of the Mississippi, Pemberton misinterpreted the constant movements of Union vessels on the river itself.[3] Perhaps falling victim to wishful thinking—one writer notes his "penchant to see good news where it did not exist"—Pemberton jumped to the happy conclusion that Grant had abandoned his campaign against Vicksburg and was moving troops to Middle Tennessee to reinforce the Yankee army in Bragg's front. Having fallen into that intoxicating delusion, Pemberton, with Johnston's approval, activated the "pipeline" and started some of his own troops for Tennessee. The Rebels in Vicksburg scheduled a grand celebratory ball for the night of April 16.

AS officers and citizens gathered that evening at the stately home of William Watts, Yankee sailors just a few miles upriver were completing their preparations to

2 J. C. Taylor, Diary. The Union cavalry force he is referencing is popularly known as Grierson's Raid.

3 The Louisiana side of the river was in the Trans-Mississippi Department, then commanded by Lieutenant General E. Kirby Smith. Smith, however, found himself distracted by Federal activity along Bayou Teche and the Red River. The 15th Louisiana Cavalry Battalion commanded by Major Isaac F. Harrison seems to have been the only Rebel unit posted in the area where Grant planned to take his main force. Either in response to some unknown arrangement or owing to his own good sense, Harrison sent information gathered by his scouts to the Confederates directly across the river as well as up the chain of command to his own superiors. Partly in response to Harrison's reports, Brigadier General John S. Bowen, commanding Confederate forces in the Grand Gulf area, sent some of his own troops to the Louisiana side of the river to observe and harass the enemy. After Union gunboats ran by Vicksburg during the night of April 16-17, Bowen pulled his men back to the Mississippi side of the river. See Grabau, *Ninety-Eight Days*, 67-72, and Ballard, *Vicksburg*, 201-203.

attempt to run a small fleet of gunboats, transports, and supply barges past the fortified bluffs at Vicksburg.

At about 11:15 p.m. the dancers heard the booming of heavy artillery over the sounds of the music. The first cannon discharges came from the upriver shore batteries, but the sounds quickly spread southward as the big guns at downriver positions took up the firing.

Going outside the revelers saw a lighted sky glowing off to the west; officers immediately realized that lookouts had ignited the bonfires that the city's defenders had placed along the riverbank to illumine the Mississippi River. Obviously, whatever was taking place was something more than just another exchange of a few artillery rounds. As officers quickly said their goodbyes and hastened off to their duty stations, the shore batteries below the city began to join in the firing.

In an hour or so it was over. One of the transport boats had been sunk, but the rest of the Union vessels had gotten past the Confederate batteries. As the great black shapes of the Yankee boats glided off into the downriver darkness, the guns along the riverbank fell silent. It was now clear that the Secessionists could not deny the Mississippi to the Federal fleet. The Rebels had lost the river. Had any of the Southerners stopped to think seriously about the matter, it would also have been obvious that Vicksburg and Port Hudson had lost almost all their value to the Confederacy.[4]

PASSAGE of the batteries on the night of April 16-17 gave the Yankees a fleet of seven gunboats and two transports in the river just below Vicksburg. Supply barges had also gone downstream, lashed to those nine vessels, and the presence of Union soldiers on the river's Louisiana bank at New Carthage and Hard Times provided the Federal navy with a secure base inside the Vicksburg-Port Hudson corridor.

During the night of April 22-23 five more transports and four additional barges made it by the big Confederate guns on the Vicksburg bluffs. With their arrival Grant had a formidable fleet with which to ferry his army across the river and protect his base. Even as carpenters scrambled aboard the boats and barges to repair the damage sustained in running the batteries, Grant hustled more troops and guns down the road leading from Milliken's Bend to the New Carthage area. By

4 Ballard, *Vicksburg*, 127, 132, 139, and 193-205; 24 *OR*, pt. 1, 238; 24 *OR*, pt. 3, 712, 713, 730, 731, 733, and 738.

the end of the month of April, he had everything in readiness he needed to cross the river.[5]

ON the thirtieth the Union navy moved 22,000 of Grant's men across to Bruinsburg, a few miles below Grand Gulf, on the Mississippi side of the river. The Yankees landed unopposed. On the following day Grant marched inland, having dropped all idea of going downriver to join the force seeking to capture Port Hudson. His objective was Vicksburg, and his immediate purpose was to isolate the river city from the rest of the Confederacy.

Grant's troops defeated a gallant but hopelessly outnumbered Confederate force under General Bowen at Port Gibson on May 1. This defeat forced the Rebels to abandon Grand Gulf, and that town quickly became Grant's major base on the Mississippi's left bank.

By May 12 the Federal commander had some 44,000 troops in the area and had accumulated enough supplies to launch his campaign into the heart of the state. He planned to put his army between Vicksburg and Jackson—a position that would isolate Vicksburg and place the Yankee army between its ultimate objective and the reinforcements that Grant knew the Rebels were trying to assemble at the state capital. He could then deal with first one enemy force and then the other.

It was Grant's crossing of the river and his subsequent march inland that set off the "crisis of April-May 1863" and precipitated Secretary Seddon's urgent telegraphic order for Johnston to hasten to Mississippi and take charge of the Confederate effort there.

JOHNSTON, still sick in Tullahoma, first learned of the Union fleet's passage of the Vicksburg shore batteries sometime early in the morning of April 17. Pemberton's telegram (from Jackson) quoting another message from Vicksburg reporting the fact was transmitted to him at 2:30 a.m. (Pemberton sent a similar report to Richmond.)

That same day Pemberton, still at his Jackson headquarters, telegraphed three more messages to Johnston. Suddenly awakened to the Federal strength in the New Carthage-Hard Times area and on and in the river below Vicksburg, Pemberton realized the danger. "The *return* of Grant and the *resumption* of operations against

---

5 By then, of course, Pemberton was aware of the danger, and on the twenty-sixth reported to Johnston that signs indicated that Grant would soon cross the river and operate against Vicksburg from the south. See 24 *OR*, pt. 1, 239.

Vicksburg [my emphasis]," he telegraphed, necessitated the recall of the troops he had so recently started along the "pipeline" to Tennessee. Now he wanted them turned around and rushed back to Mississippi. Johnston replied immediately, advising Pemberton to contact Kirby Smith and urge the Trans-Mississippi commander to operate against Grant's supply line. He also authorized Pemberton to recall the units he had started along the "pipeline" to Bragg's army.[6]

Twelve days later Union gunboats began a bombardment of Grand Gulf. When on May 1 Grant's army crossed the Mississippi at Bruinsburg, twelve miles below Grand Gulf, Confederate leaders immediately realized the seriousness of the threat and the necessity of defeating the enemy force. "If Grant's army lands on this side of the river," Johnston wired Pemberton from his sickbed in Tullahoma on May 1, "the safety of Mississippi depends on beating it. For that object you should unite your whole force." (Was this an order? Pemberton later maintained that it was not; Johnston asserted that it was.) On the same day Secretary of War Seddon telegraphed Pemberton, "Heavy reinforcements will be sent from General Beauregard's command [on the South Atlantic Coast]."

Meanwhile, Pemberton busied himself shifting what troops he thought he could spare from the Vicksburg defenses southward to oppose Grant. Eventually, he reported, he was able to send about 3,500. To transfer more, he easily convinced himself, would expose Vicksburg to capture by the part of Grant's army then still in the Milliken's Bend area. The reinforcements he sent south were far from enough.

Realizing the threat facing the Rebels, Pemberton saw that Jackson was in great danger. He accordingly advised the governor to move the state archives from the capital, and he ordered the machinery from the government arsenal there shipped "into Alabama."[7]

Knowing that Grand Gulf was lost, and that Grant was moving to the northeast, Pemberton made some changes in his defensive deployments. On May 1 he shifted his headquarters from Jackson to Vicksburg. He also began moving about three-fifths of the Vicksburg garrison to positions on the high bluffs along the Big Black River about halfway between Vicksburg and Jackson. There, he thought, he could block Grant's advance once the Union commander turned his column west from the Jackson area to regain contact with the Yankee fleet in the Mississippi. Pemberton even directed the commander at Port Hudson, Major General Franklin Gardner, to send some 5,000 troops from that town to join the

---

6 24 *OR*, pt. 3, 751, 753, 760, and 761; 24 *OR*, pt. 1, 239; J. Davis, *Papers*, vol. 9, 149.

7 The documents relating to these developments are in 24 *OR*.

concentration on the Big Black. His staff officers scurried about west-central Mississippi to obtain all the supplies they could get and move them into Vicksburg. To the governor he sent the happy news that the Richmond authorities had notified him "that heavy reinforcements will be sent here."[8]

ALTHOUGH Pemberton had telegraphed some information to Johnston about developments in Mississippi, he and President Davis had continued their direct communications. Late on Thursday, May 7—the dispatch is dated 11:30 p.m.—the President wrote out or dictated a telegram to be sent to Pemberton. Davis, who was then quite ill (bronchitis and neuralgia), apparently composed the dispatch from his sickbed.

The Chief Executive's message opened with disappointing news. General Beauregard at Charleston, who had been directed to send 10,000 troops to Mississippi to reinforce Pemberton, "insists that he cannot spare more than the 5,000" then already reported en route from the Atlantic coast. Davis followed this demoralizing report with a weak "I hope he may change his views." Then, after promising to send more weapons and some 3,000 recently exchanged prisoners of war to Mississippi, he predicted that "after a few days" Grant would have to return to the river to draw supplies from the fleet.

President Davis had a propensity to sprinkle off-hand remarks—truisms and generalizations—in some of his correspondence. It is almost as if the Chief Executive were musing to himself or thinking on paper. One suspects that Davis needed somebody with whom he could mull over and discuss the Confederacy's military situation.

Since Lee had left to take command of the Army of Northern Virginia almost a year earlier the President had had no such readily available sounding board for his ideas. Nor was there anyone in Richmond who would be likely to have major military ideas of his own to present for Davis's consideration or to raise (politely and respectfully, of course) questions about the Chief Executive's own thoughts on military subjects. Adjutant and Inspector General Cooper, the only officer above the grade of major general stationed in Richmond, was an administrator. He was most unlikely to bring up matters on his own or to differ with Davis.[9] The

---

8 Ibid., pt 3, 828.

9 Steven Woodworth (*Davis and His Generals* and *Davis and Lee, passim*) suggests that Davis had originally expected that, in addition to his administrative work, Cooper would also serve as a

secretaries of war were civilians who, except for the departed Randolph, had little or no military experience. Davis was not the sort of president to take members of Congress into confidential discussions of military (executive) matters, and in any case by early 1863 many of them were too thoroughly alienated from the commander-in-chief for any such discussions to be productive.

NOW, not long before midnight on May 7-8, 1863, a sick and doubtless exhausted President Davis added one of those truisms to his message to Pemberton. This fateful sentence read: "To hold Vicksburg and Port Hudson is necessary to a connection with [the] Trans-Mississippi." He then closed the telegram with, "You may expect whatever is in my power to do," signed it, and sent it off to the telegraph office.

On May 8, Pemberton dispatched a message to General Gardner, ordering him to return to Port Hudson with 2,000 of the 5,000 troops he was bringing north to help with the defense of Vicksburg. "President says," Pemberton concluded, "both places must be held."

The next day Seddon, at Davis's direction, sent the telegram ordering Johnston to go to Mississippi and take charge of the effort to save Vicksburg.[10]

---

military adviser. Cooper, however, was not an officer to step outside bureaucratic routine, and never fulfilled that role.

10 24 *OR*, pt. 3, 842. Why Pemberton chose to regard Davis's observation as an order is not clear. He would soon disregard even more strongly stated messages from Johnston, possibly because he did not realize Johnston was supposed to be his commander. Michael Ballard (*Pemberton*, 142-143) suggested that Pemberton's 1861-1862 South Carolina experiences led him to the belief that he had to hold to the last any place he was assigned to defend. We do know that Pemberton had long preferred to avoid field maneuvers and had thought since at least Dec. 1862, that the way to hold the river was to shut his army up in Vicksburg while other Confederates organized another army to raise the siege. (See Chapter Four.) Davis's "order," if that is what it was, coincided with this view. Davis's truism, of course, was valid as far as it went. Holding the two towns was "necessary" to preserve communication between the halves of the Confederacy, but it was not *sufficient* for that purpose. As discussed earlier in Chapter Three, the Rebels also had to control the river between the two towns, and they lost that on the night of Apr. 16-17. The real problem was that three weeks after the Cis-Mississippi Secessionists lost connection with the Rebels west of the great river, none of them realized the fact—or if any did (Johnston, perhaps) we have no record of it. As things worked out, the Confederates would lose some 40,000 to 50,000 men trying to hold what they had already lost. Pemberton was fixated on Vicksburg itself and confused occupying the town with defending it. Johnston was sick in Tullahoma, and Pemberton did not keep him as well informed as he should have. Davis was sick in Richmond, and much of his attention was absorbed by the late April - early May Chancellorsville campaign only some fifty miles north of the capital.

Chapter Seven

Confused Command (and Commanders)

"I am too late."

— Joseph E. Johnston, May 13, 1863

On May 13, the train carrying Joseph E. Johnston, David Yandell, his medical officer who came along to tend to the still ailing general, and a few other members of Johnston's party crept slowly westward along the dilapidated rail line between Meridian and Jackson. At several points beside the rickety, recently repaired track Johnston had the opportunity to observe some of the damage done a few weeks earlier by a force of raiding Yankee cavalry. The train reached the Jackson station that evening as a hard rain fell on the town.[1]

Upon arrival Johnston and his party went a few blocks north to the Bowman House, in antebellum days the capital's finest hotel, where the general took up quarters. Johnston, doubtless, was tired and feeling the effects of his illness. (He was "unfit for field duty," he had informed Richmond on May 9 when ordered to Mississippi.) He had no time to rest, however. A major crisis loomed up west of Jackson.[2]

AT the time of Johnston's arrival, the Confederates in the Jackson area numbered some 5,000 to 6,000 and were somewhat demoralized. Some of these men, mostly from the brigade of Brigadier General John Gregg, were fugitives from a Rebel force that had been defeated by Grant's troops the day before in the Battle of Raymond fought a few miles to the southwest. Others were members of the brigade of Brigadier General William H. T. Walker—the leading units of the

---

1 The closest we have to a full account of the trip and the situation Johnston found upon his arrival in Jackson is in Yandell's June 17, 1863, letter to John M. Johnson, Rowland, *Davis Constitutionalist*, VI, 2-5.

2 See Johnston, *Narrative*, 175; 23 OR, pt. 2, 825-826.

reinforcements sent from Beauregard's South Atlantic department. The rest were small fragments of other commands or state militia.

Gregg, the ranking officer present prior to Johnston's arrival, told the new commander what he knew (or believed) about the situation in the Jackson area. The Confederates had reports that some 25,000 Federals (four divisions), marching up from the south under Major General William T. Sherman, had reached Clinton on the railroad about eleven miles to the west. They were expected to advance eastward against Jackson on the fourteenth. Four brigades of Confederate reinforcements (supposed to have a total strength of about 5,000) were then en route to the capital and should arrive in a day or two. The fortifications protecting Jackson, Gregg reported, were but slight, unfinished, poorly located works and probably could not be long held against a serious attack by a vastly superior force.

After conferring with Gregg and doubtless other officers, Johnston sent off two messages. One of these communications, probably dispatched about 9:00 p.m., indicates that he saw at least a glimmer of hope. That day, when his train paused at Lake Station about halfway between Jackson and Meridian, Johnston had received a telegram from Pemberton—the first communication from his Mississippi subordinate in about ten days. From that message Johnston had learned that Pemberton had moved some 20,000 troops from Vicksburg eastward across the Big Black River to Edward's Station on the railroad eighteen miles west of Clinton. Pemberton anticipated that he would fight the Union army at Edward's when it turned west toward Vicksburg.[3]

Upon reaching Jackson, Johnston "inferred" (he later wrote) that the Yankees at Clinton had separated themselves from the main enemy force to the south and were positioned between the Rebels in Jackson and Pemberton's troops at Edward's. Combined, the two groups of Confederates would be as strong as the enemy force believed to be at Clinton.

Always a strong advocate of concentration, Johnston quickly concluded that if he and Pemberton could join their commands or launch a coordinated attack on the Federals at Clinton before the other Yankees could come to their aid, the Rebels would have an excellent chance to cripple a significant part of Grant's army. Thinking along those lines, Johnston instructed Pemberton that, "if practicable," he should come up in the rear of the Yankees at Clinton with every man he could

---

3 24 *OR*, pt. 1, 220-221 and 239. See also Arnold, *Grant Wins the War*, 136.

bring. The Rebels at Jackson, he wrote, "could co-operate." "Time," he added, "is all important."[4]

JOHNSTON'S second message, a telegram sent after his arrival in Jackson, went to the authorities in Richmond. "I arrived this evening," he reported, "finding the enemy's force between this place and General Pemberton, cutting off communication. I am too late."[5]

4 24 *OR*, pt. 1, 221. I find it most strange that so cautious a general as Johnston would issue such a directive, especially so quickly after reaching Jackson. He knew little of the area (one short visit the previous December) and nothing of the situation in central Mississippi other than what he had learned that day from Pemberton's message and what Gregg and others told him upon his arrival in Jackson. Johnston's dispatch could not possibly get to Pemberton in less than five or six hours. In fact, it did not reach the defender of Vicksburg until about 9:30 a.m. on the fourteenth (Pemberton, *Compelled to Appear*, 103). By that hour the Yankees who had been at Clinton had left and were marching east, moving on Jackson. Pemberton, furthermore, was not at Edward's when he received Johnston's message. He was then near Bovina, several miles west of the Big Black River, *en route* to join his troops at Edward's. He did not even reach Edward's until about 12:00 M. Implementation of Johnston's proposed plan would disrupt whatever Pemberton might be doing to meet the situation. It would necessitate that he redeploy his troops and adjust his logistical arrangements to feed and supply his men as they moved eastward from Edward's Station. (The Federals had torn up a couple of miles of track west of Clinton on the thirteenth so Pemberton's Rebels would not have use of the railroad beyond that point.) Nor did Johnston specify any details in his message. What did he mean by "could co-operate"? Was he to remain in Jackson or leave the town to join Pemberton in the field? Were the two forces to unite north or south of the railroad, or make two separate attacks on the enemy troops between them? If the latter, were the attacks to be coordinated as to time? If so, when were they to occur and how would the Rebels coordinate their efforts? Uniting two separate columns on the battlefield is an extremely difficult feat, especially given the slow, indirect means of communication available to Johnston and Pemberton. In July of 1861, Johnston had wisely ignored a similar proposal by Beauregard just prior to First Manassas. It is most puzzling of all that Johnston would send this "order" (suggestion?) to Pemberton without knowing where the bulk of Grant's army was or what it was doing. (This subject apparently did not come up during his meeting with Gregg.) The Yankee force at Clinton, in fact, comprised only two divisions and was commanded by Major General James B. McPherson. Most of the rest of the Union army was about ten miles south of the railroad in the Raymond-Mississippi Springs area and was approaching Jackson from the southwest. Those Federals were in a perfect position to strike northward against Pemberton's right flank or rear if the Rebels moved eastward from Edward's, or against Johnston's left flank or rear if he moved out of Jackson toward Clinton. My guess is that Johnston was so exhausted from his trip that he simply accepted Gregg's report without question and overlooked these matters. Normally such concerns would have kept him from issuing such an "order." Indeed, they might well have kept him from taking any action. For a discussion of the phrase "if practicable" in Civil War era military correspondence see Bowden and Ward, *Last Chance*, 199-209.

5 24 *OR*, pt. 3, 870; 24 *OR*, pt. 1, 215.

We would very much like to know Johnston's thinking behind this telegram and the reaction to it in the Confederate capital. Was the general pronouncing his situation hopeless so as to free himself from blame should he not accomplish his assigned mission? After all, he may very well have used the same ploy in Virginia early in 1862 when he described the task of safely moving his army from its position along the Potomac to be virtually impossible. In May 1863, was he only expressing his usual pessimism? Had he simply abandoned hope? Was he giving up even before he really started? Or did he mean only that since bad health prevented his undertaking the arduous, nighttime horseback ride in the rain (made necessary by the Yankee presence on the railroad at Clinton), he was too late to join Pemberton and take personal command of the Rebel army in the field?

If the Richmond authorities wondered about such questions, we can puzzle over the matter of why Johnston did not inform his superiors about his hastily designed plan for Pemberton's force and his own to strike the Federals at Clinton. Even if Johnston sent the disheartened (and disheartening) telegram to Richmond prior to coming up with the idea for a combined attack on the enemy at Clinton, he could have dispatched another message outlining that plan. Why did he once more choose (Covey again) not to keep his government informed about his situation and his plans?

The message to Pemberton indicates that Johnston—whatever he meant in the telegram to the Richmond authorities—thought he had at least the possibility of striking a telling blow at a significant part of Grant's army. To do so, however, he had to unite the Rebels at Jackson with the three divisions Pemberton had brought east from Vicksburg. Such a combined force would give the Secessionists a chance to beat the enemy in detail. Uniting the two could have been done in space (bringing them together in the field) or in time (having them strike the enemy simultaneously at different points).

IT was not to be. Upon receiving Johnston's message, Pemberton, at Bovina, replied that he would move on Clinton "at once." Hours later, however, after reaching Edward's Station, he realized that obeying Johnston's order involved serious risks. When he was at Bovina, Pemberton did not have access to detailed knowledge of the Federal position. Once at Edward's, however, he learned enough from his subordinates and from prisoners to realize the dangers that the Yankees to the south would pose to his right flank and rear should he move east as Johnston had directed (suggested?). The enemy, furthermore, could get in behind his marching column and cut him off from Vicksburg. Pemberton remained firmly convinced that, above all, he must not evacuate, or allow himself to be separated from, Vicksburg. He believed that President Davis had ordered him to hold the town. Pemberton, however, also felt it imperative that he do something. Contrary to what he had anticipated, the enemy was not coming west against his position at Edward's. Instead, the Yankees were heading east.

Pemberton met with his generals that same afternoon (May 14). The officers debated three proposals: pull back to defend the line of the Big Black since sooner or later the Federals would turn west; obey Johnston's "order" to move toward Jackson to join Johnston's own force; or, strike to the south to try to cut Grant's supply line to the Mississippi. Indeed, about that same time Johnston was writing to suggest such a move to Pemberton (see below in the text). Pemberton preferred the first of these options. A few days later he wrote, "My own view was expressed as unfavorable to any movement which would remove me from my base which was and is Vicksburg."[6] Most of his officers, however, favored following Johnston's "directive." Eventually, Pemberton allowed himself to be persuaded by a few of his subordinates to adopt the third course and launch a strike southward to cut the line of supply and communications between the river and to the Yankee army. By the time he determined upon this course of action it was so late, and there were so many preparations to make, that Pemberton decided not to begin the march until the morning of May 15.

DURING the night of May 13-14, after sending the "order" to Pemberton to attack the Federals at Clinton, Johnston had second thoughts. He decided to withdraw his 6,000 troops from Jackson and move toward Canton on the Mississippi Central Railroad about twenty-five miles northeast of the capital. The order for this movement is dated 3:00 a.m., May 14. A few hours later the Rebels marched out of Jackson and up the railroad toward Canton as their rear guard skirmished with the oncoming Federals west and southwest of the city.

Several historians have criticized Johnston severely for what they have labeled a premature decision to abandon Jackson without making a serious effort to defend it. With the 6,000 men he had in the capital on May 13-14, they have argued, Johnston ought to have held the city until the expected 5,000 reinforcements arrived. Then, with 11,000 troops present and more coming, Johnston could have mounted a serious and sustained resistance.[7]

---

6 24 *OR*, pt. 1, 217.

7 See, for example, Ballard, *Vicksburg*, 279-280 and *passim*, and Bearss, *Campaign for Vicksburg*, II, 554-555.

This criticism seems unfair. For one thing, Johnston had no guarantee that the reinforcing troops would arrive on schedule. Should they meet with a delay, he could find himself outnumbered at least four-to-one at Jackson (an estimate based on the information he then possessed). The brigade of Brigadier General Samuel B. Maxey, for example, had reached Brookhaven about fifty miles south of Jackson by nightfall May 12. It was scheduled to continue its northward journey the next morning. A few weeks earlier, however, raiding Union cavalry had torn up the railroad track at Brookhaven and at Hazlehurst (some twenty-five miles north of Brookhaven), and the Rebels had not repaired the damage. Maxey had only one locomotive and ten cars available for his use on the isolated section of the railroad between Brookhaven and Hazlehurst. Any derailment or breakdown of that locomotive, and Johnston would find himself without a major part of his anticipated reinforcements for at least a couple of days.

Johnston's own recent journey from Meridian to Jackson had showed him how dangerous it would be to rely upon reinforcements and supplies arriving on schedule over that rail line. A Confederate officer reported a few days later that his brigade had been delayed in Alabama because so much railroad equipment had been taken to use in evacuating material from Jackson. In July an officer traveling from Jackson to Meridian would note that at one point on that line, male passengers were required to get out and push the train to help it along.[8]

Second, Gregg and the other officers Johnston consulted had told him that the capital's fortifications were inadequate. Johnston had no opportunity to examine them personally, and he had to rely upon his subordinates' opinions. With a battle likely early on the 14th if he remained in Jackson, Johnston would have had no time to examine the works even if his own health had permitted him to do so in the heavy rain of May 13-14. Nor would he have had the time or laborers to strengthen the defenses. He certainly could not detail men from his fighting units to do the work, and time simply did not permit him to impress slaves from the surrounding area and to organize them into work parties—or to complete the work if he got them organized.

Third, Johnston had no guarantee that the 25,000 Yankees reported at Clinton would not turn on Pemberton with their superior force while he and his 6,000—or 11,000—troops sat in Jackson's fortifications (inadequate though they were) vainly awaiting an enemy attack.

---

8 24 *OR*, pt. 3, 920; Fremantle, *Diary*, 100-101.

Fourth, the Confederates at Jackson constituted at best an ad hoc force with no organization other than Johnston himself and a few staff officers above the brigade level. How well would such a collection of units operate against a much larger, compact, and thoroughly organized enemy column? How well would Johnston, who had virtually no knowledge of the area, direct the Rebels' action? How well and for how long could the scraped-together band of Confederates fight without the many support services and the equipment that an army must have to function? The commander of one of the reinforcing brigades reported a few days later that many of the troops coming to Mississippi had "left behind [at their old posts] many necessary matters."[9]

Finally, Johnston's whole approach to defending Mississippi (not just Jackson and Vicksburg) was predicated on a scheme to join his troops with those under Pemberton to strike the enemy force reported at Clinton. By marching toward Canton—even though that town was northeast of Jackson—Johnston would remain on or close to the railroad by which his force drew food from the northern part of the state and also position his men to march to join Pemberton when he ascertained by what exact route that general was approaching from the west or southwest.[10]

Much of the criticism leveled at Johnston for giving up Jackson on May 14 seems to be based upon knowledge of the great damage the Yankees did to the capital while they occupied it May 14-16 and the extent to which that damage later handicapped the Rebels in their effort to save Vicksburg and Pemberton's army. Had Johnston been able to unite with Pemberton and to operate the combined forces as a mobile field army, the loss of Jackson would have been of far less significance in the May-July operations in Mississippi.

In summary, given what Johnston knew on the night of May 13-14, what he had been told, what he did not know, his logistical and organizational difficulties, and what he hoped to accomplish, his decision to evacuate Jackson on May 14 does not loom as the major disaster it subsequently became.

Throughout the war Johnston consistently advocated concentration of Confederate forces. With the Yankees who had been at Clinton in the Jackson area

---

9 24 *OR*, pt. 3, 920.

10 As of 7:30 a.m. on the sixteenth Johnston still expected to unite with Pemberton (24 *OR*, pt. 1, 215-216). We lack adequate knowledge of the subject, but given what we know about subsequent events, it seems most unlikely that Johnston had in mid-May sufficient field transportation for even his relatively small force to operate away from the railroad for even a short time. Every hour that he could spend on the railroad, therefore, worked to his advantage.

on the 14th, it was obvious that there would be no fight at the former place. If Pemberton followed the Yankees east, he would not approach the Jackson-Canton area until late on the sixteenth or on the seventeenth. By that time Johnston would have been able to obtain food for his men at Canton, learn Pemberton's exact route, and march west or to the southwest to meet him. My guess is that Johnston willingly would have swapped Vicksburg and probably Jackson as well to unite his troops with Pemberton's. What he would have done with the combined forces we can never know.

WE can, however, legitimately fault Johnston for not being clear in his May 13 message to Pemberton (which Johnston called on "order") and for failure to communicate adequately with his subordinate after he decided to leave Jackson. He did write a belated note to Pemberton on the fourteenth from his camp seven miles northeast of the capital. (The message does not show the time it was sent, but it would have been early to mid-afternoon if not later.) Johnston informed Pemberton that the Rebels had been compelled to evacuate Jackson. He followed that statement with an expression of hope that the Confederates could prevent the Federals at Jackson from drawing provisions out of the region east and north of the capital and that the Rebels could quickly unite their scattered forces. The next day Johnston wrote again, informing Pemberton that he would march on to the northeast toward Canton—a route that would increase the distance between the two Confederate forces. Johnston also threw out a suggestion, asking if Pemberton might cut the Yankees off from their base on the Mississippi near Grand Gulf. (Implementation of this suggestion would, of course, necessitate that Pemberton move his troops to the south, thereby increasing the difficulties of communication and, therefore, of united action by the two Confederate forces.)

Two points about Johnston's May 14 message stand out. First, Johnston wrote nothing about the proposed attack on the enemy at Clinton that he had outlined in the dispatch sent to Pemberton on the night of May 13. Was that "order" still in effect? Should Pemberton march on eastward through Clinton toward Jackson to attack the enemy at the capital? If so, would Johnston's troops come south from Canton to cooperate? If not, what did Johnston want Pemberton to do?

Second, should Pemberton march southward to operate against the enemy supply line as Johnston suggested? If he moved to the south to cut the supply line, how could he even hope to join forces with Johnston to the north? Moving against the supply line was exactly what Pemberton was deciding to do at the May 14 conference with his generals. Indeed, Pemberton might well have been coming to that conclusion at the very moment Johnston was writing the dispatch.

Since Johnston's note did not reach Pemberton until after 5:30 p.m. on May 16, it had no effect on troop movements. It is important, however, for what it shows us about the Rebels' weak command structure and their clumsy, muddled, and confused response to the rapidly changing situation in mid-Mississippi.[11]

ON the morning of May 15, as Johnston prepared to resume his march toward Canton, he received Pemberton's message announcing that he had decided to disregard the "order" (or was it only a suggestion?) to march eastward against the Yankees at Clinton. Instead, Pemberton reported, he would move southward against Grant's supply line. Johnston's Rebels, whom he believed still to be in Jackson, he added, might communicate via a route through or south of Raymond. (We should note that Pemberton did not explain the reasons for his decision other than to say that he felt too weak to do more than fight on the defensive if he could compel Grant to attack in an effort to restore the Unionists' supply line.)

When he received this note, Johnston had not yet gotten Pemberton's first May 14 dispatch (the one written that morning from Bovina upon receiving Johnston's May 13 message about a possible attack on the Federals at Clinton). That message arrived some time after the note announcing Pemberton's planned thrust to the south, and Johnston disregarded it.[12]

DOUBTLESS furious at this unanticipated turn of events, Johnston— conveniently forgetting his own suggestion about attacking Grant's supply line in his May 14 note—sent off a harsh order for Pemberton to abandon the projected strike south against the Federal communications and to march "in the direction of Clinton." This message did not reach Pemberton until the morning of May 16. By then he had moved his force some distance to the south in an effort to reach and cut the enemy supply line between Grant's force and its base on the Mississippi River.

This time Pemberton obeyed Johnston's directive. He turned his army around and began to retrace his steps. Unfortunately for the Secessionists, his column ran into Grant's army at Champion Hill south of the railroad and about halfway between Jackson and Vicksburg. (One of the three couriers to whom Johnston entrusted copies of his May 13 note to Pemberton proposing an attack on the Yankees at Clinton turned out to be a Federal spy who had promptly turned his

---

11 24 OR, pt. 1, 221 and 240; Pemberton, *Compelled to Appear*, 101.

12 24 OR, pt. 3, 876-878, 882.

copy of the message over to the Federal generals.) Grant, having read Johnston's first note to Pemberton and fully alert to the importance of time and movement as well as to the necessity of keeping his enemy divided and off balance, had marched west from Jackson with most of his force.

That afternoon, in what was arguably the most important battle of the war, Grant's Federals attacked and routed Pemberton's army at Champion Hill.[13] The Rebels fled westward to the Big Black River where, on the seventeenth, they suffered another crushing defeat. After that loss Pemberton's men scurried west into the fortifications at Vicksburg. Grant followed, and within a few days the Unionists had clamped a stranglehold on the city and its garrison. Before Grant's siege lines closed off almost all communication between Johnston and Pemberton, the two managed to exchange a few more messages. After reaching Vicksburg, Pemberton reported the recent events to Johnston and ironically closed his message with "I respectfully await your instructions."

When he received instructions from Johnston to evacuate Vicksburg at least to save the army, Pemberton could not bring himself to do so. Once again he convened a meeting of his chief subordinates, who concluded the army had suffered such a battering that it was logistically, psychologically, and physically incapable of escaping from the city in condition to be of any further value to the Confederacy. He would hold the city, Pemberton informed Johnston, "as long as possible, with the firm hope that the Government may yet be able to assist me. . . . I still conceive it to be the most important point in the Confederacy."

A few months earlier Theophilus Holmes had imposed his will on Confederate geopolitical military grand strategy for the defense of the Mississippi Valley simply by refusing to send troops from Arkansas to aid in the defense of Vicksburg unless President Davis directly ordered him to do so. Now John C. Pemberton had imposed his preferred strategy on Rebel operations in the Mississippi Valley simply by disobeying Johnston's orders (or did he merely ignore Johnston's suggestions?).

When he received Pemberton's message announcing his intention to try to hold Vicksburg, Johnston replied, "I am trying to gather a force which may relieve you. Hold out."[14]

---

13 For a fine treatment on the battle, see Smith, *Champion Hill*.

14 24 *OR*, pt. 3, 689, 876, and 892; 24 *OR*, pt. 1, 222, 240, 241, 242, 372, and 373.

THE Confederates' real problem in Mississippi in mid-May 1863 was not the defense of Jackson and Vicksburg or even the difficulties of communicating between Johnston and Pemberton. The real problem was the mutually exclusive ideas held by President Davis and each of the two top Rebel generals in Mississippi: the Chief Executive's refusal to give his commanders positive orders or even adequate guidance, combined with Pemberton's absolute refusal—reinforced by his interpretation of Davis's May 7 telegram ("To hold Vicksburg and Port Hudson is necessary to a connection with [the] Trans-Mississippi")—to let go of Vicksburg, and Johnston's desire to form a strong mobile field army, but his refusal to issue a peremptory order to do so.

This was the same problem that in a different form had surfaced at the Grenada conference in late December, and one Davis, Johnston, and Pemberton had left unresolved ever since.

Chapter Eight

The Gettysburg Decision

"Take the aggressive."

— Robert E. Lee, April 9, 1863

Roughly one hundred hours elapsed between Joseph E. Johnston's arrival in Jackson, Mississippi, late on May 13, 1863, and the time that John C. Pemberton shut himself and his army up inside Vicksburg's massive fortifications on the evening of the seventeenth.

Those one hundred hours bracketed a crucial four-day period of the Confederacy's history. At about the time Johnston was making his way from Braxton Bragg's headquarters in Tullahoma, Tennessee, to Jackson, his old military academy classmate, longtime friend and (Johnston thought) professional rival Robert E. Lee journeyed from his camp near Fredericksburg, Virginia, to Richmond. Lee went to the capital to confer with Confederate authorities about how the Rebels should respond to the rapidly deteriorating situation in Mississippi and to the dangers looming on several other fronts.[1]

THE threat to Rebeldom that erupted in Mississippi in April-May 1863 was but the most recent of a host of problems besetting the Confederates that spring. Except in Virginia, the previous twelve months had been a time of virtually unmitigated disaster for the Secessionists. Rebel armies outside the Old Dominion had proved unable to reverse the major setbacks they had suffered in the first months of 1862 (see Book One, Chapter Two above), and in some cases they had suffered several additional defeats.

Most Confederates then, like most historians for decades afterward, focused sometimes almost exclusively on the military operations in Virginia. For that

---

1 Lee was in Richmond May 14-17, 1863, but the date of his arrival is not certain. He was back with his army on the eighteenth. 25 *OR*, pt. 2, 801, 805, and 807; Knight, *Arlington to Appomattox*, 270-271.

reason very few Secessionists—and very few of the later historians—seem to have understood the desperate nature of the Southern nation's plight as the third year of the war approached. One of the few contemporaries who did grasp the true situation, I believe, was Robert E. Lee.

FOR some time prior to the spring of 1863 Lee had realized that simply winning battles that produced no result beyond the immediate damage inflicted on the enemy in the field was not sufficient if the Confederates were to gain their independence. Even a great victory such as Lee had won in the Second Battle of Manassas the previous August had been barren of lasting results. The defeated Federal army had fled to safety in the nearby fortifications around Washington, and it was soon ready to take the field again.[2]

Every battle also took the lives of valuable soldiers—men whom the South found increasingly difficult to replace—and consumed vast quantities of the Confederacy's finite material resources. Even the supply of food was reduced. Unfavorable weather limited production, the contending armies took work animals and other livestock, confiscated crops to feed hungry soldiers, destroyed farms, wrecked barns, burned fence rails, and, in the case of the Federal armies, liberated thousands of the slaves who did much of the agricultural work. Increasingly, as the war went on, the Yankees also wrecked whatever Confederate railroads they could reach. In so doing, they made it more difficult for the Rebels to transport food from farms to their armies and civilian population centers.[3]

Against an enemy with virtually unlimited resources—human, financial, industrial, agricultural, and material—to throw into the conflict, the Confederacy could not indefinitely continue the war. The Rebels' ability to manufacture cannon and rifled muskets was limited. Heavy railroad equipment was captured, damaged, destroyed, or simply wore out and could not be replaced.

With a rapidly deteriorating transportation system, the Confederacy's manufactured goods and foodstuffs, even when produced in sufficient quantities, could not reach the armies that consumed them so voraciously. If the war continued for another few years along the path it had followed in 1862, the Rebels

---

2 Harsh, *Confederate Tide* and Leigh, *Confederacy at Flood Tide*, date Lee's concern about the Confederacy's plight to sometime in the summer of 1862. I am in essential agreement with them.

3 See sources listed in next three footnotes.

would exhaust their human and material resources. Unless that pattern could be broken, the defeat of secession was but a matter of time.[4]

If barren, but costly victories—simply avoiding defeat in Virginia—were ultimately meaningless, catastrophic strategic and tactical defeats were even worse. As Lee contemplated the campaigns of 1862 and surveyed the results of the year's operations, a man of his intelligence, wide knowledge, and willingness to face facts could not help but realize that his army was the only major Rebel force that had managed to hold its own. At year's end his Army of Northern Virginia stood essentially (and strategically) where it had been when 1862 began. In the West, however, the Confederate armies had suffered one defeat after another, yielding to the enemy vast stretches of valuable territory, key railroad lines, important cities, and almost all of the crucial Mississippi River. They had sustained those setbacks even in several battles and campaigns in which they had outnumbered the enemy. By the winter of 1862-1863, many of the Rebel generals in the West were locked into semi-public, poisonous, and self-destructive squabbling that did not bode well for future Confederate success.[5]

LEE also confronted more immediate trouble that winter. He was only too well aware that his army, despite its 1862 successes, faced a very serious problem that cast great doubt over its future effectiveness. On January 26, 1863, Lee warned the secretary of war, "The question of provisioning the army is becoming one of greater difficulty every day. . . . I am more than usually anxious about the supplies of

---

4 This condition held true even if the Confederates won the battles. The Unionists' superiority was so great that, as historian Allan Nevins noted, "even in [battlefield] defeat the North grew stronger, in victory the South became weaker." *Ordeal of the Union*, VI, 482.

5 See Joseph Harsh's brilliant analysis of Lee's thinking in *Confederate Tide*. Harsh attributed Lee's fall 1862 acts to this belief. I think that by the spring of 1863 Lee had come to realize that defeats in the West inevitably would doom the Rebels if they were not offset by some great success elsewhere. To my knowledge, there is no explicit evidence that Lee harbored these ideas (no "smoking gun," to use a modern term). My longstanding belief that he did hold these thoughts is based on my great respect for his intelligence and the obvious fact that the Confederacy could not survive without the West (any more than it could survive the loss of Virginia and the East). Lee also kept himself well informed about the Confederacy's general situation (as his correspondence makes clear). Finally, the fact that he held so tenaciously to his purpose in the spring of 1863 indicates that he was then working toward what he saw (correctly, I believe) as the only possible viable remedy for the Rebels' plight—an offensive into the North by his army. Quotations such as those given below in the text lend, I hope, additional weight to this admittedly speculative argument. See also the comments by Pedro Garcia in "Crossfire," *N&S*, vol. 6, no. 1 (Dec. 2002), 94, written in response to an earlier article by Richard Rollins ("Lee's Strategy and Pickett's Charge,") ibid., vol. 5, no. 5, (July, 2002), 76-83.

the army as it will be impossible to keep it together without food." On the following day he wrote a commander in the Shenandoah Valley, "Should there be any region unoccupied in which provisions can be secured, I hope you will lose no time in endeavoring to collect them." When the secretary of war informed him that the main difficulty was getting food to the troops from the regions where it was produced, Lee offered to detail men from his army to assist in repairing a vital railroad supply line.

Two months later the situation had not improved and Lee reported that he had been compelled to put his men on reduced rations. "I do not think it enough to continue them in health and vigor, and I fear they will be unable to endure the hardships of the approaching campaign." Scurvy had made its appearance in the army, and Lee had detailed men to go into the woods to gather "sassafras buds, wild onions, garlic, lamb's quarters, and poke sprouts" to supplement the rations issued by the Commissary General's department. Unfortunately, Lee added, "for so large an army the supply obtained is very small."

Three more weeks passed, and Lee again warned the War Department that while the men might be able to live on their reduced rations, they "certainly would not have the strength for an active campaign." The time has come, he wrote, "when it is necessary the men should have full rations. Their health is failing, scurvy and typhus fever are making their appearance, and it is necessary for them to have a more generous diet."[6]

THE plight of the Confederacy in general and that of the Army of Northern Virginia in particular raised serious questions in Lee's mind concerning the ultimate viability of the Rebel cause. Was final defeat for the Confederacy inevitable? Could the Secessionists find some way to attain their independence despite the many defeats and great losses they had suffered in 1862, the failure of their fall 1862 offensives, and the even greater odds they would face in the future?

Lee's whole being rebelled against accepting defeat. There had to be something the Rebels could do that would bring final success despite the obstacles in their path. Whatever that "something" might be, it seemed almost certain that only Lee and the Army of Northern Virginia could do it.

---

6 25 *OR*, pt. 2, 597-599, 610-611, 612, 686-688, and 730. See also 693 and 735-738. Lee's problems were part of a major crisis in supply, logistics, transportation, and financial matters that afflicted both the Confederate military effort and civilian life in the late 1862 and early 1863 period. Virginia and her defending army found themselves especially hard-hit. See Goff, *Confederate Supply*, Chapter 3, and the opening pages of Bowden and Ward, *Last Chance*.

Perhaps there was a means to national independence for the Confederacy, and that winter Lee began to grope his way toward it. Ever since the earliest days of the conflict, many Secessionists had favored an offensive war, at least to the extent of "liberating" the border slave state of Maryland and securing Kentucky and Missouri as members of the Southern nation. By late 1862 many Rebels also desired to shift the fighting to the North—to inflict on Yankee farms and towns a taste of the destruction and suffering that invading (and defending) armies had brought to many parts of the South.[7]

During the winter months, as Lee mulled over these matters, a plan gradually took shape in his mind. He seems to have spent some time consulting with his great lieutenant Stonewall Jackson, and the two slowly worked out their idea. Late in February Jackson called in his topographical engineer Jedediah Hotchkiss, whose antebellum career as a civil engineer had taken him over much of southern Pennsylvania, western Maryland, and west-central Virginia. Now, Hotchkiss received secret orders ("a profound secret," he noted in his diary) "to prepare a map of the [Shenandoah] Valley of Virginia extended on to Harrisburg, Pa., and then on to Philadelphia." Rebel agents slipped into Maryland and southern Pennsylvania to procure county maps and other local information that would help Hotchkiss with the task.[8]

DURING the winter and early spring while Lee in Virginia wrestled with problems of supply and grand strategy, Joseph E. Johnston, then recuperating at Bragg's Tullahoma, Tennessee, headquarters, became increasingly alarmed at the clear and mounting evidence of a massive Yankee buildup in the Kentucky-Tennessee area. By late March or early April his dire warnings had gotten the attention of the civilian authorities in Richmond.

Faced with the obvious increase in Union strength on Braxton Bragg's front, Rebel officials concluded that the enemy was shifting troops from other areas preparatory to a massive offensive in Middle Tennessee. In such a situation, implementation of President Davis's offensive-defensive strategy called for strengthening Bragg's army from Confederate forces in other unthreatened areas. Secretary of War Seddon began a search for troops he could transfer to Tennessee for that purpose.

---

7 See Harsh, *Confderate Tide, passim.*

8 See Kegel, *North with Lee and Jackson, passim,* especially Chapter 17; Hotchkiss, *Journal,* 116-119.

Seddon found Secessionist manpower resources quite limited. Other than Bragg's army, only three large concentrations of Rebel troops could be found in the Cis-Mississippi Confederacy. From Charleston, Beauregard reported that the enemy was about to launch a massive assault on that city. Charleston was crucial for its railroads, its access to the sea for blockade runners, and for its symbolic value as the birthplace of secession. It had to be held. Reinforcement of Bragg from the troops along the South Atlantic coast seemed obviously out of the question, at least for the moment.

The presence of Grant's army at Milliken's Bend just upriver from Vicksburg made it extremely risky to transfer any troops to Tennessee from Pemberton's Mississippi force. Then, in the early weeks of April, Pemberton reported the exhilarating news that the Yankees had abandoned their effort against Vicksburg and were sending troops from Grant's army up the Mississippi to Tennessee to reinforce the Federal army there (see Chapter Six above). As a result, announced Pemberton, he had begun moving troops from Mississippi along the "pipeline" to strengthen Bragg's army.

Could the authorities find additional reinforcements to meet the great emergency that Johnston anticipated on the Tennessee front? Seddon turned to the only other large source of potential help for Bragg. In late March, Rebel spies and scouts had reported that the IX Corps, which had been part of the main Federal army in Virginia, had departed for the West. Confirmation of these reports in the first days of April led the secretary of war to reason that troops from Lee's army could reinforce Bragg without increasing the danger to the Old Dominion.

On April 6, doubtless at President Davis's direction, Seddon sent a short summary of Johnston's recent communications to Lee and asked if the general would agree to release two or three brigades from the Army of Northern Virginia to go to Bragg. "It would seem natural," the secretary commented, for the Confederates to shift troops out of the area from which the Yankees had removed some of their own forces to strengthen the Rebel army at the point where the enemy had chosen to concentrate. In keeping with Davis Administration practice, however, the secretary declared that the authorities were unwilling to order any of Lee's troops to Bragg unless Lee gave his consent.[9]

9 25 OR, pt. 2, 689, 691, 697, 700-703, and 708-709. For another example of the Davis administration's unwillingness to make decisions that only the Richmond authorities could make about such matters, see Secretary Seddon's Feb. 3, 1863, message to Lee reporting that General Beauregard expected an attack on Charleston and asking Lee to "judge as to the advisability of sending any troops [from the Army of Northern Virginia]" to assist the Rebels

SEDDON'S inquiry threatened to abort Lee's partially developed plan to carry the war into the North and to feed his troops there during the summer. It also served as the catalyst that brought Lee's thoughts about what grand strategy the Confederates should pursue into a more specific dialogue about the immediate action they should take regarding the anticipated Union offensive in Middle Tennessee.

Lee seized upon the opportunity presented by his April 9 reply to Seddon to expound on the strategic ideas he had been developing over the past few months and to apply those ideas to the Rebels' then unfolding spring 1863 crisis. When the Federals reinforced one army with troops transferred from another, he noted, "it diminishes the force opposed to our troops in . . . [the area from which the Yankee reinforcements departed] and may enable them to take the aggressive and call them back."

"The most natural way to reinforce General Johnston," Lee went on, "would seem to be to transfer a portion of the troops from this department to oppose those [Yankees] sent west, but it is not so easy for us to change troops from one department to another, and if we rely upon that method we may always be too late."

As at all times, however, Lee would obey orders. He concluded, "I must, therefore, submit your proposition to the determination of yourself and the President. *If you think* it will be advantageous at present to send part of the troops [from the Army of Northern Virginia] . . . General [James] Longstreet [from whose command they would come] will designate such as ought to go [my emphasis]."[10]

The Richmond authorities (i.e., President Davis) were no more willing to take the responsibility of deciding such a matter in April 1863 than they had been the

---

on the Carolina coast. Lee, of course, was in no position to make such a determination and replied the next day, "I will do so [i.e, send the troops] if you deem the exigency requires it" (14 *OR*, 759 and 762-763). See also the following footnote and Lee's Apr. 9, 1863, reply to Seddon quoted in the following section of this chapter.

10 25 *OR*, pt. 2, 713. We should note that Lee was taking, with regard to the entire Confederacy, exactly the same position that Johnston had taken earlier (although only with regard to the West) about the impossibility of shifting Rebel troops about rapidly enough to counter enemy movements on widely separated fronts. As pointed out above (Book Two, Chapter One, Part II), the question involved a weighing of the danger to one area as opposed to that to another, and a judgment as to which was in greater danger or more valuable to the Rebels. These were geopolitical questions or matters about which the commander of an individual army did not have the information to decide. Lee could no more determine such matters about Virginia and South Carolina or Tennessee than General Holmes could about the relative value of Arkansas and Mississippi, or Johnston could about the relative importance of Mississippi and Tennessee.

previous December when the Chief Executive himself had reasoned, pleaded with, and even begged General Holmes to send some of his troops from Arkansas to help Pemberton in Mississippi but would not order him to do so. (See Book Two, Chapter Four above.)

Renewing the spring 1863 entreaty on behalf of the President, Adjutant and Inspector General Samuel Cooper wrote to Lee on April 14 to point out that the enemy threat in Middle Tennessee "makes it absolutely necessary that we should, without any loss of time," reinforce Bragg. (One wonders if Lee, upon reading this comment, thought to himself that the Rebels had already wasted more than a week because nobody in the Davis Administration would make a decision that only the civilian authorities with access to all the available information could make.)[11]

Cooper went on to report that by his calculations the Yankee force in Bragg's front totaled 106,000 men. Bragg's army, by contrast, numbered only about 55,000, and Rebel authorities wanted to add 12,000 or 15,000 more troops to his force. "In this contingency, then, I would ask if it is not possible for you to spare . . . [a division] from your command for this purpose?"[12]

Lee replied on the sixteenth, patiently pointing out the obvious (which often escaped Richmond officialdom and which the politicians and government bureaucrats often chose to ignore): "I believe the enemy in every department outnumbers us, and it is difficult to say from which troops can with safety be spared." The recent repulse of the Yankee attack on Charleston,[13] along with Pemberton's reports that the Federal army that had been menacing Vicksburg was withdrawing from that area, offered an opportunity to strengthen the Confederate army in Tennessee from Rebel forces in South Carolina and Mississippi. President Davis, Lee added, "can better decide than [can] any one else."[14]

On that same day, probably before he replied to Cooper and possibly even before he received the letter from that bureaucrat, Lee wrote directly to Davis. "I

11 As late as May 9, Longstreet pointed out to Seddon that if reinforcements were to go to the West, they ought to "be sent at once or not at all" (*OR*, Series II, vol. 5, 944).

12 25 *OR*, pt. 2, 720.

13 Ibid., 725. The Confederate defenders repulsed the April 7, 1863, attack on Charleston, and within a few days it became clear to almost everyone except Beauregard that the danger to the South Atlantic coast had been much reduced.

14 Here, too, Lee took the same position that Johnston had taken with regard to a question involving national priorities—only the civilian authorities had sufficient information to decide such questions. It was their duty to do so (Tennessee or Mississippi? in Johnston's case). See Chapter Five, Part II of this book and the following section of this chapter.

think it all-important," he informed the Chief Executive, "that we should assume the aggressive by the 1st of May. . . . If we could be placed in condition to make a vigorous advance at that time . . . and the enemy army opposite me thrown north of the Potomac, I believe greater relief would in this way be afforded to the armies in Middle Tennessee and on the Carolina coast than by any other method."[15]

SEVERAL hours after Lee completed his April 16 letters to Cooper and Davis and sent them off to Richmond, the Confederates' general strategic situation changed drastically. That was the night that Union gunboats and transports ran down the Mississippi past the Rebel cannon on the high bluffs at Vicksburg. That success gave the Yankees virtually complete control of the Vicksburg-Port Hudson corridor and effectively cut the Confederacy in half. (See Book Two, Chapter Six.)

The Yankee success led to several alterations in the general strategic situation. Pemberton finally realized that for a week or so he had completely misinterpreted Yankee movements in his front. Frantically, he recalled the units he had started along the "pipeline" to Tennessee a few days earlier.

With a major Federal force now poised on the right bank of the Mississippi River not far below Vicksburg, the area south of the great fortress became the crucial point. Rebel authorities in Richmond quickly forgot their recent anxiety over the reported threat facing Bragg's army in Tennessee. Instead, they turned their attention completely to Mississippi. Indeed, over the next eight weeks they would transfer thousands of troops from Bragg's army to the Magnolia State in a desperate effort to save Vicksburg.

WHILE the Confederate authorities studied the drastically changed situation in Mississippi and struggled to decide how to cope with it, another great crisis erupted in Virginia. During the late winter and into the spring the Federal army in Lee's front, then commanded by Major General Joseph Hooker, had been preparing for yet one more "on to Richmond" effort. As April entered its last weeks, it became apparent that Hooker's army would soon be on the move. Lee, of course, had to react to Hooker's offensive, and when the Yankees advanced in force he did so. Seizing the initiative, he outmaneuvered the enemy and waged what has been called his "greatest battle." When the massive engagement at

---

15 25 OR, pt. 2, 724-726. Lee was not the only Rebel to suggest that a Confederate offensive was the best defense. In late January or early February, Major General Sterling Price had argued that a diversion in Arkansas would reduce the danger to Vicksburg. See Thomas C. Reynolds to Seddon, Feb. 5, 1863, in 22 OR, pt. 2, 782.

Chancellorsville came to its end in the first week of May, the Federals had retreated to the positions north of the Rappahannock River from which they had launched their offensive.

While most Confederates rejoiced over the Chancellorsville victory, Lee correctly realized that it was nothing more than another barren and costly battlefield triumph. The Army of Northern Virginia had lost some 12,000 men killed, wounded, and captured/missing (Union casualties totaled about 17,000), and the organization of Lee's forces had been drastically disrupted by the death on May 10 of Stonewall Jackson, who had been wounded a week earlier.

EVEN as Lee waged the Battle of Chancellorsville against Hooker, the Rebels' situation in Mississippi became more desperate. At the end of April Grant moved his army across the Mississippi River about thirty miles below Vicksburg. After defeating a small Southern force at Port Gibson on May 1, he marched northeast to seize Jackson and thereby isolate Vicksburg from the remainder of the Confederacy.

Once the authorities in Richmond got over their panic at the threat posed by the recent advance of the Yankee army only some fifty miles north of the capital and learned that Lee once more had turned back the enemy, they again shifted their attention to events in Mississippi. What they saw greatly alarmed them. A major Union army marched almost at will through the interior of President Davis's home state. Indeed, the Chief Executive's own plantation only a short distance downriver from Vicksburg had fallen into Yankee hands.

In response to these developments, Secretary of War Seddon, acting for the ill President Davis, directed Joseph E. Johnston on May 9 to leave Bragg's headquarters in Tullahoma, Tennessee, go to Mississippi, and take personal command of the Rebel force there. Seddon also renewed his pleas for Lee to send reinforcements from the Army of Northern Virginia to the West—but to Pemberton in Mississippi now, not to Bragg in Tennessee.

LEE responded bluntly on the tenth with both a telegram and a letter. The secretary's proposal, he asserted, "is hazardous," and the whole matter had come down to "a question between Virginia and the Mississippi." That was exactly the kind of dilemma that Jefferson Davis almost always refused to face up to deciding. (Did the President, upon reading Lee's sentence, recall Joseph E. Johnston's January 7, 1863, plea for the Chief Executive to decide between Tennessee and Mississippi?)

Then, having set forth his general case, Lee got down to specifics as to why he believed dispatching some of his veteran troops to aid Pemberton's army was inadvisable. In all probability, reinforcements from Virginia could not reach Mississippi before the end of May. By then, Lee pointed out, the contest there might well have been decided.

With the troops en route for so long a time, the Rebels would run a great risk that the enemy would strike in Virginia while the reinforcements were in transit to Mississippi and the men, therefore, would not be available to help either Lee or Pemberton. (Upon reading this did Davis recall his transfer—over objections from Joseph E. Johnston and Braxton Bragg—of Carter Stevenson's division from Bragg to Pemberton the previous December, a transfer that kept the division out of important battles in both Tennessee and Mississippi?)

In addition, Lee argued, the arrival of summer in the lower Mississippi Valley with its most unhealthful climate "will force the enemy to retire." Summer in the Lower South might well prove fatal even to Confederate soldiers unacclimated to it. "I think troops ordered from Virginia to the Mississippi at this season would be greatly endangered by the climate," he wrote.[16]

Third, Lee expressed concern about what he tactfully called "the uncertainty of its [the force sent to Mississippi] application" (letter) and "the uncertainty of the employment of the troops" (telegram). By these remarks Lee seems obliquely to have been expressing his opinion of the poor quality of the Confederate generals in the West. By the spring of 1863, those Western commanders had already lost several battles in which their forces had outnumbered the enemy. What grounds, Lee implied, did the authorities have for hoping that they would perform any better now?

Finally, if his own strength were reduced—Seddon wanted to send the entire division commanded by Major General George E. Pickett (about 6,400 men)—Lee would find himself even more heavily outnumbered. Under such circumstances, he warned, he would have to abandon his projected offensive into the North and "may be obliged to withdraw into the defenses around Richmond" where he would be unable to maneuver and where defeat would be only a matter of time.

16 Lee's warnings about the effect of the climate in the Lower Mississippi Valley have drawn scorn from some modern writers who maintain that he was desperately stretching for reasons not to give up any of his troops. (See, for example, Connelly and Jones, *Politics of Command*, 40.) In fact, the concern was legitimate and the fears widely shared. See McMurry, "Marse Robert and the Fevers."

Lee quite properly refused to make a major geopolitical decision that could be made only by Davis. But, as always, he would obey orders. "You can . . . see the odds against us, and decide whether the line of Virginia is in more danger than the line of the Mississippi. . . . If necessary, order Pickett [to go west] at once."

On the following day Lee again wrote to Davis. Recent intelligence gleaned from Northern newspapers, he informed the President, indicated that Federal authorities had ordered troops from the South Atlantic coast to reinforce the Yankee army in Virginia. "A vigorous movement here would certainly draw the enemy from there," he added.

Lee carried the argument. President Davis, unwilling to overrule his most, and indeed his only, successful general, endorsed Lee's message: "The answer of General Lee was such as I should have anticipated and in which I concur." On May 13, as Joseph E. Johnston's train crept slowly along the rickety railroad from Meridian toward Jackson, Davis wrote to Lee, "Your letter is conclusive against the suggestion made."[17]

NO reinforcements would go from Lee's army to Mississippi, but the Confederates still had to determine how they would respond to the crisis they faced that spring. It was to deal with that matter that Lee journeyed to Richmond in mid-May and spent several days in meetings with Davis and members of the cabinet.

We have no record of what was said at those meetings. Lee, doubtless, listened carefully, respectfully, and politely to the views of Davis and the other civilian

---

17 25 *OR*, pt. 2, 601, 790, 797, and 814. Pickett's Division missed Chancellorsville. It, along with Longstreet and other troops from his corps, had been on foraging duty in southeastern Virginia around Suffolk. Some modern students of the war maintain that Lee was not really concerned with the situation in the Mississippi Valley. Instead, they argue, he wanted only to free his native Virginia of the burden of the war and to feed his army in the North. I believe this argument is erroneous. First, the Confederate authorities debated at length what they should do about the crisis posed by Grant's army then threatening Vicksburg and Rebel control of the Mississippi River. While some wanted to detach troops from Lee's army and send them to Mississippi, Lee himself clearly believed that the best response would be for his force to "take the aggressive." This action, he thought, would compel the Yankees to shift troops away from Mississippi. Second, Lee's chief subordinate, Lieutenant General James Longstreet, conferred with the authorities when he was in Richmond in May 1863 and urged them to send troops to Tennessee, where they were to take the offensive. After rejoining the army in northern Virginia and conferring with Lee, Longstreet wrote that his earlier idea had been based on the assumption that Lee's army was to remain idle that summer. Discussions with Lee, however, convinced Longstreet that Lee's proposed offensive was a better alternative. See McMurry, "The Pennsylvania Gambit and the Gettysburg Splash."

authorities. Doubtless, too, he expressed his own ideas forcefully, but as always respectfully and courteously and reiterated the points he had made in his recent correspondence with Davis, Seddon, and Cooper.

Lee may even have reminded his audience that the Confederates' May-June 1862 successes in Virginia (Stonewall Jackson's campaign in the Shenandoah Valley and the Seven Days' Battles just outside Richmond) had led a shaken Lincoln Administration to transfer troops from the South Atlantic coast northward to Virginia. Lee might also have pointed out that those same successes had also led the Federal government to order troops rushed east from the Mississippi Valley. Perhaps a thrust into Union territory in the summer of 1863, coming after Lee's 1862 victories and the triumph recently won at Chancellorsville, would reinforce success and add to the momentum those victories created. It might produce the same results that the Valley Campaign and the Seven Days' Battles had produced. If so, withdrawal of Union troops from other areas to defend against Lee's proposed offensive would free other Rebel forces to send additional help to Pemberton and could even lead to the withdrawal of Grant's army from Mississippi. A short time later Lee wrote Davis, "I think if I can create an apprehension for the safety of their [the Federals'] right flank [in northern Virginia] and the Potomac, more troops will be brought from their lines in the south."[18]

Did Lee go beyond these arguments to advocate the strike across the Potomac as an offensive ploy to draw the Union army away from its shelter in the Washington fortifications and then to bring on a battle on Northern soil in which a Confederate victory might so demoralize the enemy that it would decide the war? We simply do not know. (My belief is that he did not. The difficulty of arguing the authorities out of the proposal to transfer troops from Virginia to Mississippi and the probable greater difficulty of persuading Davis to undertake such a risky plan that Lee, I think, was hoping to launch argue against the general's having done so.)

Whatever Lee said proved persuasive. As the conference concluded, Davis, with the concurrence of all but one of the cabinet officers, agreed to the proposed

18 In fact, the Lincoln government, in what one Union general labeled a "stampede," had ordered troops sent from the West Tennessee-North Mississippi area to Virginia to help deal with Lee's army in June and early July of 1862. Some troops actually began such a movement. The orders were soon revoked, but somehow the Confederates learned of them almost as soon as they were issued. On May 11, 1863, Lee had informed Davis that recent intelligence gleaned from Northern newspapers indicated that the Federal authorities had ordered troops from the South Atlantic coast to reinforce the Yankee army in Virginia. "A vigorous movement here would certainly draw the enemy from there," Lee wrote the President. See 17 *OR*, pt. 2, 52, 53, 55-56, 59, 63, 70, 76, and 82; 25 *OR*, pt. 2, 791-792; and 27 *OR*, pt. 2, 290-294.

thrust across the Potomac. The lone exception was Postmaster General John H. Reagan of Texas, who naturally worried more about connections with the Trans-Mississippi than did his colleagues.[19]

LEE left Richmond, probably on the morning of May 18, to return to his camp and prepare his army for the great effort.

19 See Bowden and Ward, *Last Chance*, 237. Reagan was most impressed with Davis's thoroughness in making the decision. Cooper, *Davis*, 65-66.

Chapter Nine

Joseph E. Johnston and the Army of Relief

PART I

"Tell me if more troops can be furnished."

— Joseph E. Johnston, May 27, 1863

In mid-May, while Robert E. Lee was in Richmond conferring with President Davis and the cabinet about the Confederate response to the desperate situation then facing the Rebels, Joseph E. Johnston spent several frustrating days roaming about the area north and northwest of Jackson.

When he evacuated the Mississippi state capital in a heavy rain early in the morning of May 14, Johnston had taken his 6,000-man force to Tugaloo on the railroad seven miles to the north. There he halted. He expected to unite his army with the troops John Pemberton had brought eastward from Vicksburg and whom, he thought, he had directed (or did he only suggest it?) that general to move on toward Clinton. United, he and Pemberton would have about 25,000 men— perhaps enough to overcome isolated parts of the Union force that Johnston believed to be in the Clinton-Jackson area.

EARLY that morning Pemberton received Johnston's message to move toward Clinton to attack the Federals reported to be there. Quickly he sent word that he would march eastward as ordered (suggested?) to unite with his commander. He would bring a force he put at 16,000. (It was closer to 20,000.)

Soon, however, Pemberton concluded that the move Johnston apparently wanted him to make—to march eastward from Edward's Station—would take his troops toward the Yankee force lying between Johnston's army and his own. Such a move, he realized, would also expose the rear and right flank of his own men to an attack from the south. Even worse, it would open Vicksburg itself to possible capture should another Union force move up from the south and slice in behind his eastward marching column of Rebels.

After thinking over the matter for several hours, Pemberton decided that he would disregard Johnston's orders (wishes?). Instead, accepting the suggestions of a few of his generals, he would march south to cut the supply line between the Mississippi River and the Yankee army in the Clinton-Jackson area.

At 5:40 p.m. Pemberton, who that morning had written Johnston that he would move toward Clinton as Johnston wanted him to do, dispatched another note to his commander. In this message he announced that, instead of moving east, he would take his men south to interrupt the flow of supplies to the Union army in the interior. The enemy, he assumed, would then be compelled to turn and attack him to restore communications with their base on the river. In such a situation his own troops would enjoy the great advantage of fighting on the tactical defensive. Since Pemberton had done nothing that day to prepare his army for such a march, he decided not to begin his southward trek until the following morning.

The fiasco that passed for Confederate command continued on May 15. That morning Pemberton discovered that his troops did not have sufficient rations for the projected march. Owing to the delay necessary to bring forward food and issue it to the men, the column did not get underway until mid-afternoon. The troops had not gone far when they reached an unfordable stream and found the bridge out of service. Pemberton had to redirect the march. When the column halted for the night, the force was only a few miles from its camps of the previous day. Ominously, as they went into bivouac that evening Pemberton's troops could see the glow from thousands of campfires off to the east.

ON May 14, 15, and 16, as Pemberton's Confederates floundered about west of Jackson, the Federals busied themselves demolishing much of the state capital, especially the railroad lines in, and for short distances north, south, and east of the city. Most importantly, they wrecked the bridge that carried the railroad tracks over the Pearl River just east of Jackson. When they finished their work, what was left of the capital and all of the railroad rolling stock west of the Pearl was completely cut off from the rest of the Confederacy.[1]

On the morning of the fifteenth, General Grant left about one-third of his force in Jackson to devote a few more hours to the destruction of the capital. With the remaining two-thirds he marched west to intercept Pemberton. (From the copy of Johnston's first message to Pemberton turned over to him by the Yankee spy/

---

1 24 *OR*, pt. 1, 754-755, 762-763, and 770; 24 *OR*, pt. 2, 251; Carter, *Final Fortress*, 192-194; Bearss, *Campaign for Vicksburg*, II, 550.

courier, Grant knew the approximate location of the two Rebel forces. See Chapter 7 of this book above.) The Union commander determined to strike Pemberton before he could unite his troops with those of Johnston—and Grant, unlike the Confederates— was alive to the importance of time.

Meanwhile, that morning Johnston had received Pemberton's second May 14 note announcing that he would march south to cut the Yankee supply line rather than east to unite with Johnston's force. Undoubtedly furious at this blatant disobedience of his directions (or suggestion?) and unmindful of his other suggestion to Pemberton that he try to cut Grant off from his base on the river, Johnston immediately dashed off renewed instructions for Pemberton to move to the Clinton area to unite his force with Johnston's own. When Pemberton received this message at about 6:30 a.m. on the sixteenth, he felt that he had no choice but to turn his column around and start north in obedience to the note.

That same May 16, while Davis, Lee, and the cabinet were meeting in Richmond to discuss the crisis, Pemberton's marching column collided with Grant's force at Champion Hill, just south of the railroad and about halfway between Vicksburg and Jackson. By late afternoon the defeated Confederates were fleeing westward. The next day the Rebels attempted to make a stand at the Big Black River. Routed once again, they streamed west from the battlefield. By that evening they were huddled safely inside Vicksburg's fortifications.

WHILE Pemberton marched back and forth and fought and lost the battles of Champion Hill and the Big Black River, Johnston hovered in the area north and northwest of Jackson. On May 15 he had moved with his little force from Tugaloo some ten miles up the railroad to Calhoun. Not knowing by which route to expect Pemberton, Johnston allowed his men to rest on the sixteenth. The next day he marched to Cheatham's plantation, about eighteen miles to the west. There, that evening, he received a note from Pemberton reporting the crushing defeat at Champion Hill. A short time later Johnston learned from some civilians of the rout of Pemberton's army at the Big Black and of the flight to Vicksburg.

By this time Johnston had concluded that events of the past two weeks had stripped Vicksburg of its value to the Confederacy and that the Rebels could not hold the town once Grant reestablished contact with the Union fleet in the Yazoo and Mississippi rivers. Realizing that a siege would ultimately end in the loss of both Pemberton's army and Vicksburg, Johnston rushed off a message to his subordinate to evacuate the town and march to the northeast "if it is not too late."

To facilitate a junction with the Vicksburg army, Johnston on May 18 moved to the northwest toward Vernon and Kibbey's Ferry on the Big Black. At Vernon the next morning he received a message from Pemberton announcing that he found it impossible to withdraw his men from Vicksburg. Instead, Pemberton reported, he would endeavor to hold the town while Johnston organized an army to raise the siege.

With only 6,000 men Johnston could do nothing at the time to reinforce or relieve those trapped inside Vicksburg. He sent a message urging Pemberton to hold out as long as he could and announcing that he would try to gather a force to save the town. Then he took his small army back to Canton where it could easily receive food by rail from the north and where, he hoped, reinforcements would soon join him.

FOR the next six and a half weeks Johnston held his force—which soon became known as the Army of Relief—in an area that stretched along a rough arc north and northwest from Jackson (re-occupied by the Rebels after the last Yankees marched off to the west on May 16). "We spent the latter part of May and a large part of June roaming around the vicinity of Canton, Yazoo City, and Big Black River," remembered a member of the 27th Alabama. Throughout those weeks Johnston kept his headquarters in Canton, but he went to Jackson almost every day.[2]

The task facing Johnston was formidable in the extreme. He had to build, organize, and fully equip a force strong enough to operate successfully against Grant's army. He had to accomplish that despite the shortages that usually hampered Confederate military operations, and in the face of the massive obstacles to communication and effective cooperation that he and President Davis had allowed (chosen, Covey would point out) to grow up between them over the preceding two years—and he had to do so before Pemberton's food and other supplies ran out.

JOHNSTON'S most obvious, immediate, and pressing need was to increase the numerical strength of the Army of Relief. Within a week after Pemberton had shut himself and his army up inside Vicksburg, some 14,700 more Rebel troops joined Johnston's 6,000-man force. These reinforcements comprised units that were already on the way to Jackson when the Confederates evacuated the Mississippi capital on May 14, or were in the division of Major General William W.

---

2 Cannon, *Bloody Banners*, 34; Giles, *Letters,* 108.

Loring that had become separated from Pemberton's army during the fight at Champion Hill and had wandered into Jackson a few days later.[3]

Realizing that Port Hudson, like Vicksburg, had ceased to be of value to the Rebels and probably not yet aware that a Federal force under Major General Nathaniel P. Banks was then moving upriver threatening the town, Johnston on May 19 sent an order to Major General Franklin Gardner to evacuate Port Hudson and bring his men to join the army gathering in the Jackson-Canton area. Banks's Yankees laid siege to Port Hudson before Gardner could quit the town and thereby trapped the Rebel garrison. In fact, Gardner—probably in the belief (as relayed earlier by Pemberton) that Davis wanted the town held no matter what—had disregarded Johnston's initial directive to move to Jackson. He found himself surrounded in Port Hudson before a courier from Johnston could reach him with a peremptory order to evacuate the place.[4]

---

3 The troops in the Jackson area when Johnston arrived on May 13 included the brigades of Brigadier Generals John Gregg, John Adams, and W. H. T. Walker (major general and division commander as of May 23), a total of about 6,000 men. Arriving at Jackson on date shown: brigades of Brigadier Generals States Rights Gist (May 18), about 2,000; Evander McNair and Matthew Ector (May 19), about 2,800; Samuel B. Maxey (May 23), about 3,000; and Nathan G. Evans (May 25), about 2,000. Walker, Gist, and Evans came from Beauregard's South Atlantic coastal force; McNair and Ector from Bragg in Tennessee. The others were parts of Pemberton's command prior to Johnston's arrival in Mississippi. Loring's Division, about 4,900 strong, reached Jackson on May 20. Arriving later from Bragg: the infantry division of Major General John C. Breckinridge (June 1), about 5,200 men; and the cavalry division of Brigadier General William H. Jackson (June 3), about 3,000 men. Some sources give slightly different strength data for some of these units. Numbers from strength returns and other documents in 24 OR 3.

4 Had Gardner obeyed the initial order, he might well have put Johnston and Pemberton into an even more difficult situation than they and Davis had already created for the Secessionists. The siege of Port Hudson, which did not end until July 9, tied down far more Union troops than the number of Confederates that Gardner's force would have added to the Army of Relief. In addition, at least some of the Federal naval vessels employed at Port Hudson would have augmented the Federal fleet at Vicksburg. Johnston soon recognized this fact. On June 15 he sent a message to Gardner urging him to hold out as long as possible, adding, "It is very important to keep Banks and his forces occupied [at Port Hudson]." He also directed commanders of Rebel cavalry units in the area to harass the Yankees as much as possible. (24 OR, pt. 1, 243; 26 OR, pt. 2, 39-40). Gardner's abandonment of Port Hudson would have benefitted the Confederates only if Johnston, reinforced by Gardner, could have struck a decisive blow against Grant in the few days between Gardner's arrival at Jackson and Banks's juncture with Grant. That would almost certainly have been impossible given Johnston's numerical strength, organizational weaknesses, and shortages of transportation, supplies, and equipment (detailed below in the text). The abandonment of Port Hudson, moreover, would have meant the permanent loss of the Confederates' east-west corridor connecting the halves

By the end of May Johnston found himself at the head of a force that had grown to about 21,000. In early June the total passed 30,000. In addition to these Confederate army units, an unknown (but small) number of Mississippi state troops had been called into service in the effort to save Vicksburg.

As late as the first week or so of June the combined strength of the forces commanded by Johnston and Pemberton exceeded that of Grant's army. The Rebels, however, were divided, and Johnston and Pemberton had no reliable means of communication. Johnston's Army of Relief, furthermore, was but partially organized, armed, and equipped, and found itself especially deficient in field transportation. After early June massive reinforcements gave Grant a great (and growing) numerical superiority over the combined armies of his enemies. (Johnston then estimated Grant's force at 60,000 to 80,000.)[5]

TRUE to their customary ways, Johnston and the Richmond authorities soon fell to bickering over (among other topics) the numerical strength of the Rebel force in the Jackson-Canton area. In a May 27 telegram Johnston mentioned that when all the reinforcements then reported to be en route to Mississippi arrived, he would have only 23,000 men. "Tell me," he begged, "if additional troops can be furnished."

President Davis was shocked at this statement. "The reinforcements sent to you exceed by, say, 7,000, the estimate of your dispatch," he wired on the twenty-eighth. Two days later, after Johnston had asked for 7,000 more men, the Chief Executive reported that he had checked with Secretary of War Seddon. The secretary "reports the re-enforcements ordered to you as greater than the number you request. . . . he states your whole force to be 34,000 exclusive of militia."

It was Johnston's turn to be surprised. "The Secretary of War is greatly mistaken in his numbers," the general telegraphed on June 1. Just the day before, Johnston had sent the President some details taken from the official returns

---

of Rebeldom no matter what happened at Vicksburg, since the Federal navy would then have controlled all the river except the area immediately in front of Vicksburg. (See Book Two, Chapter Three.) An interesting "what if" is that the arrival of the Federal Port Hudson army at Vicksburg would have put Banks in command of the combined Union forces by seniority. Who knows what would have resulted from that change.

5 On May 20, Pemberton estimated the Federal strength to be "at least 60,000." 24 *OR*, pt. 3, 916 and 920. About all that Johnston himself could do to bolster his strength was to issue a proclamation granting full pardon to deserters who returned immediately to their units. Mobile *Advertiser and Register*, June 20, 1863.

showing his total strength to be only 23,000 (plus the men in two units, the strength of which he did not then know). In another telegram sent that day, based on "their own [strength] returns," he put "the troops at my disposal available against Grant" at 24,100 not counting a division of cavalry ("the strength of which I do not know") and "a few hundred irregular cavalry."

These official data settled the matter, but we must wonder if the actual returns had been sent to the War Department and, if so, how such differences arose. It would not have been the only—and probably not the first, and certainly not the last—time that officials at a higher military headquarters did not carefully study reports from the field. By the time the Rebels resolved this matter, the differences between Richmond and Mississippi had shifted to other subjects.[6]

ON June 8, Secretary Seddon, in response to Johnston's pleas for more troops, innocently asked if the general advised that additional men be taken from Bragg's army in Tennessee. "You, as commandant of the department, have power so to order, if you, in view of the whole case, so determine."

Owing to problems deciphering the telegram, several days elapsed before Johnston grasped the full meaning of the message. By the twelfth, however, with the telegram still "imperfectly deciphered," he understood enough of its contents to reply. "I have not considered myself commanding in Tennessee since assignment here [on May 9]," he telegraphed.

---

6 24 OR, pt. 1, 193-195 215, 223-224, and 242. We should note that the Richmond authorities often cited the number of men they had ordered (or, in reality, only asked other commanders to send) to Mississippi. Johnston reported the number of men who had arrived. Seddon seems for a while to have believed that Beauregard had sent the full 10,000 men he had been ordered (asked) to send. Johnston reported receiving only some 6,000—all that Beauregard actually sent. That difference alone explains much of the discrepancy. All of the data relating to numerical strength should be regarded as more-or-less educated guesses. Some accounts use "effective strength," some "present for duty," and some use other categories. As explained in Chapter Two of this book, totals in different categories were determined by different criteria and could vary significantly. The "present for duty" strength, if available, gives the best picture of a Rebel unit's size. A good approximation of the "present for duty" number can be obtained by multiplying the "effective strength" by 1.18. Johnston stated on June 1, 1863, that he was reporting his "effective strength," which he put at 24,100. Application of the above multiplier puts his "present for duty" number on that day at 28,438. His "present for duty" strength on June 7 would have been about 35,400. Readers should also keep in mind that in this case a unit's strength could decrease somewhat while the unit was en route owing to accidents, desertions, sickness, and so on. Delays along the railroads could also complicate matters. The number of men reaching Mississippi, therefore, could differ from the number that left South Carolina or Tennessee, even if both numbers were accurately reported.

Three days later Davis got into the act. "The order to go to Mississippi did not diminish your authority in Tennessee," he telegraphed, "both being in the country placed under your command in original [November, 1862] assignment." To what order or message did Johnston refer as the basis for his conclusion?

For the next month Davis badgered Johnston, repeatedly asking the general to cite the specific letter, order, or telegram that justified his assumption that the order directing him to take charge of the forces in Mississippi had terminated his command of those in Tennessee. "I do not find in my letter-book any communication to you containing the expression which you again attribute to me and cite as a restriction on you against withdrawing troops from Tennessee; and have to repeat my inquiry, to what do you refer? Give date of dispatch or letter," the President demanded on June 17. "After full examination of all the correspondence between you and myself and the War Office . . . I am still at a loss to account for your strange error in stating to the Secretary of War that . . . your command over the Army of Tennessee had been withdrawn," he wrote on June 30.

Amid all his other problems and distractions Johnston had to answer as best he could. His explanation boiled down to the fact that he had assumed that Seddon's order to go to Mississippi had relieved him of responsibility for Tennessee since he obviously could not command the Rebels in the Volunteer State while acting as the full-time commander of the field force in Mississippi. (This was essentially the argument he had been making—to no avail—since receiving the Western command seven months earlier.) This belief, added Johnston, had been strengthened when the government, in May, had transferred thousands of Bragg's troops to Mississippi without consulting him.

Johnston could cite no specific directive since there had been none. Nor had he ever bothered to inquire if his assumption was correct. On June 20, he did express "much regret for the carelessness" of his reply to Davis's inquiry.

This minor matter rolled (and roiled) on into July. On the fifteenth, eleven days after Vicksburg had surrendered, Davis sent a long letter (thirty-four paragraphs, five printed pages in the *Official Records*) to Johnston. The document was filled with paraphrases of, quotations from, summaries of, and citations to various letters, orders, and telegrams, all designed to demonstrate that Johnston's assumption had been completely unfounded.

Johnston replied to this foolish screed with his own long and silly letter dated August 8 (three and three-quarter printed pages plus enclosures and sub-enclosures). The whole matter, Johnston maintained, was of no real consequence because he would not have taken any troops from Tennessee anyway since he believed the Volunteer State too endangered to spare any of its defenders. Besides, he pointed out, he had already corrected his mistaken assumption (based on messages from Secretary Seddon) even before the matter had come to Davis's attention.

In truth, this whole episode is important only for what it indicates about the wide and widening gulf between the Davis Administration in Richmond and its general in Mississippi, and for what it shows about Davis and Johnston. The basic question that touched off the whole spat remained unanswered. Should Bragg's army be further reduced to strengthen the Army of Relief? It was a question of where the Rebels should make their stand. As such, it was—as Johnston maintained—a political question that only Davis could answer, and, typically, he refused to do so. It was the same question—Tennessee or Mississippi?—that Johnston had asked back on January 7 and to which he had never gotten a meaningful answer. In essence it was the question (Virginia or Mississippi?) that Lee had refused (politely) to answer for Davis on May 10.[7]

EVEN as the telegraph wires between Jackson and Richmond hummed with messages in which the President and the general debated the strength of the Army of Relief and whether or not the command arrangement in the West had been changed, Johnston had to get his force organized, equipped, and prepared for operations against Grant's army at Vicksburg.

In its early days, Johnston's Army of Relief comprised nine separate units—Loring's Division and eight independent brigades. As additional troops reached the Jackson-Canton area, Johnston organized his force into three divisions.

General Loring would, of course, command the division he had brought to Jackson after the Champion Hill debacle. Johnston wanted two more major generals to take charge of his to-be-organized second and third divisions. Accordingly, on May 21 he telegraphed Richmond asking President Davis to promote Brigadier Generals W. H. T. Walker and Cadmus Wilcox to fill those posts. (Wilcox then commanded a brigade in the Army of Northern Virginia and had just played an important role in the great Rebel victory at Chancellorsville.)

As with the correspondence between Johnston and the government on so many subjects, this simple request touched off a flurry of confused and confusing messages. Somehow Johnston's telegram was garbled in transmission, and it reached Davis as a request to promote Brigadier Generals "W. H. Taliaferro" and "Wilson."

---

7 24 OR pt. 1, 196, 198, 202-207, 209-214, and 226. See Chapter Eleven.

On May 22, Davis replied that he had already promoted John S. Bowen "to meet the want specified in your dispatch" and suggested Brigadier General Stephen D. Lee if Johnston's army needed another major general. In a separate telegram the President stated, "I do not understand recommendation for promotion of Brigadier General Wilson." The Chief Executive's perplexity was certainly justified since no "Brigadier General Wilson" then served anywhere in the Confederate army, and the only Rebel officer of that surname who ever held the grade would receive it posthumously several months later. (Although, as colonel of the 25th Georgia, Claudius Charles Wilson then served with Walker's Brigade in Johnston's army.) "W. H. Taliaferro" was a mixed-up reference confusing W. H. T. Walker and Brigadier General William B. Taliaferro, who served in the defenses of Charleston.

On the following day, Johnston informed the President that the request had been for Wilcox, not Wilson, and that Generals Bowen and Lee were then trapped inside Vicksburg with Pemberton and, therefore, not available for duty with the Army of Relief. This time the clerks and telegraphers got it right, and Davis promoted Walker. The June 1 arrival of Major General John C. Breckinridge and his division from Tennessee gave Johnston his third major general. (We should note that Davis had promoted Bowen to be a major general in Johnston's command without consulting Johnston or asking him for recommendations. Bowen was an excellent choice—indeed, about the only Confederate general to come out of the 1863 Mississippi fiasco with an enhanced reputation. Unfortunately for the Rebels, he died from disease soon after the surrender of Vicksburg.)[8]

WHILE these telegrams flew back and forth, Johnston repeated his request for a major general. Davis took the message as an application for yet another officer of that grade and ordered Major General Samuel G. French from Virginia to Mississippi. (Again, he assigned a general to Johnston's command without consulting Johnston.)

When Johnston learned of the President's action, he wired the Chief Executive on June 9 that he had heard "that the troops in this department are very hostile to officers of Northern birth, and that on that account . . . French's arrival will weaken

8 24 *OR*, pt. 1, 190-192; 24 *OR*, pt. 3, 929.

instead of strengthening us. I beg you to consider that all the general officers of Northern birth are on duty in this department."[9]

On June 11 Johnston's protest brought forth a reply from an apparently annoyed Davis. French, the President lectured Johnston, although born in New Jersey, was a citizen of Mississippi where he had lived for years. He had been a wealthy planter in the state before "the Yankees robbed him." He had also served as the chief of artillery and ordnance in the Mississippi State Army prior to entering Confederate service "and has frequently been before the enemy. . . . If malignity should undermine him as it has another,[10] you are authorized to relieve him. . . . Surprised by your remark as to the general officers of Northern birth, I turned to the register [of army officers], and find that a large majority of the number are elsewhere than in the Department of Mississippi and Eastern Louisiana." Davis might have added, but did not, that French's local knowledge and Mississippi contacts could prove of considerable value to Johnston and that, other than the recently promoted Walker, French would be the only West Point-trained major general in the Army of Relief.

When French reported for duty on June 11, Johnston gave him a leave of absence to visit his Mississippi home. (What does that say about Johnston's sense of urgency?) Upon French's return a few days later, Johnston scraped together a three-brigade division for him.[11]

AS his army slowly took shape, Johnston had to deal constantly with its shortages of equipment. Many of the units that arrived to reinforce him came without at least some of their artillery, field transportation, baggage, or other necessities. For example, by the time Loring's Division reached Jackson it had lost its wagons, baggage, and almost all its other equipment—down to and including its cooking utensils—in its flight from Champion Hill. Some of the reinforcements coming from South Carolina experienced delays in reaching the Jackson area

---

9 Did Johnston mean to write, "I beg you to consider all the general officers of Northern birth who are on duty in this department"? We cannot know, but by his own admission on several occasions he was "a careless writer."

10 A reference to the Pennsylvania-born Pemberton then under criticism for his recent handling of the Army of Vicksburg.

11 24 *OR*, pt. 1, 195 and 220; 24 *OR*, pt. 3, 929; French, *Two Wars*, 169 and 178. Grabau (*Ninety-Eight Days*, 169 and 178) comments on Johnston's "lack of urgency" during this time.

because the evacuation of material from Jackson tied up so much of the Rebels' railroad equipment.[12]

For the army as a whole, the most serious deficiency seems to have been the shortage of field transportation. Without an adequate number of wagons and the mule teams to pull them, the Army of Relief simply could not operate in the area west of Jackson. With the capital's railroads destroyed for a distance of several miles in all directions and for many miles west of Jackson, the Rebels had to have wagon transportation sufficient to haul food, forage, ammunition, medicines, and other supplies for the army's individual units from the rail termini (points that railroaders call "ends of track"—in this case simply the places where the Yankees had stopped wrecking the railroads). Since only one train at a time could reach any of the ends of track and there be unloaded and since there were no transshipment facilities at the ends of track (turnouts, yard tracks, side-tracks, platforms, turntables, cranes, warehouses, and so on), the whole process would consume far more time than normal. Then, there was the problem of the wrecked bridge over the Pearl River that cut the track from the east. Johnston's need for wagon transportation, therefore, was unusually great. On May 23 the general wrote Seddon that he did not have enough field transportation to operate for more than four days away from the railroad.

We lack detailed knowledge as to how the Confederates went about solving their transportation problem. We do know that in June Johnston had some of his officers scouring eastern Mississippi and even going as far afield as Alabama and Georgia in search of wagons and teams for his army. The matter proved even more complex than it first appears because Johnston's force needed big, sturdy, heavy-duty army wagons that could haul large loads and could operate on rough roads and even in off-road terrain. What the officers usually found on the farms and plantations would have been smaller and lighter civilian buggies and farm wagons. Such vehicles would have been much less serviceable for military purposes and far more prone to break down under the harsh demands of army use.

Since each civilian wagon taken for military use could haul much less than an army wagon, the Rebels needed more of them, more animals to pull them, more teamsters to drive them, and more food for the drivers and teams. In addition, the Army of Relief—should it manage to break through the Yankee siege lines around Vicksburg—would have to have with it enough additional transportation to bring in supplies for Pemberton's army or for that army to use in making its escape. (We

---

12 See 24 *OR*, pt. 1, 191; and 24 *OR*, pt. 3, 920.

should also remember that every wagon and mule taken for military use would inflict some degree of suffering on civilians in the area and weaken their support for the Rebel cause.)

Not until late June did Johnston judge his wagon transportation adequate. By then he had also had built in Canton carriages for his artillery, and he had even managed to procure a "floating bridge" for possible use in crossing the Big Black River.[13]

PART II

"Come Joe! Come quickly!"

— Lieutenant John Cowdery Taylor (from inside besieged Vicksburg), May 29, 1863

All through the weeks of May and June 1863, as he labored to organize and equip the Army of Relief, Joseph E. Johnston faced major problems with communication—with Pemberton inside Vicksburg; with Rebels in the Trans-Mississippi; and, as usual, with the Confederate government in Richmond.

Johnston could exchange messages with the Vicksburg commander only by using daring couriers. These men might cling to some piece of floating debris and drift down the Yazoo and Mississippi rivers at night, passing through the Yankee fleet to reach the besieged city. Others could try to sneak through the Federal siege lines around Pemberton's army—an increasingly hazardous undertaking as time went on and the Yankees perfected their fortifications.[14]

13 24 OR, pt. 1, 224-225, and 242; 24 OR, pt. 3, 901; Johnston, *Narrative*, 190-191 and 202-203. Many thanks to Jim Ogden for pointing out the need for heavy-duty wagons. It seems logical that the taking of large numbers of civilian farm wagons and their teams would have hampered the production and distribution of food for Confederate civilians and other Rebel armies. Food for the Army of Relief seems not to have been a problem for Johnston. (See CLINT's June 10, 1863, letter, Mobile *Advertiser and Register*, of June 16.) The counties north and northwest of Canton produced what he needed to feed his men despite occasional raids into the area by elements of the Yankee army besieging Vicksburg. His difficulty was to get the food from the end of the track south of Canton to the units in the field. 24 OR, pt. 3, 132-133 and 932-933.

14 What purports to be an account of such a trip into and out of besieged Vicksburg by Lamar Fontaine ("the hero upon crutches") with dispatches and forty pounds of percussion caps appeared in the Richmond *Daily Dispatch* on Aug. 1, 1863 (reprinted from the Mobile *Advertiser and Register* of unknown date).

Pemberton's replies and reports would be carried out of Vicksburg through the Yankee lines or by men who floated down the Mississippi for miles until they could wade ashore. Once on the riverbank, they sought out a Confederate cavalry patrol or outpost somewhere southwest of Jackson. From there couriers could rush the documents to Johnston.

Such roundabout means of communication meant that, at best, reports, orders, and other documents reached the addressee only after long delays. Couriers from Johnston, for example, took ten days to get a May 19 dispatch to Pemberton. A message sent on May 29 reached the Vicksburg commander on June 13. Some messages, of course, were delivered in shorter times.

Until Johnston or Pemberton received the other's reply to one of his own dispatches, sometimes two weeks or longer after sending it, he had no means of knowing if his couriers had gotten through the Yankee net around the city. During such a delay, circumstances could change drastically, rendering much of the information in the message irrelevant and making any orders or plans laid out in the dispatch impossible to execute.

Since any effort to resupply Pemberton or to extricate his trapped army should be coordinated as to time and place, such delays multiplied exponentially the difficulties facing the Confederates. At least, so far as is known, no more Yankee spies served as Confederate couriers and delivered the documents they carried to the Federal generals, although Grant's soldiers did intercept some of the messengers.

Communication between Johnston and Pemberton could be even more problematical. What would happen if Johnston sent two copies of an order and only one got through while the Yankees captured the other? In such a case Grant would be prepared to deal with Pemberton's Rebels when they put the order into execution.

Eventually Johnston gave up trying to coordinate some plan for joint action with the Vicksburg garrison. On July 3, he wrote to Pemberton that he hoped to attack Grant's lines east of Vicksburg four days later. "Our firing will show you where we are engaged," he wrote. At that time presumably Pemberton was to plan, prepare for, and position his troops for the breakout either at the point where Johnston had chosen to strike the Union siege line or at some other place where Pemberton judged the chances for escape to be more favorable. Since preparation for such an effort would require at least several hours, success was most unlikely.

It didn't matter. The message did not reach Pemberton until July 10—six days after he had surrendered both Vicksburg and his army.[15]

JOHNSTON'S problems with communications and coordination were not limited to the Cis-Mississippi half of Rebeldom. Several times during the April-July struggle for the Mississippi stronghold, Pemberton, officials in Richmond, and Johnston desperately appealed for assistance from their countrymen in the Trans-Mississippi. As was the case with similar entreaties to Theophilus Holmes the previous winter, their pleas produced little effort and no results. As with those earlier cases, the basic problem was the absence of anyone other than President Davis with the authority to make decisions and to direct the armies on both sides of the Mississippi—and of anyone willing to do so.

Like many younger officers, Edmund Kirby Smith greatly admired Joseph E. Johnston. He had served with distinction in Johnston's Virginia army in the first year of the war. Early in 1863 when Smith received the assignment to take charge of the Trans-Mississippi, he promised cheerful cooperation with his former commander. Although he would be independent of Johnston's authority and subject only to directives from distant Richmond, Smith vowed that he would regard any suggestion from Johnston as an order.

When Smith had conferred with Seddon in Richmond prior to departing for the West, he and the secretary of war had "coincided in thinking that the most important operation in . . . [the Trans-Mississippi] department for some time would be directed to aiding the defense of the Lower Mississippi [River], and keeping that great artery of the West effectually closed to Northern occupation or trade."

Smith journeyed to his departmental headquarters, then in Alexandria, Louisiana, and on March 7 formally assumed command of the Trans-Mississippi. Eleven days later Seddon wrote, directing Smith's attention to "an even more pressing necessity" than keeping the Lower Mississippi River closed to the Yankees. This imperative emergency was the crisis resulting from "the disorder, confusion, and demoralization" then reported "everywhere prevalent, both with the armies and people" in Arkansas. "You should at once," Seddon directed, "visit that portion of your command and use your known ability and influence to restore order and confidence and to reorganize and recruit the scattered forces."

If two major and mutually exclusive missions were not sufficient to confuse and discombobulate poor Smith, Seddon added a third. Before leaving ("at once")

15 24 OR, pt. 1, 281.

to visit Arkansas, the secretary wrote in the same March 7 letter, Smith should "I hope, have been enabled to plan and direct operations which will protect [from Federal raids] the valuable districts lying on the smaller rivers and bayous back from the Mississippi."

What was Smith to do? He went off to spend three weeks in Little Rock and then came up with the answer. "My duties now and for some time, must be principally of an administrative character," he later reported to President Davis from his headquarters which he had moved to Shreveport. "It is in that field that my usefulness will be felt. The department has to be made self-sustaining. . . . I must begin de novo in . . . [an] attempt at a general systematizing and development of the department resources."

Thus, while Grant pounded Vicksburg, Banks hammered away at Port Hudson, Pemberton and Gardner grimly held their men in the trenches, Johnston labored to cobble together the Army of Relief, and Lee marched north into Pennsylvania, Smith went up the Red River to Shreveport. There—even farther removed from Vicksburg, Port Hudson, Pemberton, Gardner, and Johnston—he would devote his attention to completing telegraph lines to various points in his department, planning an arsenal, erecting a foundry, constructing textile mills, and creating the bureaucratic machinery for implementing, enforcing, and administering the tax-in-kind and conscription laws. He considered his three chief subordinates (the commanders of the Districts of Arkansas; Louisiana; and Texas, New Mexico, and Arizona) to be, he wrote, "officers of merit and ability, and . . . they have my confidence." Thus, he saw "no need to take the field in person . . . unless a large concentration of troops becomes necessary." Meanwhile, Secretary of War Seddon wrote Johnston expressing his hope that aid for the defenders of Vicksburg by the forces in the Trans-Mississippi "is a policy so apparent that it will be voluntarily embraced and executed"—but, we must note, not ordered.

Distance, poor communications, and the menacing presence in the Mississippi of the Federal navy made any sort of coordinated action between Rebel forces east and west of the river impossible. Johnston and Pemberton could do no more than appeal to Smith for help. On May 13, for example, Pemberton asked Smith to operate against Grant's Louisiana supply line which then stretched from Milliken's Bend and Young's Point sixty-three miles down the Mississippi's right bank to New Carthage. Eighteen days later Johnston wrote requesting help for Port Hudson. On June 26 Johnston again wrote to Smith. By then, he confessed, the Confederates' only hope to save Vicksburg was for Smith's troops somehow—he could not come up with a really good idea as to how—to act.

All during the crucial days of April and through the first three weeks of May, Smith occupied himself with a threat to his own department. A Union column had advanced up Bayou Teche and occupied Alexandria, thereby closing the Red River to the Rebels. Fearing that the Yankees would continue on to Shreveport, Smith pulled together what few troops he could scrape up (about 10,000, many of them drawn from Arkansas) to meet the enemy in northwestern Louisiana. He had little time during those days to worry about events east of the Mississippi.

By May 22 the Federals had abandoned Alexandria and gone down the Red River to operate against Port Hudson. Smith, finally, could give some attention to Vicksburg. In true Confederate fashion, he and his Louisiana commander, Major General Richard Taylor, fell into an argument over how best they might aid the Rebels in Mississippi. Smith favored undertaking direct operations along the right bank of the river across from Vicksburg. Taylor argued for an attack on New Orleans to draw Banks downriver from Port Hudson and thereby free the garrison of that town to join the Army of Relief.

Eventually Smith overruled Taylor and ordered his subordinate to the area across the river from besieged Vicksburg. To their dismay, the Rebels found that the Yankees were no longer moving any significant quantity of supplies down the Louisiana side of the river. Grant, it turned out, had established his siege lines about Vicksburg and was drawing his supplies by boat directly down the Mississippi.

The Federals, however, still held Milliken's Bend and Young's Point as supply depots and maintained a presence at Lake Providence (north of Milliken's Bend) where they were undertaking to grow cotton. Taylor decided to attack the three Union posts even though it was obvious that if he captured or destroyed all three, his success would not in any way seriously interfere with Grant's operations against Vicksburg.

Taylor's attacks on June 7 and 9 proved farcical even by Confederate standards. Whatever slight chance they had for success was literally blown away by the big cannon on the Yankee gunboats in the Mississippi. The Rebels pulled back from the river. For several weeks they occupied themselves by burning cotton, with attempts to harass Federal shipping from the riverbank, and with a harebrained scheme to provision the Vicksburg garrison by swimming a large herd of cattle across the Mississippi. Nobody seems to have given much thought as to where the cattle were to come from, how they were to get to the area, or how they were to avoid drifting downstream on the current to become food for the sailors on the Yankee boats or for the catfish in the river.

Finally, on July 5, Kirby Smith himself arrived in the area to see what might be done. Unable to formulate any plan to help Pemberton, he was still there a few days later when the Trans-Mississippi Rebels learned that Vicksburg had surrendered on July 4.[16]

IN communicating with Pemberton and Smith, Johnston had to overcome more than just geographical obstacles and the barriers put up by the enemy. In communicating with the authorities in Richmond he was free from those problems, but he faced the even greater hurdles that he and President Davis had created between themselves. The predictable result was an almost complete failure on the part of the government to comprehend the enormity of the difficulties facing Johnston in Mississippi and the extremely limited possibilities that the Rebels had there after early May. Another, and equally predictable result, was a great increase in the level of bitterness, frustration, and distrust between Davis and Johnston.

The May-July correspondence between Johnston on the one hand and Davis and Seddon on the other comprises a series of letters and telegrams that dealt largely with subjects that might be classified as "low-to-mid-level" matters (as opposed to the nitty-gritty minutiae of daily command and administration on one side and over-arching strategic geopolitical-military topics on the other).

Not once while he was in Mississippi did Johnston give the President a thorough, detailed overall catalog of the numerous problems he would face supplying his army west of Jackson. Not once did he describe Grant's position and detail the great obstacles the Confederates would encounter in undertaking an operation against the Federal lines around the besieged city. Not once did he openly question the value of the President's desire to hold the Vicksburg-Port Hudson corridor after Union gunboats had occupied the river between the two towns. Not once did he inform Davis that Pemberton had thrice disobeyed his "orders" (or ignored his suggestions) to unite and fight Grant in early May, to move east against Clinton on May 14, and to evacuate Vicksburg after the defeat at the

---

16 24 *OR*, pt. 1, 219; and 24 *OR*, pt. 3, 979. See also the late May Confederate correspondence in 26 *OR*, pt. 1, 180-214. In fairness to Smith, we should note that on May 8, President Davis had written him referring to the widespread belief that the summer heat and the diseases associated with the Lower Mississippi Valley would soon bring large scale operations to a halt. Therefore, he pointed out, a delay in dealing with the enemy threatening Vicksburg might be wise. By July 2, the desperate situation in Mississippi had moved the Chief Executive almost to the point of giving an order to Kirby Smith: "I am convinced that the safety of Vicksburg depends on your prompt and efficient co-operation. As far as practicable, I desire you to move your forces to the Mississippi River and command in person operations for the relief of the besieged city." J. Davis, *Papers*, vol. 9, 172, and 22 *OR*, pt. 2, 902.

Big Black. In summary, once again Johnston—true to his ways—chose (Covey again) not to communicate fully with his government about the situation with which he had to cope and the extremely limited options he had in trying to deal with it.

JUST what, he might have inquired, did the government want him to do? The May 9 telegram ordering him from Tennessee to Mississippi had directed him to "take chief command of the forces, giving to those in the field, as far as practicable the encouragement and benefit of your personal direction." The general had arrived in Jackson too late to join Pemberton, and that officer had three times refused to obey Johnston's orders (or follow Johnston's suggestions). He and Gardner had elected to shut themselves up in the towns they held. What did the government now wish for Johnston to do?

ONCE the Army of Relief had been organized, its transportation provided for to the extent possible, requests for more reinforcements dispatched to Richmond, and letters pleading for help sent off to the Trans-Mississippi, Johnston turned to the matter of how best to use his force in an effort to rescue the trapped garrison of Vicksburg.

In theory, Johnston had five options. First, he could move west to make a direct attack on Grant's besieging army and attempt to destroy it or at least to drive it away, thereby saving Vicksburg and maintaining a Confederate presence on the Mississippi. Next, he could attempt to break through the Yankee siege lines to resupply and perhaps reinforce Pemberton's garrison. Third, he could abandon all thought of saving Vicksburg and try only to open an exit route by which as many men as possible might escape. Fourth, he could move north to threaten Corinth or Memphis or south to attempt to relieve Port Hudson. Finally, he could simply hover about the Jackson area and hope that he could prevent the Yankees from doing more damage after Vicksburg's inevitable surrender.

Had Johnston asked—and, of course, he did not—the authorities (i. e. President Davis) would have favored the first option. Indeed, throughout May and June Richmond frequently bombarded Johnston with messages urging him to attack Grant's army. Johnston, however, surely realized, even if Davis and Seddon never did, that destroying Grant's army was clearly far beyond Confederate capabilities. Even defeating it or pushing it away from Vicksburg to open a route by which the garrison could escape was probably impossible given its position and the wide margin by which it outnumbered the Army of Relief. (On May 23 Johnston estimated Grant's strength at 60,000. On June 3, he reported 30,000 more troops en route to the Federal army at Vicksburg.[17]) To make matters more difficult, the Unionists would be fighting on the defensive from a strongly fortified position with their flanks resting securely on navigable rivers where they would be protected by the ubiquitous gunboats, and with the Mississippi River itself as their unbreakable line of supply.

Breaking into Vicksburg—if it could be done at all—to resupply or reinforce the garrison might prolong the siege, but in the end doing so would simply increase the number of Rebels who finally surrendered when their supplies eventually ran out. Grant himself is reported to have said, "If Johnston tries to cut his way in, we will let him do it, and see that he don't get out." Even worse for the Confederates should such an event occur, the absence of Johnston's army from the region east of Grant's position would remove the only major Rebel force standing between the Lower Mississippi Valley and the South Atlantic coast. In so doing it would expose the crucial agricultural and industrial areas of Alabama as well as the rail lines in that state and those in Georgia. It would also open the way for Grant's Unionists to operate against the rear of the Rebel army in Tennessee and North Georgia. So, too, would a march of the Army of Relief to threaten Federal forces in northern Mississippi or those at Port Hudson.

Since it was politically unacceptable for Johnston simply to hover about Jackson and await events, he reached the conclusion by May 29 that Vicksburg could not be saved and that the only thing he might be able to accomplish would be to open a route by which Pemberton and his army could attempt to escape. Such an effort faced many massive obstacles. These ranged from communications to logistical, tactical, and terrain problems standing in the way, to the physical strength of Pemberton's troops as the days and then weeks of reduced rations and exposure in the trenches took their toll. (In fairness, Johnston probably did not know about this last difficulty or, at least, about the extent to which the siege had weakened the strength of Pemberton's soldiers, reducing both their physical ability to march and to fight in the open field.)[18]

AS was the case so often during the war, the geography of the western Confederacy worked against the Southerners. Vicksburg sat near the western end of what was, from a military point of view, a peninsula bounded by the Yazoo, Mississippi, and Big Black rivers. The Yazoo flows roughly from east to west and

17 24 *OR*, pt. 1, 192-194 and 374; Symonds, *Johnston*, 212.

18 See 24 *OR*, pt. 3, 929; and 26 *OR*, pt. 2, 26.

the Big Black northeast to southwest. At their closest point the two streams are only a little more than twelve miles apart. At times of "normal" rainfall both rivers were navigable for a considerable distance.

To reach Vicksburg or to open an avenue of escape for Pemberton's army, Johnston had two possible routes of advance, neither of them promising. He could move the Army of Relief directly west from the Jackson area—a move that would take his force to the Big Black River, which he would then have to cross. His only other realistic option was to shift northwest of Jackson and try to advance down the narrow neck of land between the Yazoo and the Big Black. This isthmus was known as the Mechanicsburg Corridor.

Should Johnston elect to move directly west from Jackson, he faced the formidable problem of getting his army across the Big Black. We lack detailed and reliable information on the river's depth in late June 1863, but it was said, at various times, to have been fordable at many points. Fordable or not, the Big Black presented a major obstacle to the Confederates. The river could be fordable one day and impassable the next. In mid-May, General Loring reported it "deep and difficult . . . to cross." On June 5 it was said to be "falling rapidly." A week later a Union general noted that it was "swollen considerably." Two days later he pronounced it "fordable at almost any place."[19]

The lighter Union gunboats ("tinclads") drew only a few feet of water and could operate in shallow streams. (Indeed, Lincoln is supposed to have once quipped that they could operate wherever there was a little dew.) The Big Black, in fact, could have been fordable and navigable at the same time and place. In addition, sudden heavy rains, not uncommon in the region in the summer, could quickly if temporarily raise the water level in the streams. A Union general reported that during the night of July 5 a heavy rain raised the water level in the Big Black by four feet.

Should Federal naval vessels ascend the Big Black after the Confederates crossed the river, they could cut Johnston's supply line and trap his army on the right bank between the Union army and the river. Even if the Rebels could drive the gunboats off with their artillery, doing so would consume part of their ammunition supply and divert some of their not-very-great strength from operations against the Federal siege lines at Vicksburg. Such action would also show Grant where Johnston was preparing to strike.

---

19 24 *OR*, pt. 2, 78, 222, 449, and 521; and Grabau, *Ninety-Eight Days*, 446 and 448-449.

Finally, the banks along much of the Big Black were so steep at many points that they would have presented serious logistical problems even had the riverbed been completely dry. The Confederates would have had to construct the means of getting artillery and wagons across the stream bed—approach roads, cuts, fills, and so on. They had neither the resources nor the time to do so.

The Mechanicsburg Corridor posed equally serious difficulties of its own. That route involved an approach march along narrow ridge-top roads leading down a thin isthmus with a river open to enemy vessels on its right flank and another potentially open to such vessels on its left. Would the Yankees ascend the Yazoo and/or the Big Black and fall upon the flank(s) or rear of the Army of Relief as it moved southwest down the corridor toward Vicksburg? Equally serious was the possibility that, while Johnston was making his way down the corridor, a Yankee column could cross the Big Black downstream and strike east. In such a case the Army of Relief would find itself cut off from its Jackson-Canton base.

THE Federal generals, of course, could read a map as well as the Confederates, and they knew at least as much about the immediate area as did Johnston. They, too, were well aware of his possible routes of advance. In June, as reinforcements brought Gant's strength up to more than 70,000 men, the Federal commander deployed about half of his force to defend against any attack that Johnston might make from the east. This force, sometimes called the Army of Maneuver, obstructed the roads that the Confederates would have to use and built fortifications across the corridor and to cover the rivers' likely crossing points. It was ready to dispute any attempt Johnston might make to reach Vicksburg from the east, and by itself, outnumbered Johnston's force. If necessary, it could draw upon the remainder of Grant's army for thousands of additional troops.[20]

Even had Johnston managed to break through Grant's lines and reach Pemberton's position, he could not have long remained there—unless he wanted simply to add his army to the trapped Vicksburg garrison. He would have had to hold an escape route open long enough for the Army of Vicksburg to march out. Doing so would have presented the Rebels with even more insuperable problems.

Johnston had no way to coordinate his efforts with Pemberton, and the latter had no way of knowing when and where his would-be rescuers would strike. To evacuate his army from Vicksburg, Pemberton would have to withdraw his troops from their long defensive line around the city and assemble them for the breakout

---

20 32 *ORS*, 40, 160, 288, and 422.

effort at whatever point he had chosen for the attempt. Such a redeployment would take at least several hours and could not even begin until Johnston's attack on Grant's lines alerted Pemberton (and Grant) to the fact that, at long last, the rescue effort had gotten underway.

Even had Pemberton known when and where to gather his troops for the breakout in advance of Johnston's arrival, abandoning his defensive line to form the escape column would have allowed the Yankees to walk through the empty Rebel fortifications into the city. They could then attack the assembled Army of Vicksburg as it awaited word indicating that the escape route was open. Leaving a sufficient force in place to hold the city's defenses would have reduced the number of escapees so much that Johnston's casualties could well have exceeded the number of men who made it out of the city to safety. If all that came to pass, could the garrison troops, worn down by six weeks of constant service in the trenches and weakened by exposure, malnourishment, and sickness, have mustered the physical strength for a breakout, let alone for an open field battle?[21]

FROM the beginning of the siege the Confederates trapped in Vicksburg had looked toward Johnston to rescue them. As early as May 17 a citizen in the town wrote in his diary, "The enemy have a line entirely around us, leaving no outlets. Our only hope now is that we can hold out until Johnston arrives." One of Pemberton's soldiers wrote soon afterward, "We were exhorted to hold the place for only twelve hours longer, being assured that General Johnston would join us by that time, at the head of a heavy force." Another citizen noted, "we were repeatedly informed that he was coming." On May 29, Lieutenant John Cowdery Taylor, a member of Pemberton's staff, wrote, "Courier from Genl. Johnston—he will come to our relief as soon as he can collect a sufficient force—Come Joe! Come quickly!" The Vicksburg *Citizen* told its readers on June 18 that "we may look forward at any time to his [Johnston's] approach. We may repose the utmost confidence in his appearance within a very few days. . . . relief is close at hand. Hold out a few days longer."[22]

---

21 William Pitt Chambers, one of Pemberton's men, noted ("Journal," 279, in a "catch-up" entry), "In view of the condition of the men such an attempt would have been utter madness. We were wholly unfit for such exploits because the weakness from hunger and the stiffness of limb engenered by weeks of crowding behind our works." See also the June 12 entry in the John Cowdery Taylor "diary."

22 Chambers, "Journal," 274 and 276.

IN late June and early July, as Johnston finally put the Army of Relief in motion and inched cautiously westward, he sought to determine the best point at which to make the rescue attempt. His first inclination was to try to launch his effort down the Mechanicsburg Corridor. After several days, however, he concluded that that route simply was not practicable. He then turned his attention to the area along the Big Black south of the railroad.

As Johnston carefully probed the Yankee positions along the river in the early days of July, the sounds of gunfire that for so long had been heard from the west died out. On July 4 Pemberton surrendered Vicksburg and the city's defending Rebels (a total of about 30,000 men), all of his artillery, equipment, and supplies, and all possibility of a significant Confederate presence on the Mississippi River.

AS Joseph E. Johnston had realized in early May (at least at some level), once Grant came ashore on the Mississippi side of the river below Vicksburg, the Confederates' only chance was to concentrate immediately and defeat him, even if doing so meant at least a temporary abandonment of Vicksburg. Therefore, Johnston from his sickbed in Tullahoma had sent instructions (suggestions?) to that effect to Pemberton on May 1. The Vicksburg commander had chosen to ignore the message—as he chose to disregard those of May 13-14 to march east from Clinton as well as that of May 17 to evacuate Vicksburg and save his garrison.

The seeds of the Vicksburg disaster that had been planted the previous December at the Grenada conference, when Davis, Johnston, and Pemberton left so many questions unanswered, took just over six months to come to fruition.

Chapter Ten

Aftermath of Disaster

". . . the pain of such disastrous intelligence . . ."
— Secretary of War James A. Seddon, July 7, 1863

On Friday, July 3, Joseph E. Johnston's Army of Relief remained in its camps a few miles east of the Big Black River. Out along the river the army's skirmishers occasionally exchanged shots with their Yankee counterparts as they fought duels at various possible crossing points.

General Johnston summoned several of his chief subordinates to his headquarters that day, where he and they spent some nine hours questioning locals and poring over maps and reports from scouts. The officers were seeking information about the roads leading to and along the Big Black and those between the river and Vicksburg. (Why Johnston had not had at least the area east of the Big Black thoroughly reconnoitered during the preceding weeks is not known.) The day proved very frustrating for the Confederate commanders, since they learned little of value.

The next morning, Saturday the fourth, a strange silence descended upon west-central Mississippi. For the first time in seven weeks the almost constant chatter of small-arms fire and the heavy boom of artillery and big naval guns did not roll eastward from besieged Vicksburg. Speculation about the silence doubtless ran through the Rebel camps, and some of Johnston's soldiers must have correctly guessed its meaning.[1]

Inside Vicksburg that day Pemberton's troops, having surrendered their flags and weapons, awaited their formal paroles—a procedure that took about a week. East of the Big Black Johnston's Rebels, ignorant of the city's fate, went on with their preparations to march west and attempt to extricate the Army of Vicksburg.

---

1 The firing from Vicksburg could sometimes be heard at least as far to the east as Jackson. See, for example, the telegrams from the Mississippi capital of June 4, 9, and 11, 1863, published in the Richmond *Examiner* of June 6, 11, and 15, 1863.

Johnston's preparations continued throughout that Saturday and some elements of the Army of Relief began to shift westward to positions closer to the Big Black. Orders were for the army to begin its attempt to cross the river at midnight. At about 10:00 p.m., however, an officer who had left Vicksburg that day reached Johnston with news that the town had surrendered. The bearer of this sad report may well have been Lieutenant Colonel Louis M. Montgomery, an acting aide-de-camp on Pemberton's staff, sent out by his general to arrange food and quarters for the surrendered troops once they had received their paroles and marched back into Confederate lines.

Correctly anticipating that Grant would quickly turn his forces eastward against the Army of Relief, Johnston immediately cancelled the orders to cross the Big Black and directed his troops to move back to Jackson.[2]

JOHNSTON'S Rebels reached the state capital early in the afternoon of July 7. As the troops filed into the line of fortifications that guarded the approaches to the western side of the city, Johnston, Samuel French, and perhaps other officers rode

---

2 The account in the text is the best reconstruction I have been able to make from incomplete, unsatisfactory, and sometimes contradictory sources. For example, the Mobile *Advertiser and Register*, n. d. (quoted in the Richmond *Dispatch,* July 20, 1863) reported that the advance was set for 2:00 a.m. on July 5. See French, *Two Wars*, 182; unsigned letter, dated Jackson, July 16, 1863, in the Atlanta [*Southern*] *Confederacy*, n. d. (reprinted as "THE WESTERN CAMPAIGN," in the Charleston *Mercury,* July 28, 1863); 24 *OR*, pt. 1, 230; and the July 11 report from Jackson in the Charleston *Courier*, n. d., (reprinted as "Why Vicksburg Fell," in the Memphis *Daily Appeal* (published in Atlanta), July 22, 1863. This last source refers to "A Col. Montgomery, who was on Pemberton's staff, escaped with two hundred men; they were the only ones, I believe, who made their escape." Louis M. Montgomery had participated in the July 3 surrender conference. Rather than escaping from Vicksburg, he was sent by Pemberton to arrange details of the paroled garrison's march eastward (24 *OR*, pt. 1, 230. See also Ballard, *Vicksburg*, 397; Ballard, *Pemberton*, 179; and Bearss, *Campaign for Vicksburg*, II, 6 and 43-49). In his *Narrative* (204), Johnston wrote that he received intelligence of the surrender late on July 4. Since news of the capitulation reached Jackson on the fifth (24 *OR*, pt. 1, 230), it is possible that he did. In writing his Narrative a decade later, however, Johnston seems to have confused the dates—or he may have regarded the accounts received on July 4 as mere rumors and, therefore, continued preparations to cross the Big Black until he had more reliable information. A report by an officer of Pemberton's staff who had assisted in making arrangements for the surrender (Montgomery) would have been reliable enough. On July 8, a telegram from Jackson reported that Col. Montgomery had reached that city. It was published in the Richmond *Daily Dispatch* on July 10 and in many other papers about the same time. On July 16, the Macon *Daily Telegraph* reprinted an item from the Montgomery *Advertiser*, n. d., reporting that Johnston did not receive news of the surrender until late on July 6. This was clearly an incorrect date. See also 24 *OR*, pt. 3, 992.

out to inspect the line. "It is miserably located and not half completed," French observed. Two days later the Yankees appeared before the Confederate position.

Very little rain had fallen in central Mississippi in recent weeks, and the resulting drought seemed to offer Johnston a slight hope. In the hot mid-summer weather many of the area's streams had run dry and the water level in the ponds had dropped. The Federals "suffered much from excessive heat and the scarcity of water during the recent campaign," reported a member of the 13th Illinois on July 27. Knowing that the Jackson defenses were much too weak to withstand a heavy attack, Johnston counted on a shortage of water to defeat the Union column that had followed him east. To that end he had his men foul the ponds as they fell back toward Jackson by leading animals out into the water and killing them. The Rebels had also tossed dead animals into the farm wells as they passed. (What did any civilians still in the area think of that?)

Lack of drinking water, Johnston anticipated, would compel the Federals to choose between abandoning their effort against Jackson and launching an immediate assault on the Rebel works. In the latter event Johnston's troops would enjoy the advantage of fighting from behind the city's fortifications, slight though they were. (Upon reaching Jackson on the seventh, the Confederates had gone to work to bolster the town's defenses, but one must wonder why Johnston had not had them strengthened in late May and June.)[3]

UNFORTUNATELY for the Secessionists, a heavy rain on the night of July 7-8 gave the Yankees a sufficiency of potable water. Soon the Federals were deployed west of Jackson along a semi-circular line stretching from the Pearl River north of the capital around the west side and then back to the stream south of the city. Major General William T. Sherman, commanding the Union force, planned to smash Jackson and Johnston's army with a massive artillery bombardment.

When Rebel cavalry failed in an attempt to destroy a wagon train bringing ammunition for Sherman's cannon, Johnston realized that he could no longer remain in Jackson. During the night of July 16-17 he evacuated the city, crossed the Pearl River, and slowly moved his army to Morton on the railroad about thirty miles to the east.

After a brief half-hearted pursuit the Federals pulled back and inflicted even more damage on what remained of the Mississippi capital and its railroad network. When they finished, on the twenty-third they marched back to the area west of the

3 French, *Two Wars*, 182; 21 *ORS*, 30.

Big Black River. Like the Rebels, they were exhausted by the long struggle for Vicksburg.

Once Johnston ascertained that the Unionists were not pursuing him eastward toward Morton, he put his army into camps along the Jackson-Meridian railroad. With his cavalrymen out to the west and the area between Jackson and the Big Black a sort of desolate no-man's land, he could anticipate having several weeks to rest, refit, reorganize, and resupply his troops as he awaited whatever transpired next.[4]

FOUR days before he evacuated Jackson, Johnston received word that the Rebel garrison at Port Hudson had surrendered on July 9. All of the great Mississippi River was back under national control. On July 16, even as the Confederates prepared to evacuate the state capital, the civilian steamboat *Imperial* reached New Orleans from St. Louis.[5]

THE last weeks of June and the first week or two of July must have seemed an eternity to Confederate authorities in Richmond. In mid-June, Robert E. Lee's army had marched off to the northwest from its central Virginia encampments and then headed north down the Shenandoah Valley. Within a week its leading units were across the Potomac River and into Maryland, pressing on toward Pennsylvania. Once Lee crossed the river and passed into Maryland, his

---

4 Such a rain, of course, raised the water level in the Big Black and in so doing justified Johnston's insistence on obtaining a pontoon bridge for his thrust westward. (See discussion of river obstacles in preceding chapter.)

5 The disaster was massive. In addition to losing Vicksburg, Port Hudson, and the Mississippi River, the Rebels suffered 9,091 casualties in the campaign and siege of Vicksburg. On July 4 they surrendered 29,491 officers and men, five locomotives, "a number of [railroad] cars," 172 cannon, 38,000 artillery shells, 58,000 pounds of black powder, 50,000 rifles, 600,000 rounds of ammunition, 350,000 percussion caps, 38,681 pounds of bacon, 5,000 bushels of peas, 51,241 pounds of rice, 92,234 pounds of sugar, 428,000 pounds of salt, and 731 rations of flour (Ballard, *Vicksburg*, 398-399; 24 *OR*, pt. 3, 553. See also the letter from "One of the Garrison," to the Mobile *Advertiser and Register*, n. d. (reprinted in the Charleston *Mercury*, July 28, 1863). Casualties at Port Hudson and in the other engagements of the struggle for the Lower Mississippi (such as Arkansas Post), as well as desertions, raised total Confederate losses to more than 50,000. All of the Rebel troops killed, wounded, and captured after the night of Apr. 16-17 (when Union gunboats gained control of the Vicksburg-Port Hudson corridor) fell defending something the Confederates had already lost—communication between the eastern and western halves of their country. I wonder if Johnston, with his ability sometimes to see (or sense) the military significance of such developments, might have pointed that fact out to Davis and Pemberton if he had been asked, or if he had had the initiative so to advise Davis.

communications with Richmond were tenuous at best, and Rebel officials in the capital knew virtually nothing about the activities of his army.

Nor did the authorities immediately learn anything about what was transpiring in west-central Mississippi. Apparently, Johnston had sent no word that he had finally moved out toward the Big Black River, and press reports that the Secessionists had left Jackson lagged many days—sometimes a week or more—behind the events.[6]

To make matters even worse for the harried government officials, Federal troops in southeastern Virginia began to show signs that they were moving against Richmond. On July 2 the authorities called the capital's local home guard units, which included clerks in the government departments, into the field to man the city's defenses against what was reported to be an advancing force of 25,000 enemy troops. The government clerks were out until Monday, July 6, so the normal slow pace of government work became even more slothful.[7]

AT 1:00 p.m. on Tuesday, July 7, three days after Pemberton's surrender and the day after the War Department clerks had returned to their desks, a telegram from Jackson, Mississippi, came in over the wires to the telegraph company's Richmond office. The message, dated July 5, was a "press dispatch" signed "Woodson" and endorsed "Approved" by Lieutenant Colonel T. B. Lamar, an assistant adjutant general on Johnston's staff then on duty in Jackson. The message reported the capitulation of Vicksburg based on statements by an unnamed officer who had reached the state capital after coming through the enemy's lines from Pemberton's army.

Shown the message, the president of the telegraph company doubtless was surprised and shocked. Instead of releasing the telegram to the press, he sent or took it to the War Department. So far as the records show, this was the first news of Vicksburg's fate to reach the capital. By nightfall, reports (probably originating with

---

6 For example, the Richmond *Dispatch* of July 7 announced that "The indications are strong that Gen. Johnston is at last making a move upon the rear of Grant's army." The Atlanta *Southern Confederacy*, n. d. (reprinted in the Charleston *Mercury*, July 28) published a July 16 letter that opened with the ringing declaration, "The movement for the relief of Vicksburg commenced on the 1st inst."

7 Kean, *Diary*, 78; Richmond *Sentinel*, July 10, 1863; letter, July 1, from "Dixie," Memphis (Atlanta) *Daily Appeal*, July 3 and 6, 1863.

some telegraph company employees) that the Mississippi stronghold had fallen were "about the streets" of Richmond.[8]

SECRETARY of war Seddon may well have found himself annoyed at the source of the news in the telegram—the press rather than his general on the scene—but he could not have been greatly surprised at the contents of the message. Johnston had informed him as early as June 15, "I consider saving Vicksburg hopeless." Three days later the general had telegraphed, "I will do what I can, without hope of doing more than to aid to extricate the garrison."

On June 17 a British officer on a visit to the Confederacy to observe military operations talked with Rebel officials in Richmond. He noted in his diary: "I was sorry to hear in the highest quarters the gloomiest forebodings with regard to the fate of Vicksburg. The fortress is in fact given up, and all now despair of General Johnston's being able to effect anything towards its relief." Vice President Alexander H. Stephens, who after a sojourn at his Georgia home reached the Rebel capital on June 26, was surprised to learn from some officials that Vicksburg might surrender at any moment.[9]

---

8   The press reports on which this account is based (Richmond *Examiner*, July 8 and 9) say only 1:00 o'clock. I assume it was in the afternoon since it seems unlikely the telegraph company president would have been at the office at 1:00 a.m. to take or send the message to the War Department. Will O. Woodson, a reporter for the Confederate Press Association, worked in Jackson at that time. My guess is that since the telegram dealt with a very sensitive subject, the telegrapher or manager of the Jackson telegraph company office refused to transmit the dispatch unless a member of Johnston's staff cleared it. Woodson's telegram itself has not been found, so we do not know how he worded it or to whom he addressed it. See also 24 *OR*, pt. 1, 230.

9   24 *OR*, pt. 1, 227; Fremantle, *Diary*, 164; and Schott, *Stephens*, 378. See also Seddon's comment on Johnston's July 7 telegram quoted in next section of this chapter. In the days prior to the surrender, Rebel newspapers carried numerous reports to the effect that Vicksburg was certain to hold out for a long time. For example, the Selma (AL) *Dispatch*, June 28 (reprinted in the Macon *Daily Telegraph* on July 3), predicted that "The armies of Kirby Smith, Taylor[,] and [Maj. Gen.] Sterling Price, now under the complete control of the wary chieftain [Johnston], are each in position for moving at a moment's warning towards the common centre— Vicksburg—and will be most likely to afford an early relief to its heroic garrison by the total annihilation of Grant's army—a consummation not in the least improbable. . . . the hour of action is at hand . . . and the fearful fire from the rear [is] about to open upon the weary, wasted forces of Grant." The *Dispatch* claimed that it based its forecast on a "special interview" with a "highly intelligent and reliable gentleman" who served as Johnston's "confidential agent" and who was then *en route* to Richmond bearing "important dispatches for the War Department."

BY the time Woodson's telegram reached Seddon it was a day-and-a-half or two days old (depending on the time of day Woodson dispatched it from Jackson), and as usual the government had received no recent news from Johnston. Quickly Seddon sent off a telegram to the general summarizing the Woodson message's contents and directing Johnston to "Telegraph if this be true and any particulars known."

Some time after Seddon dispatched this inquiry a message from Johnston, sent soon after he reached the state capital on July 7, arrived in Richmond. (Why Johnston had not sent a staff officer or courier ahead to Jackson earlier to telegraph the authorities is not known.) Upon receipt of Johnston's telegram, Seddon sent it to President Davis "with the deepest regret at being compelled to inflict the pain of such disastrous intelligence, tho only confirmatory of our fear." On the eighth Johnston, in replying to Secretary Seddon's inquiry of the previous day, repeated his message of the seventh.[10]

NEWS of the fate of Vicksburg was but one of the discouraging reports that reached Confederate authorities in the first half of July. A few days before Johnston moved the Army of Relief out of the Jackson-Canton area to attempt to save Pemberton's trapped Vicksburg garrison, the Federals under General William Rosecrans at Murfreesboro, Tennessee, awakened from their long hibernation. Through the last week of June, they maneuvered against Bragg's Army of Tennessee at Tullahoma, and in a brilliantly planned and well-conducted operation forced it to fall back. Unable to find a place suitable for making a stand, Bragg retreated southeast. On July 4, as the Vicksburg army surrendered to Grant, he crossed the Tennessee River and moved into Chattanooga. The Rebels had lost all Middle Tennessee along with that part of Alabama north of the Tennessee River.

10 24 OR, pt. 1, 238 and 243; J. Davis, Papers, vol. 8, 264. Press reports indicate that many initially doubted the authenticity of both Woodson's telegram and Johnston's first message. The latter was reported to have been signed "JOSEPH E. JOHNSTON," rather than the usual "J. E. JOHNSTON," and some citizens thought that it might have been a hoax perpetrated by speculators in sugar. See Richmond Examiner, July 9, and the Richmond letter from DIXIE in the Memphis (Atlanta) Appeal, July 13. Unfortunately, gaps in the microfilm files of several important newspapers deprive us of what would have been very valuable sources. The microfilm file of the Memphis Appeal, for example, is missing the issues of July 7-11; that of the Richmond Sentinel those of July 4-7, and, most serious of all, the Mobile Advertiser and Register is missing July 1 through Sept. 30. Scattered issues of some of these papers are available. Other papers frequently reprinted material from now-missing issues of many of these papers—as will be seen below.

Even as news of the disasters in Mississippi and Tennessee trickled into Richmond, the Rebel government began to get unverified word of a major battle in southern Pennsylvania. Initial reports indicated success for Lee's army, but as more details were received, it became clear that the Confederates had met with a great defeat and were retreating to Virginia. Indeed, their retreat began on July 4—the day Pemberton surrendered and Bragg crossed the Tennessee River. By the middle of the month Lee's army that had marched northward with such high hopes a few weeks earlier was back in the Old Dominion.

ON July 10 Josiah Gorgas, the Rebel chief of ordnance, noted in his diary, "On the whole our affairs look gloomier now than ever." A week later he asked his diary, "Can we believe in the justice of Providence, or must we conclude that we are after all wrong?" On the twenty-eighth he observed,

> Events have succeeded one another with disastrous rapidity. One month ago. . . . All looked bright. Now the picture is just as sombre as it was bright then. . . . It seems incredible that human power could effect such a change in so brief a space. Yesterday we rode on the pinnacle of success—to-day absolute ruin seems to be our portion. The Confederacy totters to its destruction.[11]

11 Gorgas, *Diary*, 74-75.

Chapter Eleven

Searching for a Scapegoat

PART I

"[Mrs. Johnston apprehends] that the whole power
of the government is preparing to overwhelm me."
— Joseph E. Johnston to Louis T. Wigfall, August 12, 1863

The Federal forces posted between Vicksburg and the Big Black River did not constitute the only serious problem with which Joseph E. Johnston had to concern himself during the first days of July 1863. At about the time he ordered the Army of Relief to move out from its camps in the Jackson-Canton area in what became the aborted effort to relieve Vicksburg, the general received a telegram from President Davis. In this message, dated June 30, the Chief Executive dredged up once more the issue of whether the War Department's order for Johnston to go to Mississippi and take personal command there had also terminated his authority over Bragg's army in Tennessee. "I am at a loss to account for your strange error in so thinking," scolded Davis.

On July 5, even as he readied his troops for the attempt to cross the Big Black to reach Vicksburg, Johnston had taken the time to try yet again to explain to the Chief Executive why he had assumed that the order had also relieved him from command of the Rebel forces in Tennessee. Davis responded on the eighth, the day after the government learned of the capitulation of Pemberton's army. "The mistakes . . . [your dispatch] contains will be noted by letter," the President promised. He then went on to state that he had been "painfully anxious" about Vicksburg and had "remained without information from you as to any plans proposed to raise the siege. Equally uninformed as to your plans in relation to Port Hudson, I have to request such information in relation thereto as the Government has a right to expect from one of its commanding generals in the field." Johnston replied the next day. "I have never meant to fail in the duty of reporting to the

Executive whatever might interest it in my command," he telegraphed, listing items he had communicated to the secretary of war.[1]

Seddon's War Department clerks soon went to work, digging through their files to gather material for Davis's promised letter of reply to Johnston's July 5 telegram. Meanwhile, the government's newspaper mouthpiece, the Richmond *Sentinel*, loosed a bitter editorial broadside at Johnston. In its July 9 issue the paper commented:

> The people are asking, and the world will ask, where was General Johnston and what part did he perform in the grand tragedy. In answer it will be said that with an army larger than [that which] won the first battle of Manassas, he made not a motion, he struck not a blow, for the relief of Vicksburg. For nearly seven weeks he sat down in sound of the conflict, and he fired not a gun . . . he has done no more than sit by and see Vicksburg fall, and send us the news.[2]

BY the middle of the month Davis's letter was ready—the fifteen-page screed described in Chapter Nine above. The document, in fact, much resembled a legal brief, and I strongly suspect that Johnston's old nemesis Judah P. Benjamin, a highly regarded lawyer and Davis's secretary of state, played a major role in drawing it up.[3]

As mentioned earlier, the document was a compilation of quotations from letters, telegrams, and other sources arranged to demonstrate that the government had never officially relieved Johnston from authority over Bragg's army in Tennessee. It seems clear that what Johnston in his July 5 telegram clearly intended as an explanation of why he had believed as he did was read by Davis as an assertion that the general's belief was valid. If so, we do not know if this apparent presidential

---

1 24 *OR*, pt. 1, 198 and 199.

2 Whoever penned this editorial was most unfair to Johnston. It was true that the Army of Relief outnumbered the Rebel force at the 1861 Battle of Manassas (about 35,000 to 31,000). It was also true—but left unsaid—that Grant's army at Vicksburg numbered about 70,000 as opposed to about 31,000 in the Federal army at the earlier battle. Johnston's 1863 force, furthermore, did not exist as an army on May 13 when he reached Jackson. Not all of his troops arrived until early June, and then he had to build, equip, supply, and organize the Army of Relief.

3 Some in Richmond thought the same thing at that time. See Kean, *Diary*, 97-98. Wigfall, writing to Johnston on August 9, asserted that "Jerusalem" had been involved in producing the document. On the copy of this letter in the Johnston Papers (W&M), the word "Benjamin" has been inserted above "Jerusalem" in what appears to be Johnston's handwriting.

misreading stemmed from haste and carelessness, willful disregard of Johnston's meaning, or (more likely, I think) the President's frustration, anger, poor health, and exhaustion.

The document seems, in fact, to have been at least in large part something of an emotional catharsis for a sick, sad chief executive suffering in body, mind, and spirit. The issue of Johnston's erroneous assumption offered an escape mechanism from his own despair. Surely Davis must have recognized at some level that he bore a very large share of the responsibility for the spring-summer disasters in both Mississippi and Tennessee.

The President had devised the defensive strategy that had failed. He had created the command arrangement that had not worked, and he had refused several times to modify it when his generals on the scene had recommended that he do so. He had selected Pemberton to command in Mississippi, and he had sustained that officer in that post—even to the extent of communicating directly with him without keeping Johnston posted. He had put Johnston in overall command in the West even though that general made it obvious at the time of his assignment that he had absolutely no confidence in the President's whole arrangement of the Western command. Davis had transferred thousands of Bragg's men to Mississippi against the advice of his Western commanders. He had not provided any real guidance for his generals in the region. Finally, he had refused to order Holmes to help Pemberton despite Johnston's pleas that he do so and his own clearly expressed conviction that such a step was crucial to Rebel efforts to hold the Vicksburg-Port Hudson corridor.[4]

HAVING completed the letter and derived from it whatever psychological and emotional satisfaction it offered, Davis would have been well advised to burn it, or at least to file it away and get on with the war. Such an act, however, would have constituted a tacit admission (at least to himself) that he could not blame Johnston for all that had happened.

---

4 The Rebels' 1863 Western disaster reverberated through the late summer and on into the fall. In addition to the immediate losses inflicted on the Secessionists, the Federals captured or destroyed massive quantities of railroad rolling stock (to be discussed in the following chapter), and on Sept. 10, the Federals marched into Little Rock, AR. In effect, Davis had failed (refused?) to implement his own offensive-defensive strategy. He had reverted to the cordon defense of 1861-1862. The result was the same as it had been in early 1862. By trying to hold everything through a passive defense, the Confederates had lost all the major Western points they sought to defend.

In refusing to acknowledge—or to recognize—the flaws in his system for defense of the West, Davis seems to have convinced himself that the general must be held responsible for the disaster. On July 17 an officer remarked to Davis that Vicksburg apparently had surrendered "from a want alone of provisions." "Yes," snapped the President, "from want of provisions inside and a general outside who wouldn't fight." Davis was, the officer noted, "bitter against Johnston." Four days earlier Johnston's political ally, Senator Wigfall, had reported to his friend Senator C. C. Clay of Alabama, that the Chief Executive was denouncing Johnston "in the most violent manner . . . & attributing the fall of Vicksburg to him & to him alone."[5]

ON July 28 in Mobile, where he had gone to inspect the city's defenses, Johnston received the President's letter from the hands of a special messenger. The general's anger doubtless rose as he read the document. A short time later one of his staff officers wrote that his chief was "disgusted" by it.

In the opening paragraph Davis pronounced Johnston's assumption a "grave error" (a term he repeated twenty paragraphs later). The Chief Executive went on to label Johnston's decision to limit his attention to the forces in Mississippi "your abandonment of your duties as commanding general of the geographical district to which you were assigned." In summary, Davis held, the government had not in any way changed Johnston's assignment or limited his authority over any part of the area placed under his command in November 1862.

Lydia Johnston's outrage at this reprimand seems to have exceeded even that of her husband. Writing to Charlotte Wigfall on August 2, she branded the presidential letter "15 pages of such insults as only a coward or a woman would write." She reported that she had tried to get her husband to resign, but he had replied that "No indignity from Davis could drive him from the service." Lydia's wrath extended to Varina Davis as well as to the President, and she went on to denounce "the vengeance of one wicked man" and declared that "nothing can make me forgive either of . . . [the Davises]." Johnston himself wrote Wigfall that his wife "apprehends that the whole power of the government is preparing to overwhelm me." Davis's letter, he noted, proved "ill feeling towards me—for which certainly I have given no cause." (The last eight words give a damning insight into Johnston's great weakness when it came to relations with his commander-

---

5 Gorgas, *Diary*, 74; Wigfall quoted in Govan and Livingood, *Different Valor*, 225.

in-chief. He, too, bore a great deal of the responsibility for the disasters in the West.)[6]

WHEN he penned his reply to Davis (dated August 8, but not sent for another two weeks or so), Johnston had gotten enough of a grip on himself to compose a more or less civil document. The general argued that his erroneous assumption had had "no practical results" and, in fact, had been corrected by a June 8 message from the secretary of war even before the matter came to Davis's attention.

Johnston, however, felt special concern with Davis's statement, which he viewed as an accusation, that the assumption constituted "a serious military offense." Such an assertion, Johnston feared, would be seen by many as a slur on the general's reputation. Even worse was the statement (charge?) that Johnston had abandoned his duties as commanding general. "I respectfully deny the commission of such a military crime," he wrote. He did not think, he added in closing, that he had been "obnoxious [liable] to the imputations of your letter."

Davis's answer, the last document in this silly exchange, was dated September 7. His sole purpose in writing the July 15 letter, the President asserted, was to show the mistake in Johnston's belief regarding the limits of his authority. He had not, Davis wrote, accused Johnston of "a serious military offense" but only of "a 'grave error.'" He "cheerfully" accepted the general's admission that he had erroneously assumed that a change had been made. "I do not deem it necessary now to make any answer to the remaining parts of your letter, which are principally directed to defending yourself from charges that I do not think are contained in the letter to which you were replying," explained Davis. Since Johnston had admitted his mistake "in attributing to me orders which I had not given . . . it is not necessary to dwell on these extraneous subjects."[7]

IN mid-SUMMER 1863 an interesting series of letters and editorials began to appear in some of the major newspapers published in Richmond and across the Deep South. These articles were preceded by at least two private letters (dated July 8 and July 15) from Louis T. Wigfall to Johnston regarding the campaign for Vicksburg.

---

6 24 *OR*, pt. 1, 209 and 233; Symonds, *Johnston*, 220-221; Govan and Livingood, *Different Valor*, 227-229.

7 24 *OR*, pt. 1, 209-213; 30 *OR*, pt. 1, 618; and 30 *OR*, pt. 4, 618-619.

Writing from the Confederate capital, the Texas senator notified his friend that some of the Richmond papers, in anticipation of the loss of Vicksburg, were building an argument that Johnston would be responsible for the disaster. Pemberton, Wigfall added, had already written to President Davis blaming the defeats at Champion Hill and the Big Black River on Johnston. Since Davis had appointed the inexperienced Pemberton to the Mississippi command, Wigfall warned, he would seek to protect himself from criticism by placing responsibility for any defeat on Johnston.[8]

As if to prove Wigfall's point, the Richmond *Sentinel* printed an accusation a week or so prior to Vicksburg's surrender:

> Johnston must at least try and show that the fault was not his. . . . If Vicksburg falls without
> a blow from him, his reputation, were it ten times what it is, would not survive it. It would
> be impossible to imagine ["Stonewall"] Jackson, were he alive, sitting by inactive while his
> gallant brethren were being assailed by night and by day, and starved into capitulation; and
> Jackson's example and his great success have taught our people to attach great value to
> daring and activity, and to place large calculation on such qualities. On the other hand the
> sleeping fox catches no poultry. Let Johnston bestir himself.[9]

On July 1 the Richmond *Daily Dispatch* pointed out that while the Confederates held Vicksburg they prevented "the separation of our mighty empire into two parts. . . . [T]he question is continually and naturally asked, 'Why does not General Johnston strike at least one blow for the relief of the heroic garrison? Why does he not at least make the attempt? . . .' If there be no intention to relieve Vicksburg, or make an effort to relieve it, why keep that large army [the Army of Relief] in that deadly climate? . . . If Vicksburg should fall without an effort from him his military fame will be gone forever."

EVEN before Vicksburg surrendered, articles defending Johnston had also begun to appear in the newspapers. Sometime in late June or the very earliest days of July a correspondent of the Augusta *Constitutionalist*, writing from Jackson,

---

8 Wigfall also wrote to C. C. Clay (June 12) that he had no doubt that the Davis Administration would attempt to make Johnston the scapegoat for any disaster in Mississippi. See Govan and Livingood, *Different Valor*, 210; and Symonds, *Johnston*, 221.

9 Richmond *Sentinel,* n. d. (quoted in Charleston *Mercury*, July 4, 1863). "DIXIE," writing from Richmond on July 10 noted that the *Sentinel* was then "regarded, properly or improperly as the government's organ."

penned a lengthy letter portraying the difficult situation in which Johnston found himself. The terrain west of the state capital through which Johnston's force would have to march to reach Grant's army and Vicksburg, the correspondent wrote, presented a major obstacle:

> The hills are in many places nearly perpendicular, with but little room on their tops. . . . This almost interminable succession of steep hills and deep valleys for miles and miles around Grant's camp has been fortified with all the skill that the devilish ingenuity of these rascals could secure. The hills are crowned with heavy guns, and every gorge is ready to belch forth destruction.
>
> He [Grant] has devastated the country all around him for 20 or 30 miles, leaving nothing that could contribute to the support of an army advancing on him.

Grant, the writer reported, had 70,000 to 80,000 troops and secure lines of transportation (the rivers) to feed and supply his men. "Johnston has to work hard to buy every mouthful his army eats, and then is obliged to haul it many miles— sometimes 40 or 50—and the farther he goes towards Vicksburg, the farther he must wagon his supplies." The writer put Johnston's strength at a reasonably accurate 30,000 and closed with the hope that Johnston would not be driven by public opinion to sacrifice his army, which was the only force protecting central and eastern Mississippi, Alabama, and western Georgia.[10]

On July 15 the Montgomery *Advertiser* printed a letter written sometime earlier while Vicksburg remained in Confederate hands. "General Johnston, indeed," wrote the unnamed correspondent, "has the hardest work before him, that has been laid out for any General during the war." Grant's position at Vicksburg, he reported, was very strong and he can get "as many men as he wants or is pleased to call for, with perfect communications and abundance of supplies." His position "is as strong to the full as [is] Vicksburg."

ONCE Vicksburg fell some of the comments in editorials and letters to the press became both more defensive with regard to Johnston's lack of action and much sharper in terms of their criticism of Pemberton and the Davis Administration. As early as July 10 the anti-administration Richmond *Examiner*

---

10 Letter, n. d., in Augusta *Constitutionalist*, n. d. (reprinted in Charleston *Mercury*, July 11, and in Montgomery *Daily Advertiser*, July 22, 1863). Note that this and several of the other letters quoted in these pages gave more detailed information about the situation in Mississippi than Johnston was furnishing to the government.

criticized what it called "this filthy effort" to shield Pemberton, "a General by favour (for where were his battles, where the service which earned his commission?) and those who are justly responsible for him, from the consequences of his incompetence, by making a brave old soldier the victim and scapegoat." Many, the paper commented, had said for months that if Vicksburg fell Johnston could be made to bear the blame.

At about the same time another correspondent penned a letter from Jackson to the Mobile *Advertiser and Register.* "General Johnston," he began,

> could not by possibility, with the troops at his command have relieved Vicksburg. All that skill, energy and zeal could do has been done. . . . He had to create an army and all its appliances before he could move with any reasonable hope of success, and to have moved at an earlier day without adequate preparation . . . would have been but to expose his army to the blows of the enemy with the certainty of its defeat.

The writer went on to argue that the "root of the disaster is two-fold." First, Grant's movement into the state of Mississippi from the river below Vicksburg could have been defeated "with competent and prompt action." [Johnston, of course, had advised Pemberton to concentrate and drive Grant back as soon as he crossed the river.] Instead, the Yankee invaders met only a "feeble resistance with inadequate numbers." The second reason, he continued, was because "There has been a crying incompetency in the antecedent management of affairs" in the west-central Mississippi area.

The "antecedent" commander who had failed to demonstrate "competent and prompt action" was, of course, Pemberton, although he was not mentioned until the next sentence. Pemberton, the writer went on,

> was beyond question loyal to the Confederacy and has certainly done the best he knew how—If he lacks capacity it was his misfortune and not his fault. *The appointing power must take the responsibility before the country* with respect to Vicksburg and the Trans[-]Mississippi Department [My emphasis].

The unnamed "appointing power" was, of course, President Jefferson Davis, who was also the only man with authority over both Vicksburg and the Trans-Mississippi.

The correspondent closed with a promise ". . . in my next I will proceed to show that the responsibility [for the loss of Vicksburg] rests with persons a thousand miles away to the east, from which the light is breaking that will relieve the darkness in the west."[11]

The barrage of pro-Johnston writings continued. On July 10, the Macon *Daily Telegraph* printed an unsigned editorial under the title "THE FALL OF VICKSBURG." Johnston, the writer asserted, "was never in condition to strike a blow, as we are informed [by whom he did not state], and any attempt at it would have been a useless sacrifice of life."

On the following day a writer in Jackson sent a letter to the Charleston *Courier*. Johnston, he wrote, almost certainly could not have broken through Grant's lines without "an immense sacrifice of men. . . . [H]ad Johnston crossed the Big Black he would never have returned. This he well knew, but he yielded to public opinion contrary to his own judgment and was on his march to the relief of Vicksburg when the sad intelligence reached his ears that it had fallen, and thus, perhaps, he and his army were saved from impending ruin."[12]

On July 15, the Montgomery *Advertiser* reminded its readers in an unsigned article that "we some weeks since defended Gen. JOHNSTON against the implied imputation of that journal [the Richmond *Sentinel*] representing those in authority at Richmond." The *Advertiser* then went on to present a summary of Johnston's standing objections to the whole command structure that Davis had imposed on the West. This summary—be it well-noted—echoed Johnston's complaints that "he had no power to more than inspect BRAGG'S and PEMBERTON'S armies." (See Johnston's comments in his letter of quoted in Part III of Chapter Two of this study.) "Therefore," asserted the paper, "the responsibility of bad management and disaster rested upon the President."

In a passage written some time earlier, the *Advertiser* had thundered:

> If Vicksburg falls, it will take something more than the perverse prejudices it [the *Sentinel*] represents [i. e. the Davis Administration] to shake public confidence in the tried and able soldier who commands in Mississippi, and that unless facts plainly appear to the contrary, the censure will fall heavily upon those who having the power to assist seem to have used it

---

11 This letter was dated July 8 or 9 (the date on the microfilm cannot be read with certainty). It appeared in the Mobile *Advertiser and Register* on an unknown date and was reprinted in the Charleston *Mercury* on July 16. As reprinted, it bears no signature. If the writer did send the promised second letter and it was printed, I have not found it.

12 Letter from Charleston *Courier*, n. d., reprinted in Memphis (Atlanta) *Appeal*, July 22, 1863.

rather to thwart and retard the movements of Gen. JOHNSTON. In this we are far from attributing to the President any intention to injure the service, but we conscientiously believe that his personal predilections or prejudices are so great that they frequently warp the dictates of his better judgment, and that the country suffers by it.

On July 18, the Charleston *Mercury* reprinted an undated report from the Mobile *Advertiser and Register* of unknown date. Had the effort to relieve Vicksburg lasted another day, the writer claimed,

> Johnston's army would, without any doubt, have been cut to pieces. From what has since been learned of Grant's position, it is now known that if Johnston's force had been doubled and tripled it could never have got through the works of Grant.

The writer reported that the Federals had so thoroughly obstructed the roads east of Vicksburg that after the surrender some of Pemberton's paroled officers required fifteen hours to ride fifteen miles through the felled trees. "We claim that we have been fortunate," he summed up, "in saving the gallant little army of Johnston as well as the Vicksburg garrison from further loss."

CLINT, in Brandon, Mississippi, on July 17, wrote defending Johnston's delay of the effort to relieve Vicksburg. "He had to supply himself with everything anew; in a word begin at the beginning, save the men and guns" to organize the Army of Relief. Despite the outcome of the campaign, CLINT asserted, Johnston's troops "are by no means dispirited and have unbounded confidence in their leader."[13]

Nine days later another soldier, writing from Morton, Mississippi, to the Memphis (Atlanta) *Appeal*, praised Johnston for not yielding "to the pressure of the public" and destroying his army "by hurling it against superior numbers, sheltered by elaborate field works, and on ground of their own choosing. . . . To have ended the siege would have required fully as large an army as that of the enemy."[14]

At about the time this letter to the *Appeal* was written, the Mobile *Advertiser and Register* printed an unsigned editorial entitled "THE CAMPAIGN IN MISSISSIPPI." The column opened with the ringing declaration that "The attempt to make General Johnston responsible for a situation, which was irretrievably lost

---

13 Letter in Mobile *Advertiser and Register*, n. d. (reprinted in Macon *Daily Telegraph*, July 27, 1863).

14 Letter, July 26 to the *Appeal*, n. d. (reprinted in the Charleston *Mercury*, July 31, 1863).

before he was ordered to the scene of the disaster, strikes every honest mind as an outrage upon right and justice." Pemberton, the writer asserted, knew that he did not have sufficient food in Vicksburg to withstand a long siege and that the Confederates could not "mass force enough in the rear of Grant to relieve him before starvation should do the work." He had disobeyed Johnston's orders to unite the two Rebel forces in Mississippi. [How did the writer know this?] He now "attempts to fasten his glaring blunders on the shoulders of another high and distinguished officer, who enjoys the confidence and admiration of the nation, and who never for one instant had it in his power to remedy the evil done before his appearance on the scene or avert the disaster which became inevitable." Pemberton, however, "is not responsible for failure, but the power that placed him there [in command at Vicksburg] is." "The press," the column concluded, "has the highest duties . . . to utter and uphold the truth, sustain the right and defend those who are unjustly pursued."[15]

DID Joseph E. Johnston or any members of his "military family" write any of these articles or encourage others to write them? Did Jefferson Davis and other members of the administration read any of them? We simply do not—and can never—know. We do know, however, that another communication similar to those quoted above did appear in the press; that in its original version it predated those quoted above; that a member of Johnston's staff did write it; that President Davis did read it; and that it worsened relations between the Chief Executive and the general.

ON the front page of its July 18 issue, the Memphis (Atlanta) *Appeal* printed a long (thirty paragraphs) letter dated Chattanooga, July 13, entitled "GEN. JOHNSTON AND THE FALL OF VICKSBURG." The letter was addressed to the *Appeal's* editor and it was signed "VINDICUS."

The letter's first eight paragraphs presented a more or less routine account of the recent Confederate retreat from Middle Tennessee to Chattanooga. "The retreat," VINDICUS reported, "has been accomplished; Middle Tennessee is given up, the growing crops are sacrificed, and our army is safe, while the enemy has gained no advantage, but has lengthened his communication and weakened his position." General Braxton Bragg's army, he pointed out, "is now concentrated

15 Letter to Mobile *Advertiser and Register* (reprinted in Macon *Daily Telegraph*, Aug. 3, 1863).

south of the [Tennessee] river and will soon be ready for more successful operations in another direction."

After narrating this brief history of the recent events in Tennessee, VINDICUS transitioned to a discussion of the campaign in Mississippi. The recent Federal success in the Magnolia State, he claimed, was "inevitable, almost, from the first." A knowledge of the facts "would satisfy the public that whatever blunders may have contributed to our reverses in that quarter, must be attributed to some other than the illustrious General who was assigned to the command of our armies there when it was 'too late' to save Vicksburg and defend the State." Johnston, "the true hero," did everything possible, and he "fairly earned the reputation of one of the greatest military chieftains of the age."

VINDICUS went on to detail some of the many obstacles Johnston had faced. "The Government," he wrote, "realized when 'too late' the danger which threatened that department. . . . it awoke when 'too late' to the imperiled condition of the army in Mississippi. . . . 'Too late!' Prophetic words! How rapidly have they become a historical formula!" "With his little army, General Johnston could do nothing. . . . With the force under him, increased by reinforcements, though still inadequate, General Johnston could not break the enemy's lines." VINDICUS continued:

> The country will determine whether blame attaches anywhere for the fall of Vicksburg. An intelligent public will fix the blame, if blame there be upon the guilty one. Gen. Johnston could not succor the gallant defenders of Vicksburg, but he has not been idle. He has raised, organized, equipped, mobilized an army, insufficient, it is to be feared, for the work before him, but second in organization, discipline, and morale to none on the continent. All that it was possible to do, he has done. All that can be done he, will do. He possessed the confidence of the country. His claim to it is stronger to-day than ever before.

ON July 22, the Charleston *Mercury* reprinted the VINDICUS letter from the *Appeal*, and a few days later President Davis read it in that paper. Five days after the letter's appearance in the *Mercury*, Davis telegraphed Pemberton, who was then about to commence work on his official report of the campaign. The Chief Executive directed Pemberton's attention to the letter, pointed out that it included several passages critical of the former Vicksburg commander, and urged him to make his own report as "promptly and fully" as possible.

A week later Pemberton replied from Demopolis, Alabama, where he was seeking to reform what remained of his army of paroled prisoners. He had obtained a copy of the published letter, he informed Davis, and he agreed with the President that "the article . . . is as the signature indicates intended for the vindication of an individual." "I shall endeavor in my report," Pemberton promised, "to present my official acts in a light which will justify me before . . . [the government], and disprove many charges made against me through ignorance or malice."

On August 9 Davis again wrote to Pemberton telling him that he had called the letter to his attention because it contained "some points which should be noticed in your report . . . [that] sufficiently warn you of an attempt to place on you the responsibility" for some of the disasters of the campaign, especially the defeat at the Battle of Champion Hill. The President then took a swipe at the "unscrupulous men who resort to the newspapers to disseminate falsehood and forestall the public judgment."[16]

DAVIS clearly regarded the VINDICUS letter as a document written to shift responsibility from Vicksburg's loss from Johnston to the administration. It would not have been appropriate, however, for him officially to stoop to question the general about an anonymous article in a hostile newspaper. In late July, however, the President got a break. A manuscript copy of the original letter, dated July 17, turned up in Richmond among papers sent to the War Department for forwarding to Europe. Someone in the department opened and read the document, and in due course it came to the attention of the President.[17]

With the intercepted letter in hand, Davis had the pretext to write to Johnston about the document. Sending a copy of the letter to the general on August 1, the President pointed out that the letter contained passages quite similar to those that had appeared in the version of the letter published in the newspapers, and that its numerous lengthy quotations from official communications indicated that its author clearly "was some one having access to your correspondence." In closing his letter, Davis wrote—probably tongue in cheek—"It is needless to say that you are not considered capable of giving countenance to such efforts at laudation of yourself and detraction of others and the paper is sent to you with the confidence that you will take the proper action in the premises."[18]

16 J. Davis, *Papers*, vol. 9, 306, 313-314, and 334; 24 *OR*, pt. 3, 1033. Champion Hill also known as the Battle of Baker's Creek.

17 The Confederacy had no postal arrangements with other governments, so international communications had to be carried out through Mexico or by blockade runner and then put into the Mexican, British, or Spanish (Cuban) postal systems. The Davis Administration believed the letter was sent abroad for publication in England. See next footnote.

18 This account is pieced together from the the following sources: Davis to Johnston, Aug. 1, 1863 (J. Davis, *Papers*, vol. 9, 316; 24 *OR*, pt. 3, 1070); W. P. Johnston to Davis, Oct. 6, 1874

Davis's August 1 letter and its enclosures did not reach Johnston until August 11. Writing in response, the general denied all knowledge of the document ("I have neither seen nor heard of it before") and reported that "My staff officers present know nothing of it."[19] He did admit, however, "It is clearly based upon information only to be had in my office" and promised an investigation of the matter.

Two days later Johnston reported to Davis that the original letter had been written by David W. Yandell, a distinguished physician and the medical officer who had come with Johnston from Tullahoma to Mississippi to look after the general's delicate health. Yandell, Johnston informed the President, said that the letter had been a private communication sent to his friend and colleague John M. Johnson, chief medical officer on the staff of Lieutenant General William J. Hardee. Johnson denied that he had submitted the letter for publication and claimed that a journalist had seen and copied parts of it for publication.[20]

Davis was not mollified. Believing that the letter had been written for publication (an opinion that Yandell's biographer finds plausible), Davis wrote Johnston that the doctor should be punished for "surreptitiously" obtaining the documents and publishing them. Johnston replied that the documents were not obtained surreptitiously, but that crowded conditions had compelled the general to live in close quarters with his staff officers. That fact, he asserted, accounted for Yandell's acquaintance with the official correspondence. In addition to his medical

---

(Rowland, *Davis Constitutionalist*, VII, 406-407); Davis to W. T. Walthall, Nov. 23 and 28, 1874 (ibid., 408-409) and Apr. 28, 1875 (ibid., 421); and W. P. Johnston to Davis, May 25, 1885 (ibid., IX, 370). It is also clear from the Oct. 6, 1874, letter cited above that Davis and his friends believed John Forsyth of the Mobile *Advertiser and Register* had a copy of the letter during the war. The rest of this note is pure speculation: Henry Hotze, a former Rebel soldier who in 1863 served as an agent in Europe and as publisher of *The Index,* the pro-Southern newspaper issued in London, had worked with Forsyth on the *Advertiser and Register* in the late antebellum years. It may, then, have been a copy of the letter sent by Forsyth to Hotze that Rebel authorities intercepted. Who else in England might have published the letter? (Hotze's biographer Lonnie A. Bennett does not mention the letter in *Henry Hotze, Confederate Propagandist.*)

19 Had some of them stepped out of the room?

20 24 *OR*, pt. 3, 1070; and J. Davis, *Papers*, vol. 9, 342. Barring the unlikely discovery of more evidence, it now seems impossible to trace the letter's path to publication beyond this point. Several questions, however, present themselves: Who was the journalist? Did the journalist add the paragraphs on Bragg's recent campaign? If so, why? If he did not, who did (Johnson, perhaps)? Did the journalist remove the long quotations taken from General Johnston's official correspondence? If so, why? If not, who did? Who decided that the published letter should be signed "VINDICUS" and why? The fact that Johnston replied to Davis in only two days also raises suspicions. Did the general know of the letter before he received Davis's inquiry? Had Yandell and Johnson worked out the story of the journalist as their defense?

duties, Yandell helped Johnston with headquarters paperwork and at times probably acted as an amanuensis for the general who suffered from poor eyesight. Davis noted that Johnston's explanation did not address the question of whether the official material had been improperly used.

Davis referred the whole file to the secretary of war "for official action," and there the matter rested. The letter, however—like Johnston's intemperate protest about his rank, the matter of state brigades, and Davis's July 15 reprimand over the extent of Johnston's command authority—added more deadly poison to the deteriorating relations between the general and the Confederate government.[21]

TO repeat the question asked above: did Johnston and the members of his staff, other than Yandell, have anything to do with the July barrage of newspaper publications favorable to the general and harshly critical of the Davis government? The answer remains that we simply do not know.

Was it coincidence that the barrage began with Yandell's letter written at about the time that Wigfall's June 8 message would have reached Johnston with its warning that the administration was preparing to blame the general for the impending loss of Vicksburg? Was it any coincidence that the articles written from the army originated at points at or near which Johnston and his staff were at the time they were written? Was it coincidence that the barrage came to an end (or

---

21 J. Davis, *Papers*, vol. 9, 339, 342, 353, and 379; 24 *OR*, pt. 3, 1070; 30*OR*4, 625; Symonds, *Johnston*, 224; Baird, *Yandell*, 51-52. On Dec. 22, Yandell, writing from Brandon, Mississippi, to his uncle David D. Wendel provided a narrative of the letter's history (as above in the text) and asserted that it reported the "unvarnished truth," and that his friend Johnson "indiscreetly" allowed a reporter to see it. That (unnamed) journalist copied "large abstracts" from it and sent it to the *Appeal*. Yandell's explanation satisfied General Johnston but not President Davis. See Jakes and Campbell, *Wendel Papers*, 196-198. Thanks to Jim Ogden for bringing this source to my attention. The only concrete action to result from this kerfuffle came a few weeks later. The War Department relieved Yandell from duty in Johnston's department and transferred (exiled?) him to the Trans-Mississippi. A friend writing in late 1863 called the assignment to the Trans-Mississippi "banishment" and "a great outrage," and described Yandell as "the victim of petty tyranny." Once Yandell reached the Trans-Mississippi, his medical and administrative abilities so impressed Kirby Smith that the general appointed him chief medical officer for the entire Trans-Mississippi Department. In 1864, when Confederate authorities in Richmond learned of Yandell's new status, they ordered Smith to remove him as departmental medical director and replace him "with any surgeon of your choice." Yandell held minor medical posts in the Trans-Mississippi for the rest of the war. After the war he returned to Louisville and resumed his medical practice. In the early 1870s he served as president of the American Medical Association. He died in 1898. In 1874, after the publication of Johnston's *Narrative*, Davis undertook a brief effort to obtain more information about the letter. See Baird, *Yandell*, 54-56; J. Davis, *Papers*, vol. 13, 244, 252, and 253; and the biographical material in the Yandell Papers.

seems to have done so) about the time that Johnston became aware of the President's anger at the Yandell letter?

We can never know.

PART II

". . . an untruth. . . . a false statement. . . . his misstatements were intentional."

— Joseph E. Johnston, September 12, 1863

Newspaper articles and editorials constituted but one front in the escalating war between General Johnston and the Davis government over responsibility for the Vicksburg disaster. President Davis soon ordered a military court to "investigate the campaign in Missi. and East Louisiana . . . [to] develop the real causes of events and give to the public the means of doing justice to the actors." Special Orders 184 of August 4, 1863, established the court and named its three members: Major General Robert Ransom of North Carolina and Brigadier Generals Howell Cobb of Georgia and John Echols of Virginia. The court was to meet in Montgomery on August 15 "or as soon thereafter as practicable." On August 8 the War Department authorized the court to assemble in Atlanta.[22]

Warned by friends in Richmond that it was "extremely important" that he attend the court's sessions to defend himself, Johnston asked that the inquiry be postponed until circumstances would permit him to be present at its sessions. In reply, the War Department assured the general that he would be temporarily relieved from duty to appear at the court hearings. On September 2 Johnston left Mississippi for Atlanta. In the Georgia city six days later, Johnston learned that the court had been directed to suspend its business until further orders. The court never met.

---

22 Some Johnston partisans assert that Davis rushed the establishment of the court to hamper Johnston's chances to defend himself and cited the wording of the order to substantiate the charge. In fact, the wording was standard practice in such cases to set a formal date for the court to come into official existence. On July 28, Pemberton had suggested a court of inquiry to Davis (24 OR, pt. 3, 1034), and that may have been the catalyst behind the President's order.

Johnston expressed disappointment at this turn of events. As he wrote Wigfall on September 15, he had viewed the court as his only chance to "show the position I have occupied—& how completely my military opinions were disregarded in relation to what was called my command." Wigfall responded that Johnston's case was so strong that Davis would not dare allow the general's version of events to get before the public.[23]

AS if a presidential letter of reprimand, newspaper articles critical of one side or the other, and a formal court of inquiry were not enough, yet one more outburst over Vicksburg arose between Johnston and the government that fall. To the harried general it must have seemed that the Davis Administration was launching one assault after another against his reputation and his honor.

On August 25, John C. Pemberton forwarded to the War Department what became the first of his three official accounts of the Vicksburg Campaign. (This report was dated August 1.) Pemberton submitted his second report on November 10, this being in large measure a response to some leading questions put to him by Secretary of War Seddon. Pemberton added a third account on December 14, this one written in response to Johnston's report of November 1 (itself largely a reply to Pemberton's first account).

Pemberton's initial report was relatively mild in its comments regarding Johnston. Vicksburg's defender noted that his major weakness in trying to protect Mississippi the previous spring had been a "great deficiency of cavalry," and that when he several times requested the return of the mounted units Johnston had transferred to Bragg's army in Tennessee early in the year Johnston had declined to send them. Pemberton also claimed that obeying Johnston's May 13 directive to march east from Edward's Station against the Federals at Clinton would have placed his troops in a very dangerous position because of the strong Federal forces to the south that would have been on his right flank. In the belief that he had to do something, however, Pemberton had elected to abandon his plan to fight at Edward's Station and instead move south to endeavor to cut the Yankee supply

23 J. Davis, *Papers*, vol. 9, 334; 24 *OR*, pt. 3, 1045 and 1058; Govan and Livingood, *Different Valor*, 229-231; Symonds, *Johnston*, 224-225. In justice to the administration, we should note that the fall's active military operations would have made it difficult, if not impossible, for many key witnesses to testify at the court's hearings. On Aug. 13, a War Department official noted that he had "been recently getting up documents for the court of inquiry." The evidence, he confided to his diary, seemed to show that "the incapacity of Pemberton was as glaring as the President's abusers allege. It comes in every shape and especially from some of the general officers under his command." (Kean, *Diary*, 90-91).

line. Upon receiving Johnston's positive order of May 14 to move to Clinton, he had turned his column around and marched to the north. Soon after doing so, he wrote, he had encountered Grant's army at Champion Hill with unfortunate results.[24]

ON September 12 in Montgomery on his return trip to Mississippi after the aborted court of inquiry, Johnston saw references in a newspaper to Pemberton's report. He immediately wrote Adjutant and Inspector General Samuel Cooper to request a copy of the document which, he pointed out, should have been forwarded through his headquarters since he had been Pemberton's commander during the time covered by the report.[25]

Along with the request Johnston also sent to Cooper a letter clipped from the Montgomery *Advertiser* (reprinted from the Mobile *Advertiser and Register*). Signed "A PAROLED PRISONER," the letter offered a fairly aggressive defense of Pemberton's conduct of the campaign for Vicksburg. The writer stressed the great handicaps under which Pemberton had had to operate after Johnston ordered 6,000 of his cavalrymen to Tennessee. With these horsemen, A PAROLED PRISONER asserted, Pemberton would have defeated Grant soon after the Federal army crossed the Mississippi. Pemberton, he commented, had fought the Battle of Champion Hill (Baker's Creek) "under protest, against his own judgment, and in obedience to positive orders."

Somehow Johnston soon learned that A PAROLED PRISONER was Major William H. McCardle, Pemberton's assistant adjutant general. When he forwarded a copy of the letter to the War Department, Johnston also sent along a statement of his own in response to McCardle's allegations "to point out an untruth and a great exaggeration" in the document. The only positive order he had sent to Pemberton, Johnston wrote, had been the May 13 directive to march east, not south, to attack the Federals at Clinton. Second, Johnston pointed out, he had transferred only

---

24 The report is in 24 OR, pt. 3, 249-320. Large sections of the document, especially the appendices, deal with matters that did not involve the Johnston-Pemberton spat. Pemberton, for example, devoted many pages to defending himself against newspaper allegations that he had not adequately provisioned Vicksburg.

25 We might wonder what the result would have been had Johnston early in 1863 ordered Pemberton to forward correspondence through channels in the months prior to the siege of Vicksburg. Did Johnston's statement indicate that he did not understand that Pemberton had been authorized (ordered?) to communicate directly with Richmond under Davis's impracticable scheme? (See Chapter Two, Part III and Chapter Five, Part II of this book.)

about 3,000 cavalrymen to Tennessee. "I therefore accuse this officer," wrote a bitter Johnston, "of publishing a false statement of a military matter about to be investigated by a military court. His position in the Adjutant General's department makes it certain that his misstatements were intentional."[26]

When this squabble reached President Davis, he—true bureaucrat that he was—commented that Johnston should prefer formal charges so the case could be submitted to a military court for adjudication. The War Department so informed Johnston with the notation, "As soon as your charges are put in [proper] form and forwarded to this office, a general court martial will be ordered for the trial of Major McCardle."

Learning of Johnston's assertions, McCardle on October 28 wrote the War Department requesting a copy of any charges the general had preferred against him. "If General Johnston has formally declined to prefer charges," he added, "I respectfully solicit a copy of the letter (if received) in which he so declines." On December 4, General Cooper notified McCardle that no charges had been preferred against him. There, so far as the record shows, the matter rested.

With Johnston's accusations of "an untruth," "a false statement," and "intentional" misstatements, however, the general had given vent to a much harsher tone in his official correspondence. The Johnston-McCardle (Pemberton) differences—and behind them the Davis-Johnston quarrels—had become even more caustic.[27]

JOHNSTON'S September 12 letter—dated two years to the day after his 1861 protest regarding his rank—together with its enclosures, would have reached Richmond in about a week. Several days after it arrived, Secretary of War Seddon met with President Davis. The two discussed Pemberton's report and probably Johnston's recent letter. They soon realized that the key to the argument over responsibility for the loss of Vicksburg had come to focus on Johnston's May 13 order (suggestion?) to Pemberton to move from Edward's Station eastward against

---

26 Johnston had forgotten or elected not to mention his May 14 suggestion that Pemberton operate against Grant's supply line. (See Chapter Seven of this book.)

27 Montgomery *Advertiser*, Sept. 8, 1863. This correspondence is in 24 OR, pt. 3, 1061-1065. Other parts of McCardle's letter covered matters that did not concern Johnston but mirrored Pemberton's own assertions. Johnston, therefore, could conclude that the major was writing at Pemberton's request. The issue of the Mobile paper (date unknown) in which the letter first appeared, if extant, may contain information bearing on the document.

the Federals at Clinton, and Pemberton's decision not to do so, but instead launch a thrust south to strike the enemy line of communications.

In his initial report Pemberton had not discussed in much detail his reason for disobeying the May 13 "order." He had stated only that he regarded the movement that Johnston had directed (suggested?) to be "extremely hazardous" and "suicidal" because of the large Federal units that would have been only a few miles south of his right flank had he moved toward Clinton. He had marched to the south, reported Pemberton, only because he believed that he must do something, and cutting Grant's communications with the Yankee base on the Mississippi seemed to offer "the only possibility of success."

On October 1 Seddon, "At the suggestion of the President," wrote to Pemberton to "call your attention to several points in your recent report" and to have them "elucidated or explained." Seddon wanted Pemberton to discuss more fully his decision to disregard Johnston's May 13 message. In framing his inquiry, however, the secretary hinted at some possible phrases that Pemberton might use to strengthen his case and at some points that he might emphasize.

Was it possible, Seddon wondered, that in considering Johnston's message, Pemberton had realized "that [Johnston] must necessarily be very imperfectly acquainted with your position and resources, as well as with the movements and forces of the enemy." The secretary also referred to "your better knowledge" and to "your superior knowledge of the position" of the opposing forces between Jackson and Edward's Station as factors that might have influenced Pemberton.

I find it impossible to escape the conclusion that, in asking Pemberton to elaborate upon his report in response to such questions, Davis and Seddon (or perhaps only Davis acting through Seddon) sought to lead Pemberton so as to strengthen the government's case against Johnston. It was not the last time that the Davis Administration would attempt to use a subordinate's official report to pin responsibility for a military disaster on Joseph E. Johnston.[28]

WHILE Pemberton mulled over Seddon's letter and worked on his response (his second report), Johnston, back at his Meridian headquarters, labored over his own account of the spring and summer operations in Mississippi. In late May Johnston had submitted a brief narrative of events up to that time. Now, he wished

---

28 See 24 *OR*, pt. 1, 261, 269, and 321-322. Seddon also asked about several minor matters. See McMurry, *Hood*, 185-187, for another attempt by the Davis Administration to use a subordinate against Johnston.

to file a much more elaborate document covering his role in the campaign for Vicksburg. By that time, too, Johnston had a copy of Pemberton's report or knew details of its contents from excerpts that had been published in the pro-administration Richmond *Sentinel*. The report he submitted on November 1 did not differ much from Pemberton's narrative of the facts. It was, however, in large measure a response to Pemberton's accusations and a defense of his own conduct.

With regard to the crucial May 13 "order," Johnston had an easy and seemingly irrefutable argument. Pemberton had disobeyed his instructions and disaster had followed. No one, furthermore, could prove that a different disaster would have resulted had Pemberton obeyed the directive. It was not the last time that Johnston and his reputation were to benefit from such a counterfactual situation.

Johnston closed his report with a summary of his position and a declaration that in his report Pemberton,

> by direct assertion and by implication, puts upon me the responsibility of the movements which led his army to defeat at Baker's Creek [Champion Hill] and the Big Black Bridge; defeats which produced the loss of Vicksburg and its army.

> This statement has been circulated by the press in more or less detail, and with more or less marks of an official character, until my silence would be almost an acknowledgment of the justice of the charge.

> A proper regard for the good opinion of my Government has compelled me, therefore, to throw aside that delicacy which I would gladly have observed toward a brother officer suffering much undeserved obloquy, and to show that in his short campaign General Pemberton made not a single movement in obedience to my orders and regarded none of my Instructions, and, finally did not embrace the only opportunity to save his army—that given by my order to abandon Vicksburg.[29]

ON November 10 Pemberton, then in Richmond, submitted his response to Seddon's October 1 letter. Taking up the strong hints in the war secretary's questions, Pemberton declared that, when Johnston wrote the message of May 13,

---

29 Johnston's May 27 report is in 24 *OR*, pt. 1, 220-223; the later report is in ibid., 238-249. See also Symonds, *Johnston*, 222 and 225, and Govan and Livingood, *Different Valor*, 234-235. Johnston's reports, of course, covered other topics and omitted some important subjects. For example, he never addressed the crucial matter of how the major Union force south of the railroad (and, therefore, in position to strike Pemberton's right flank if he moved as Johnston suggested), would have affected the situation.

he "seemed to be entirely ignorant of the dispositions of the enemy." Pemberton, on the other hand, claimed to have been well aware of the massive Union forces south of the railroad although his weakness in cavalry had prevented his obtaining detailed information. Once Johnston evacuated Jackson in the forenoon of May 14 and moved to the northeast, declared Pemberton, "By no possibility . . . [could he] have effectually co-operated with me" against the Yankees at Clinton. Thus, had he obeyed the "order," Pemberton would have found his force isolated from Johnston and engaged with a considerably larger enemy army in the Clinton area with another strong body of Federals off to the south and in position to strike the flank or rear of his army or to cut it off from its base in Vicksburg.

In summary, Pemberton maintained, Johnston had issued the order in virtually complete ignorance of the positions of both the enemy and Pemberton's own force as well as of Pemberton's plans.

His own preference, Pemberton noted, would have been to await the enemy at Edward's as he had first planned to do. His own officers, however, had not backed such a plan. Feeling that he had to act, he had chosen to move against the enemy's line of communications.[30]

PEMBERTON'S second supplemental report, dated Richmond, December 14, 1863, was written after Rebel authorities had permitted the former Vicksburg commander to read Johnston's November 1 account. "In justice to myself," explained Pemberton, "I request to be permitted to make the following additional report."

Reiterating the points of his earlier accounts, Pemberton stressed his belief that Johnston had issued the May 13 order in ignorance of the location of most of the Yankee army and in the erroneous belief that the Federals at Clinton would be the only enemies encountered by the Rebels in marching east from Edward's. To have obeyed the order, he wrote, would have led to "the entire destruction or capture of my army and the immediate fall of Vicksburg."

Pemberton explained that he had deployed his force in line of battle at Edward's when he had received the May 13 order. Then, "when it was known that General Johnston had ordered an advance, the weight of his name made the pressure upon me [from his subordinate generals] too heavy to bear and a movement became necessary." Most of his generals had favored obeying the order, apparently because they believed Johnston to be a great general and assumed that

---

30 24 *OR*, pt. 1, 322-325.

he must, therefore, know what he was doing. Pemberton's senior subordinates, however, had advocated the move to the south, and in the end that was the course he adopted. Given the belief that he no longer could wait at Edward's, Pemberton asserted yet again that a strike against the enemy supply line was the only proposal that offered any real hope of success.

Having come this far in arguing his case, Pemberton went on to inject his own harsh accusations:

> The various suggestions and instructions in these dispatches [Johnston's of May 13-16] seem to me to evidence a want of clear and well-developed plans and all, however, seem to ignore Vicksburg, the defense of which I had conceived to be the main purpose of the Government in retaining the army in Mississippi.

> Then, since Johnston's directive had brought on the movement south from Edward's, and the entire consequences of my movement resulted from General Johnston's order, and he is in part responsible for them, for if that order had never been given the battle of Baker's Creek [Champion Hill] would not have been fought.

Somehow Johnston learned (probably from friends in Richmond) of Pemberton's supplemental reports. As late as January 30, 1864, he was still attempting to obtain copies of the documents. The reports, he again maintained, should have been sent to Richmond through his headquarters since he had been Pemberton's commander during the campaign for Vicksburg.[31]

THE wartime wrangling between Johnston and the government over responsibility for the loss of Vicksburg died out by the late spring of 1864. In part this development was owing to events that soon brought other military matters to the fore. In part, too, it may well have stemmed from a realization by the Davis Administration that Pemberton's writings did not really offer solid grounds for criticizing Johnston.[32] If Pemberton really understood the situation on May 13 and 14, for example, why did he not advise Johnston of the facts?

---

31 24 *OR*, pt. 1, 325-331 and 237. In his postwar account published as *Compelled to Appear in Print*, 99-140, Pemberton expanded his case and even accused Johnston of "a criminal negligence" in not keeping the Vicksburg commander well informed. Pemberton, of course, made no mention of his own failure (refusal?) to keep Johnston informed during the Dec. 1862 – May 1863 period.

32 Wigfall so wrote Johnston on Oct. 6. See Govan and Livingood, *Different Valor*, 229-231.

While Pemberton made a strong case that obedience to Johnston's May 13 order (suggestion?) most likely would have led to disaster, his argument beyond that point was extremely weak. In his October 1 letter, Seddon had hinted at the belief that if he were not going to follow the "order," Pemberton should have kept to his plan to fight at Edward's rather than marching off to the south to attempt to cut the enemy's line of communications. Pemberton's reasoning beyond this point was, in fact, so poor and weak that it undermined his entire argument that responsibility for his battlefield defeats rested on Johnston.

A reading of the documents inevitably leads back to the real source of the Rebels' problem: the Confederate leaders had no clear-cut, plainly stated, fully understood idea of what they should have been trying to do in the West in the first half of 1863. Nobody ever faced and answered the basic questions: Should General Holmes concentrate on Arkansas or help to defend the Lower Mississippi? Tennessee or Mississippi? What changes had been brought about after mid-April when the Federal fleet ran by the Vicksburg batteries? What adjustments should the Confederates have then made? Hold Vicksburg and Port Hudson at all costs, or evacuate them to save their garrisons?

ALL of these matters (except the dilemma posed by the Federal gunboats in the Vicksburg-Port Hudson corridor) had come up in one form or another in the early weeks of 1863. In fact, they had surfaced at the Grenada conference in late December 1862, and had arisen several times in the months that followed. Never had the Rebels resolved or even addressed them.

Only one man could decide such matters, and President Jefferson Davis resolutely refused to do so.

Chapter Twelve

A Five-Month Interlude

"Alas, for our prospects this winter."

— Robert G. H. Kean, October 18, 1863

While the feuding over responsibility for the loss of Vicksburg raged between Johnston on the one hand and Pemberton and the Davis Administration on the other, the Confederate government moved to alter its Western command arrangements.

Six days after the Mississippi stronghold's surrender President Davis notified Major General Daniel Harvey Hill, then commanding Rebel forces in southeastern Virginia and northeastern North Carolina, that he would be promoted to lieutenant general and sent to Mississippi. Two days later, while en route, Hill received a telegraphic order changing his assignment. Davis now directed him to report to Braxton Bragg to replace Lieutenant General William J. Hardee as commander of one of the infantry corps in the Army of Tennessee. Hardee, in turn, would go to Mississippi as Johnston's second in command.

Robert G. H. Kean, head of the War Department's Bureau of War, noted in his diary on July 26 that he had "positive information" that President Davis had made these changes in order to ease Johnston out as commander in Mississippi and Alabama and to replace him with Hardee. Four days earlier the President had detached Tennessee and North Georgia from the Western department. The move reduced Johnston's command to Mississippi, East Louisiana, and West Tennessee, along with that part of Alabama south of the Tennessee River.[1]

---

1 24 OR, pt. 1, 232 and 234-235; Kane, *Diary*, 83. My guess is that Davis made these alterations in his command scheme because: (1) Hardee, as the senior and far more experienced lieutenant general, should have the independent command after replacing Johnston, while Hill would serve under Bragg's guidance; (2) Hill would have been outranked in the department by Pemberton who, once exchanged, might return to his old command; (3) neither Hardee nor Hill could exercise authority over Bragg should his army have remained a part of what had been

Davis seems quickly to have realized that simply relieving Johnston from command "would have produced an explosion against the Administration," to quote Kean. The cabinet, he reported, was said to be divided on the question, and Johnston still had numerous "influential supporters."

Davis, therefore, decided that, at least for the moment, he would retain Johnston in the truncated Mississippi-Alabama command. There was no suitable post to which a full general could be sent (or, in Johnston's case, exiled), and Johnston's powerful and vocal supporters constituted a difficult obstacle to the traditional ploy of sending him away from the army to "await orders" (that never came). The President may well have hoped that the court of inquiry he was establishing would produce findings that would provide him with the political cover he needed to remove Johnston. (See preceding chapter.)

As matters worked out, Hardee, in effect, replaced Pemberton as Johnston's chief Mississippi subordinate. Davis, doubtless, hoped that since it proved politically impossible to remove Johnston, he could simply leave that general in his now relatively unimportant backwater command until the war ended.[2]

EVEN in his reduced command, however, Johnston soon found himself entangled in yet another unsavory squabble with the Richmond authorities. This time the aggravating matter concerned railroad equipment and rolling stock. As usual, the basic problem stemmed from Davis's and Johnston's mutual failure (refusal?) to communicate.

Back in early May 1863, Union troops had crossed the Mississippi River below Vicksburg and fanned out in the area south and southwest of Jackson. They then pushed to the northeast to destroy Jackson before turning west to trap Pemberton's army against the river. As they did so, alarmed railroad officials in the Magnolia State acted to protect the property of their companies. To do so, managers of the New Orleans, Jackson, & Great Northern Railroad, the Southern Railroad of Mississippi (the Vicksburg-Jackson-Meridian line), and the Mississippi Central Railroad (running north from Canton to Grand Junction, Tennessee), had

---

Johnston's old Western command; and (4) Hill was not then involved in the anti-Bragg cabal in the Army of Tennessee, while Hardee was one of its leading members. (Soon after joining that army, however, Hill became infected with the Western virus and gleefully joined in the plotting against Bragg.)

2 Bridges, *Hill*, 193-194; Kean, *Diary*, 83 and 97. Pemberton soon resigned his lieutenant general's commission (Provisional Army) and served loyally for the rest of the war in his Regular Army slot as a lieutenant colonel.

moved as much of their rolling stock as they could up the Mississippi Central tracks to the Grenada area some 105 miles north of Jackson. The Mississippi & Tennessee Railroad (Grenada to Memphis) also parked much of its rolling stock around Grenada.

When the Yankees seized Jackson on May 14 and destroyed most of the capital area's railroad facilities, more than seven hundred locomotives and cars were trapped north of Canton. That rolling stock would be invaluable to the Confederates if they could secure it. With the Yankees in firm control of the rail lines' northern termini (Memphis and Grand Junction in Tennessee, and Corinth in Mississippi), the only way the Rebels could save the cars and locomotives at Grenada was to bring them south through Jackson and then move them east. To do that, they would have to repair the railroads that the Yankees had so recently wrecked at the state capital.

Once the Rebels re-occupied Jackson on May 16-17 Johnston directed his chief quartermaster, Major Livingston Mims, to furnish railroad officials with materials to make repairs and authorized Mims to impress area slaves to do the work. Johnston did not, however, detail any of his soldiers to do part of the repairs. Nor did he place much emphasis on rebuilding the railroads even though he sometimes had to walk part of the way from Canton to Jackson because several miles of the rail line remained out of service.

By early July the railroad had been brought back into use except for the bridge over the Pearl River just east of Jackson. That gap, however, was crucial. The track ran eastward from Jackson to Meridian, where it connected with the Mobile & Ohio running south to Mobile. The line east from Jackson was the only rail outlet from Mississippi left in Confederate hands. If the cars and locomotives stranded at Grenada could get across the Pearl at Jackson, they could continue on into eastern Mississippi and western Alabama. If they could not get east of the river at Jackson they would remain trapped in Central Mississippi where they would be, at most, of only limited use to the Confederates even if the Yankees did not capture or destroy them.

After Johnston's second evacuation of Jackson on July 17, the Yankees tore up the city's recently repaired rail structure. This time they extended the scope of their destructive work as far north as Canton. In all, they wrecked five locomotives, thirty cars, two turntables, and thirteen railroad buildings. They also thoroughly demolished the by-then partly repaired Pearl River bridge.

Meanwhile, on July 14, as he prepared to flee Jackson for the second time, Johnston sent an order to Brigadier General James R. Chalmers, who commanded Confederate forces in the Grenada area. The Confederate commander directed

Chalmers to "Hold your troops in readiness to move east, if it becomes necessary, destroying the railroad bridges and rolling stock." Although Johnston could have worded this order more clearly, the directive's intent is plain enough. Chalmers was to destroy the railroad equipment if he had to evacuate the Grenada area. This meaning was reinforced that same day when a member of Johnston's staff telegraphed that the equipment was to be destroyed "*when* it becomes necessary [my emphasis]."[3]

Several people, however, misread Johnston's instructions as an order for Chalmers to destroy the cars and locomotives immediately. On July 19, Walter A. Goodman, president of the Mississippi Central, wrote to his close friend Jefferson Davis protesting Johnston's order to Chalmers (which he had misunderstood). Four days later Goodman sent a second plea. Estimating the value of the equipment at $5,000,000, he pointed out that if destroyed, it could not be replaced at any cost.

On July 22 Davis overruled what he understood to be Johnston's order and directed that the railroad equipment at Grenada be saved if possible. Only if necessary to keep it out of the enemy's hands was it to be destroyed. Two days later Secretary of War Seddon sent instructions to that effect to Johnston, and on several occasions in August the Confederacy's chief military engineer prodded Johnston on the effort to save the cars and locomotives.

Even with such obvious high-level political interest in the matter, Johnston did little for two weeks. He did "authorize" railroad officials to impress slaves and to begin repair work, and he offered them military protection. He did not, however, detail any of his own engineers and troops to help with the effort. In fact, early in August Johnston rejected out-of-hand suggestions from the Rebels' chief engineer that he use some of his troops to assist with the repair work.

Not until August 15 did Johnston act or even show much interest in the rescue effort. By then he had learned of a massive Union cavalry force moving toward Grenada. He was too late. Chalmers's troops were routed and fled south, setting fire to some of the railroad equipment as they left. On August 17 the Yankees destroyed much of Grenada, the town's railroad facilities, and the cars and locomotives stored there.[4]

---

3 30 *OR*, pt. 4, 493-504; Johnston, *Narrative*, 567-568.

4 Lash, *Destroyer*, Chapter 3, covers this matter in harshly critical detail. See also 24 *OR*, pt. 1, 232 and 235; 24 *OR*, pt. 3, 1003-1004; and 30 *OR*, pt. 4, 493-504. Some Confederate newspapers did not help matters when they published reports of "ninety to one hundred locomotives" and

JOHNSTON'S conduct in this matter offers yet another illustration that reveals much about his generalship and his role in the Confederate war effort, as well as about his passive-aggressive attitude toward the Davis Administration. He seems simply not to have grasped the desperate (and growing) logistical plight of the Confederacy or to have realized that the cars and locomotives stored at Grenada could have helped to ease it. He may have believed that since the matter far transcended the limits of his military command, it did not concern him and his soldiers. Therefore, he had no responsibility for it. In this sense, it was yet another example of his parochial, limited outlook on military command—an outlook bad enough for any officer, but one wholly inappropriate for a general at Johnston's level.

It was typical of Johnston's relationship with the government that he did not inform the authorities of the equipment stored at Grenada or of his July 14 order. It was also typical of Davis that he overruled at Goodman's urging what he understood to be Johnston's order without the courtesy of inquiring about the order and asking why Johnston had issued it. It was also typical that once Johnston informed Seddon on August 2 that his order had been to destroy the equipment if it became necessary to do so to prevent its capture, it turned out that the general and the President had arrived at the same position and had been there from the beginning of the matter.[5]

JOHNSTON found little in the way of military operations to occupy his mind during the five months after the end of the Vicksburg Campaign. He did have to respond to the occasional Yankee raid sent out from one of the Federal bases on the Mississippi River (Baton Rouge, Natchez, Vicksburg, and Memphis) to destroy Rebel resources and supplies in the Magnolia State. Johnston seems most to have

---

many railroad cars trapped north of Jackson. If the Federals did not already know of this valuable collection of rolling stock, they could have learned of it from such irresponsible reports. In July, for example, the Memphis (Atlanta) *Appeal* published such a story datelined July 23 (reprinted in the Charleston *Mercury*, July 31 from the *Appeal* of unknown date).

5 One could make a strong case that the Rebels would have found it extremely difficult to get the rolling stock out of central Mississippi. Many at the time, however, believed that a temporary bridge could have been built over the Pearl River in a few days and at least some of the equipment saved. Getting it out of Mississippi and to where it was most needed would have been a formidable task involving track gauges and political conflicts with state politicians and railroad companies. Still, to make no a real effort to save the cars and locomotives was to guarantee they would be lost to the Confederates, one way or another.

feared that the Unionists would next turn their attention to Mobile. He accordingly gave considerable time and thought to the defenses of that crucial city.[6]

Almost every day Johnston encountered difficulties with matters that held little interest for him. These problems included attempts to retrieve some of the paroled Vicksburg garrison troops from the Trans-Mississippi, difficulties arising from encoded messages that could not easily be deciphered, illegal civilian trade with the Federals (especially cotton for food and supplies), conscription and the assignment of conscripts to various army units, secret service funds, and the great confusion that grew from the Confederacy's increasingly chaotic currency situation. Although important, these problems involved matters that Johnston would like to have ignored. Fortunately, they did not generate any more serious controversies with Richmond officialdom. With General Hardee available to handle many of the daily tasks of troop command, Johnston found himself with little to do.[7]

In early August Johnston began to lose many of the troops from his old Army of Relief. The War Department ordered one of his brigades sent from General Beauregard the previous spring back to the south Atlantic coast. Johnston obeyed the order, but did not acknowledge it or report that he had dispatched the troops. This act of omission drew from an obviously irritated Adjutant and Inspector General Samuel Cooper a telegram inquiring if Johnston had complied with the directive.[8]

WITHIN a few weeks the larger Western military situation changed drastically. The Union army under Major General William Rosecrans, which had maneuvered Braxton Bragg out of Tennessee in late June and early July, renewed its advance. Crossing the Tennessee River in northeastern Alabama and moving eastward through the mountains, the Yankees threatened the Chattanooga-Atlanta railroad and forced Bragg to fall back from Chattanooga into North Georgia.

With yet another disaster looming in the Western theater, Confederate authorities moved to counter the new threat. Bragg called upon Johnston for help. Securing the government's approval and taking care to specify that the reinforcements he sent were for battle only and were to be returned as soon as

---

6 On Aug. 7, for example, the Richmond *Sentinel* reprinted a column from the Mobile *Advertiser and Register* of unknown date with an account of Johnston's recent trip to inspect the coastal city's defenses.

7 These subjects can be followed in the correspondence printed in 24, 30, and 31 *OR*.

8 Symonds, *Johnson*, 243.

possible, Johnston dispatched all told about 12,000 men to North Georgia (two infantry divisions, followed by two more brigades).

Bolstered by the reinforcements sent by Johnston and by others from Virginia and East Tennessee, Bragg pounced on the Yankees on September 19 and 20 along Chickamauga Creek in northwestern Georgia. Aided by a great deal of luck, Bragg's army routed the Federals and sent them streaming back into Chattanooga. The Rebels moved onto the heights southwest and east of Chattanooga and settled down to starve the enemy into surrender.

This change in Western Rebel fortunes presented Johnston's troops in Mississippi with an opportunity to help their comrades in Bragg's army. If Johnston's cavalrymen could move into Middle Tennessee, they might be able to disrupt Federal efforts to send supplies and reinforcements to the Yankees besieged in Chattanooga. Accordingly, Johnston in early October ordered his mounted troops northward in an effort to assist the Rebels on the heights at Chattanooga. Nothing came of the effort. Federal raids out of Memphis into northern Mississippi led to the recall of some of the Rebel cavalry units to protect the Magnolia State; the officer commanding the others found Union strength in southern Tennessee too great.[9]

MEANWHILE, as the post-Chickamauga euphoria faded and Bragg's army moved onto the heights outside Chattanooga, the generals of the Army of Tennessee renewed their customary squabbling and bickering. Their brawling soon became so tumultuous that it brought President Davis scurrying west from Richmond to try once again to see if he could quell what amounted to an uprising against Braxton Bragg. As usual, Davis refused to deal with the real problem. He made but one significant change. He transferred Lieutenant General Leonidas Polk, the leader of the Army of Tennessee's malcontents, to Johnston's Mississippi command, and shifted Hardee (another of Bragg's harsh critics) back to the Tennessee army at Chattanooga. Having replaced one of Bragg's bitter foes with another, and still naively believing that the generals would heed his pleas to support Bragg and cooperate, Davis set out to pay a visit to Mississippi.

---

9 See, for example, 30 *OR*, pt. 2, 757-762; 31 *OR*, pt. 1, 25, 30-31, 247-249, and 588-589. Ironically, a few months later Johnston, then commanding in Georgia, harshly criticized the Confederate authorities for not using mounted units in Mississippi to cut the railroads that supplied the enemy in his front. In 1864, the authorities held those horsemen to meet Yankee raids into the Magnolia State.

The President arrived at Johnston's Meridian headquarters on October 20. Over the next few days he traveled with Johnston to Jackson, Mobile, and Montgomery. We know nothing about what the two discussed during those days. It is a safe bet that their time together was marked by at best a strained, formal, and official politeness. It is also reasonable to assume that they held no honest substantive discussion of their views about the Confederacy's parlous situation, and what the Rebels might do about it.[10]

ONCE Davis departed for Richmond, Johnston returned to the dull routine of command in his unimportant peripheral theater of the war. There, it seemed most likely, he would remain for the duration of the conflict. It was not to be. In late November Bragg's army was routed in the Battle of Missionary Ridge outside Chattanooga and fled into North Georgia.

An official in Richmond had noted in his diary as early as October 18, "Alas, for our prospects this winter."[11]

---

10 Davis to Hardee, Oct. 30: "I rely greatly upon you for the restoration of a proper feeling [in the Army of Tennessee], and know that you will realize the comparative insignificance of personal considerations when weighed against the duty of imparting to the army all the efficiency of which it is capable." (31 OR, pt. 3, 609).

11 Kean, *Diary*, 111.

Index

About the Author

Richard M. McMurry earned his Ph.D. at Emory University in Atlanta studying under Bell Wiley and was a professor of history at North Carolina State University in Raleigh. He is the author of numerous articles and books, including the award-winning *John Bell Hood and the War for Southern Independence* (1982), *Two Great Rebel Armies: An Essay in Confederate Military History* (1989), and *Atlanta 1864: Last Chance for the Confederacy* (2000). He makes his home in Georgia outside Atlanta.